Richard III

Richard III

A Ruler and His Reputation

David Horspool

BLOOMSBURY

LONDON · OXFORD · NEW YORK · NEW DELHI · SYDNEY

Bloomsbury Continuum

An imprint of Bloomsbury Publishing Plc

50 Bedford Square
London
WC1B 3DP
UK

1385 Broadway
New York
NY 10018
USA

www.bloomsbury.com

**Bloomsbury, Continuum and the Diana logo are trademarks of
Bloomsbury Publishing Plc**

First published 2015

British Library Cataloguing-in-Publication Data
A catalogue record for this book is available from the British Library.

Library of Congress Cataloguing-in-Publication data has been applied for.

ISBN: HB: 978-1-4729-0299-3
ePDF: 978-1-4729-0301-3
ePub: 978-1-4729-0300-6

2 4 6 8 10 9 7 5 3 1

Printed and bound in Great Britain by CPI Group (UK) Ltd, Croydon CR0 4YY

MIX
Paper from
responsible sources
FSC
www.fsc.org   FSC® C020471

To find out more about our authors and books visit www.bloomsbury.com.
Here you will find extracts, author interviews, details of forthcoming events and the
option to sign up for our newsletters.

In memory of Christopher Horspool (1940–2013)

Table of Contents

List of Illustrations

1 The Falcon and Fetterlock badge of the Yorks (p.14) from *Heraldry for Craftsmen and Designers* by William St John Hope (New York: Macmillan, 1919).

2 The seal of Richard of Gloucester as Admiral of England (p.94) from *Heraldry for Craftsmen and Designers* by William St John Hope (New York: Macmillan, 1919).

3 The Middleham Jewel (p.140). Image courtesy of York Museums Trust: http://yorkmuseumstrust.org.uk/: Public Domain.

4 A facsimile of Richard's own addition to a letter to the Lord Chancellor, 12 October 1483 (p.194) from *The Handwriting of the Kings and Queens of England* by W. J. Hardy (London: The Religious Tract Society, 1893).

5 A replica of the 'Bosworth Boar' badge (p.240). Photograph: Thea Lenarduzzi.

Introduction

A famous portrait: a man gazes distractedly off to the left, his hands held lightly together in front of his chest. The eye is drawn to those hands. In a nervous gesture, the left thumb and forefinger pinch off, or on, the ring on the little finger of the right hand, one of three rings he is wearing. The man is sumptuously dressed and ornamented, his sleeves lined with fur, a ruby and pearl jewel in his hat, and a rich collar in which fourteen more rubies and twenty-four more pearls are visible. These are the trappings of very high status, but the sitter has none of the placid self-assurance associated with the wearers of such finery. His eyes seem those of a youngish man, perhaps in his early thirties. They are bright and keen, if mournful, while his skin is pale and his features are drawn. The lines on his brow and around the eyes age the face. Here is a picture of nervous energy, and of gnawing conscience.

This painting, hanging in the National Portrait Gallery in London, a detail of which is reproduced on the cover of this book, remains the most familiar of all images of Richard III, though it is not the oldest. It was painted long after its subject's death in 1485, probably around a hundred years later. It is based, like dozens of others that once decorated the corridors of great houses throughout the country, on a portrait in the Royal Collection, which was painted between 1504 and 1520 – that is, also not from life. Intriguingly, despite the hints of troubled conscience, the National Portrait Gallery version is far more sympathetic than the earlier Royal Collection one. That portrait was touched up fairly soon after it was first done, to thin the lips and set the mouth in a hard line, and to raise the right shoulder – only very slightly elevated in the National Portrait Gallery version – rather more acutely. The skin in the Royal Collection portrait is sickly pale, almost yellowing, and the eyes are harder, while the thumb on the right hand, which is bent in the National Portrait Gallery version, seems to have sharpened into a point. This picture, recorded in the collections of Henry VIII and Edward VI, son and grandson respectively of the man who replaced Richard III on the throne, seems to have been painted to capture the classic 'Tudor' view of Richard, as an incarnation of evil, a usurper and mass murderer, deformed in mind as in body. Here is the wicked uncle, killer of the Princes in the Tower (among others), awaiting his deserved comeuppance in battle against the rightful king.

The fact that the Tudors themselves kept a deliberately exaggerated version of 'bad King Richard' on their walls is less puzzling than the fact that, towards the end of the sixteenth century – by which time Shakespeare's monster had probably already appeared onstage and the material on which he based his version was certainly well established – somebody should have commissioned a portrait that turned out to be so broadly sympathetic. The Richard in the National Portrait Gallery *doesn't* look like a bad man: he looks like a man with a lot on his mind. The portrait prompted similar reactions in Richard's most famous (fictional) advocate, Inspector Grant, hero of Josephine Tey's extraordinarily successful pro-Richard detective novel *The Daughter of Time* (1951). This is, Grant thinks, a painting of 'Someone too-conscientious. A worrier; perhaps a perfectionist'. It is emphatically not an image of villainy. For Grant, the painter, whoever he was, turns out to be on to something, after the policeman has conducted an investigation into Richard from his sickbed. The last words of the novel, spoken by a nurse, are: 'When you look at it for a little it's really quite a nice face isn't it?'

What neither the nurse nor Inspector Grant reflect on is that this 'nice face' was as much a work of imagination as any of the nastier faces of Richard made by painters or conjured by chroniclers or playwrights. The National Portrait Gallery painting reminds us that there has very rarely been a settled opinion about Richard III, even in the supposedly propaganda-filled Tudor years. But it also cautions us that all our efforts, like those of the anonymous artist who decided to give back to Richard a little humanity, are prey to some form of wishful thinking. The National Portrait Gallery describes its picture of Richard as using 'the pattern from an original likeness', and art historians think that the very earliest surviving portrait of Richard, now in the collection of the Society of Antiquaries, was *based* on one 'painted from life'.[1] But we are still at one remove, at the very least, from Richard himself. There is no contemporary portrait of Richard, no record of his sitting for one. Here, in visual form, is the problem for anyone approaching a life of Richard III. For a king who spent just over two years on the throne, he has received an extraordinary, perhaps even an unsustainable, level of attention and range of opinion. Some of that material was contemporary, but the most powerful, the bits that have stuck in the public imagination longest, like Richard's portrait, are not. Reconstructing Richard is often an exercise in admitting our ignorance – in stark contrast to the confidence of those who wrote about him shortly after, or even long after, his death – and deciding on the balance of probabilities. We can demonstrate how Tudor 'propaganda' or Ricardian advocacy has, in the past, overstated its case, but being sure what isn't right is not the same as knowing what is.

The confirmation that Richard's remains had been discovered in Leicester in 2012 offered the hope that in some areas, science could replace speculation about him. But most of the problems with understanding Richard have not been solved by the discovery. These can be summed up as too little to go on, and too much. Too little, because the evidence for Richard's life, particularly his life before he became king in 1483, is not exactly super-abundant. He features in royal grants and parliamentary rolls, and is mentioned in near-contemporary chronicles of the period, though the tradition of monastic chronicle-writing was in terminal decline, and the town chronicles that survive are mostly terse records of events, with little embellishment. There are mentions of Richard or things to do with him in the chance survivals of private family correspondence, chiefly that of the Pastons of Norfolk, whose business just happened to overlap with his on occasion. There are a few letters dictated, and fewer lines still actually handwritten, by Richard. The great majority of this material is available in printed editions, of which this book will make copious use. We know about some of Richard's own books, though for most of them we can't be sure he read them, let alone what he thought about them. In almost all his earlier appearances on the historical stage, Richard is not the protagonist. As a child he is often invisible, and, even in his 'formative years' as Duke of Gloucester, he is frequently missing from the record. For much of his life we don't know precisely where Richard was at specific times, nor when some very major personal events happened.

We don't know, for example, exactly when he got married, nor when his legitimate son or (at least) two illegitimate children were born.

But those gaps are nothing compared to the difficulty of reconstructing Richard's personality. Overwhelmingly, the imprint that Richard left on his time was impersonal. It is a record of acquisitions, of political and judicial decisions, of hiring and firing, of public building and foundation, and military planning. The personality that lay behind those acts is thus ripe for speculation. For centuries, Richard has tended to be characterized as a puzzling bundle of contrasts: loyal yet treacherous, pious yet ruthless, courageous yet paranoid. It will be part of the contention of this book that many of these contradictions are more explicable than at first appears. One way of doing that is by trying to stick closely to chronology. The order in which things happened can often go a long way towards explaining why they happened. In the case of Richard, he seems to have been able to adapt to change in an often changeable world. It may seem strange to argue that a man who was killed before he reached his thirty-third birthday was a born survivor, but given the circumstances of his upbringing and the fact that two of his older brothers had died violently, he must have learned to be one. As for the remaining contradictions, they may be due to lack of evidence, or to a Walt Whitman-like multitudinous character. Nobody is consistent throughout their life, and acting in ways that seem to contradict a perceived personality trait is hardly unique. To take an example from Richard's own family, his brother, Edward IV, is often characterized (including by contemporaries) as indolent and given to sensuality rather than vigour. Yet he was undoubtedly the greatest military leader of the Wars of the Roses, and despite years of relative peace, was apparently gearing up for a renewed assault on France when he died in 1483. Richard is often categorized, some might say dismissed, as a 'man of his time'. One eminent historian of the Tudors went further, calling him a 'bore'.[2] He lived at the heart of one of the most dramatic periods in English history, and it would be strange if those experiences had not shaped him. But the fact that he could be so unpredictable makes him more than a typical fifteenth-century aristocrat, and very far from boring. Of course, Richard was a man of his time and class. But he was also an individual, and one who has constantly attracted attention over the centuries.

This leads us to the problem of too much to go on. In the century or so after 1485 a picture began to emerge that read back the drama of Richard's brief reign into the life that preceded it, in some ways taking advantage of the lack of contemporary accounts of Richard to create a villain in the making. This was also the beginning of an age of national historiography, a tradition begun by Polydore Vergil and carried on through the writings of Edward Hall (1548), Richard Grafton (1568) and Raphael Holinshed (1578). The influence of Shakespeare, who drew on this tradition, is naturally the most powerful in the construction of a myth of Richard that makes uncovering the reality so difficult. But the later development of a counter-myth, if not as dazzling as Shakespeare's monster, has been almost as influential. The pattern was set for a debate over Richard's merits very early. As the National Portrait Gallery painting reminds us, this was not a case of an unchallenged version of history holding sway for hundreds of years before finally being swept away in more enlightened times. Richard has had historical defenders from the early seventeenth century to the present day. But on the other side, he has continued to be attacked. His great Victorian biographer James Gairdner, for example, after a thorough immersion in contemporary sources, was still convinced of the 'general fidelity of the portrait with which we have been made familiar by Shakespeare and Thomas More'.[3] More recently, at least since Paul Murray Kendall's sympathetic account published in 1955, a more charitable view has taken hold. Subsequent academic historians, including the author of what remains the authoritative biography of Richard III, Charles Ross (1981), have tried to move beyond the study of Richard as being a matter of taking sides. Most continue to find Richard guilty of the murder of his nephews, for example, but are sanguine rather than censorious about it. This book aims at neutrality, too, taking account of the latest historical and archaeological arguments and discoveries to present a comprehensible Richard, without keeping a foot in either pro- or anti-Ricardian camps. Readers will learn my conclusions about the perennial Ricardian mysteries, but they will also read that there is a lot more to him than whodunnits, and that making moral judgements about medieval monarchs, while perfectly legitimate, is a very small part of any attempt at historical biography. I am also interested in the reasons why, more than five hundred years after the event, there are still people apparently keen to fight the Wars of the Roses.

Biographers and historians often write about 'stripping away' the myths created by later writers, but it is probably worth admitting that, for Richard, this is an almost impossible task. Part of the fascination of Richard is that he has become a myth, a model of evil or of wronged righteousness, depending on the storyteller. The task of anyone trying to reconstruct the life of Richard III is to be alert to the temptations that these myths and counter-myths offer, and to make use of them to understand how we have ended up with the composite figure who is at once so familiar and so alien. In most of this book, consequently, while I tell Richard's story based on contemporary or near-contemporary accounts, I also discuss later versions where those have come to dominate the received view of events. In the last, 'posthumous' section of the book, I focus more closely on the constructors of Richard's reputation, as well as following his final journey to reinterment in Leicester Cathedral. The sustained excitement following the discovery of his remains in Leicester in 2012, culminating in the burial of the king with full royal honours in March 2015, shows how much Richard continues to matter to contemporary Britons. The debates occasioned by the discovery show that his reputation is still by no means a settled argument. The same pattern of competing narratives – and even, despite the fact that Richard has been dead for over five centuries, of competing loyalties – has re-emerged. Our continuing fascination with Richard III offers a reflection of what British history means to us, and how we interpret it.

***

On 2 March 2013 all 485 seats in the Peter Williams Lecture Theatre at Leicester University were taken. The occasion was the first big meeting of the Richard III Society since the confirmation that the bones discovered at the Grey Friars dig the previous year were, indeed, those of the missing king. There was something of the air of a party conference about the event, though it would be beyond the fantasies of the most authoritarian of mainstream political party leaders to have followers of such loyalty and broad agreement. And there was, too, a sense of celebration, as if a minority party had, against all the odds, won a general election.

The Society had attracted many new members in the wake of the discovery, we learnt, but a fair number of those in attendance were old hands. Some wore their allegiance proudly. Here was a lady in a home-knitted cardigan featuring the Yorkist Sun in Splendour, and men and women of all ages sported white-boar T-shirts and badges – Richard's own device. Others were more discreet, and claimed no great expertise, but could point to more than thirty years of membership, and quietly revealed an intimate knowledge of fifteenth-century dynastic politics. There were more women than men, and while the best known of them, the newly famous Philippa Langley, the screenwriter who had pushed the project to dig for Richard forward, laughed off suggestions that she was 'in love' with a man who had lived and died so long ago, other attendants were less shy. I spoke to one woman who admitted that, yes, she was 'a little bit in love' with Richard, a man who fought for what he believed in – went down fighting, too.

The stall that opened between sessions was typical of the day's combination of scholarly antiquarianism and outright fandom. Facsimiles of the Beauchamp Pageant and volumes of the Society-sponsored scholarly edition of a vital British Library manuscript source sat alongside Richard III headscarves and white-boar pendants. The father and son that I sat next to, both new members with a passion for medieval history, proudly showed me their new lapel badges from the stall.

The discovery of the 'king in the car park' is undeniably an extraordinarily unlikely thing to have happened. Who could blame the backers of the project for exuding an atmosphere of festivity, even of triumph? The keynote speaker, Chris Skidmore, a historian who also happens to be a Member of Parliament, duly sounded a note of caution, like a new minister warning the party faithful not to expect miracles in the first year of office. But the theme of the conference, 'A New Richard III?', even with that concessionary interrogative, was more in keeping with the mood. What had been the 'Looking for Richard Project' could move into a new phase now that the king had been found.

Speakers who had been involved with the dig, with the tracing of genealogical evidence, with the reconstruction of Richard's face based on the bone structure of his skull, all addressed the conference. The discovery was proof that the efforts of devoted amateurs and professionals with open minds could bear fruit. These men and women had set out their case, carefully, doggedly, at times even obsessively, and been proved right. For a Society that is habituated to outside scepticism, such spectacular success must be all the more gratifying.

But can his bones help us find a new Richard? The pervasive influence of myth on the subject of Richard III was in evidence again from the moment his bones were uncovered. The most obvious thing about them was, at first, the hardest to assimilate to the pro-Richard, 'Ricardian' view. As the pictures of the newly laid out spinal column made very clear, Richard suffered from scoliosis. It was pointed out that this is very different from kyphosis, which results in the classic 'hunchback' of the Shakespearean Richard. Nevertheless, it had been an axiom of Ricardian discourse that the 'venomous hunchback' was a Tudor fabrication, and that contemporary witnesses left no impression of any deformity whatsoever. Scoliosis, even of the severe type evident in Richard's case, is not always visible on a clothed body. But Richard's body was not always clothed. He would have been dressed and undressed by others throughout his life (the affliction is estimated to have begun around the age of ten); and even if his body servants never gossiped about their master's unusual shape, the public display of his naked corpse, thrown across a packhorse on the battlefield at Bosworth, and laid out for all to see before its final interment at Grey Friars church in Leicester, would have revealed the truth.

Of course, Richard's defenders as early as Clements Markham at the turn of the last century have pointed out that it is 'an unreasoning prejudice against Richard' to associate 'his alleged crimes' with 'his personal repulsiveness'.[4] But here we run up against the peculiarity of Richard's case, as posterity treats it; while his defenders are scrupulously keen to base their defence on research and evidence, to counteract Tudor 'propaganda' and its later disseminators, there is still an emotional resonance to Ricardianism. At the Peter Williams theatre, this was nowhere more in evidence than when the wax reconstruction of Richard's head was unexpectedly revealed to be in the room. As it was unveiled, the contents of the glass case were greeted with a gasp, not of astonishment – the bust was familiar from television and newspaper reproductions by now – but of admiration. Here was the 'bonny lad', as a TV presenter had described him, if not in the flesh, then the next best thing.

When Dr Caroline Wilkinson, Professor of Craniofacial Identification at the University of Dundee, finished her description of the extraordinary lengths to which she had gone to reconstruct Richard's face, one of the first questions from the floor was whether his body could be reconstructed as well. The scientific or historical benefits of such reconstruction, even if it could be afforded, were not immediately apparent. The potential emotional payoff was clear.

At the very least, the testimony of Richard's body and the numerous insults and blows it received, peri- and post-mortem, will expand our knowledge of the king's last stand. It must be admitted, however, that even his harshest critics never alleged that he had ended in any other way than 'fighting manfully in the press of his enemies', as the Tudor historian Polydore Vergil put it.[5] Even Thomas More – another of the king's earliest and most eloquent critical historians, and indirect inspiration for his most eloquent critic *sine rivale*, Shakespeare – conceded Richard's soldierly qualities in his unfinished *History of King Richard III* (printed in 1543, though, like Vergil's *History*, it was written in the decade after 1510). In this instance, the discovery would seem likely only to confirm what few disputed, that Richard died violently at Bosworth. Earlier archaeological investigations, such as those at the site of the greatest battle of the Wars of the Roses (and probably of any war on English soil), Towton in Yorkshire (1461), had already shown the extreme violence perpetrated, and how the blows focused on the faces of the victims, in some cases splitting the skull almost in two, causing 'injuries that are far in excess of those necessary to cause disability and death'.[6]

Other contributions to the conference raised the prospect of new insights, without truly delivering them. The discipline of modern experimental psychology, for example, might be applicable to Richard. However, Professor Mark Lansdale's decision to base his findings, or suggestions, not on contemporary evidence but on 'reliable biographies' such as the (stirring, persuasive, deeply researched but frequently rather imaginative) work of Paul Murray Kendall, meant that, while thought-provoking, those findings could hardly be historically convincing. Richard, Lansdale argued, was not a psychopath, but may have suffered from 'intolerance to uncertainty syndrome'. For a man surrounded by (never mind responsible for) premature death from his first years, a man who had had to run for his life in childhood and later, uncertainty must have been an almost everyday experience. Medieval life was uncertain at the best of times: hence the attractions of living *sub specie eternitatis*. But how could someone unable to tolerate uncertainty take such big risks, including putting himself on the throne, and deciding to gamble everything on defending his position? We are more likely to get close to Richard's psyche by considering the alternatives open to him and the choices he made, than by seeing his psychological make-up as predetermining those choices.

The conference was on more familiar ground with the contributions that provided first impressions of how Richard's injuries might be used to reconstruct the course of his last battle. An expert on medieval armour also showed how the calibre of armourers Richard is likely to have drawn upon would have ensured that any evidence of his scoliosis was cunningly concealed, without restricting his movements or disadvantaging him in battle.

So this New Richard looked rather a lot like the Old (Ricardian) Richard, for all the unexpectedly 'bonny' facial features. He was brave, tough, no-nonsense (intolerant of uncertainty) and loyal. In a way, the most revealing talk was that of Philippa Langley and Annette Carson (author of *Richard III: The Maligned King*), which, as well as detailing the heroic lengths to which the former went to persuade archaeologists to dig in the now famous car park of Leicester social services, set out a view of the king that would not have been unfamiliar to any of Richard's staunchest posthumous defenders – from Horace Walpole, whose *Historic Doubts on the Life and Reign of Richard III* was published in 1768, to Josephine Tey in the twentieth century. We were returned to a world of bad Tudors and good Yorkists, of a blameless king who took power for the reasons he said he did (his brother Edward's children had, on his death, turned out to be illegitimate). As for the Princes in the Tower, well, this crowd didn't really need persuading that he 'didn't do it'.

The stated aim of the Richard III Society is 'to secure a more balanced assessment of the king'. Over the years since its foundation in 1924, this has led to the publication of editions of primary sources, to hundreds of scholarly articles, to a reconsideration of all aspects of Richard's life and reign – and of course, to the discovery of the king's body itself. No reputable historian now would perpetuate the 'black legend' of Richard, the one that Thomas More and Shakespeare give us. But to prosper as a popular organization, rather than a dependable, but somewhat dry, sponsor of scholarly debate, the Society needs the black legend. Shakespeare may have given us a monstrous Richard for all time, but the most popular modern versions of the king have all been 'revisionist'. The fact that Richard is a monster only onstage cannot be allowed to stop Ricardians from 'fighting against' a Tudor picture that has long since become a straw man.

If we are to find a new Richard, it is unlikely to come in any great measure from his bones. As we will see, the diligent work of scientists since the excavation has led to some fascinating conclusions about Richard's lifestyle, his health and his last hours. But it would be too much to expect that his bones would be eloquent enough to answer the most profound and persistent questions about the last Plantagenet king. What led him to take the momentous steps he did in 1483, by which in a matter of weeks he put aside his nephew, Edward V, and replaced him on the throne, violently clearing away opposition; what sort of a noble was he before he became a king, what sort of a king was he, and what sort of king might he have been if he had survived the Battle of Bosworth; what effect did the violent times and spectacular elevations and demotions all around him have on Richard; how do we square the evidence of piety, loyalty and pragmatism with the apparent record of murderous violence, ruthless lack of scruple and risk-taking? All these questions remain as urgent today as they have for centuries. And we might add some newer ones. Was Richard's a uniquely English experience, or should we view it in the context of power struggles across continental Europe? Was Richard a typical magnate when he was Duke of Gloucester, or did he take a unique approach to his position? As king, was he an innovator, or did he not have time to do more than try to hold on to what he had?

In some ways the discovery has told us far more about the way modern Britons view history, or about the importance of accessibility to modern academic research, than about Richard. (The University of Leicester's ability to involve almost every department in the find is remarkable; I remarked to a Leicester lecturer that De Montfort University, the city's other higher-education institution, must envy its neighbour, whose discovery threatens to remove entirely from the popular imagination the name of another medieval celebrity from association with Leicester. 'Yes,' she replied, with only the barest hint of embarrassment, 'and De Montfort is so much closer than our University to the site of the dig.') Almost immediately, there was an outbreak of controversy about Richard's new final resting place: Leicester, where he was found; York, his 'spiritual home' (according to some); London, where his wife Queen Anne is buried in Westminster Abbey; Fotheringhay, where he was born? This controversy was played out in the media, the House of Commons and the law courts. This was a reflection of modern Britain. It offered few insights into the life of a fifteenth-century king.

The discovery can, nonetheless, be seized as an opportunity to bring to public attention the more comprehensive picture of the king and the age in which he lived that has been emerging for the past thirty years. Richard lived through and fashioned pivotal moments in British history. His character will always remain a puzzle and a source of fascination. Of all the waxworks in the popular pageant of the country's past, fashioned and refashioned in the public imagination by the competing influences of historians, dramatists, novelists, enthusiasts, fantasists, and now of scientists and archaeologists, he remains the most controversial. Looking for Richard is not a quest that ended in a Leicester car park. The discovery of the physical remains of the king only encourages us to keep on looking for Richard in different ways.

The Falcon and Fetterlock badge of the Yorks, as seen on the bronze gates of Henry VII's Chapel in Westminster Abbey. Henry VII's wife Elizabeth of York was Richard's niece.

1

Son of the 'high and mighty Prince'

Fotheringhay Castle, by the banks of the River Nene in Northamptonshire, was a statement in stone made by one of the most powerful families in England. It was granted in 1377 to the first Duke of York, Edmund of Langley, one of Edward III's many sons. Over the next two decades, Edmund rebuilt the motte and bailey fortification into a fine aristocratic residence as well as a military stronghold. At its centre, raised up on earthworks and surrounded by a moat, was the irregular octagonal shell keep, known as the 'Fetter lock' (like a modern 'D'-lock) after the heraldic device that the Yorks adopted. That would have been the redoubt if the castle was under attack, but the residential buildings were in the rectangular upper courtyard, beside the keep. From here Mary, Queen of Scots was taken to her execution in 1587. Here, too, a woman who was the mother and grandmother of kings, but who never became queen consort herself, Cecily Neville, Duchess of York, gave birth to a son on 2 October 1452. He was named after his father, Richard, the third Duke of York.

The church in which Richard was probably baptized can still be visited at Fotheringhay. But the castle where he was born has all but vanished, 'slighted' by the son of the Scottish queen who was killed there, and dismantled not long afterwards. What remains are only earthworks and a small section of stone now reserved behind railings. There are two plaques on the railings to commemorate the castle's most famous residents. The ruin is a reminder right at the beginning of Richard's story of how much is lost, how much can only be put back in the imagination.[1]

Children – even the children of senior noblemen such as Richard, Duke of York – did not make much of an impression on the historical record in medieval England. The exceptions were the eldest sons of nobles and royalty, whose futures as bearers of great titles and holders of great patrimonies meant that onlookers took an interest in them from birth. But when Richard, the future Duke of Gloucester – and king – was born to Richard and Cecily, Duke and Duchess of York, he was the couple's eleventh child, and their fourth son (of those who had survived infancy). To inherit his father's title he would have to outlive his brothers Edward, Edmund and George – and their future heirs. Even in the turbulent age into which Richard was born, and the ordinary perils of disease and accident notwithstanding, this must have seemed a very unlikely fate. That he eventually assumed, not his father's title, but the throne, despite the fact that his brothers' heirs did survive their fathers, is testimony to the sheer unpredictability, not to mention the force of personality, that became the most distinguishing feature of Richard's life almost from the start. The role of chance, the sense that nine times out of ten, events would have taken a different course, is perhaps the main element in the 'mystery' of Richard III. As much as disputes over facts or interpretations of motive, it is chance that makes his life so inexhaustibly intriguing.

Richard's physical odds of survival were the long ones dictated by the age, only compounded by the dangers of the political world of mid-fifteenth-century England. As his own parents could attest, surviving childhood, even for the most privileged in society, was an achievement in itself in the Middle Ages. Five of Richard's siblings did not see adulthood, and we now know that, from some point in his childhood or adolescence, he lived with the effects of a curvature of the spine. One of the most significant points of the discovery of Richard's skeleton at Grey Friars in Leicester was evidence of this spinal abnormality. This was, of course, not confirmation that the future king was 'rudely stamped' from birth, let alone 'deformed, half finished, sent before my time/Into this breathing world, scarce half made up'.[2] But did the condition of his spine affect Richard's chances as a child, especially given the state of medical knowledge at the time? The short answer is 'no'. The team who discovered the remains have concluded that Richard 'had severe idiopathic adolescent-onset scoliosis'.[3] That is, at birth and through early childhood at least, Richard's body would have shown no signs of the later condition.

We may discount the views of the chronicler John Rous, who rewrote his previously sympathetic account of Richard's reign after the king's death to reflect that his later 'crimes' were foretold in the circumstances of his birth. Where Shakespeare made Richard a premature delivery ('sent before my time'), Rous pictured him as cursedly (and fantastically) overdue. Richard, Rous wrote, was 'retained in his mother's womb for two years and emerged with teeth and hair to his shoulders'.[4] But there is one other fleeting glimpse of the infant Richard in contemporary records. It comes in a poetic dialogue written by an Augustinian friar, Osbern Bokenham, in Clare Priory, Suffolk. The 'Dialogue at the Grave of Dame Johan of Acres', better known today by the name of the manuscript in which it is preserved, the Clare Roll, ends with an encomium to Richard of York's family. It was written in May 1456, when Richard was three. In a list of the third duke's family, living and dead, including his youngest son's elder brothers Edward, Edmund and George, as well as other children who 'had passed to God's grace', Osbern mentions Richard, who 'liveth yet'. It is indicative of just how little survives about Richard's childhood that these two words should have occasioned the amount of debate that they have. By the time that James Gairdner, the first 'modern' biographer of Richard III, writing in 1898, considered this 'honest rhymester's' evidence, it was in the light of at least two previous discussions of it, as potentially indicating that Richard was 'slender and sick' and had 'serious illness as a child'.[5] More recently, the lines in context have merely been taken to mean that Richard was alive, by contrast to five of his siblings. That view is made more convincing when it is observed that earlier in the same poem Osbern refers to Richard's father, Richard, Duke of York, 'which yet liveth'.[6] As the duke was a fully grown, vigorous (and fecund) man, it would seem obvious that the poet meant no comment on his subject's state of health when he used the expression.

Richard, then, was no less robust than any other fifteenth-century child, but his world was a dangerous one. It was also one that his own father, in the years just before Richard's birth and of his childhood, began to shape for decades to come. To begin to understand Richard, whose path was so often laid out by the actions or precedents of his father and his elder brothers, it is necessary to see the world they made. The effects of the decisions taken by Richard's immediate family would reverberate for centuries; naturally, they had their most forceful impact on those, like Richard, who were closest to them. Not only that, but it seems clear that he took the examples given by his close family as models – to be followed or avoided, but in either case, the best guide as to how to act, and how to succeed.

The most important political fact of the age, almost universally agreed upon, was that a strong king made for a strong country. Poets throughout the 1400s, as England's royal fortunes waxed under Henry V and waned under his son, Henry VI, returned to the theme. From the Privy Seal clerk Thomas Hoccleve – who addressed his *Regiment of Princes* (1411–12) to the future Henry V – to the author of *Three Considerations Necessary to the Good Governance of a Prince* from around the time of Richard's birth, commentators agreed that 'A Kyng is maad to keepen and maynteene/Justice'. They also emphasized the importance of good counsel, 'For whan a man yfelle into errour is,/His brother owith him conseil and rede [advice]'.[7]

That was the ideal, but the man who sat on the throne when Richard was born fell very far below it. If Richard III has suffered the insults of posterity, he has, at least, benefited from an urge towards rehabilitation that has been evident in one form or another since the seventeenth century. Henry VI has experienced almost the opposite trajectory. Even those who opposed his rule most forcefully during his lifetime made most of their accusations against those 'evil counsellors' who surrounded him. The king himself was above direct criticism. In the centuries after his death, his piety even earned him a shot at sainthood. But by the twentieth century, most measures of sympathy for this pious, ineffectual and periodically deranged man had run dry. Henry has suffered from the eloquence of a variety of exasperated observers of the late Middle Ages, as for example the great Dutch historian Johan Huizinga, condoling with Margaret of Anjou for having 'married at 16 an imbecile bigot'.[8] He had come to the throne as a baby, and the tensions between powerful men with competing interests and outlooks that characterized the minority period of Henry's rule did not end with his majority. In fact, while the personnel altered, the same dynamic persisted – of a divided nobility who thought that they and their adherents should direct all policy, with the royal presence incapable of enforcing its own will. This was the era of the 'over-mighty subject', but it has been pointed out with justification that the precondition for over-mighty subjects is an 'under-mighty ruler'.[9] That was what England had in Henry VI.

In June 1450, two years before Richard was born, anger at the conduct of domestic and foreign policy, the (largely accurate) perception that government was in the hands of a self-serving clique and revenues were being squandered, and fears of rumoured reprisals for the murder of the disgraced but senior nobleman the Duke of Suffolk, all combined to spark a popular rebellion in Kent, led by a mysterious figure, Jack Cade. The circumstances of and support for the rebellion were different from those of the Peasants' Revolt some seventy years earlier, but the impression of a country descending into unholy chaos would have been frighteningly familiar, particularly when the rebels made for the capital. What would have been of interest, and of concern, to Richard's family was one of the names that began to be ascribed to Cade, 'Mortimer'. This was the family name of the Duke of York's mother, whose title, the Earls of March, Richard of York had inherited. Importantly for the dynastic arguments that developed from Richard of York's intrusion into royal politics, his mother's royal bloodline could be traced back to the third son of Edward III, Lionel of Antwerp, Duke of Clarence. As Henry VI was descended from Edward's *fourth* son, John of Gaunt, this would emerge as a crucial point, more significant than York's paternal descent, from yet another of Edward III's sons, his fifth, Edmund of Langley, the first Duke of York. Crucial, that was, if maternal inheritance counted – a moot point.[10]

In 1450 Cade's rebels demonstrated that they, at least, valued this pedigree. In their articles of rebellion, they pushed for the Duke of York to take a leading part in government. The king, they petitioned, should 'take about his noble person his trew blode of his ryall realme, that is to say, the hyghe and myghty prynce the Duke of Yorke'.[11] The subject of the rebels' ardour was not, in fact, in the country at the time. Richard of York had spent much of his life on the king's business abroad, latterly as Lieutenant of Ireland, but first as Lieutenant of France, where he was one of a succession of magnates who struggled to salvage something from the remains of the Hundred Years War. English policy in France moved from the expansionist glory days of Henry V, to retrenchment, negotiation and surrender during the minority and early personal rule of his successor. At his father's death, the infant Henry had inherited his claim to the French throne as well as the English, and he was even crowned King of France in Notre-Dame shortly after his tenth birthday. Although Henry's government had by then seen off Joan of Arc, the tide was already turning, and under the 'rival' King of France, Charles VII, the French continued to make progress in clawing back territory.

The Duke of York's record in France was complicated but by no means disastrous. On separate tours of duty, he was responsible for the successful defence of Rouen and Pontoise, and was involved in the negotiations that led to the truce of Tours (1445), which arranged the marriage of Henry VI and Margaret of Anjou and the surrender of Maine. All the more conspicuous military failures of the period were the work of other royal appointees, the Beaufort brothers John and Edmund, successive Dukes of Somerset, whose campaigns in France resulted in no significant gains in the first instance, and critical losses, including the prized city of Rouen, in the second.

Richard of York's French experiences began the long disaffection with Henry's government that eventually ripened into outright rebellion, and ultimately into designs on the throne. In France he had found himself out of pocket – not only when the government failed to pay his wages, but from massive loans he made to the same government, which by 1446 stood at £26,000, the equivalent of around £13 million today – and sidelined, when John Beaufort's French expedition, and elevation to a dukedom, had compromised York's standing. He returned to England in 1445, only to be replaced as Lieutenant of France by John's brother Edmund Beaufort, who had succeeded as Earl of Somerset in 1444 and was, too, made Duke of Somerset, in 1448. It was he who handed over Maine, as agreed under the terms of the truce of Tours – and who took compensation for it. But it was also Somerset who failed to halt the French recapture of Normandy, a Lancastrian gain, in 1449–50, or, later, Gascony, an Angevin one (i.e. a loss of a province that had been in English hands for centuries before the Hundred Years War). Whether or not Richard of York resented or blamed the Duke of Somerset from the beginning, or only grew to equate Somerset's involvement with government as the source of misrule, it was on Somerset that he focused his attack when he first involved himself at the heart of English domestic politics after Cade's rebellion in 1450.

Richard of York had been in Ireland during the rebellion itself. His appointment as Lieutenant there may have been envisaged as a compromise, or even a calculated demotion, by Henry's advisers. It certainly gave the duke an effective platform from which to launch himself. He returned to England via Wales in September 1450, in the aftermath of the rebellion. Historians used to think that, as he progressed via his own lands towards Westminster, York gathered an impressive retinue of up to 5,000 men.[12] But a recent discovery in Surrey county archives, of a letter dated 21 September from Humphrey Stafford, Duke of Buckingham, to William Beauchamp, Lord St Amand, describes an approach of an army, its commander's name lost in the damaged part of the document, of only 300–400 men.[13] If the letter dates to 1450 and the missing leader is Richard of York – the timing and people involved make it difficult to think of other candidates – this fresh evidence could be taken to indicate two things. Any idea that York was even contemplating an all-out attack on the Lancastrian regime at this time is premature; secondly, perhaps York was confident of a hearing in any case and so didn't need an overwhelming show of force.

As he approached London, York also made a rhetorical gambit, issuing two bills that summarized his grievances, the slanders that he wished to repudiate, and the 'mysrewlers' who were bringing the kingdom – and the duke's own 'myth and powere' – into disrepute, though the last went unnamed.[14] In his reply to the first bill, King Henry seems nervous and conciliatory. Although he maintains his dignity, thanking his 'cosyn' for his 'humble obeisance', he also reveals how much anxiety York's reputation has generated at court. Henry speaks of being menaced by 'untrue schypmen', just the kind of lawless sailors on shore leave who had set upon and killed the royal servant Adam Moleyns, Bishop of Chichester, in the prelude to Cade's rising. These 'fals pepill' have, Henry reveals, said that 'you [York] schuld be fechid home with many thousandis'. Perhaps York did not need to gather thousands behind him right away when even the king was aware he had such a groundswell of support.

By the time Richard of York arrived in London on 27 September 1450, it is likely that his complaints had already been aired. In his reply to the second bill, Henry or those around him seemed to have regained their confidence. While appearing to take York's complaints about misrule seriously, he plays the duke at his own game by refusing to take the hint that the chief culprit might be the king's closest adviser, the Duke of Somerset. In effect, Henry fobs off York, merely promising to appoint a 'sad and so substancial consaile', which he wants 'yow to be oon'. For any change of substance, York had to try a different approach. He was able to secure a significant representation in the Westminster Parliament in November, including the appointment of his chamberlain, Sir William Oldhall, as Speaker. There, York's representatives moved against Somerset and his followers. During this session of Parliament, York did put on a show of force, in common with other magnates, giving a grim foretaste of the clashes between nobles to come. He was reported as arriving in the city with more than 4,000 men at his back, 'his sweerd born a fore him'. In Parliament a petition was formally presented for the removal of Somerset and other 'persons . . . behaving improperly around your royal person and in other places', for them to be 'withdrawn and removed from your most noble presence, person and estate for the term of their lives'. There was also an outbreak of mob violence in London, and an attempt on Somerset's life, at which York may have connived, though his men foiled it. The moves appeared to have succeeded when Somerset was imprisoned for two months in the Tower, but Henry's underlying loyalty to him, or perhaps Somerset's hold over the king, could not be so easily broken. By January 1451, Somerset was free, and accompanying Henry on a tour of Kent, the heartland of Cade's rebellion.

It is likely that the spectre of violence was too much for neutral observers, who naturally gravitated towards the king. Richard of York was sidelined again and he retired to his estates, though he stayed in England. The May session of Parliament came to an abrupt end after one of York's supporters, Sir Thomas Young, Member for Bristol, petitioned the Commons to acknowledge the duke as heir presumptive to the throne (Henry VI's marriage had so far been childless). There is no record of such a petition being formally delivered in the Parliament Rolls, but in 1455 Thomas Young did put in a petition for recompense 'for his imprisonment in the Tower for things said by him in the house of commons, notwithstanding the commons' old liberty to say what they wish without challenge, charge or punishment'. It sounds as if even raising the subject of the succession informally had got Young into trouble. York's principal supporter in the 1450 parliament, Speaker Sir William Oldhall, also felt the heat that year. In November he took sanctuary in St Martin's-Le-Grand in the City. York's first attempt to stamp his authority on national politics seems merely to have exposed the weakness of his position while loyalty to the king prevailed.[15]

Back in Ludlow, Shropshire, Richard of York had two courses open to him. He could make his retirement from national affairs permanent, or he could await an opportunity to reassert himself. Given his birth and background, as well as the fact that he was a royal lieutenant still owed a massive sum of money by the Crown, the first option was hardly attractive. A dispute in the West Country in September 1451 became the occasion for a demonstration of York's continuing ambition, as he intervened to arrest the warring parties in a way that could only be interpreted as usurping the king's authority. York then moved to an even more open breach, by refusing to attend a royal council in January 1452, before publicly charging the Duke of Somerset, in February, with the loss of Normandy. To make good his threat to arrest Somerset, the Duke of York gathered his forces again and marched towards London. But he was diverted by a royal army towards Kent.

The long-anticipated defiance took place at Dartford in Kent, but Richard of York had once again misjudged the strength of his support. Instead of Henry and Somerset conceding to York's demands, he was forced to back down, and without a fight. According to the *Great Chronicle of London*, York was even tricked by Henry. As he entered the king's tent, having disbanded his army in the belief that he had secured the rearrest of Somerset, York instead discovered his nemesis at Henry's side. 'Lyke a prisoner,' York was forced to cross into London, and to swear an oath of loyalty to the king at St Paul's Cathedral.[16] The same source tells us that it was the announcement of the approach of York's ten-year-old son, Edward, Earl of March, at the head of 10,000 men that secured his father's release. That may sound an unlikely tale, even in a medieval world where boys grew up fast, but it is possible that York's retainers had gathered a force and put his eldest son in nominal charge. York could return home, but even then, his humiliation was not complete. Henry, or rather Somerset, chose to follow York to Ludlow, and there to hear in person cases brought against his retainers, in July 1452. One (admittedly partisan) account has tenants of 'divers of the duke of York's townships . . . compelled to come naked with choking cords about their necks in the direst frost and snow'. The justice meted out to these unfortunates was peremptory, and there was no doubt who was really administering it: 'And the king himself having pardoned them, the duke [of Somerset] ordered them to be hanged.'[17] Small wonder that by the time the Duke of York's new son Richard was born on 2 October 1452, his household had decamped to another of his estates, Fotheringhay Castle.

'His wit and reson wt drawen'

In the very year of Richard's birth, the Duke of York had taken the most decisive steps on the path to outright confrontation with the Crown. The conflicts that became known – many years later – as the Wars of the Roses spanned almost exactly the period of Richard's life. Although he was in the beginning only a peripheral figure – not just a child, but a fourth son – it is true to say that Richard never experienced a time before civil war. There were, of course, times of peace during his life. But he was born into, and died in, a time of violence, uncertainty and strife.

Richard's earliest childhood experiences can only be surmised from the evidence of the upbringing of children in a similar position. Even the experiences of his own eldest brother, the future Edward IV, who as his father's heir drew far more attention, are barely recorded. A letter survives from Edward and his younger brother Edmund, to their father, thanking him for clothes, asking for more, and complaining of the 'odieux reule & demenyng of Richard Crofte and of his brother'. The letter, written at Easter, has been tentatively dated to 1454, when Edward was twelve (and Richard not yet two). It is not known, however, whether the Crofts were the boys' tutors or their elder contemporaries – whether, that is, the boys were complaining of bullying or harsh discipline. It seems even more unlikely, despite some suggestions to the contrary, that Croft or his wife had anything to do with Richard's education.[18]

Up to the age of six or seven it was the custom for aristocratic boys to live with their families and to have a nurse. It seems likely that Richard and George, the two youngest sons, would have stayed with their mother, Cecily, either at Fotheringhay or at Ludlow, along with their nearest elder sister, Margaret, born in 1446. It has been suggested that as the youngest son of an aristocratic family Richard may have been destined for the Church, using the evidence of what survives of his book collection – particularly the fact that some texts would have required good knowledge of Latin, which is probably more significant in this connection than Richard's ownership of several religious volumes.[19] But it is impossible to be sure.

In later life Cecily became noted for her piety, but earlier she was a vigorous and active supporter of her husband and her sons, with no qualms about taking her part in high politics. The Wars of the Roses are sometimes portrayed as the tragic consequences of aristocratic personal feuds, of men behaving badly. That interpretation has some force, but one of the many remarkable features of the period is the number of influential high-born women. As well as the Yorkist matriarch, this was the age of Margaret of Anjou, of Isabel and Anne Neville and their mother, Anne Beauchamp, of Elizabeth Woodville (who may not have been high born as far as the English were concerned, but whose mother, of the House of Luxembourg, certainly was, and who took to queenship naturally), and Henry Tudor's mother, Margaret Beaufort. In Cecily's case, both George and Richard would receive her active support in their intrigues, while her relationship with her eldest son seems to have been irreparably damaged by his choice of consort, namely Elizabeth Woodville. And as with several other influential women of the period, Cecily's own family connections were an important ingredient in the power games that turned into civil war. Cecily was a Neville by birth, daughter of Ralph Neville, Earl of Westmorland, sister to Richard, Earl of Salisbury, and aunt to another Richard Neville – who inherited the earldom of Salisbury and married into the earldom of Warwick, by which title, and a nickname, 'the Kingmaker', he is best known. The rivalries of the age were always complicated by the fact that so many of them were also family matters.

Whatever the exact arrangements made for Richard's early upbringing, they were dramatically disrupted by his father's next encounters with government. At first, the Duke of York's fortunes appeared to be on the rise. His revival after the humiliation of Dartford in 1452 came as a result of an unprecedented development in English royal history. Towards the end of July 1453, Henry VI was 'indispost sodenly was take and smyten wt a ffransy and his wit and reson wt drawen'[20]. Another chronicler recorded that 'the king suffered a sudden and unexpected fright, becoming so ill that, for a year and a half, he lacked both natural sense and intelligence sufficient to govern the realm'.[21] Neither doctor nor medicine could be found to cure him. What had frightened the king out of his wits? It has been suggested that the news of what would come to be seen as the final defeat of the Hundred Years War, at the Battle of Castillon in Gascony, and the death of the English commander John Talbot, Earl of Shrewsbury (after a brief revival in English fortunes), was the trigger, but no specific contemporary reference makes the connection. And while English kings had not suffered mental collapse before, a French king, Charles VI, had from 1393 succumbed to various delusions, including the belief that he was made of glass. Charles was Henry's maternal grandfather. Whether genetic or not, Henry's decline lasted so long that it could not be ignored.

In France the power vacuum created by Charles's mental illness had led directly to factionalism and civil war, and encouraged the encroachments of the English. In England in 1453, however, for eight months, during which time a royal son and heir, Edward, was born to the oblivious Henry, those around the king did try to ignore his affliction, conducting government in his name as if they were the mere executive of a functioning monarch. But tensions continued to rise. In November the Duke of Somerset was arrested, charged with his past failures in Normandy and Gascony, a move engineered in the Great Council by the Duke of Norfolk, rather than Somerset's arch-enemy York, who had joined the Council in October. Somerset was sent to the Tower, where he remained without trial for a year. Before Parliament assembled in February 1454, armed retinues began to gather: in the north and west, around the king, and from the estates of York and those of his allies the Neville Earls of Salisbury and Warwick.

When Parliament opened, the queen, Margaret of Anjou, moved to establish her son as heir to the throne, having Edward declared Prince of Wales on 15 March. If this was a rallying point for all who wished to emphasize their loyalty, it was also an assertion of royal power in the absence of personal royal will. But the Duke of York's moment was coming. The Archbishop of Canterbury and chancellor, Cardinal John Kemp, who had been acting as head of government (without any additional official title), died suddenly on 22 March. The king had to be told. A deputation of twelve lords and bishops rode to Windsor to give Henry the news and ask him to nominate a successor to the two highest offices in the realm. They were shown in to see the king after dinner. Three times the Bishop of Chichester, a scholarly Welshman, Reginald Pecock, who had succeeded the murdered Moleyns, tried to address Henry on the lords' behalf. But 'they cowede gete noo answere ne signe, for no prayer ne desire, lamentable chere ne exhortation, ne eny thyng that they or eny of theim cowede do or sey, to theire grete sorowe and discomfort'.[22] Two days later the Lords appointed the king's closest relative, Richard, Duke of York, Protector. With Somerset imprisoned, York appeared to have everything he wanted: a place at the head of government, and his great rival humbled.

Up to this point, it could be argued that Richard of York's political interventions had all been personally motivated and factionally defined. He had aimed at removing the Duke of Somerset from government and placing himself there instead, he had complained of plots against him and moneys owed to him, though he had also adopted the language of conciliation and national interest ('the tranquillity and conservation of all this his realm').[23] Now, with Somerset removed, the Duke of York had a chance to show that he could act for the realm as a whole, not just his own affinity. Remarkably, that is what he did. He made sure his supporters were placed in important positions, such as his brother-in-law Richard Neville, Earl of Salisbury, who was appointed chancellor. But Richard of York also imposed a reduction in the royal household, which the open-handed Henry had allowed to expand uncontrollably. York ensured, too, that the Council over which he presided had representation from across the political spectrum, including supporters of the queen. Disturbances continued in the west and north, but York at least seemed to have the will to address them. He could rightly argue that he was doing his best to live up to the promise he had made on assuming the office of Protector, to do 'that that may be to the honour, prosperite and welfare, of thestate and dignite of our said soveraine lord'.[24] For York's youngest son, his father's record not only as defender of his own honour and promoter of his family's interests, but also as a guardian of the realm and of the 'reste and tranquilite of the people', was a powerful blueprint.

But the Duke of York's power was one with an expiry date. Or two dates – the first uncertain, depending on when Henry regained his senses, and the second more predictable, if distant, the time when the Prince of Wales reached 'the age of discretion', or was close enough to it for his mother and her followers to begin to wield power on his behalf. Around Christmas 1454, almost a year and a half after he had lost his faculties, Henry as suddenly regained them. The king greeted the son he had been unable to acknowledge at birth, and was saddened and surprised to hear of the death of Cardinal Kemp. Almost immediately, Henry ordered the release of the Duke of Somerset, who quickly resumed his role at the head of government.

The events of the previous months had allowed York to make alliances, most notably with the Neville family, his brother-in-law Richard Neville, Earl of Salisbury, and Salisbury's son, York's nephew by marriage, the other Richard Neville, Earl of Warwick. The combined holdings of the two Nevilles were a match for York's own. Their regional rivals were the Percy family, Earls of Northumberland, and the Cliffords of Westmorland, who naturally adhered to the Duke of Somerset and the royal party. The groupings that later observers came to know as 'Yorkist' and 'Lancastrian' were beginning to form. The Duke of York and his supporters were spooked by a summons to a Great Council in Leicester, fearing that it would be another occasion for Somerset to get his revenge. As Henry and Somerset set out from London for the Council in May 1455, they were confronted by a larger armed party of York and his allies at St Albans. A last attempt to negotiate came to nothing, and the opening battle of what became known as the Wars of the Roses was joined.

It was more of a street fight than a pitched battle, fought around the marketplace and abbey of St Albans. There were no more than 3,000 men on either side, though the Duke of York's army outnumbered the king's; but, as one contemporary report had it, 'because the place was small few of the combatants could set to work there'. Nevertheless, the outcome was decisive, and the casualties significant. Chief among them was the Duke of Somerset himself. Surrounded by York's men as he took refuge in an inn, Somerset broke out, and 'was felled to the ground with an axe and incontinent being so wounded in several places that there he ended his life'.[25] Henry Percy, Earl of Northumberland, and Lord Clifford were also killed. Richard of York entered the abbey at St Albans, where the pious, consistently unbellicose Henry had been placed for his safety (having been wounded in the neck), and submitted himself to his king. Once again, York was pre-eminent in the kingdom, even if the king's symbolic rights were reasserted a month later at a ceremonial crown wearing that York attended. His status was confirmed when he was reappointed Protector in November. Once again, there remained far too many internal contradictions and external critics for this state of affairs to last.

The young Richard, of course, being only two, was nowhere near the battle scene. His appearance there in the second part of Shakespeare's *Henry VI* is pure fantasy, only compounded by the starring role he is given in Somerset's death 'underneath an alehouse' paltry sign'.[26] For Richard, the beginning of the civil war was significant because of his father's leading part, because of the direct effects it would have on him as he grew up, and because the consequences of these disputes would be played out, sometimes submerged but always reappearing, for the next thirty years – that is, over his entire lifespan. One effect of Shakespeare's premature introduction of Richard is to cement the impression that he was a participant in the Wars of the Roses from the beginning. It also ages him, so that by the time of Bosworth he seems far older than his actual thirty-two years. When historians discuss the impact of Shakespeare's portrayal of Richard III in skewing the popular mental picture of him, they mostly concentrate on the 'bottled spider' king-monster of the play that bears Richard's name. But from his first appearance in the cycle of Shakespeare's Wars of the Roses plays, Richard is recast as the supreme agent of his own fate, pitiless ('priests pray for enemies, but princes kill,' he declares, long before any Yorkist could have thought of himself as a prince) and unrelenting. In fact, Richard began life as a victim of the Wars of the Roses, absolutely at the mercy of the changing fortunes of his family.

In the months that followed St Albans, Richard's father discovered how limited was his own room for manoeuvre. Despite the Duke of York's apparent success in removing his strongest opponents, he encountered a constitutional impasse. When Henry had been incapacitated, a more or less explicit scheme to operate government in his absence could be implemented. But during York's second protectorate, Henry was merely weak, not incapable. In the absence of the Duke of Somerset, the king did not become his own man, he merely attracted a new puppet master. It was his queen, Margaret, who now took the leading role in manipulating him. Although Richard of York managed to pacify a long-running murderous quarrel in the West Country, his next attempt to foster good government merely lost him powerful support. When York backed the Commons' introduction of an Act of Resumption in Parliament, under which numerous royal grants would be overturned, the Lords, who would suffer as a result, opposed it. With the loss of this body of support, any attempt at a government of national unity was doomed. Henry was duly brought out of mothballs to declare York's protectorate over, in February 1456. He had lasted only three months.

The Duke of York returned to his estates. Perhaps he saw his three-year-old son. For the next three years he did spend more time on his lands, though we have no idea how much time he spent with his family. Although he made appearances at Great Councils, he was not the power behind Henry's throne. That remained the queen, who moved the centre of royal power to the Midlands, building up support around Coventry. One chronicler reported that 'The quene with such as were of her affynyte rewled the reame as her lyked, gaderyng ryches innumerable.'[27] Thomas Gascoigne, an Oxford don who kept notes in Latin on contemporary goings-on amid his scholarly works, recorded that 'Margaret did much in the realm of England, they say, after her husband, the king of England, declined into obvious simple-mindedness'; and 'the queen herself ruled, in the year 1456, because almost all the business of the kingdom was done according to the said queen's will, for right or wrong, as many different people say.'[28] She also made further moves to ensure that her eldest son, Edward, was established as Henry's heir. When a council for the Prince of Wales was set up, an unusual clause was inserted into the announcement, mentioning the 'approval and agreement of . . . the queen'.[29]

Henry's own part in these manoeuvres was non-existent, except for his sponsorship of an act of reconciliation for the bloodshed at St Albans, a solemn 'Loveday' held on 25 March 1458 in London, at which Yorkists atoned for the deaths of Somerset, Northumberland and Clifford, and processed arm in arm with their opponents. Richard of York escorted Queen Margaret into St Paul's. But as a sermon preached around this time before the king at Coventry pointed out, shows of reconciliation could conceal treacherous intent: 'they hadde made love days as Judas made whythe a cosse'.[30] And by this time, there were already clear signs that the country was sliding towards lawlessness. 'The reame of Englonde was oute of alle good gouernance . . . for the kyng was symple and

led by couetous counseylle, and owed more then he was worthe.'[31] The port of
Sandwich was attacked and plundered by a French raiding party. The Earl of
Warwick, the Duke of York's close ally who retained the captaincy of Calais
secured for him during the protectorate, resorted to acts of piracy to provide
for his garrison. He had only retired across the Channel after surviving an
assassination attempt at court. In May 1459 there were riots in London.

'Infants, who have not offended against the king'

The riots prompted another royal move out of the capital. The court repaired
to Coventry, and there the crisis deepened further when a summons was
issued to York, Salisbury and Warwick. With no great speed, the final
chances of avoiding war were played out. Seeing the summons as a trick to
lure them from their centres of power and places of safety, the Yorkist lords
failed to respond, and began instead to arm. In September 1459 the Earl of
Warwick crossed from Calais, and made to join up with his father, the Earl
of Salisbury, and with Richard of York. Salisbury defeated a royalist army
that attempted to bar his way at Blore Heath in Staffordshire, though his
two younger sons, John and Thomas Neville, were captured. York, Warwick
and Salisbury met at Worcester, where they took communion and swore
their allegiance to the Crown in the cathedral. Making their way towards
York's stronghold at Ludlow, they drew up their armies at Ludford Bridge on
12 October, faced by a royal force that outnumbered theirs. Overnight, the
Yorkists appear to have had second thoughts. They had been abandoned by
one of Warwick's retainers, Andrew Trollope, whose contingent of troops
from Calais switched sides when they realized that Warwick's protestations
of loyalty were a sham.

In the morning the Yorkists fled. Richard of York himself, with his second
son Edmund, Earl of Rutland, made for Ireland. Warwick, Salisbury and
Edward, Earl of March, York's eldest son, crossed over from Devon to Calais,
via Guernsey. They left behind Cecily, Duchess of York, and her younger

children: Margaret, George – and Richard, who had just turned seven. The debacle of Ludford is the second time Richard enters the historical record – if not by name, then as one of his mother's 'infants, who have not offended against the king' – after his fleeting appearance in the Clare Roll.[32] Over the previous two years, it is likely that Richard would have seen more of his father, and of his two eldest brothers, Edward and Edmund, than ever before. But without warning, they were gone. The very fact that the duke did not take his wife and younger children with him shows how sudden was his flight. His ally, Salisbury, had been forced to abandon his own sons after Blore Heath. But they were grown men, taken on the battlefield.

What happened to Cecily and her three youngest children after Ludford Bridge is a matter of some dispute. There are two chronicle accounts detailing the aftermath of Richard of York's flight, and both paint a picture of a victorious army let off the leash. The 'kyngs galentys' entered the town of Ludlow and helped themselves to the contents of its cellars, smashing open barrels with such zeal that 'men wente wete-schode in wyne'. This drunken mob then plundered the town 'and defoulyd many wymmen'.[33] The chronicle known as 'Davies's' confirms the story that Ludlow was 'robbed to the bare walles', adding that Richard's mother, 'the noble duches of York unmanly and cruelly was entreted and spoyled'.[34] In a memoir written around sixty years after the event, known as Hearne's fragment after the 'keen scavenger in the neglected dustbins of history'[35] who rediscovered it, Thomas Howard, Duke of Norfolk, a Yorkist who had ridden his luck into the Tudor age, put Cecily and her two sons face to face with 'King Harry' as he 'rode into Ludlow, and spoiled the town and castle'. If that picture is unlikely for the active impression it gives of the king, it is weakened further by the fact that the memoirist gave the brothers' ages as thirteen and ten, when they were in fact ten and seven. (Margaret, unmentioned, was fourteen.) Howard himself would not have witnessed any encounter. He was sixteen years old and several hundred miles away at the time. This episode has been coloured in subsequent retellings into a dramatic confrontation between the duchess and the king 'at the market cross', with her children in attendance, though Cecily is surely more likely to have kept to the relative safety of Ludlow Castle. The suggestion in Davies's chronicle that Cecily might have been raped, which is certainly one meaning of 'spoyled', should also be treated with caution. The word also means 'robbed', and it would doubtless have formed a much more explicit part of Yorkist accounts if such an accusation had been widely made. For all that, the experience after Ludford must have been a traumatic one for Richard, witnessing at first hand what going against the Crown and losing could mean.

Cecily did meet Henry. She came 'unto Kyng Harry and submyttyd hyr unto hys grace' at Coventry in November 1459, where her husband had been declared a traitor by Parliament and had forfeited his lands in an act of attainder.[36] The extension of this process at the so-called Parliament of Devils to include York's wider alliance was controversial.[37] Cecily was spared the full treatment herself, receiving instead a generous annual allowance of 1,000 marks from her husband's estates, now in others' hands. But her children's inheritance had been removed. Richard and his siblings had at a stroke gone from being members of one of the wealthiest and most powerful families in England to being without power or prospects. Or freedom. Cecily was consigned with the three children to the care of her sister, the Duchess of Buckingham; one chronicler described less than sisterly treatment (her brother-in-law, Humphrey Stafford, Duke of Buckingham, was a Lancastrian loyalist with a volatile reputation). The Duchess of York 'was kept fulle strayte and many a grete rebuke'.[38]

It is not known at which of the Buckinghams' houses, or for how long, Cecily and her children were confined. A reference in the Paston Letters to 'my lady Duchesses . . . stille ayen receved yn Kent'[39] in January 1460 may account for the assumption that they were kept at the Buckinghams' castle in that county at Tonbridge, though the manor of Writtle in Essex has also been suggested.[40] The family's fortunes depended on what her husband and his allies did next. Left with nothing by the acts of attainder, but still at liberty, none of them was likely to give up now. Warwick, Salisbury and the Earl of March in Calais, and the Duke of York with his second son Edmund, Earl of Rutland, in Ireland, were able to prepare their next move carefully. Warwick even risked the voyage to Ireland to meet Richard of York in Waterford, to discuss their plans.

In June 1460, while Richard and his siblings were still in the custody of the Buckinghams, their eldest brother, Edward, Earl of March, landed at Sandwich in Kent in the company of the Earls of Salisbury and Warwick and their men.

This army was welcomed by the people of Kent, who had sent messages to Calais to invite the earls, and posted a ballad praising 'Edward Erle of Marche, whos fame the erthe shalle sprede,/Richard Erle of Salisbury named prudence,/ Whythe that noble knyghte and floure of manhode Richard Erle of Warrewyk sheelde of oure defence' on the doors of Canterbury Cathedral.[41] As they marched towards London, proclaiming 'yet ayene' their true allegiance to the king and their determination to restore the realm (and their inheritances), they could have passed close to young Richard's temporary home at Tonbridge. Perhaps Cecily might even have been reunited with her eldest son, and proceeded to London along with him. The Archbishop of Canterbury, Thomas Bourchier, who had greeted Warwick's party in Sandwich and had his cross carried before them, was Buckingham's half-brother: could he have engineered an early release? Buckingham himself, along with other magnates loyal to the king, was away, mustering at Northampton.

The capital, when the Yorkist earls arrived, was not quite as unequivocal in its support as Kent had been. But Lord Scales and Lord Hungerford, loyal to the Crown, were forced to retire to the safety of the Tower when the city authorities welcomed the Yorkists on 2 July 1460. At St Paul's Cathedral the Archbishop of Canterbury presided over a clerical convocation, where Warwick rehearsed the Yorkists' grievances, and plans were made to go to King Henry at Northampton. While their brother Edward marched north to confront the king, Richard, George and Margaret were left behind, in London or elsewhere. If they were still in the Buckinghams' custody, it may be thought surprising that the fact that Henry had hostages does not seem to have formed part of the negotiations that preceded the confrontation at Northampton on 10 July. The main voice raised against any compromise, brokered by Bourchier and his fellow bishops, was, in fact, that of Humphrey Stafford, Duke of Buckingham. Dismissing the peace delegation 'nat as bysshoppes for to trete for pease, but as men of armes', Buckingham ensured that battle was joined.[42]

There were orders not to attack the king's person, and to spare the 'common people'. This was a fight between aristocrats, who had accumulated insults and grievances over the years of Henry's misrule. At Northampton, in a downpour that incapacitated the Lancastrian guns, it was the loyalist lords who suffered. 'On the king's side there fell the Duke of Buckingham, the Earl of Shrewsbury,

Viscount Lord Beaumont, Lord Egremont and other nobles.' But the same chronicler also reported that the order to spare the lesser ranks had not been followed: 'a countless number of commoners' were killed, too.[43] Although the nobles talked of 'the commonweal' and made gestures towards limiting casualties, the reality of war was that all manner of men would suffer. For the Yorkists the most important result of Northampton was that the king was now in their hands. This would allow them to rule in Henry's name, but without the interference of his queen and her supporters, who had fled, with her son Edward, to Wales, before sailing to Scotland.

At Fastolf's Place

Victory at Northampton, and the death of the Duke of Buckingham, gave Cecily and her children their freedom, if they had not already won it. They were brought to the capital. In London the house of the Duke and Duchess of York, Baynard's Castle beside the Thames, was their usual residence. But by 15 September 1460, with the duke's arrival still awaited from Ireland, the duchess and her three children had in fact moved into a house formerly belonging to an old supporter, Sir John Fastolf, which on his death had passed to John Paston. It is to one of the Paston family's surviving letters that we owe a rare glimpse into Richard's childhood. Christopher Hansson, a retired German soldier who had charge of the house in Southwark, wrote to Paston on 12 October with news of their guests. Although Hansson had offered to put the duchess and her three children up until Michaelmas (29 September), Cecily 'had not ley here ii dayes but sche had tythyng of the londyng of my lord at Chestre. The Tewesday next after [23 September] my lord sent for hir that scho shuld come to hym to Harford [Hereford], and theder scho is gone, and sythe y left here bothe the sunnys and the dowzyter, and the Lord of Marche comyth every day to se them.'[44]

For a moment, the Yorks look almost like an ordinary family, one in which a husband separated from his wife for almost a year cannot wait to be reunited with her; and one in which the younger children are tended to by a solicitous elder brother. Edward comes 'every day' to see his siblings. Of course, this is no ordinary family, and the times are extraordinary, too. The eighteen-year-old

Edward had just commanded a division in a battle against the king. His
father, moreover, was raising the stakes even higher. When Cecily joined
him, conducted in a 'chare i-coveryd with blewe felewette', the couple began
to put on a display that could only mean he now meant to claim the throne
himself. The duke hired trumpeters as he made his way to London, giving
them banners with 'the hole armys of Inglonde with oute any dyversyte'. Only
royalty was preceded by such a device, and only a king could order his sword,
as the Duke of York now did, to be 'borne uppe ryghte be-fore hym'.[45]

While this conspicuous display of royal pretensions was paraded through
the country, the actual king was said to be hunting at Greenwich, 'bydyng the
parlement' – doubtless under close watch. We may not be surprised that
Henry was unaware of Richard of York's plans, and, in any case, he could do
little about them. What is more surprising is that York's allies seem not to
have known his intentions either. There could scarcely be any more dramatic
political move than to claim the throne. But it was not an unprecedented
move, and when it had been made before, as by the king's grandfather Henry
Bolingbroke, Duke of Lancaster, in 1399, it was carefully stage-managed. The
Duke of York, too, seems to have primed all the principal actors. It is difficult
to believe that in their discussions in Ireland, Warwick and York hadn't raised
the question of the latter claiming the throne. By his actions since landing, he
had made it clear that this is what he proposed to do. And yet, when he arrived
at Westminster Hall, filled with his supporters for the opening of Parliament,
and 'walked straight on, until he came to the king's throne, upon the covering
or cushion of which laying his hand, in the very act like a man about to take
possession of his rights', Richard of York was met not by a shout of acclamation
but by an embarrassed silence. As the duke 'looked eagerly for their applause',
Thomas Bourchier, the Archbishop of Canterbury, asked him instead if he
wanted to see the king.[46] For ten years the Duke of York had fought to establish
his rights without directly asserting his claim to the throne. Emboldened at
last to take the final step, he had apparently been abandoned by his allies. Had
the Nevilles, Salisbury and Warwick really been taken by surprise by York's
gambit? Had no word of the manner of his progress through England – and
thus of his clear intentions – reached them? That strains credibility: what else
was such an explicit show for than to prepare the way? It can only be surmised

that York's supporters gauged the mood of the assembly of lords at the moment he went to claim the throne, and decided it was not with them.

Richard of York could not back down straight away. He told Bourchier that he knew no one in the kingdom who shouldn't come to see him rather than he go to them. But he did go to the king, breaking down doors and making Henry move into the queen's apartments. He also tried to put his claim more formally, requesting first the House of Lords, then the justices, and finally the serjeants at law to rule on the matter. The basis for his claim was the priority of the Mortimer descent over a junior branch of the royal family, descended from Henry IV. Of course, nothing about this blood claim had changed. Richard of York could always have argued that he had a better right to the throne than the reigning king. As early as 1450, when Jack Cade was associated with the name Mortimer, this alternative claim had been in the political air. So why now? The fact that York would not, or could not, say, illustrates the quandary of any pretender to the throne. Merely ruling badly was not enough reason to be deprived of a Crown. But having a superior claim meant nothing if it was not accompanied by political support.

The Duke of York's youngest son had just turned eight years old when all this was happening. We should hardly expect Richard to have understood the niceties of a debate on which ostensible experts were reluctant to pronounce. But the drama of these events, as they were relayed to him, must have made an impression. Nor can he have been unaware that his father had declared that he was the rightful king, and had been denied. Whatever the psychological impact of such a public humiliation, recalling the practical lessons of risking such a claim would have given the adult Richard pause for thought.

The responses of those consulted on the Duke of York's petition, and the tortuous debate surrounding his genealogy, were all enrolled in the parliamentary records. This was a far cry from the neat legal *faits accomplis* that accompanied previous – and subsequent – depositions. Each body, put in an impossible position that would risk treason whatever they said, refused to give an answer. Eventually, a compromise was reached. Under the Act of Accord, enrolled on 31 October, Henry would remain king, but York and his descendants would succeed him. This was exactly the formula that had been used to end a much earlier civil war, when King Stephen gave up his inheritance in 1153, paving the way for the succession of Henry II. It was also the principle on which the Treaty of Troyes had made Henry V and his descendants heir to the French throne in 1420. In 1153 the disinherited prince, Stephen's son Eustace, died before his vociferous objections could ripen into rebellion. In 1420 the claims of Charles's son, later Charles VII of France, were passed over, an arrangement understandably rejected on his father's death. In 1460, however, the Act of Accord ignored a far more formidable figure than either Eustace or Charles on those earlier occasions: Queen Margaret, who could be relied upon to defend with relentless tenacity the interests of her son Edward, Prince of Wales.

Margaret had taken refuge in Scotland with her son, in whose name she now called on followers in the north to rise up against the Duke of York's government. They gathered in Hull. A month after the Act of Accord had become law, York, Rutland and Salisbury had to leave London to confront Lancastrian forces in Yorkshire. The Earl of March, meanwhile, went west, to deal with trouble in Wales. The duke and his allies arrived at his castle of Sandal in Yorkshire on 21 December. The Lancastrian force included the Duke of Somerset, the Earl of Devon, and the Earls of Northumberland and Westmorland, as well as Lord Clifford. Somerset, Northumberland and Clifford were the heirs of men killed by Richard of York; the Earl of Westmorland was a Neville, but one who had seen his inheritance swallowed up by the junior branch of the family represented by Salisbury and Warwick; the Earl of Devon was a Lancastrian loyalist who had married the queen's cousin. These were formidable foes, personally wounded by the violence of the previous decade, and they were likely to take any chance they could of revenge. Although a truce was agreed over Christmas, somehow the Lancastrians managed to lure the Duke of York from his castle on 30 December by attacking a foraging party at Wakefield. The duke had ridden into a trap. Outnumbered, Richard of York was killed along with his second son, the Earl of Rutland. The Earl of Salisbury was captured, taken to Pontefract Castle, and executed. Lord Clifford was reported to have killed the seventeen-year-old Edmund of Rutland personally. The Duke of York's head was taken from the battlefield and placed on a spike at the gates of the city of York, wearing a paper crown. The victorious Lancastrians turned south, apparently set on retaking the capital, liberating the king, and re-establishing Henry, his queen and his son at the head of government.

'Into the parties of Flanders'

For Richard and his family, awaiting news in London, this was a terrifying reversal of fortune, as well as a personal tragedy. Rumours of the conduct of Margaret's army, pillaging as they marched down the country, put the whole city into a state of panic. For Cecily, the threat to her children was surely much greater. She decided to get them out of harm's way, 'fferyng the ffortune of that world sent ovyr the See hyr yonger sons George & Rychard into a toune in Flaundres named uteryk [Utrecht] where they Restid a whyle'.[47] The date of this journey is unknown, though it seems unlikely that Cecily would have waited as late as February 1461, when the Lancastrians were closing with the Yorkists on two fronts, to act. For this latest upheaval, the boys were not accompanied by their mother or their sister. The details of an annuity later granted by Edward IV record that one Alice Martyn took in the brothers, keeping them 'from daungier and perill in thair troubles vnto the tyme of thair departing out of this owre Reame into the parties of fflaundres'.[48] She is described as 'of our Citie of London, Widowe', but no details survive of where she lived nor how long she had charge of George and Richard – though it was long enough for her to be remembered by a grateful older brother two years later.

George and Richard are likely to have stayed with widow Martyn only long enough for arrangements to be made to get them to safety. The fact that neither the Yorks' usual London residence, Baynard's Castle, nor Fastolf's house where they had stayed before, was thought safe enough, is indication of the danger they were felt to be in. Alice Martyn's house was perhaps suitably anonymous, unknown to potential enemies who may, even before the arrival of the Lancastrian army, have been looking for the Yorks to deliver them to the victors when they reached the city gates. The arrangements Cecily made for her sons were initially rather complicated. The duchess wanted her children to fall under the protection of the Duke of Burgundy, Philip the Good. Philip, however, decided to wait for the outcome of England's civil war. If he showed too much favour to the Yorks, and Margaret's Lancastrians triumphed, as must have seemed very likely after Wakefield, then he would be in a difficult diplomatic position. If, on the other hand, he refused to welcome the young sons of York, and the Yorkist cause suddenly revived, then he would be out of a favour with a new regime.

Philip's solution was an elegant one. He allowed his illegitimate son, David, Prince-Bishop of Utrecht, to take George and Richard in. There is no record of how they made it there, or who took charge of them on the way (though unnamed 'merchants' were later mentioned in connection with the brothers, so perhaps they were entrusted to men who had regular business in the region).[49] Utrecht was not part of Burgundy's lands, though Philip's manoeuvrings to have David installed in 1456 were certainly aimed at increasing Burgundian influence there. It was also a place where English exiles had found refuge before (such as the Lancastrian Earl of Wiltshire, in the city in 1460, but shortly to face Richard's brother in battle). While uncertainty continued, Philip would keep the children safe, but at arm's length.

So, until there was a settled outcome to the fighting over the North Sea, Richard, still only eight years old, could add Bishop David's stronghold of Duurstede to his parents' castles at Fotheringhay and Ludlow, the Buckinghams' residence in Kent or Essex, Baynard's Castle by the Thames, Fastolf's house in Southwark and Alice Martyn's refuge somewhere in London to the list of his temporary homes. True, the children of the nobility often lived peripatetic lives, which was one of the principal differences between their experiences and those of the vast majority of their contemporaries, whose horizons might extend little beyond the parish boundaries. But added to constant movement in the case of the York children was near constant apprehension. The two boys – their father and one elder brother killed, their mother far away, and threatened by a Lancastrian army on the rampage at the gates of London – can have had little hope of yet another turn of fortune's wheel.

At first, the news that arrived from England only added to the confusion. In the space of just over two weeks at the beginning of February, the Yorkists experienced a great victory, and then an apparently more significant defeat. On 2 or 3 February 1461, Richard and George's brother Edward, the new head of the family, defeated a Lancastrian army led by Jasper Tudor, Earl of Pembroke (and half-brother to Henry VI), and James Butler, Earl of Wiltshire (himself returned from Utrecht), at Mortimer's Cross in Herefordshire, in the Welsh marches. The teenager's army was initially 'aghast' at the sight of three suns rising at dawn (a phenomenon caused by atmospheric conditions now known as a parhelion), but the quick-thinking Edward interpreted this as a sign of the blessing of the Holy Trinity.[50] This mark of heavenly favour was later said to have inspired Edward's adoption of the device of the 'sun in splendour'. The Earl of Wiltshire was certainly rattled enough to cement a reputation for cowardice that he had initially acquired from fleeing the first Battle of St Albans in disguise. At Mortimer's Cross the earl who 'fought manly with his helys [heels]',[51] didn't even wait for the fighting to begin before once again getting into mufti and slipping away. Jasper Tudor, too, made his escape, to remain a thorn in Yorkist sides.

Richard's eldest brother was beginning to look more and more like a man of destiny, able to win in battle, and demonstrate how God and the heavens were on his side. But the Earl of March still had something of his father's hesitancy in him, moving cautiously after Mortimer's Cross, and the now predictable reprisals that followed it: Jasper's uncle Owen Tudor, grandfather of the future Henry VII, former husband of Henry V's widow Queen Katherine, went to the executioner's block in Hereford in a state of denial, unable to comprehend how it had come to this. ('That hede shalle ly on the stocke that was wonte to ly on Quene Kateryns lappe', he was heard to murmur.)[52] Thus Edward was not present when the Earl of Warwick and his brother John Neville, recently created Baron Montagu, were unable to halt the Lancastrian advance at St Albans; on 17 February they fled the battlefield in defeat before they suffered the same fate as their father after Wakefield. What was worse, they lost control of the king, who was taken back by the Lancastrians and reunited with his wife and son. As for Henry, he now seemed to have little idea of what was happening all around him. It was reported that during the battle, 'The king was placed under a tree a mile away, where he laughed and sang.'[53]

If Margaret had been welcomed into the capital after seeing off the Earl of Warwick, support for the Yorkists might well have drained away. Richard and George would have been consigned to a childhood in exile – the fate that lay in store for Richard's future rival, Henry Tudor, in Brittany. But the Lancastrian army had established a fearsome reputation on its march south.

It was rumoured that the unbridled conduct of the soldiers, living off the land in lieu of pay, had encouraged more widespread lawlessness, witnessed by alarmed monastic chroniclers, such as the prior of Crowland in the East Anglian fens, who wrote in a fit of zoological mixed metaphors of 'paupers and beggars . . . flock[ing] forth . . . in infinite numbers, like so many mice rushing forth from their holes', attacking religious houses and 'covering the whole surface of the earth just like so many locusts'.[54] At St Albans, where the Abbot, John Whetamstede, could be forgiven for feeling even more in the thick of unwanted drama, the 'Northerners' drew unfavourable comparison with despoilers of sacred spaces from Antiochus Epiphanes and Nebuchadnezzar to Attila the Hun.[55] If these timorous monks were exaggerating (and it was not just monks: Clement Paston wrote to his brother in January that 'þe pepill in þe northe robbe and styll and ben apoyntyd to pill all thys cwntré'),[56] they give the lie to the view that the Wars of the Roses was just a vicious spat between blue bloods, of little consequence to society at large. And even if rumours of the Lancastrians' lawlessness were overplayed, they also had the effect of making up Londoners' minds not to allow Margaret's forces into the capital. An advance party sent by the Duke of Somerset was repulsed, and although there were some voices raised on the side of the queen, the people seemed to be decided against: 'the comones, for the sauacione of the cyte, toke the keyes of the yates were they shulde have entred, and manly kept and defended hit fro theyre enemyes, vnto the commyng of Edwarde the noble erle of Marche'.[57] The path was open for Edward, who had made contact with Warwick in the Cotswolds, to enter the city unopposed, on 26 February 1461.

Edward moved rapidly to claim the prize that had always eluded his father. He could present himself as victorious, wronged (after the Lancastrians had broken the Act of Accord by attacking the Yorkists) and legitimate (he had been established as successor to his father the Duke of York by the same Act). Henry VI, it was now argued, had forfeited his right to rule by breaking the Act of Accord. In London at least, where the alternative presented by Queen Margaret's marauders had been explicitly rejected, Edward was welcomed as king. The Neville family were conspicuous in arranging the public formalities that opened the way for Edward, in a manner that contrasted markedly with their role when Richard of York had made his bid for the Crown. George

Neville, chancellor and Bishop of Exeter (and Edward's first cousin), made a declaration in favour of Edward on 1 March, at St John's Fields in Clerkenwell, to a crowd of up to 4,000. And George's brother Richard Neville, the Earl of Warwick, now began to earn his later sobriquet of 'Kingmaker', as part of the Great Council that met at Baynard's Castle to urge Edward to accept the crown. On 4 March 1461, Edward formally took up the offer after celebrating Mass and hearing a Te Deum at St Paul's. After George Neville had preached a public sermon at St Paul's Cross, the party made their way to Westminster Hall, where Edward took his seat on the King's Bench, sitting as sovereign where his father had merely placed his hand.

These events were swiftly reported across the Channel, and conveyed to Bruges, in Duke Philip's territories, by 9 March. But Philip, like Edward, understood that these formalities, as extraordinary and impressive as they undoubtedly were, would not effect a permanent change in English politics until the Lancastrians commanded by Margaret of Anjou were finally and comprehensively defeated – and, preferably, the now deposed King Henry could be returned to the Yorkists' custody, his fate to be decided. And so it was not until further news arrived from England, rumours at Middelburg on 3 April passed on to the duke, that Philip finally saw fit to welcome his now princely guests with honour. On 10 April it was reported back in London that 'the Duke of Burgundy is treating the brothers of the king with respect'.[58]

What had happened to change Duke Philip's attitude was nothing less than the greatest battle in English history. Edward had wasted no time in gathering an army to march north and confront the Lancastrians. They met outside the village of Towton in Yorkshire. Vast estimates were made of both of the armies on either side, and of the ensuing casualties, but even today, as archaeologists continue to dig up more evidence of the slaughter, astonishing figures of up to 28,000 dead, first reported in a newsletter preserved among the Pastons' correspondence, are still given credence.[59] The battle was fought through the whole of Palm Sunday, 29 March 1461, in freezing conditions.[60] Artillery was used, but most of the dead met their ends in more time-honoured fashion, either from volleys of arrows fired by longbowmen, or, in the words of the battlefield archaeologists, from 'blade wounds occurring in the front and back of the head. The majority of these wounds penetrate the endocranium, indicating trauma to the brain.'[61] The bitterness and violent hatreds of more than ten years of conflict seem to have erupted at Towton. 'One is left to wonder when a rout ends and a massacre begins.'[62]

At the end of the hardest day of fighting in the Wars of the Roses, the new king's army held the field against supporters of the old king. The dead on the Lancastrian side included the Earl of Northumberland and the younger son of the Duke of Buckingham, as well as Andrew Trollope, the captain who had defected at Ludford Bridge. Noble losses on the Yorkist side were not so significant. Among the Yorkist ranks was a contingent led by the Dauphin of France, Prince Louis, who, in opposition to his father (Charles VII), had thrown in his lot with Richard and George's host, the Duke of Burgundy. It was Duke Philip who bankrolled the Dauphin's party at Towton. Perhaps having his own ally on the battlefield meant that Philip received news of the outcome all the faster. The presence of the Dauphin as Philip's proxy makes it even more intriguing to consider what might have happened to Richard and George if their brother's army had been defeated.

The rewards of victory, even at several hundred miles' remove, were certainly handsome. The boys were taken from Utrecht to Sluys, in Burgundy itself, and finally to Bruges, where they were entertained at Philip's court, one of the finest in Europe. The duke himself paid them a visit, before laying on a banquet at the Aldermen's Hall. The Milanese ambassador to the court of France, staying at Bruges, wrote that 'two younger brothers of March, son of the Duke of York, are coming here, and the Duke of Burgundy has given notice for great honours to be shown to them'. He also remarked that, for all the slaughter visited on the Lancastrians at Towton, this was unlikely to be the end of the matter: 'If the King and Queen of England [i.e. Henry and Margaret] . . . are not taken, it seems certain that in time fresh disturbances will arise.'[63]

Duke of Gloucester, Squire of Warwick

When Richard and George finally departed Burgundy, on 24 April 1461, returning to England via Calais, they were travelling to a coronation. The sun of York had risen. For Richard, the next few years would bring princely promotion and, for the first time, a settled situation in which he could receive a less sporadic education in the knightly and royal virtues. For a few weeks, ceremony, celebration and pageantry dominated the new princes' lives. They landed in Kent and were greeted at Canterbury on 30 May. As well as attending three services at Christ Church priory, they were presented with another feast, which gives an idea of the size of their party: 3 capons, 2 oxen, 20 sheep and 3 gallons of wine.[64] By 2 June they had reached London, to be greeted at Billingsgate by the mayor and aldermen decked out in crimson, accompanied by the liveried wardens of the city guilds. Richard and George would have been used to certain marks of respect, as members of one of the greatest families in the country. But even an eight-year-old would have noticed the change in their treatment now.

In London, Baynard's Castle is likely to have been their home while they waited for the return of their victorious brother. Edward arrived at Shene palace, Richmond – the principal residence of Henry V, who had rebuilt it – on 14 June, and was reunited with his brothers shortly afterwards. The eldest sibling, who had visited his younger brothers 'every day' at Fastolf's house, had, in the space of six months, become King of England (and, by tradition, of France and Ireland, too).[65] In less than a fortnight, George and Richard would be made Knights of the Bath at the Tower of London, the night before they accompanied Edward IV, 'proceeding before the king, in their gowns and hoods, and tokens of white silk upon their shoulders', to his coronation at Westminster Abbey.[66] It could have been remarked that among the venerable judges and trusted servants of the Yorkists who represented the Order of the Bath at the coronation procession, such as Sir John Markham and Sir William Blount, there were several young faces to match the king's own. As well as the eight- and eleven-year-old brothers of the king, there was John Mowbray, heir to the dukedom of Norfolk, who was sixteen; Thomas Fitzalan, future Earl of Arundel, ten; Lord Strange, sixteen; and Sir William Stanley, twenty-six.

All these new Knights of the Bath, young and old, had been through the same elaborate purification ceremonies and preparation, washed naked in the ritual bath, dressed in red, white and black silk, before receiving the sword and spurs of the order, together with a blue robe and a hanging of lace, to be worn on the left shoulder until the new knight had earned the right by his deeds to remove it. Although George, as Edward's nearest brother, and heir while the king remained unmarried, took a more formal part than Richard in the coronation ceremony itself, confirmed by his creation that day as Duke of Clarence, Richard would have been impressed by the rituals in which he had featured so prominently. He may have been a child, with only the faintest understanding of the politics that had so altered his circumstances, but from those experiences in June 1461, he would have known that his whole life had changed course.

At first, this alteration was manifested in yet another change of address. It has been speculated that George and Richard had apartments in Greenwich Palace, but the only surviving records of this period that refer to them (the Great Wardrobe accounts for April 1461 to April 1465) show clothing, saddlery and armour being delivered not only to Greenwich but also to Westminster and Leicester – at dates that coincide with the king's movements. There is also the evidence of Edward's grant, not made until a decade later in 1471, to 'the king's kinsman Thomas [Bourchier], cardinal archbishop of Canterbury . . . because in time past at the king's request he supported the king's brothers . . . for a long time at great charges'.[67] What form this support took, whether the brothers spent time staying with the archbishop at Canterbury or Lambeth, is unknown. While Richard's exact movements may not be clear, it is obvious that his existence remained peripatetic.

There were other big changes. George had already been made Duke of Clarence at the coronation. Richard had to wait until after his ninth birthday to receive a similar promotion. On 1 November 1461 he was made Duke of Gloucester. By February of the following year, he had joined Clarence in the highest order of chivalry in the country, as a Knight of the Garter. On turning ten, he gained yet another title, 'Admiral of England, Ireland and Aquitaine, with all accustomed profits and powers'.[68] To accompany these titles were the beginnings of an income, if not yet a power base. Richard received a package of manors and offices, including the castle of Gloucester and constableship of Corfe in Dorset, as well as, potentially most significantly, the estates of the Earl of Oxford, who, along with his eldest son, was executed for treason in February 1462.[69] But the Oxford lands were returned to the new earl, younger son of the executed twelfth earl, when he was restored to his inheritance in 1464. By comparison with Clarence, Gloucester received relatively little, less securely, and it was income rather than influence that was the early governing principle of these grants.

Of course, all these honours, offices and grants were held for Richard during his minority by those who looked after his interests, though the names of these individuals are lost to us. Richard was, however, about to come under the influence of an individual whose name and reputation are only too well known. In 1464 or 1465, at the age of twelve, Richard was deemed ready to take the next important step in his princely upbringing. He was sent to the household of his cousin the Earl of Warwick, Edward's close ally and most powerful subject, the man who some said had put him on the throne and remained the real power behind it. The famous remark reported to King Louis XI (who had ascended to the throne a few months after Edward), that the English 'have but two rulers, M de warwick and another whose name I have forgotten', is one of those witty phrases whose wit has allowed it to do a lot of historical heavy lifting. It was made by the Governor of Abbeville, a town two days' ride from Warwick's garrison at Calais, and as it was passed to a man who had fought (while the Dauphin) with both Warwick and Edward at Towton, where Edward's generalship was never doubted, it isn't likely to have gained much credence.[70] Warwick was a formidable figure, and his was a suitable household for the king's younger brother to grow up in. But it was he who had failed to stop Margaret's army at St Albans after Edward had presided over the miracle of Mortimer's Cross. Richard was not being sent to live with a man whom Edward feared, but a magnate and kinsman whom he trusted to impart the necessary knightly virtues. For all that, Richard's formative years were spent in the orbit of a supreme practiser of late-medieval realpolitik. We shouldn't be too swift to dismiss the notion that some of Warwick's attitude to the manipulation of power rubbed off on an impressionable son of York.

On the cusp of adolescence, a much shorter period in a young person's life then than now, Richard might have reflected on the great upheavals that had seen him made a duke along with one brother, while the other had seized a throne. There would be practical lessons to learn from these events, of the importance of loyalty, of timing – and of luck. But however pragmatic an age this could be, it was also an age of faith, and of a conception of science and history that to modern eyes looks more like magic and myth. Henry VI's ineffectual kingship and his sickness were widely seen as part of the same affliction. That is, one was not just a consequence of the other: they amounted to the same thing, the body politic sickening with the king's corporeal body. Attempts to diagnose and cure his malady, and failing that, to find and legitimate an alternative, preoccupied philosophers and alchemists (which were not two distinct professions) in the 1450s and 1460s. The catapaulting of Edward to the pinnacle of power – particularly after his family's fortunes had sunk so low – was seen not merely as the culmination of decades of misrule and factionalism. It was the providential triumph of a dynasty – one that Edward's court sages portrayed as fulfilling ancient legends from the time of Merlin and Arthur, and classical models both mythical and historical: Caesar, Alexander, Brutus and Achilles.

As Mortimer's Cross and Towton had demonstrated, the coming of Edward had sacred implications, too. A flurry of public literature, produced in the form of great rolls to be hung on open view, portrayed the new king in alchemical and religious terms, as the risen sun in contrast with Henry VI's weak and watery moon, and as a number of biblical figures or their descendants, from Joshua, Noah and Moses, to Christ himself. These symbolically illustrated rolls, depicting, for example, Edward in majesty, not just at the summit of Fortune's wheel, but secure there because Reason has placed a spar between the spokes to stop it turning, were meant to be seen, and their message assimilated, by the wider public – the 'commonweal' to whom Edward and his father had appealed, and who, in Edward's case if not his father's, had given him their acclamation. They were also the kind of striking visual statements that were likely to have left a lasting impression on those closest to the king, such as his youngest brother.[71]

When tracing Richard's development into adulthood, the sparseness of our records might lead us to view it in purely conventional terms. Here was a young (fatherless) prince, whose chivalric education was entrusted to the king's cousin, his closest ally (and mightiest subject). If we do not have records of exactly how his education was undertaken at, presumably, Warwick's fine, fortified residences of Middleham, Sheriff Hutton or Warwick itself, there is enough evidence of the regime of similarly high-born (or high-thrust) young men to have a fair idea. Edward's own son was the recipient of a programme of instruction that survives. The king's 'Black Book' of his household specifies instructions for his 'henxmen' – squires or pages – the role that the young Richard is likely to have played. The Master of these young men is entrusted with a complete programme of education, including lessons in riding a horse fully armed, in courtesy, manners, music, and 'sondry langages and othyr lernynges vertuous'.[72]

These were the expected accomplishments of one in Richard's station. But as well as having no idea how this regime might have been adapted in his case, we cannot say how he reacted to it. Warwick may well have been a formidable, not to say overbearing presence, but, until late 1467 at least, when relations with Edward cooled, he was more often an absence, away on the king's business, or his own. Again, it has often been argued that Richard's 'love of the north' stems from this period of his life, spent among the great families of Yorkshire. Richard's northern leanings have become one of the generally shared 'counter-myths' about him, but it is worth examining, at least to the extent that we can really take it as representing an emotional, rather than a purely pragmatic connection. That Richard became a magnate whose power base was in the north is incontrovertible. That he came to rely on that affinity after he seized the throne is also true. But these were the practical long-term consequences of decisions taken by his brother Edward when Richard was made his northern lieutenant after 1471. That based Richard in the north and meant he found his support there, though he also had holdings and supporters in other parts of the country. A natural result was that some in the north benefited, and regretted his death in 1485. The lament of the city of York for Richard after Bosworth, 'late mercifully reigning upon us', who was 'pitiously slane and murdred to the grete hevynesse of this citie',[73] is often quoted to show the special affection in which Richard was held 'in the north', and was even used as an argument for his remains to be transferred there when a legal challenge was brought in 2014. But York soon became a loyal Tudor city, receiving Henry VII with pageants in 1486, and resisting the army of the 'Yorkist' impostor Lambert Simnel the following ear. However honest the expression of affection, it surely stemmed from the reciprocal relationship between Richard, first as Duke of Gloucester, then as king, and York, rather than the unique place the city held in his heart.

Richard spent a lot of time in the north, but as a boy and as a young man it was not his choice to go. As an adult duke, with most of his estates and then military command in the north, his presence there was natural. As king, however, he spent about 60 per cent of his time south of Nottingham. He kept a permanent household in the north as king, at Sandal Castle in west Yorkshire, but given the fact that the children housed there included two whose claim to the throne was arguably better than his own, it may also have been convenient that Sandal lay at the heart of Richard's northern affinity, and away from sources of rebellion.[74] The north remained important, but not to an overwhelming degree. Perhaps the most remarkable geographical fact about his short time on the throne was not to do with a north-south bias, but an east-west one. After the rebellion towards the beginning of his reign, Richard never went west of Leicester. As we shall see, he was at one point being groomed as Edward's representative in Wales. If that had lasted, it would not have made him a 'Welsh king' when he took the throne. He was not a 'northern king' either, except by force of circumstance, and any attempt to portray him as one should not rely too heavily on his adolescent experiences to make the case.

Some people who were also under Warwick's roofs at this time would become Richard's loyal friends and companions, even to their deaths. It may be tempting to suggest that Richard's future wife, Anne Neville, Warwick's younger daughter, would have been among them. Certainly Edward IV's own example gives the lie to the idea that all high-level medieval marriages were matters of diplomacy and political calculation. But Anne was four years younger than Richard, and it is perfectly possible that they lived at different Warwick houses – and boys and girls were, in any case, educated separately. So while Richard's future bride would not have been unknown to him, it is fantasy to conclude that 'in childhood they had known each other well'.[75]

Those who *are* likely to have shared Richard's table and his tasks in Warwick's estates included a man whom Richard came to trust absolutely, Francis Lovell. Lovell passed to Warwick's wardship in 1467 after the death of his father, John Lovell, along with the 'custody of all [Lovell's] lordships, manors, lands, rents, services and possessions'.[76] Two other companions whom Richard remembered in 1477 as among his 'servanders and lovers' (the latter meaning friends in fifteenth-century English) may also have been with him under Warwick's care: Thomas Par and Thomas Huddleston. Their names were later listed among the souls to be prayed for by four newly endowed Fellows of Queens' College, Cambridge, 'the which were slayn in his service at the batelles of Bernett, Tukysbery or at any other feldes . . .'[77] The training for knighthood that Richard and his fellows undertook was a preparation for a life of risk.

There is one other piece of evidence that can be tentatively dated to this period and gives us a glimpse of the effect this chivalric education had. Among the books and manuscripts Richard is known to have owned is a collection of fifteenth-century texts, including Chaucer's *Knight's Tale*, John Lydgate's *Siege of Thebes*, and the prose version of the story of Ipomedon, an Apulian prince who disguises himself to perform heroic labours and win the hand of his love. On a page of the manuscript are the handwritten words, 'Tant le desieree/ RGloucestre'. The most recent scholarship has given a date before 1469 for the manuscript and its decoration, and suggested a provenance in York, so it seems very likely that this book, as either gift or purchase, served as improving entertainment for the young duke while he was with Warwick. If the dating is correct, the very first indication we possess of Richard's own thinking shows him as a conventional product of his time and class. He ached with desire to emulate the deeds of legendary knights.[78]

'Little body and feeble strength'

One way in which Richard's experiences differed from those of his contemporaries is that around this time he is likely to have developed the condition identified by modern observers as scoliosis. The distinctive 's' shape of the spine began to develop, with the eventual result that Richard's 'true' height was reduced, and his shoulders became uneven. Following the recent discovery of Richard's body in Leicester, we can now speculate that the rumours of genuine spinal abnormality are the origins of the myth of the spectacularly 'deformed' king that reach their apogee in Shakespeare's 'bottled spider'. But when did those rumours begin? It is noticeable that none of the physical descriptions from eyewitnesses who saw Richard when alive referred to any abnormality. What was observed was that Richard was small, and 'slightly built' in the reported words of Niclas Von Popplau, a Silesian visitor to the royal court in 1484 (though Niclas must himself have been diminutive, as he says that Richard is 'three fingers taller' than him).[79] When the archdeacon of Lothian, Archibald Whitelaw, described Richard in the same year as having 'such a small body',[80] there is no suggestion that he was aware that the king's spinal condition would have reduced his height by several inches.

After Richard's death, and the exposure of his naked corpse on the battlefield and in Leicester, descriptions began to change. Less lurid than Shakespeare, if still hostile, Tudor historians, who had never set eyes on Richard alive (such as Thomas More, Polydore Vergil and Raphael Holinshed), described him as having one shoulder higher than the other, which is exactly the effect of scoliosis – and not of kyphosis, the more debilitating condition of a 'hunched back', which Shakespeare foists on to Richard ('an envious mountain on my back,/Where sits deformity to mock my body'; 'that foule hunch-backt [or bunch-backt] toade').[81] What Shakespeare's exaggerations, or those of Thomas More, who tells us that Richard had a withered arm since birth, do indicate is that had Richard's condition been widely known during his lifetime, his enemies would surely have made much of it. Yet in the various published attacks on the king, the association between physical deformity and unfitness to rule is not made. We need only compare the well-meaning attempts of alchemical medicine to cure Henry VI, whose mental slackness was associated with the decline in the body politic, to see that such connections readily occurred to contemporaries.

While scoliosis is not usually associated with excessive pain, for Richard it would surely have been a source of confusion and perhaps of shame, especially at a time when physical demands and expectations were growing. It is worth considering too that young men such as Lovell, Huddleston and Par might have been among those few who would have seen him in a state of undress, and observed the beginnings of the condition. Such shared experiences could have created a personal bond to Richard that was almost unbreakable. If such was Lovell's case, the bond lasted beyond his future lord's death. Lovell not only fought with Richard in the Scottish borders and at Bosworth, but tried to raise a rebellion shortly after his king's defeat, and joined the invasion of

Lambert Simnel (and his potential replacement, Richard's nephew John, Earl of Lincoln), which was defeated at Stoke in 1487.

There was, of course, no accepted treatment for scoliosis, but it is possible that a life spent in 'harness', as armour was known, would at least not have accelerated its progress (modern non-surgical treatment relies on the 'Milwaukee brace', a device to keep the spine as straight as possible). Richard was to become an experienced soldier and ultimately a commander who, like his brother Edward, led by example. None of that career seems to have been affected by his scoliosis, and even Richard III's later critics were prepared to grant his prowess as a warrior. John Rous, for example, in the altered version of his history written after Richard's death, still wrote that 'he bore himself like a noble soldier and despite his little body and feeble strength, honourably defended himself to his last breath'.[82]

So the clearest addition to the historic record provided by the find at Grey Friars – the fact of Richard's spinal condition – can only offer us the smallest of adjustments to what we 'know' of Richard. There is no record of his ever referring to the condition, nor of anyone else doing so during his lifetime, so we can only speculate as to the effects it had on him. If, physically, it did not change the course of his life, the determination to overcome a secret 'shame' must have had some psychological consequences. On the evidence of the life of relentless activity which he pursued, the most that can be suggested is that mastering scoliosis provided Richard with the confidence that his abilities and his prospects were not limited by any physical frailty. Then again, even Shakespeare's Richard, the 'elvish-mark'd, abortive, rooting hog',[83] was hardly encumbered by the deformities the playwright heaped on him, and it did not take the discovery of Richard's bones to lead us to the conclusion that, whatever the state of his body, his mind and the extent of his ambitions were not determined by it.

Being a member of the second greatest household in England provided Richard with some experiences that required physical endurance of a very different kind, as well as offering memorable lessons of the importance, in the circles he would move in, of putting on a show. The grandest of such occasions came right at the beginning of his time with Warwick, when he joined the lavish celebrations of the enthronement of his host's brother, George Neville (the chancellor and Bishop of Exeter who had preached a sermon in favour of

Edward's claim to the throne), as Archbishop of York, on 22 September 1465. The ceremony was held 'cum maxima solemnitate et cum maximis expensis', as one contemporary put it.[84] The seventeenth-century antiquary John Leland reproduced the contents of an 'Old Paper Roll' that gives the seating plan and menus for this event 'within the close' of York Minster, hard by the chantry priests' college established by the Nevilles four years earlier.[85] The plan tells us that at the first table 'in the cheefe chamber' (but not in the Hall itself) was seated 'The Duke of Glocester the kynges brother', still aged twelve, with the Duchess of Suffolk (Richard's elder sister Elizabeth) on his right, and to his left, the Countesses of Westmorland and Northumberland, along with Warwick's daughters (including Richard's future wife Anne).

The celebration went on for a week, and has come to be seen as the epitome, if not the parody, of a medieval banquet. Three separate feasts are recorded, at which 6,000 guests were served vast quantities of meat, including 2,000 pigs and 1,000 capons, as well as hundreds of game (and not so game) birds from partridges to peacocks. The more exotic confections of medieval cuisine were also on offer, including a dozen 'porpoies and seales', and various 'subtleties' – sugar and marzipan creations – representing York's patron saint, William, 'with his coate armour betwixt his handes' and even 'a dragon'.[86] The archaeologists who discovered Richard's remains reported the evidence 'that the individual had a high protein diet, including significant amounts of seafood (amounting to some 25 per cent of the diet), suggesting high status': this was an extreme example.[87]

The most significant absentee from the enthronement feast was Edward IV himself. A year before, in September 1464, the king had made an astonishing announcement. At a council in Reading, he told the assembled lords that he had secretly married Elizabeth Grey (née Woodville), the widow of a Lancastrian knight who had been granted an audience with the king to plead for her inheritance. They had been married since 1 May, in a private ceremony conducted in the presence of the bride's mother, two gentlewomen, a priest and 'a young man to help the priest sing'.[88] The circumstances of Edward's marriage, and the background of the woman he married, were to make an impact not just on his reign, but on that of his successors, including Richard III and, arguably, the Tudors who displaced him.

Elizabeth was no foreign princess, but she was the daughter of one – albeit the product of a marriage of similarly 'unequal' stations to her own. Her mother was Jaquetta of Luxembourg, who had herself been married to the brother of Henry V, John, Duke of Bedford. But Jaquetta's second marriage in 1437, just like that of Henry V's widow to Owen Tudor, was an almost scandalous match with a member of her former husband's household, Sir Richard Woodville, a knight in Bedford's service (though he was made a baron, and took the title Lord Rivers, in 1448). For her part, Elizabeth, Richard and Jaquetta's daughter, was the widow of another faithful Lancastrian soldier, Sir John Grey, with whom she had two sons, Thomas and Richard. Elizabeth's husband was killed fighting against the Yorkists at the second Battle of St Albans in 1461, while both her father and brother had fought against Edward the same year at Towton.

It was Elizabeth's frustrated attempts to be granted the jointure settled on her by her Lancastrian husband that brought her into contact with Edward, the only person who could ensure that legal formalities were followed when the beneficiaries were the relatives of an enemy killed in battle. Thomas More tells the story that Edward 'waxed enamoured' of Elizabeth, but was frustrated when 'after many a meeting, much wooing, and many great promises', she told the king that 'she knew herself too simple to be his wife, so thought herself too good to be his concubine'.[89] More wrote long before Anne Boleyn was thought to have employed similar tactics with his master, Henry VIII. But the result was apparently the same: the frustrated sovereigns married their reluctant subjects. More introduces the possibility of drawing another parallel, too. Was Edward IV, like Henry VIII, already married? More writes that it was rumoured the king was already betrothed, for much the same reason as with Elizabeth Woodville, to one Elizabeth Lucy, who was expecting his child. But More also confirms that Elizabeth Lucy denied any such arrangement under oath. When the legitimacy of Edward and Elizabeth Woodville's offspring came to be questioned, as Richard made his bid for the throne after Edward's death, the story of a pre-contract with another woman would re-emerge, with Eleanor Butler named as the third party.

The fact that the biased More, writing some fifty years after the event, and Richard's own claim to the Crown made in Parliament, are the sources of the two stories about Edward's other betrothals may be enough to discredit them. But there is a further circumstantial case to answer. If we accept that Edward and Elizabeth were married in May, as the chroniclers William Gregory and Robert Fabyan agree, then why did the king wait until September to announce it? One answer is that it was at this moment that his hand was forced. As part of a diplomatic agreement with France, a marriage between Edward and the sister-in-law of Louis XI, Bona of Savoy, had been proposed. At the Reading council in September, plans were being finalized to send the Earl of Warwick to negotiate the match in France. Edward had to admit his marital status before he caused a diplomatic incident (and made a fool of his senior nobleman). But that doesn't explain why he delayed the announcement so long. Fabyan gave his own explanation for that: 'What obloquy ran after of this maryage, howe the kynge was enchaunted by the duchesse of Bedford [Elizabeth's mother], and howe hereafter he wolde have refusyd her, with many other thynges concernyng this matier, I here passe it ouer.'[90]

Elizabeth's first modern biographer dismissed the idea that Edward 'repented of his hot passion' as 'without the least foundation', though as he relies on Fabyan's account of the nuptials in all other respects, it is hard to see why.[91] As with speculations about Richard's deformity, we do not need to conflate a medieval interpretation of causes with a concession of the (potential) facts. Just as Richard's scoliosis doesn't mean he was cursed or wicked, so Edward does not have to have been the victim of sorcery to have had second thoughts about a marriage that – whatever the merits of the bride – brought complications. (Whether he might have *believed* himself to have been the victim of sorcery is another question. Like Fabyan, Edward lived in a world where witchcraft was an accepted part of life, with trials increasing throughout the century. In 1470 he dealt with a case in which his mother-in-law was indeed accused of witchcraft, after it was alleged that she had made lead images, 'the length of a man's finger broken in the middle and made fast with a wire . . . to use with witchcraft and sorcery'.[92] On that occasion, the king dismissed the 'slander', but Jaquetta clearly took it seriously enough to want the decision to be placed on record.)

The complications included the large number of family members that the Woodville marriage brought with it, including the new queen's two sons, her father, and her ten siblings, all of whom would expect preferential treatment. Sure enough, in the years that followed, advantageous Woodville marriages multiplied. In 1464 Elizabeth's sister Margaret Woodville married Thomas Fitzalan, the son of the Earl of Arundel (and the Earl of Warwick's nephew). In 1465 her brother, the twenty-year-old John Woodville, was married to Warwick's aunt, Katherine Neville, the sixty-five-year-old dowager Duchess of Norfolk, a match that offended court sensibilities and was described by one chronicler as a 'maritagium diabolicum'.[93] Sisters Anne Woodville married the son of Henry Bourchier, Earl of Essex; Eleanor Woodville married Edmund Grey, son of the Earl of Kent; Katherine Woodville married Henry Stafford, Duke of Buckingham; and Mary Woodville, at the age of ten or eleven, married the fifteen-year-old son of William Herbert, Earl of Pembroke. Thomas Grey, Elizabeth's son by her first marriage, was married to the daughter of Henry Holland, Duke of Exeter.

Another difficulty was that Elizabeth Woodville came with no diplomatic advantage, which was of course the premise of the proposed continental matches. The wider popularity of the royal marriage was also in question. While Elizabeth's father, Lord Rivers, had received notice that the people of East Anglia and Essex 'ar despossed in the beste wysse and glade ther of', a newsletter from Bruges reported the marriage and the opinion that 'the greater part of the lords and the people in general seem very much dissatisfied at this, and for the sake of finding means to annul it, all the nobles are holding great consultations in the town of Reading, where the king is'.[94]

These were certainly reasons enough to repudiate the marriage if it had been possible to do so. Perhaps the four-month delay between wedding and announcement can partly be accounted for by Edward's investigating the possibility of breaking the arrangement. If so, the fact that he couldn't may be thought to cast further doubt on those later allegations that the marriage was invalid. If 'means to annul' the marriage couldn't be found immediately after it was made (and before there was any issue from it), how believable is it that the marriage was void all along, a 'fact' apparently only revealed in 1483? Whether there is any merit in the speculation or not, it remained the case that, by making the Woodville marriage, Edward had reduced his diplomatic options in Europe, embarrassed his principal subject, Warwick, whose diplomatic efforts had been wasted, and introduced a potential source of internal conflict in the shape of Elizabeth's Woodville relatives. The repercussions were still being felt almost twenty years later.

A rift between Edward and Warwick that would affect the whole kingdom, rekindle the Wars of the Roses and introduce Richard to the political stage in dramatic fashion, certainly developed in the later 1460s. The events of 1464 cannot have helped. Years afterwards, when Richard was newly installed as king in 1483, the Spanish ambassador confirmed that this was the view of one continental court at least, that Edward's choice of bride was the cause of 'mortall werre betwixt him and the erle of Warrewyk'.[95] But it is not necessary to read the differences back too far. Edward's absence from George Neville's enthronement, for example, need not have been a snub. He was content, after all, not only for his brother Richard to attend the feast, but to join Warwick's household. And the astute author of the Crowland Chronicle's 'second anonymous continuation', who is thought to have been an active participant in, or at least eyewitness to, some of the events he narrates, ascribed the 'real cause of dissension between the King and the earl' to a dispute over whether to make an alliance with Burgundy, which Edward favoured, or France, Warwick's choice. When a marriage alliance was made between Edward's sister Margaret and Charles, eldest son of the Duke of Burgundy, Warwick, the chronicler writes, 'was deeply offended'.[96] The timing of the break to this event, in July 1467, rather than the king's own marriage, in 1464, after which relations continued civilly between the two for more than two years, also makes sense.

Even so, Warwick was not only present at the elaborate send-off in June 1468, after almost a year of negotiation, for Margaret, when she processed from London via Canterbury to Margate, where a flotilla took her to her bridegroom at Sluys. He even shared a horse with her as she rode from St Paul's into the City.[97] Warwick returned to court and his place beside Edward afterwards, so if a break was already mooted, the earl was biding his time before making it. Margaret's brothers were also present, the fifteen-year-old Richard accompanying his sister down to the Kent coast, along with Clarence and the king. It was Richard's last appearance in public as a minor and member of Warwick's household. When he is next heard of, it is as a trusted royal duke with grave responsibilities.

2

Exile and Recovery

W hen he was king, Richard summoned a group of senior judges to the Star Chamber in Westminster Palace for a legal discussion. The talk, which became quite technical, revolved around the extent to which judges enacted or interpreted the king's law. Richard's conclusion was that 'to say "by his justice" and "by his law" is to say one and the same thing'.[1] This is a rare insight into Richard's personal interests, and in this case his interest in the law went back a long way. Because of who he was, and the times he lived in, however, Richard's own legal education was a complex, compromised affair. His first taste of a political and judicial role was intertwined. In 1468, when Richard was tasked with sitting in judgement on two of the king's subjects, he had already been made a beneficiary of the downfall of one of the accused.

Richard was almost a man, his time under Warwick's tutelage coming to an end. With approaching adulthood came the first marks of responsibility. On 25 October 1468, just over three weeks after his sixteenth birthday, he received a grant from his brother Edward IV of lands formerly belonging to Lord Hungerford, who had been executed as a traitor after the Battle of Hexham four years earlier. In December 1468 Richard was appointed to his first political task, as part of a commission of 'oyer and terminer' (that is, a specially appointed body to deal with – hear and determine – specific events, such as a rebellion). When the commission sat in Salisbury in January 1469, Richard presided. The case before the young Duke of Gloucester was the trial of Hungerford's son, Thomas, and of Henry Courtenay, whose brother had been Earl of Devon. They were charged with treason, for having conspired on

21 May 1468 with Margaret of Anjou to bring about 'the final . . . destruction of the Most Christian Prince, Edward IV'.[2]

It was one of a number of Lancastrian plots that Edward's government claimed to have uncovered that year, including one by the Earl of Oxford, who managed to save himself (bad news for Richard, who had been granted his estates before and might have hoped to receive them again). Less fortunate were two servants of the Duke of Norfolk, John Poynings and William Alford, who were accused of having conspired against the king with the Duke of Somerset. They were beheaded at Tower Hill, along with a London skinner, Richard Steris. The plot had allegedly been cooked up during the ceremonies to see off Margaret of York to Burgundy. How much truth there was in any of the accusations is impossible now to tell. By the time the Earl of Oxford was brought to the Tower, it had been host for more than two years to the almost forgotten figure of Henry VI. The deposed king had been captured in Lancashire in July 1465, and brought, tied to his horse, to London. But with his former queen and son Edward still at large, Lancastrians had much to work for. Despite their defeats at Towton and the mopping-up operations of Hexham and Hedgley Moor in 1464, despite the capture of Henry VI, it was as recidivist Lancastrians that Hungerford and Courtenay met their fate in Salisbury.

In the presence of his brother the king, Richard passed the customary sentence on the traitors who had, inevitably, been found guilty, by a jury of sixteen. They were hanged, drawn and quartered on 18 January 1469. For Richard, this was an uncompromising introduction to the iron realities of high politics. He had played his part in various public ceremonies since his brother's accession, from the coronation to the enthronement feast of George Neville. This was very different, although he might have reflected that during his recent participation in another such display, his sister Margaret's grand departure for Burgundy, the messier business of treason was apparently being fomented. So it was that Richard's first public act as an adult prepared him for a professional life of violence and the use of the law as an instrument of implacable, though sometimes very personal, royal will. In the brutal public spectacle of the executions themselves, Richard was also witness to the other side of the dramatic performance of power, as rich with symbolism as any crown-wearing or royal progress.

This swift, possibly arbitrary exercise of justice appeared to have quietened the realm. But a threat from an unanticipated quarter was about to emerge. Warwick made his move. The ramifications played out over the next two years, and for Richard it was another hard lesson in his political – and military – education. For the country it was another lurch into civil conflict. It may matter to historians that this latest trouble should not really be classified as part of the 'Wars of the Roses'. Warwick's rebellion did not begin as a 'Lancastrian' attack on a 'Yorkist' king. But to those swept up into the fighting, that was less important than the fact that, once again, England was at war with itself. The trouble began in April and May 1469, when two rebellions broke out in the north of England, which were not Lancastrian in inspiration.

The first, led by someone calling himself Robin of Redesdale (possibly a Yorkshire knight and retainer of the Nevilles, Sir John Conyers), was put down by John Neville, Warwick's brother, who also dealt with the second uprising in the East Riding, led by 'Robin of Holderness'. No sooner had Neville dealt with this unrest (and had Holderness executed) than the Redesdale rebellion re-emerged. Whether it was really under the same leadership or the name had been adopted as a standard for the rebels to rally round is not clear. But by opportunism or design, the more threatening power behind this rebellion now revealed itself. The Earl of Warwick and his other brother, Archbishop George Neville, who had been very publicly deprived of his office of chancellor in 1467 – issued a call to arms against the 'disceyvabille covetous rule and gydynge of certyne ceducious persones'. These included the queen's parents (Lord Rivers and the Duchess of Bedford), her brothers Anthony (Lord Scales) and Sir John Woodville 'and his brethern' the Earl of Pembroke, and John Tuchet (Lord Audley).[3] Warwick's break had been a long time coming, and it was no surprise that one of his brothers, at least, broke with him. But the manifesto had one more signatory: Richard and Edward's brother George, Duke of Clarence.

Three years older than Richard, Clarence had been, until 1466, when the queen gave birth to Elizabeth of York, Edward's heir presumptive. He had begun his career as a magnate at the age of sixteen, as Richard would do. But even before then, Edward had recognized his nearest brother's greater importance by granting him lands and offices that far outweighed Richard's. During his minority, Clarence had been made Steward of England (in which role he appeared, aged eleven, at his brother's coronation, and again four years later at that of Elizabeth Woodville as queen). He was also Lord Lieutenant of Ireland (though that office was performed by a deputy) and, like Richard, a Knight of the Bath and of the Garter. As for his estates, Edward had set Clarence up with vast holdings that made him second only to Warwick in wealth and influence, centred in Staffordshire. His annual income of 5,000 marks (£3,666) was huge, even if it was barely more than a third of that of the man with whom he had now thrown in his lot, Warwick. But Clarence seems to have had ambitions that extended even beyond such lavish means. His household expenses, revealed in an ordinance made at Waltham Abbey in 1469, amounted to more than £4,500.[4] Even if that document represented a statement of ambition rather than actuality (it would have made his household the most costly in the country after the king's), it shows that Clarence wanted cash, despite his brother's generous provision for him. It was in part his solution to that problem that drew him into conflict with Edward. Clarence proposed to marry money, in the form of the elder daughter of the richest man in the kingdom (who had no sons), Richard Neville, Earl of Warwick.

Edward had refused the proposed match with Isabel Neville, possibly because he wanted to make use of his brother in a continental marriage alliance, or perhaps because he had other plans for Isabel (which might have included one of the many Woodvilles). Perhaps, though, he feared exactly what did happen when, defying Edward's command, Clarence and Isabel were married after receiving the necessary papal dispensation (as cousins) in her father's castle at Calais, on 11 July 1469. That is, Clarence became Warwick's creature. With the earl at his back, Edward had gained a throne. When news came that Warwick and the newly married duke had landed in Kent and issued their manifesto less than a week after the wedding, it is conceivable that the earl thought he had found a more biddable candidate to make into a new king. The manifesto included references to the way that Edward II, Richard II and Henry VI, all of whom had been deposed, had been led astray by false counsellors 'to the distruccion of them'.[5] If Edward refused to deal with his Woodville equivalents, the implied threat that he would follow in the footsteps of these predecessors was clear. And if that happened, a new king would be needed: who better than the Duke of Clarence, Warwick's new son-in-law?

Initially, Edward had seemed content to leave the suppression of the northern rebellions to John Neville. The fact that he relied on Warwick's brother suggests that he did not at first suspect the earl's complicity – and indeed Warwick may not have had anything to do with the first risings. Even before Warwick and Clarence landed back in England and showed their hand, however, Edward had decided to intervene personally. The king had been accompanied by his youngest brother on a pilgrimage to East Anglia, to visit the shrines of St Edmund, the Anglo-Saxon king murdered by an invading army (and the saint after whom his own slaughtered brother had been named), and Our Lady of Walsingham. Towards the end of June 1469, he ordered Richard to go north with him.

Still more than three months short of his seventeenth birthday, the Duke of Gloucester was expected to raise forces too. But the loyal Richard, unlike his treacherous brother Clarence, did not have the money to do so, at least not in hand. In his earliest surviving letter, sent from Castle Rising in Norfolk on 24 June, he wrote to Sir John Say, several times speaker of the House of Commons, and chancellor of the Duchy of Lancaster. Edward, Richard told Sir John, has 'appoynted me to attende uppon his Highnesse into the North parties of his lande, whiche wolbe to me gret cost and charge, whereunto I am soo sodenly called that I am not so wel purveide of money therfore as behoves me to be, and therfore pray you as my specyal trust is in you, to lend me an hundreth pounde of money unto Ester next commyng'. Richard was exercised enough to add a postscript written in his own hand: 'Sir J. Say I pray you that ye fayle me not at this tyme in my grete nede, as ye wule that I schewe youw my goode lordshype in that matter that ye labure to me for.'[6] In his very first surviving communication, Richard displays an essential understanding of the way he would have to operate throughout his life, in the give-and-take world of medieval nobility, where 'good lordship' was not a simple matter of master and servant, but of quid pro quo. We don't know what Say's 'matter' was, but Richard knew that if he wanted assistance, he had to do more than pull rank.

In the event, Richard did not get to lead his hastily acquired retinue into battle. As Edward and Richard marched north, the Earls of Pembroke and Devon, William Herbert and Humphrey Stafford, both newly elevated to their titles by the king, and both named in the rebels' manifesto, were also gathering an army to meet the threat. Marching from the west towards Edward, who was waiting for them at Nottingham, they clashed with 'Robin of Redesdale's' rebels at Edgecote, near Banbury in Oxfordshire. The two earls' forces had become separated, but it was the larger party of Pembroke's Welshmen who met the rebels. On 25 July 1469 their royalist army was defeated, with substantial casualties.[7] Pembroke and his brother Sir Richard were captured and executed on Warwick's orders. Others on Warwick and Clarence's list followed: Humphrey Stafford, 'that was Erle of Devynschyre but half a yere', was killed 'by the comons' at Bridgwater in Somerset[8] (that the rebellion had some popular backing cannot be doubted. It began as a popular uprising, and attracted support as soon as Warwick landed. For all the ruthlessness of which the earl now showed himself capable, he could certainly command widespread support, probably because of his piratical exploits against trading rivals on the high seas, which went down well in the seaside southern towns and, apparently, beyond); more members of the Herbert family;[9] and the last significant victims of Warwick's murderous power grab, Lord Rivers, the queen's father, and his son, her brother Sir John Woodville, who were executed on 12 August in Warwick's castle at Kenilworth.

The defeat of his allies at Edgecote left Edward – and Richard, though he is not mentioned by name in contemporary sources during this time – exposed. It seems likely they were trying to evade capture when at Olney, near Coventry, Warwick's brother George Neville (the Archbishop of York whose enthronement feast Richard had attended, and whom Edward had deprived of the office of chancellor with scarcely less publicity) took the king prisoner. He had been all but abandoned after Edgecote, and now found himself at the mercy of Warwick and Clarence.

Faced with a similar situation to that encountered by Richard of York, Edward's father, in the 1450s, Warwick seems to have attempted a similar solution. The result was similar, too. Warwick tried to make Edward his puppet, and rule in his name. If Clarence had ambitions for the throne, Warwick was, as yet, unwilling to back them, just as he had been with Clarence's father. As in that case, it could be argued that Warwick gauged the likelihood of popular support for such a move correctly. Edward was taken first to Warwick and then to Middleham Castle, Warwick's stronghold further north, away from the king's most likely sources of support in London and the south. Like Richard of York, however, Warwick found it almost impossible to act as regent for an adult king in possession of his faculties. And while Henry VI had been, even when not suffering a mental collapse, a weak and malleable king, Edward was perfectly capable of looking after himself. His chance to get free came when there was a pro-Lancastrian uprising in September on the Scottish borders. Warwick's attempts to raise forces to deal with the trouble in Edward's name came to nothing, because 'while the king was still manifestly a prisoner people were not ready to obey such commands, not until he had appeared in person at York in full possession of his freedom'.[10] Edward took his chance, and 'by fayre speche and promyse' escaped the Nevilles' clutches, making his way to London, where he summoned the Great Council to Westminster, 'and dyd what hym lyked'.[11]

Richard of Wales

Richard's own part in this episode is unknown. Whether he found himself back at Middleham as a prisoner, or avoided Warwick and Clarence by being sent elsewhere by Edward, we are not told. What did become clear was that, after Warwick and Clarence's first rebellion, Edward was prepared to reward his youngest brother for his loyalty, even if he wasn't yet ready to punish the chief rebels for their offences. Although the rebels were included in a general pardon and stripped only of those lands and offices they had snatched during their ascendancy, Edward made Richard the main beneficiary of the vacancies created by their actions. The first of these was the office of Constable of England. This, the senior military office in the realm, had been held for life by Lord Rivers, whom Warwick had summarily executed. Although the original grant had specified that Rivers's son Anthony, Lord Scales, should succeed him, Edward appointed Richard to the role on 17 October 1469, 'with the accustomed fees and profits'.[12]

Edward's next series of moves affecting his brother took advantage of the loss of another of Warwick's victims, William Herbert, Earl of Pembroke, to establish a genuine sphere of influence for Richard in Wales. Herbert had been Edward's man in the principality. After he was killed, Warwick had divided his

Welsh appointments between himself and William, Lord Hastings. (Hastings had fought alongside Edward at Towton, and had been ennobled by him in 1461 and made chamberlain of the royal household. Although he had dealings with Warwick during his ascendancy, his loyalty does not seem to have been questioned, and he would prove it several times in the years that followed.) Between October 1469 and February 1470, in a series of appointments and grants, Edward would put Richard in Pembroke's place. When the king appointed commissions of array (the usual means of raising troops to deal with trouble) throughout the country in October 1469, Richard received his in the Welsh marcher counties of Shropshire, Gloucestershire and Worcestershire.[13] In December, Richard was given 'full power and authority to reduce and subdue the king's castles' of Carmarthen and Cardigan, which had been taken by Welsh rebels.[14]

The offices that accompanied such commissions established that this was not intended as a temporary mission. Richard was made chief justice of north Wales, replacing Hastings, as well as 'chief steward, approver and surveyor of the principality of Wales and the earldom of March' (Edward's former earldom) in November, and in February 1470, chief justice of south Wales, to which post Warwick had been appointed (or had appointed himself) 'by the death of William Herbert'. (Note the cynicism behind the bland official language, as if Herbert's death was a mere accident, and had not been ordered by the man who now took his office.)[15] Unlike the Warwick appointment, which had been for life, Richard's was made during the minority of Herbert's heir. The second Earl of Pembroke was, in fact, only three years younger than Richard himself, but there was no guarantee that Richard's role would not be made permanent at his expense later.

As with so much in Richard's career, a series of unpredictable incidents had given him a role. His well-known association with the north, of which Richard's modern defenders have often made so much, arose later. But it is intriguing to speculate that, if Warwick and Clarence had accepted Edward's decision to pardon them and, while reining them in somewhat, not to strip them of influence, the Duke of Gloucester might instead have been known for his special affinity with Wales. Neither region was, in truth, any more 'natural' a base for him than anywhere else. With the lack of a patrimony that was the lot of a younger son, Richard would make a role for himself wherever he was given a chance. He did not, for example, turn his nose up at the grant of two manors in Cornwall that he also received at this time.[16] It is noticeable, though, that his knack of retaining loyal servants, of showing the 'good lordship' that was evident in his first surviving letter, can also be seen in Richard's Welsh period. Not only did former servants of William Herbert become Richard's servants, such as John Milewater, who died serving Richard at the Battle of Barnet in 1471, and was among those 'servants and lovers' later memorialized by him. Even Herbert's son, who had reason to resent Richard for eclipsing him, seems instead to have become attached to him. He agreed to marry Richard's illegitimate daughter Katherine in 1484, and may have acted as chamberlain for Richard's (legitimate) son, Edward.[17] If Richard's so-called motto, the phrase 'Loyauté me lie' (Loyalty binds me), which appears on a couple of documents in 1483 and 1484, was ever anything he really aspired to live by, it certainly describes what he expected – and often received – from followers, as well as what he offered his own royal master.

But Richard as a Welsh prince was not to be. Warwick and Clarence made sure of that. They renewed their rebellion, again by proxy, in March 1470. In Lincolnshire, Lord Welles and his son Sir Robert attacked a royal servant, Sir Thomas Burgh. While Lord Welles responded to the king's inevitable summons to explain himself in London, his son remained in Lincolnshire, mustering at Ranby Hawe in the west of the county. Edward made Lord Welles join him as he rode north to deal with the rebellion, and let it be known that if Sir Robert did not give up, his father would be executed. On receiving this news, Sir Robert, who, unbeknown to the king, had been on his way with his force to join Warwick and Clarence in Leicester (they had been gathering strength in Coventry), decided instead to turn due south and try to rescue his father. The two forces met at Empingham, about five miles from Stamford, Lincolnshire. In a show of ruthlessness to match anything Warwick had perpetrated, Edward carried out his threat to execute Lord Welles, along with fellow conspirator Sir Thomas Dymmok, 'in the field and under his banner displayed'. Sir Robert's forces were routed on 12 March 1470, the battle becoming known as 'Losecote Field', possibly because the rebels tried to get rid of their offending garments ('that time being in the field divers persons in the duke of Clarence livery'), though it may also simply be a common name for fields in this part of the country. It was reported too that the rebels' war cry had been 'A Clarence! a Clarence! a Warwick!', and when Sir Robert Welles and other rebel leaders were interrogated, 'of their free wills uncompelled, not for fear of death ne otherwise stirred, knowledged and confessed the said duke and earl [Clarence and Warwick] to be partners and chief provokers of all their treasons'.[18]

Whether they feared death or not, Sir Robert suffered the same fate as his father, along with other rebel commanders, and Edward, continuing up the Old North Road from Stamford to Grantham, turned his attentions to the ringleaders – his own brother and his most powerful former ally. Clarence and Warwick had been told of Edward's victory, and were subsequently informed of Welles's confession of their leading part in the rebellion. Edward continued to offer to receive them, while keeping on their trail; as they moved from Coventry to Burton-upon-Trent, Derby and Chesterfield, Edward shadowed them on a parallel route to the east. Refusing to meet the king, they went towards Lancashire, stopping at Manchester, while Edward rode as far as Rotherham before halting, unsure of his safety and provisions for his troops in a part of the country loyal to Warwick. On 24 March at York, Edward 'published as full traitors and rebels' Clarence and Warwick, but despite an offer of reward for their capture, and the threat of execution for assisting them, they got away.[19] Rather than risk an armed confrontation, the duke and the earl turned around at Manchester and headed south-west, eventually taking ship from Dartmouth, accompanied by the heavily pregnant Isabel, Clarence's wife, and making the long crossing to Calais, trying unsuccessfully to reinforce their fleet on the way at Southampton. Even as they approached the normally loyal Calais, however, the journey was extended further. As Isabel went into labour while still aboard ship, Warwick found that Calais was closed to him, by his deputy John, Lord Wenlock.[20] Within sight of the port, Isabel gave birth to a daughter, Anne, who died very shortly afterwards. Warwick's party eventually landed at Honfleur in Normandy, where they were welcomed by Warwick's admirer and Edward's enemy Louis XI.

Richard was not by the king's side during this latest outbreak of treachery on the part of his brother and his erstwhile mentor. He had first been attending to his Welsh duties, but from two references to him after the rebels had been turned back, we can see that, in fact, he had been summoned to assist Edward. Interestingly, he had apparently not been ordered to make from west Wales straight towards the rebellious earl and duke in the west Midlands. Instead he had gone north, shadowing the rebels on the other side of the country as they sought support in Lancashire and Yorkshire. He also embroiled himself in a regional dispute in a way that cannot have been welcome to his brother the king, who had so much to contend with.

Warwick's brother, John Neville, had been created Earl of Northumberland and granted the Percy lands that went with the title in 1464. Although Edward had begun the process in October 1469 of rehabilitating Henry Percy, releasing him from the Tower where he had been since his father was killed and attainted fighting for the Lancastrians at Towton, he had not gone as far as reinstating Percy to his earldom, and Neville, the man in possession, had stayed loyal. But there was another big landowner in the region whose reliability was more questionable. Thomas, Lord Stanley, was married to Warwick's sister, Eleanor, and had maintained an equivocal position in the disputes that blew across his lands ever since he had kept himself out of the Battle of Blore Heath in 1459. (He was on the losing Lancastrian side at Northampton the following year.) It may have been a deliberate attempt to weaken his influence in Cheshire and Lancashire that led Edward to pass two honours in the royal patrimony of the Duchy of Lancaster – Clitheroe in Lancashire and Halton in Cheshire – to Richard in May 1469, with rights that had formerly belonged to Stanley.

Stanley had refused to pay the money owing to the Duke of Gloucester in connection with these honours, so some sort of dispute was likely. On 25 March 1470, as the rebel lords fled south, Edward issued a proclamation at York referring to the 'variance late fallen' between his youngest brother and Lord Stanley. The following day a grant from Richard issued from Hornby Castle gives another hint about a different factor in the dispute.[21] For four years the original incumbents of Hornby, the Harrington family, headed by James Harrington, had been refusing to yield their property, or the wardship of Harrington's nieces, whose father and brother had both been killed fighting on the Duke of York's side at Wakefield in 1460. The man who had been made the nieces' guardian, and who had arranged marriages for both of them to his son and nephew, thereby securing their inheritance for his own family, was none other than Thomas Stanley. By being received as the Harringtons' guest at Hornby, Richard was setting his face against the Stanleys' claim. He may even have been actively engaged in resisting an assault on the castle. The Stanleys and Harringtons would not have been unusual in taking advantage of a national crisis to attempt a little local score-settling. That Richard was prepared to do so too shades the picture so often painted of the young Duke of Gloucester as totally loyal to his eldest brother.

The Stanley family's choices and activities are the perfect illustration of why there was so much more to the Wars of the Roses than 'Lancaster versus York'. Not only did this latest rebellious episode on a national scale stem from a split in the York family engineered by a York ally, with no 'Lancastrian' input to speak of. Under its cover, a principal like the Duke of Gloucester found himself taking sides in an essentially private dispute. The implications were complex. On the one hand, Richard's crossing of the Stanleys can be seen to have helped Edward's cause. Warwick and Clarence were certainly hoping for their in-laws' help when they diverted towards Stanley's Lancashire heartland and stopped at Manchester. A letter received by John Paston sent on 27 March 1470 from an unnamed 'cosyn' says that Clarence and Warwick 'wente to Manchestre in Lancashire hopyng to have hadde helpe and socoure of Lord Stanley; butt in conclucion ther they hadde litill fauour . . . and so men sayn they wente westward'.[22] In the dispute that Richard joined, however, Stanley happened to have royal backing; the grant of the Harrington wardship and lands had been made by the king. Thus, if Richard was choosing to back the Harringtons against the Stanleys, the Duke of Gloucester might just have been placing other interests above his supposedly unshakable loyalty to the king. In this instance, however, the effect of challenging Stanley was beneficial to Edward. The result of their 'variance' in March 1470 was that one of the canniest reckoners of political fortunes of the period decided not to bet against the king this time. Without his support, the rebels had little choice but unequal battle against Edward – and, probably, his youngest brother – or flight. They chose to run.

What followed need only be viewed as an astonishing change of allegiance on Warwick's part if we cling to the fixed polarities of 'Lancaster' and 'York'.[23]

In truth, Warwick, who had by now demonstrated his absolute fidelity to only one cause – that of Richard Neville – probably saw that, if he wanted to regain his former position in England, he had no choice but to try to form an alliance not only with King Louis XI, to whom as Edward's negotiator he had always been well disposed, but to Louis's royal cousin Margaret of Anjou, who had been living in exile in France, dependent on her father. While Margaret's husband Henry VI had been removed from any active role since his capture and imprisonment in the Tower in 1465, Margaret had never stopped working to keep alive the claims of his heir, their son Edward of Westminster, who was now sixteen years old. With the arrival of the Earl of Warwick in France, an opportunity presented itself, however distasteful the means, to restore Henry to his throne and secure Edward's inheritance. Although there had been suggestions made since 1465 that a grand alliance between Louis, Margaret and the man widely credited with putting Edward IV on the throne might be possible, only now did it become practicable.[24]

The greatest obstacle to such an alliance was Margaret herself. She, it appears, found it harder than Warwick to forget past enmities in the name of expediency. The 'said queen', it was reported, 'was right difficile'.[25] The Milanese ambassador to Louis' court was of the same opinion. Margaret was being 'molto difficile', but he expected she would come round. Less than a month later, in an act of reconciliation at Angers on 22 July 1470, 'with great reverence Warwick went on his knees and asked her pardon for the injuries and wrongs done to her in the past'.[26] Two days later Louis dispatched messengers to request a papal dispensation for the match that would seal this reconciliation, between Margaret's only son Edward and Warwick's younger daughter Anne. If his older daughter Isabel had been married to Clarence as a potential candidate for a crown, this second match seemed an even better prospect, for Edward was already a Prince of Wales, albeit the heir to a deposed king. Shortly afterwards, without waiting for papal permission for a marriage between parties related by the 'fourth degree of consanguinity', Edward and Anne were publicly betrothed in Angers Cathedral.[27] Margaret continued to have her doubts. One contemporary says that she held out against the match for fifteen days.[28] And the couple would not be married until the end of the year. That might have been for a number of reasons: in expectation of the papal dispensation (which was issued in August); or because Warwick decided to bide his time until after he had made his attempt to eject Edward IV and reinstate Henry VI; or because Margaret of Anjou, for the same reason, preferred to wait, even after her assent in principle.

Back in England, Edward was busily redistributing Warwick's power. The two biggest beneficiaries were Richard and the former Lancastrian loyalist Henry Percy. The first signs of Richard's realignment towards the north of England came in August 1470, with his appointment as warden of the West March towards Scotland, while Percy received the wardenship of the East March. These were vital roles for the defence of the realm, roles which had arisen piecemeal out of English dealings with the Scots over a period of around two hundred years. The office of warden itself had only come into being around 1300, but it grew in scope and formal power, so that by Richard's time it encompassed not only the right to summon to arms able-bodied men between the ages of sixteen and sixty within the area of the wardenship, but also custody of royal castles and jurisdiction over breaches of any truces between the two countries, and upholding ancient, hybrid 'march law'. These were not the sort of responsibilities usually offered to any but the most able. They tended to be held by magnates with local power bases, because the authority to summon men to arms did not in this period equate to the ability to do so, unless the summoner already had a following on which to rely. For Percy, with his family's deep roots in the area, the wardenship was a natural fit. For Richard, still two months shy of his eighteenth birthday, it was an even more significant promotion than the offices he had been granted in Wales.[29]

Edward had completed the rehabilitation of Henry Percy on 26 March 1470, restoring him as Earl of Northumberland in a grant issued at York.[30] The loser was John Neville, the brother who had stayed loyal. He was deprived of the earldom of Northumberland when it was returned to its traditional Percy holder. Neville was compensated with a marquisate, becoming Marquess Montagu, and a number of grants of former Stafford lands of the earldom of Devon in the west, as well as his son being promoted to a dukedom. But he had been deprived of a power base built over four years. With the attainder of his brother the Earl of Warwick, John Neville also lost the prospect of inheriting that part of Warwick's titles and estates that was held 'in tail male' – that is, the portion that couldn't be inherited by Warwick's daughters or their spouses (Warwick had no direct male heir) – which included the earldom of Salisbury. Edward knew that Warwick would make another attempt on the kingdom. The king was gambling on three things to secure the north: that Neville's compensation was enough to retain his support; that the re-establishment of Percy to his earldom would secure his retainers' loyalty to the Crown through their traditional lord; and that the installation of Richard as warden of the West March would replace the missing Neville authority. When the crisis came, it was not the untried younger brother who let the king down.

What the Milanese ambassador called 'the enterprise of England', the invasion that would put Edward's gamble to the test, was launched on 15 September 1470. The Earl of Warwick had been offered 25,000 crowns and 2,000 archers for his invasion, as well as the assistance of Louis's brother Charles. Warwick, Clarence, the Earl of Oxford and Jasper Tudor, former Earl of Pembroke, landed at Dartmouth. By 12 October it was being reported on the continent that 'Warwick has pursued his enterprise with spirit and has practically the whole island in his power. Edward is a fugitive and in hiding, his whereabouts being unknown.'[31] Edward and Richard had not even given battle. The invasion force began its march north, gathering a force that included the Earl of Shrewsbury and Thomas, Lord Stanley. This was ominous enough, and showed the advantages of Warwick's espousing Henry VI's cause, rather than merely finding a figurehead (Clarence) for his own. Henry may in fact have been a far feebler character than Clarence, but he was an anointed king, not a potential usurper, and that counted for a lot more than personality when it came to commanding wider loyalty. But it was the decision of Marquess Montagu to bring his army, estimated at more than 6,000 men, over to the invaders, that seems to have been the tipping point for Edward. Faced with such a loss of support, the king felt he had little choice but to escape. Edward would have known exactly why John Neville had switched sides. It had little to do with lately uncovered family loyalty and everything to do with aristocratic politics. Montagu scorned Edward's efforts at compensation as a 'pye's nest to maintain his estate with'.[32] What is more, Percy, who had been busy putting down an uprising in the north timed to coincide with the invasion, had been unable or unwilling to tip the balance in Edward's favour.

'My lord of Gloucester travelled to Holland'

The band that took ship from the busy port of King's Lynn, on the Norfolk coast, was sadly reduced. The town records, inserted into an account of a meeting arranging security for the unexpected royal visit after the king had safely departed, note that Edward arrived accompanied by his brother-in-law, Earl Rivers, Lord Hastings (Edward's chamberlain), Lord Cromwell (Humphrey Bourchier, son of Edward's steward, the Earl of Essex) and Lord Say. They also say that he had 3,000 armed men with him, though at least half of these would have stayed behind, along with Lord Cromwell, when the principals left on Tuesday, 2 October 1470.[33] In his memoirs, Louis XI's ambassador Philippe de Commines says that Edward arrived in Holland with 1,500 men. They were harried by a Hanseatic fleet as they sailed across the North Sea. (The Hanseatic League was a commercial confederation of originally Prussian towns with which England had often come into conflict as rival traders, and more than occasional pirates.)

On arrival, they apparently had no money to pay their passage. Edward gave the master of his ship a 'gown lined with beautiful martens'[34] in recompense. By 11 October they had reached the relative safety of The Hague, where they were received by Louis de Gruthuyse, governor of Holland and twice Burgundian ambassador to England, in which capacity he had come to know Edward. The royal party was accommodated in de Gruthuyse's house in The Hague, and he made representations to Charles of Burgundy (who had succeeded his father Philip in 1467) to receive them. This extended stay among some of the most sophisticated courtiers in Europe had some effect on Edward's book-collecting habits, which ever after had a Flemish tinge. He may even have met the 'governor of the English nation' in Bruges, a cloth merchant called William Caxton, who at the time was working on his translation of Raoul Lefèvre's *History of Troy*, which would in due course become the first English printed book, dedicated to Edward's sister Margaret of Burgundy; the original manuscript of Lefèvre's book was in the ducal library. Caxton's follow-up, dedicated to Edward IV's first son, was an even more appropriate subject for the exiled king and his followers: the story of Jason, and his legendary quest for the Golden Fleece. If Edward needed inspiration for the task ahead, he was in the right place.

Was Richard with Edward in Holland from the start? It used to be assumed that he was in the group that originally sailed from King's Lynn. Philippe de Commines says as much, but more recently that assumption has been questioned. Commines's description of the Duke of Gloucester, 'who was called afterwards Richard III', makes it possible that he is inserting the name of someone whom he knew would loom very large in the future. Richard is not mentioned elsewhere – perhaps most tellingly, not in the records of Edward's embarkation in King's Lynn that list four other, lesser lords: why would they have omitted the royal brother? After Edward's arrival in The Hague, Richard is not mentioned in a letter from the Duke of Burgundy (who was, after all, Edward and Richard's brother-in-law), which gives details of Edward's presence, and names ten distinguished companions, including Hastings and Rivers, as well as giving Edward an allowance for the period of his stay.

Added to these conspicuous absences are the evidence of the town accounts of Veere, more than fifty miles south of The Hague, and almost 100 miles away from the island of Texel at which Edward is recorded as having first landed. At Veere, in the second week of November 1470, in other words a month after Edward is known to have arrived in The Hague, Richard's debt to the bailiff for a sum of money lent to him when 'my lord of Gloucester travelled to Holland' was repaid. It is possible that this refers to a month before, at a time when Richard had landed initially in the south at the same time as his brother, having been deliberately or accidentally separated from Edward's ship. An undated reference to Lord Rivers (mistakenly still called Lord Scales, the title he held before he inherited his father's) receiving wine in the nearby town of Middelburg in 1470 used to be taken as confirmation that he had been with Richard when they first arrived from England. But this could just as easily refer to a separate occasion and, in any case, does not put Richard by Rivers' side.[35] Similarly, a reference in the fifteenth-century chronicle of Caspar Weinreich mentions 'Lord Scalis' (i.e. Rivers) arriving in the south when Edward arrived in the north, but not the

Duke of Gloucester. Taken all together, it seems more than likely that Richard spent at least three weeks in England before he joined his brother.

If Richard wasn't with the original royal party, what was he doing, and how and when did he leave? To these questions we have no certain answers, other than to say that by mid-November, as the Veere account confirms, he had come to the Low Countries. But we can at least suggest what Richard could have been doing by reference to what came afterwards, namely, the return of Edward IV and the campaign to recapture his throne from Henry VI.

The re-establishment of the Lancastrian regime under Henry VI was the apogee of Warwick's career as the 'kingmaker'. The 'Readeption', as this restoration was known, after the Latin phrase used on official documents of the time, was sealed by a public performance. Henry himself was brought out of the Tower of London, to which he had been consigned for almost five years, by the Bishop of Winchester. Henry 'was not worshipfully arrayed as a prince, and not so cleanly kept as should seem a prince . . . they had him out, and new arrayed him, and did to him great reverence, and brought him to the palace of Westminster . . . Whereof all his good lovers were full glad, and the more part of his people'.[36] Meanwhile another resident of the Tower left for Westminster, not to seek political acclaim, but for safety. Elizabeth, Edward's displaced queen, was expecting a child, and she chose to make for the sanctuary of Westminster Abbey, where she gave birth to her first son, named Edward after his father and the patron saint of his birthplace, Edward the Confessor.

As things stood, this Edward was not heir to the throne. That was now the Lancastrian Prince of Wales (the son of Henry VI), another Edward of Westminster, recently married to Warwick's younger daughter. They remained, for the time being, with the Prince of Wales's mother Margaret on the other side of the Channel. While Henry's wife and son stayed in France, the king himself presided over a new parliament, in November, at which the sermon preached by the Archbishop of York was a variation on the verse of Jeremiah, 'Return to me thou backsliding Israel . . . for I am merciful, saith the Lord.' It is tempting to see the hand of the restored king, still sticking to his belief in the power of a loveday, in the choice of text, though Henry plays so small a role in accounts of this period that his involvement at any level is a matter of doubt. In the main, however, Yorkists were not excluded or punished. (The exceptions were Edward and Richard, who were attainted, and the loyalist John Tiptoft, Earl of Worcester, who was executed. Tiptoft was a fascinating combination of cruelty, with a reputation as a 'fierce executioner and horrible beheader of men', and scholarship, a great collector of humanist works, and a translator of Cicero.) The chief beneficiary of the Readeption, however, was – naturally – the Earl of Warwick. Among other restitutions, he recovered his captaincy of Calais, and the office of Chamberlain. Henry VI also chose to welcome his Welsh half-brother Jasper Tudor, and Jasper's nephew Henry, to court.

If Edward was to 'go out by the door and then want to enter by the windows', without 'leav[ing] his skin there' as the Milanese ambassador put it, he would have to contend with a restored regime that had not, at least initially, simply reopened the factional wounds of the past.[37] Could Richard's time in England before joining his brother in The Hague have been spent in trying to find ways of unpicking the recently restitched polity? Two powerful men would be crucial to any attempt to return: the Duke of Clarence and the Earl of Northumberland. The first, whose betrayal may seem to an outside observer the hardest to forgive, had the best reason to switch sides again. The Readeption made Clarence not a potential royal claimant, a king-to-be-made by Warwick, but an embarrassment. Clarence must have known it. As the author of a near contemporary account of Edward's attempt to retake the throne explained, Clarence under the Lancastrians 'considred well, that hymselfe was had in great suspicion, despite, disdeigne, and hatered, with all the lordes, noblemen, and othar that were adherents and full partakers with Henry, the Usurpar, Margaret his wyfe, and his sonne Edward, called Prince'.[38] Richard played no part in persuading Clarence back into his family's embrace. As Clarence had always showed himself jealous of any favour offered to his younger brother, Richard would hardly have been the best candidate. This task was left to his mother Cecily, his sisters the Duchess of Exeter and, especially, the Duchess of Burgundy. Commines actually dates the beginning of the campaign to tempt back Clarence to an episode before the invasion and Readeption, when an unnamed 'lady' spoke to him in France and 'exploited the situation so well that she won over the duke of Clarence who promised to join his brother, the king, as soon as he came back to England'.[39] That may be an exaggeration, as Clarence did no such thing, allowing Warwick's invasion force to oust his brothers. But it is credible that efforts were made as early as possible to offer Clarence a way out of his treachery that would help Edward back into power.

The Earl of Northumberland, the restored Henry Percy, had been unable, or unwilling, to help Edward when Warwick made his move. If Percy resisted Edward's return, then a successful invasion, particularly one that tried to raise the north, was out of the question. There is evidence that Edward recognized the importance of securing the assistance of Percy, who might have been wavering because the man he had replaced, John Neville, Marquess Montagu, was in an ideal position to reassert his claim now that his own brother was back in his accustomed position at the right hand of a king. Intriguingly, the Yorkist negotiations with Percy involved men who would later become loyal servants of Richard, Duke of Gloucester, and even of Richard III. One was Nicholas Leventhorpe, a yeoman of Edward's chamber who claimed expenses in June 1471 for 'coming in the king's message from the Hague in Holland unto the Earl of Northumberland and over again to his highness in Middelburg in Zeeland'. Leventhorpe continued to serve the Yorks, and specifically Richard, when the latter was elevated to a new role in the north following Edward's restoration. Another man mentioned in the same document was Ralph Ashton, who also later strengthened his ties with Richard. When Edward and his followers landed, they were able to pick up more support in the north, including one of Marquess Montagu's men, Ralph Snaith, bailiff of Pontefract, and John Pilkington, who had been with Richard in Wales and lent Edward 100 marks when he came to Doncaster. At Nottingham, Sir James Harrington, head of the family in whose dispute over Hornby Castle Richard had become involved, also joined Edward, along with William Par, whose brother Thomas would be remembered by Richard as one of his 'servanders and lovers' after Barnet.[40]

The presence of so many of Richard's current or future adherents among those – relatively few – who would rally to Edward's side may add substance to the speculation that the young duke had been shoring up support in the north among people he could trust after being left behind by his brother; perhaps he was even drawing on the authority that his wardenship of the West March – which, as far as the Yorkists were concerned, he still held – could offer. An entry in a chronicle written by a Cistercian monk in Flanders mentions that

Richard had come to Edward in The Hague 'cum pluribus', with many men.[41] If there is any truth to that, it is more likely that Richard had promises of help than much manpower. The English accounts of this period do not mention the Duke of Gloucester in any special capacity, however, so it cannot be stated with any certainty that Richard was left behind. Moreover, Edward, as Richard's patron, was the origin of many of the loyalties that the duke secured, so claiming men as 'his' rather than his brother's can stretch the evidence. The fact that they became loyal Ricardians may be because they had been loyal Edwardians, rather than the other way round. But men such as Harrington, Par and Pilkington *were* particularly connected to Richard, and their presence at Edward's side when he returned may have had something to do with the younger brother's influence. Richard never let his brother down while he was alive (his fidelity to his posterity is another matter).

Whether or not Richard was engaged in domestic preparation for Edward's return, Edward himself had to wait for the dynamics of foreign politics to align in his favour. When we think about the Wars of the Roses, it is easy to seal them off, as if the infighting of an extended English aristocratic family had nothing to do with the outside world. It has begun to be accepted that the conflicts did move and involve popular opinion. The wars may have been 'just' a clash of dynasties or aristocratic power games, but without people willing to fight in those causes, they could not have happened. The European dimension to the wars, however, is still too easily marginalized. And yet the end of the Hundred Years War provided the backdrop to the first blows of the conflict, Burgundy and France provided refuge from it, and crucially, neither Warwick's campaign for the Readeption nor Edward's attempt to snatch back the crown could have been launched without continental help, from France and Burgundy respectively. Add to that the influence of Hanseatic shipping, the importance of the two Margarets, of Anjou and of Burgundy, to Lancastrians and Yorkists respectively, and the sporadic involvement of the Scots, and it becomes clear that the Wars of the Roses were an extended episode in a European conflict, not just a murderous private dispute.

Throughout Richard's life, England was part of a finely poised three-way balancing act with Burgundy and France. When the Earl of Warwick had been pushing Edward towards a French alliance, before the king's inconvenient marriage to Elizabeth Woodville, Burgundy manoeuvred to protect their position. Even now that Edward's sister Margaret was married to the Duke of Burgundy, Edward's brother-in-law Charles the Bold did not live up to that epithet. While allowing Edward and his entourage to seek refuge in his territory, he waited, as his father had done ten years before, to see how the Lancastrian regime, now with Warwick as its prime mover, would work with the French government of Louis XI that had helped to reinstate it. In early 1471, when a French declaration of war was followed by Warwick's order to the Calais garrison to attack Burgundy, Charles had his answer, and threw his support behind his guests. By March, with Burgundian assistance, Edward and Richard were ready to sail back across the North Sea to reclaim the kingdom. Warwick, Clarence, Montagu and who knew how many other newly adopted or loyally long-serving Lancastrians awaited them. In addition, Margaret of Anjou was finally preparing to sail herself, bringing her newly married son Edward, the Prince of Wales, with her.

Richard had been on this journey almost exactly ten years before, when as children he and George were recalled to England after their brother's triumph at Towton. Then, they were greeted as the honoured relations of a new king, feasted and blessed as they travelled from Canterbury to London to attend Edward's coronation. The situation could hardly have been more different in 1471. Now, Richard was with his eldest brother Edward, while his elder brother Clarence was, for all he knew, preparing to fight him. Edward and Richard's fleet was substantial but hardly a vast one, carrying a total of 2,000 men, according to the Yorkist account written shortly after the expedition, known as the 'Historie of the Arrivall of Edward IV in England and the Finall Recouerye of his Kingdomes from Henry VI'. Even that figure may have been an exaggeration; other chroniclers reported it as only 1,200.

Among the forces were 300 Flemish gunners. That was only part of the Burgundian contribution, which included some of the ships that Edward used and a private offering from Charles of the equivalent of £20,000. Edward had also succeeded in negotiating with representatives of the Hanseatic League so that rather than being pursued by their ships, as he had been on his outward voyage, he now sailed in fourteen of them. The whole party boarded ship in Flushing on 2 March 1471, but a great storm prevented them from crossing for nine days. Edward refused to disembark, demonstrating his determination to take his chance. Richard was in command of 300 of the company, perhaps amounting to two ships (he may have been Admiral of England, but that didn't imply any special affinity for the sea). When they eventually made landfall on 14 March, having been warned off landing at Cromer in Norfolk, after more bad weather, Richard initially found himself four miles away from Edward's party. It took a day before the whole force was reassembled. Edward had chosen to land further north at Ravenspur in Yorkshire, at the mouth of the Humber – the same port, as the *Arrivall*'s author pointed out, at which Henry of Lancaster, the future Henry IV, had landed, when he invaded to depose Richard II.

In the *Arrivall*, the author seems ambivalent about this comparison. Henry IV was, of course, Henry VI's grandfather, so he too is characterized in this narrative as 'the Usurpowr', like his grandson 'at this tyme'. But he was also successful. For his part, Edward discovered that, if he were to succeed, he would have to adopt some of his predecessor's tactics. Whether Richard had been involved or not, the Yorkists had been unable to stir up much popular support. Although pitched battles always depended on the men that major landowners could bring out, wider popular support was important. By that measure, Warwick (as against the cipher Henry VI) was more successful than his rivals. Edward had been more popular when Warwick was on his side. When Warwick deserted him, the earl seems to have taken much popular opinion, particularly in the north, with him. Norfolk had been closed to Edward as a landing place, and the town of Hull now shut its gates. When they approached York, the city's recorder Thomas Conyers rode out to advise him that he would either be refused entry, or if he did get into the city, 'he was lost, and undone, and all his'. By letting it be known that he was only interested in reclaiming his inheritance as Duke of York, however, Edward was able to persuade the citizens to admit him.

The *Arrivall* author proposes that it was this tactic that allowed Edward's army safe passage. It is worth questioning how subtle a ploy this was, however. First, it was unoriginal. Henry IV had used it, and although almost seventy years had passed, the fact had not been forgotten – as the *Arrivall* author demonstrates. Secondly, when Henry of Lancaster had used the gambit, he was a dispossessed duke, who had never yet claimed the throne. Edward was a crowned and anointed king of ten years' standing. How innocent would people have to have been not to have suspected that reclaiming his crown was really Edward's plan? More likely that his was a fiction that the invader and populace could agree upon. If Edward failed, they could say that they had never supported an attempt on the throne. In the *Arrivall*, much is made of the efforts to which Warwick had gone to ensure loyalty, sending men 'afore into those partes for to move them to be agains his highnes'. For people pulled in two directions, the 'Duke of York' fiction gave them at least some protection from reprisal.

In York, Edward only stayed a night. The chronicle of the Burgundian Jean de Wavrin, which otherwise follows the *Arrivall* fairly closely, mentions that Richard, on witnessing an argument between Edward and another citizen of York, Martin de la Mere, said to Lord Rivers that they should kill de la Mere. Instead, Rivers mustered his men and rapidly cleared out of the city, hustling Edward on to his horse.[42] As this anecdote is the first in which Richard's much disputed streak of ruthlessness appears, it is worth pausing over. Wavrin was a compiler rather than an original author, and he died in 1473 or 1474, years before Richard's reputation had begun its long posthumous 'blackening'. Much of what Wavrin includes in his accounts of earlier periods is mythical, but closer to his own time, and as he writes about an enterprise that owed much to Burgundian involvement, there is less reason to mistrust him. Moreover, Wavrin's book became one of Edward's prize possessions. The British Library still holds a copy of the manuscript that was presented to and probably adapted for the king, with an initial illumination showing the author presenting his work to Edward, who wears the Burgundian Order of the Golden Fleece. One eighteenth-century authority even identified Richard himself in the same picture – a rather sour-faced, if snappily dressed courtier in a green hat with a feather, and a fur-trimmed crimson doublet, wearing the Order of the Garter on his out-turned left leg.[43] Richard could have been intended as this figure (though the model was certainly *not* Richard), in which case the idea that the text within contained a libel on him seems even less likely. None of this is to offer a contribution to the 'blackening' of Richard. The anecdote actually shows him as fiercely protective of his brother, prepared to act decisively, and courageous. If the proposal was ruthless as well, it is arguable that ruthlessness was called for. Finally, the suggestion was also impulsive. By acting with equal speed but slightly more consideration, Rivers was able to avoid bloodshed. This would not be the last time that Richard would show a tendency towards impulsive violence.

After York, the route for Edward's army would test whether any preparations had achieved the desired effect. The next destination was Tadcaster, ten miles south, and 'a town of th'Erle of Northumberland'.[44] They were able to pass without incident. Henry Percy might not have managed to raise a force to come to the king's side himself, for, as the author of the *Arrivall* explained, memories of sufferings at Edward's hands at the 'great battaile in those same parties' – Towton – were still fresh. But 'for soo muche as he sat still', refusing to challenge Edward's advance, the restored Duke of Northumberland 'dyd the kynge right gode and notable service'. What is more, Percy's ability to hold his men to inaction meant that his rival for the duchy, Marquess Montagu, had to do the same. The people of the region, loyal to the Percy family, would not come to Montagu's aid 'in ne cawse, ne qwarell'. When Edward neared Pontefract Castle, where Montagu was staying, the Marquess 'sufferyd hym to passe in peascable wyse'. Not only that, but, as we have seen, the bailiff of Pontefract, Ralph Snaith, was even able to join the army as it marched south. Edward was gathering strength. As he moved through Yorkshire, more men joined him, though 'not so many as he supposed wolde comen'.[45]

Edward's increasing force was, however, enough to frighten 'his great Rebell', the Earl of Warwick, who had marched up from London with an army that initially outnumbered his opponent's. Warwick refused to face Edward, making for the 'strong wallyd towne' of Coventry. The delay only allowed Edward to gather more strength: at Leicester, the largest force yet, of 3,000 men, was brought to him by Lord Hastings, who had accompanied Edward into exile but could now call upon his retainers with confidence. Again, Edward offered battle, and again, Warwick refused. At times, Edward has been criticized for acting too hesitantly when his kingdom was threatened. The charge can more fairly be made of Warwick, whose refusal to risk battle while Edward's army was substantially weaker than his own allowed the king to turn the tables on him.

The last ally that Edward hoped to recruit was his own brother, the Duke of Clarence. The *Arrivall* says that as soon as Edward arrived, Clarence gathered an army to bring over to him. It is likely that he was more circumspect than that, waiting to see whether Edward's gamble had any chance of paying off before jumping his way. The encounter happened around 28 March 1471, three miles outside Banbury in Oxfordshire as Edward continued his march south. The two armies halted less than half a mile apart, and Edward, taking Richard, Rivers and Hastings with him, walked towards his perfidious younger brother, as Clarence, with a similarly reduced party, did the same. It must have been a moment of high tension, even if the principals might have made some prior private agreement, which was merely being sealed for more general consumption. In the event, there was 'right kynde and lovynge language betwixt them twoo', and the reconciliation was made for all to see. Clarence and Gloucester also 'spake together', 'and then the trompetts and minstrels blew uppe, and, with that, the kynge brought his brother Clarence . . . to his felowshipe'.[46] Later in April their sister Margaret of Burgundy wrote a letter in which she described how Edward and Richard watched as Clarence sank to his knees before, convinced by his professions of humility, they pulled him up and kissed him, 'plusieurs fois'.[47] The Italian historian Polydore Vergil, no friend to Richard in other respects, makes him the lead actor in this very public drama in his *Anglica Historia* (completed with the encouragement of Henry VII in 1513). '[A]s thoughe he had bene apoyntyd arbyter of all controversy', Virgil writes, Richard 'first conferryd secretly with the duke; than he returnyd to King Edward, and dyd the same with him. Fynally, not warre but peace was in every mans mouth.'[48]

Perhaps Vergil was exaggerating the role of a man he knew would feature heavily later in his narrative, as Commines had done. When war returned to men's mouths, however, Richard certainly did have a part to play. The long-delayed confrontation between Edward and Warwick finally took place outside Barnet, just north of London, on 14 April, Easter Day. By that time Warwick had surrendered the initiative even further. He had been unable to prevent Edward from entering London, and taking Henry prisoner. Henry's last public act, like so many in the disastrous reign that preceded the Readeption, had been scripted for him. Warwick's brother, the Archbishop of York, had taken Henry from the Bishop's Palace at St Paul's and paraded him around the city to instil confidence in its defenders. The move had the opposite effect. 'The powre of the sayde Henry, and his adherents, was so litle and feble' that the city's governors determined not to resist Edward, by now at St Albans. Even the Archbishop of York capitulated, contacting Edward in secret to reconcile with him. When Edward entered London on Maundy Thursday, it was not to the sort of rapturous reception that had greeted his first triumphant arrival after Mortimer's Cross ten years before – still less the greeting that the future Henry IV had received on his attempt at the throne, when it was alleged that the crowds had shouted 'Blessed is he who comes in the name of the Lord, Hosanna in the highest.' But the pitiful showing of Henry VI, and Warwick's failure to stop Edward, had shown London which way to lean.

'Ledyng the vaward of Kyng Edward'

Edward had enough time to seize Henry, who greeted his cousin of York and trusted that he would come to no harm at his hands, say his prayers at Westminster, and greet his firstborn son born in sanctuary there.[49] Edward stayed one more night, Good Friday, before marching north out of the capital to face Warwick's army, ten miles away at Barnet. They apparently spent the night within yards of each other: so close that Edward ordered his men to keep quiet in order that Warwick's artillery, far better equipped than Edward's, overshot them. In the morning, under a deep mist, the two armies met. How exactly they were deployed, and what exact role Richard played, is not known. The *Arrivall* describes the two armies drawing up unevenly, so that on either side the flanks overwhelmed each other. Luckily for Edward, the flight of one of his flanks was so well concealed by the mist that it did not spread panic to the rest of the army. Even more fortunate, when the Earl of Oxford's men returned to the battle after chasing a contingent of Edward's from the field, they rejoined at the wrong place, where their livery, of a star with streams, was mistaken for Edward's, of a sun with streams. Warwick's allies began to fight each other and the Earl of Oxford's men cried treason. Oxford fled, but neither Warwick nor his brother John Neville, Marquess Montagu, was so lucky. Both were cut down, and their bodies displayed at St Paul's, so that their deaths could be confirmed. There they remained for three days, before being turned over to their brother George, Archbishop of York, who presided over the burial at Bisham Abbey, traditional resting place of the earls of Salisbury.

One chronicler, Robert Fabyan, puts Richard in the thick of the action at Barnet, 'ledyng the vaward of Kyng Edward',[50] though he is not mentioned by others. But other evidence that Richard was in the thick of the fighting, even if he wasn't yet a field commander, comes both from the memorials of those killed by his side, such as Thomas Par and John Milewater, and a newsletter written by a Hanseatic merchant from Cologne, Gerhard von Wesel; he wrote that Richard and Rivers ('Lord Scales' again) were wounded 'slightly', though 'thanks be to God they suffered no further harm'.[51] Certainly, any injury did not trouble Richard enough to keep him out of the next – and last – battle to secure Edward's throne, at Tewkesbury, where the eighteen-year-old Duke of Gloucester indisputably did receive a substantial command.

On the same day that Edward's army had defeated Warwick's at Barnet, Margaret of Anjou, with her son Edward, finally arrived in England. Their ships had been held up by bad weather, but on Easter Day they landed at Weymouth in Dorset. Immediately their force began to strengthen, apparently encountering rather less resistance than had Edward on his arrival on the other side of the country. They welcomed the retinues of the Duke of Somerset (Edmund Beaufort) and John Courtenay, the restored Earl of Devon who preferred to throw his weight behind a true Lancastrian force rather than prop up Warwick's pragmatists at Barnet (which had weakened Warwick's forces, possibly significantly). They were also able to drum up popular support as they passed through Exeter, Bath and Bristol. Further reinforcements awaited in Wales where Jasper Tudor, Earl of Pembroke (accompanied by his nephew Henry), was ready.

Edward was kept informed of this growing threat, and acted quickly to meet it. He marched out to Windsor, where, after celebrating St George's Day, he replaced his injured or exhausted troops with new recruits, and set out westwards. He was not fooled by a movement of the Lancastrian army towards Yeovil, as if it would turn towards London. The capital city had never been particularly fertile ground for Margaret. The plan was surely to pull together so much support in the west and north that London and the east would be forced to capitulate. By acting very quickly, Edward was in a position to challenge the Lancastrians. Within a week his forces were within a few miles of Margaret's. Outside Bristol on 1 May 1471 the Lancastrians gave Edward the slip. But the pursuit continued at a punishing pace. The Lancastrians were trying to cross the Severn to link up with Jasper Tudor, and made for Gloucester, where there was a bridge over the river. Finding that crossing barred to them, they marched a further twenty-four miles 'in a fowle contrye, all in lanes and stonny wayes, betwyxt woodes, without any good refresshynge', towards Tewkesbury. There, Edward's army finally caught up with them. On 4 May the two armies met. The king's vanguard was 'in the rule of the Duke of Gloucester',[52] though it is unclear whether this means that Richard had command of the left or centre of the three 'battles' into which Edward's army was divided (the third fought under Hastings).

At Tewkesbury, Edward carried the fight to his opponent, advancing 'directly upon his enemyes' who had been softened up with arrows and artillery fire. The Lancastrians were led by the Duke of Somerset, who responded in kind, launching his own outflanking attack on Edward's division. Edward's response pushed the enemy uphill, towards his brother. Richard was assisted by a sudden attack from a group of 200 spearmen whom Edward had kept in reserve. This broke Somerset's line, which took flight, 'into the parke, and into the medowe that was nere, and into lanes, and dykes, where they best hopyd to escape the dangar'. But 'many of then were slayne, and, namely, at a mylene [mill pond], in the medowe fast by the towne, were many drownyd'.[53] In the pursuit, according to the *Arrivall*, Prince Edward was killed along with the Earl of Devon, the Marquess of Dorset (Somerset's brother) and Lord Wenlock, whose decision to desert the Yorkist cause and follow his old master Warwick over to the Lancastrians had not paid off. Those who outran their pursuers made for the sanctuary of Tewkesbury Abbey. Queen Margaret avoided detection by taking refuge at another abbey, on the road from Tewkesbury to Worcester, where she was eventually taken prisoner three days after the battle.

Most of those who sought sanctuary in Tewkesbury were spared by Edward, though the author of the *Arrivall* is at pains to make clear that this was an act of generosity on the king's part: 'there ne was, ne had at any tyme bene grauntyd, any fraunchise to that place for any offendars agaynst theyr prince'.[54] The ringleaders were not included in the amnesty. As Constable of England, it fell to Richard to pass judgment on Edmund, Duke of Somerset, the Lancastrian treasurer Sir John Langstrother, Prior of the Hospital of St John of Jerusalem, Sir Thomas Tresham, Sir Gervase Clifton, and 'othar notable parsonnes dyvers'. They were condemned to death, and beheaded straight away on a scaffold set up in the middle of Tewkesbury. The bodies were, at least, dismembered no further, and were allowed Christian burial. Considering the now routine brutality of the Wars of the Roses – compare the treatment of Edward and Richard's own father and brother after Wakefield – this should be acknowledged as the gentle rain of royal mercy, which had also been in evidence in the decent treatment of Warwick and Montagu's bodies after Barnet. But in the violating of the abbey's sanctuary, notwithstanding the special pleading of the *Arrivall*, Edward had once again shown that he could be as unscrupulous as his opponents. Richard was beside him for all of it.

Tewkesbury was the making of Richard, in more than one sense. By his conduct on the battlefield, he had shown himself a courageous, trustworthy and effective military commander. In carrying out his judicial obligations after the battle, he had done his duty and given no indication of squeamishness: though that could have been predicted from his earliest appearance as a political actor, in the Hungerford treason trial of 1469. But it is also to Tewkesbury and its aftermath that we can trace the first sources of the black legend of Richard, the reading back of the events of 1483 into his conduct from years before.

So any account of Richard and Tewkesbury must deal with the story that the Duke of Gloucester killed the Lancastrian Prince of Wales, Edward of Westminster, in cold blood, after the battle. Shakespeare, if not the source, certainly provides the most memorable version of this accusation, and for a particular reason. In *Richard III* the tale is spiced up by the fact that Prince Edward's widow, Warwick's younger daughter Anne Neville, became Richard's wife. Shakespeare's extraordinary scene in which Anne is seduced by her husband's murderer would not work if Richard were a mere soldier on the winning side, fighting under the prevailing code of honour, and Prince Edward a mere casualty of war. The scene depicting the murder of Prince Edward in *Henry VI Part Three* implicates all three brothers, Edward, Clarence and Gloucester, in the crime.

No contemporary or near contemporary account of the battle and its aftermath, however, says that Richard or his brothers killed Prince Edward after the battle. Most say that he died on the battlefield, and of the few that give an account of his being taken prisoner, it is an insult to the king that seals his fate, carried out by unnamed servants. In Fabyan's *Great Chronicle of London*, for example, the king 'smote him [Prince Edward] on his face with the back of his gauntlet. After which stroke by him received the Kings servants rid him out of life forthwith.'[55] Other accounts written, like the *Great Chronicle*, after Richard's death, and otherwise unsympathetic to him, nonetheless don't pin this crime on Richard and his brothers directly – if they detect a crime at all. It is not until Polydore Vergil, writing forty years after the event, that Edward is 'crewelly murderyd' – by Clarence, Gloucester and Hastings (whose part is taken by Edward IV himself in Shakespeare's version). The idea that Richard was the posthumous victim of 'Tudor propaganda' has lost much of its power over the years. In no sense can Henry VII, still less his successors under whom Shakespeare lived, be accused of orchestrating a rewriting of history along modern 'propaganda' lines. But when it comes to the story of the 'murder' of Prince Edward, it seems clear that Shakespeare is embellishing a story from the sixteenth-century historians Raphael Holinshed and Edward Hall, which they have lifted from Vergil, writing in the early part of the same century. What is more, it is only retrospectively even in Shakespeare's scheme that Richard's part in the murder looms largest, when the whole guilt for the crime the playwright has previously shown being committed by three men devolves solely on Richard.[56] This is an example of the way that Richard's reputation went through successive blackenings, even within the work of the man who did most to cast him as a villain for posterity.

Edward's progress after the Battle of Tewkesbury took him first to Worcester and then on to Coventry. There, he was joined by Henry Percy, who assured him that, contrary to his fears, the north was not inclined to rise in support of the Lancastrians. The king's two victories had crushed any enthusiasm for what now looked like a lost cause. Among those who fled the country around this time were Jasper Tudor and his nephew Henry, who took ship from west Wales towards France. They ended up in Brittany, where they spent the next dozen years, almost, but not quite, forgotten. Edward and his brothers were free to turn back towards London, and prepare for a third triumphant entry into the capital. There was, however, one remaining obstacle, which briefly threatened to be the most serious of any that Edward and his followers had to face since their return in March. It was led by a man who has remained at best a shadowy figure, but whose ties were to the leaders of opposition to the Yorkists. He was Thomas Neville, illegitimate son of William Neville, Lord Fauconberg, the Earl of Warwick's uncle.

Thomas's father had died serving Edward in the north, but the Bastard of Fauconberg, as Thomas was universally known, threw in his lot with his cousin Warwick in April 1470, when Warwick's fleet crossed to France after his unsuccessful rebellion. Thomas was with Warwick again on his return in October, after which the Readeption government appointed him (he later claimed) 'Captain of the navy of England and men of war both by sea and land'.[57] It was in this capacity that Fauconberg's fleet menaced Portuguese shipping. When Edward invaded in March 1471, Fauconberg may have been distracted off the coast of Brittany, and by the time he landed in Kent he was too late to help his cousin Warwick, who had been defeated and killed at Barnet.

We can only guess at the exact motivation, or that of the apparently substantial force, including local gentry, which Fauconberg was able to gather in Kent and Essex, for continuing the fight. If he had taken this decision between the battles of Barnet and Tewkesbury, we could interpret his actions as carrying on the Lancastrian cause, in the expectation of holding London and the south-east for a victorious Margaret of Anjou. But by the time Fauconberg had put together a large enough force to send a threatening proclamation to the mayor and citizens of London, he had again been outpaced by events, in the control of the impatient Edward IV. The mayor's reply reminded Fauconberg of the outcome of Barnet, and informed him of what had just happened at Tewkesbury. Nevertheless, Fauconberg and his followers – not only those who had served him at sea and might have been expected to stay by his side, but also many of those who had joined him as he marched through Kent – kept on towards London. For several days they assaulted the capital by land and water, bombarding the city and making attempts to breach its gates or London Bridge. Led by the Yorkist lords Earl Rivers and the Earl of Essex, whom Edward had left in charge when he marched west, London held firm, though the bridge was partially burned, and Aldgate, in the east, was taken by Fauconberg's men for a short time.

It was not enough. By the time Edward arrived back in the capital, on 21 May 1471, Fauconberg and most of his men had fled. It was not the last that the Yorkists, and Richard in particular, would hear from him. After stopping briefly in London, Edward and his brothers made for Canterbury, where the mayor Nicholas Faunt, who had fallen in with Fauconberg, was sentenced to be hanged, drawn and quartered. Fauconberg himself had made for Sandwich. One contemporary source says that Richard preceded his brothers to Kent, so it is possible that the beginning of this mopping-up operation, as after Tewkesbury, was entrusted to the Duke of Gloucester as newly reappointed Constable of England.[58] However, no one but the king himself could have been behind the offer of a pardon to Fauconberg on 10 June, while others of his followers in Kent and elsewhere were fined (if rich) or beheaded (if not). The condition of Fauconberg's pardon seems to have been a partial deprivation of liberty, and the man appointed to oversee this late-medieval control order was none other than Richard, Duke of Gloucester. Thus Fauconberg accompanied Richard, one assumes under duress, when he went north that summer. By September the same year, however, something happened to exhaust Fauconberg's chances, though we don't know what. 'On account of a new offence', Fauconberg was beheaded in September. His head was placed over London Bridge, where his bid to turn the tide of the Wars of the Roses against the Yorkists one last time had foundered.[59]

Richard's role in the demise of the Bastard of Fauconberg is unclear, but the 'new offence' must have been committed when Fauconberg was in his care, or charge. By the time it happened, the victorious Yorkists had rid themselves of a far more significant Lancastrian loose end: Henry VI. While his son was alive, there was a good reason to keep Henry in captivity. If the Yorkists had killed Henry, then they would have swapped a king in their hands for a new one at large, thereby actually strengthening the Lancastrian challenge. When Prince Edward died at Tewkesbury, the prisoner Henry might once again have become the sole focus of rebellion, particularly while his wife survived. Fortunately for Edward IV, Henry took the news of Tewkesbury badly: 'he toke it to so great dispite, ire, and indignation, that, of pure displeasure, and melencoly, he dyed',[60] on 23 May, two days after Edward's return to London. That of course was the Yorkist line. The idea of dying of melancholy was admittedly not unheard of at the time. Bishop Spens of Aberdeen was also said to have died of it in April 1480. Melancholy was a medical diagnosis to medieval doctors, an excess of black bile that could affect the internal organs. But other accounts make it clear that Henry was put to death, in the Tower of London, probably two days before, where he had been held since the capital had fallen to the Yorkists.

Rumours of Richard's involvement in this crime are more consistent than in the death of Prince Edward. All, however, date to after his reign and are more interesting as evidence of reasonably early and persistent stories about Richard's bad character ([Henry was] 'slain, as it was said by the Duke of Gloucester', as the 'Vitellius' London chronicler puts it) than proof of guilt. What is surely beyond doubt is that Edward IV, not the Duke of Gloucester, ordered the murder of his anointed and inconvenient predecessor. As with Henry IV's dispatching of Richard II in 1400, it didn't do to accuse an undisgraced king of such a crime, so a more convenient fiction was dreamed up: Richard II starved himself to death, Henry VI simply pined away. Perhaps the official version created the vacuum for Richard, Duke of Gloucester's alleged guilt to fill. But not only is there no proof of his guilt: it is untenable that he could have committed the crime unless his brother the king meant him to. It is worth recalling, however, that as Constable, Richard might well have been expected to take a role in this event, as he did at Tewkesbury and with Fauconberg.

The summer of 1471 saw Edward's Yorkist regime well and truly re-established. With a new son and heir, and the king's principal rivals all dead, there was every prospect that England was witnessing the beginning of a royal dynasty to offer reliable government and to lay to rest the long years of misrule, faction and fighting. On 3 July, Richard followed his brother Clarence in signing an oath of allegiance to the new Prince of Wales, also an Edward, 'verey and undoubted Heyre of our said Sovereigne Lord. . . . in cas hereafter it happen You, by Goddis dispocion, to outleve our said Sovereigne Lord, I shall then take and accepte You for true, veray and rightwis Kyng of Englond, etc'.[61] Richard's own role in this new regime, moulded by his eldest brother the king, was about to be expanded unprecedentedly. To begin with, Richard owed his establishment as a great lord in his own right almost entirely to Edward. But the role Edward created for Richard also allowed the Duke of Gloucester, for the first time, to emerge from the king's shadow.

The seal of Richard of Gloucester as Admiral of England, 1461–2, bearing his ducal arms; now in the British Museum.

3

Warwick's Heir

There is a volume in the British Library's holdings of the collection of the seventeenth-century antiquary Sir Robert Cotton that consists of four separate manuscripts, bound together in a single codex, about the dimensions of an A4 sheet of paper. The book contains a list of families who came over from Normandy with William the Conqueror; an account of the creation of the future Henry VIII as Duke of York in 1494; a record of the trial of the Knights Templar in England; and what the Library describes as a 'Register of Richard, Duke of Gloucester'. This last item, taking up roughly two hundred pages of the whole, does not in fact contain much that cannot be found elsewhere about the duke's holdings, for example, in the records of grants and appointments contained in the Patent and Closed Rolls, and those of the Chancery of the Duchy of Lancaster, or in the Rolls of Parliament. The fact that this record, kept up by someone in Richard's household between the beginning of his rise in 1472 and his great leap into the unknown in 1483, runs to such a length, is one indication of quite how much influence and wealth, in the form of estates and royal appointments, Richard acquired over these years. But even more than the contents themselves, it is the very existence of Richard's register that is worth noting. In this careful record of all that Richard had, in its itemization of some of what he had lost but perhaps, with the evidence gathered here, hoped to regain, the Register is a compilation made under the direction of a very careful owner. All medieval magnates of note were acquisitive, jealous of their patrimonies, and concerned in a world of disputed possession to provide legal backing for any potential challenges.

Few have left behind evidence of quite so determined an approach to this business of getting, holding and expanding.[1]

J. R. Seeley famously remarked of the British Empire that it seemed to have been acquired 'in a fit of absence of mind'. Viewing the way that Richard acquired and maintained what eventually amounted to a personal empire within his brother's kingdom, in the twelve years between Edward's return to the throne in 1471 and his early death in 1483, creates the opposite impression – of a sustained bout of presence of mind. Richard's guiding principle was to extend his influence, mostly in the north, but elsewhere as well. Much of his activity was in response to changing circumstances – the death of rivals, the fortunes of war – and it seems that, unusually, he was more interested in expanding his own holdings and the power that went with them than securing an inheritance for any offspring. In contrast to the Shakespearean picture, he did not seem to look far into the future: he reacted more often than he took the initiative. Whether the usurpation that followed Edward's death, both immortalizing and permanently tarnishing Richard's name, was a culmination of this process, or a near inexplicable rupture of a hitherto single-minded, steady, but (mostly) scrupulously legitimate pattern of take and occasional give, will be discussed later. For now, we must concentrate on the years during which Richard became Richard – before he transfigured himself into Richard III.

The creation of a role for Richard as the inheritor of the Earl of Warwick's lands and duties in the north began almost as soon as Edward was securely reinstated. One office, the Wardenship of the West March towards Scotland, had already been granted to him. In May 1471 he was appointed to Warwick's ceremonial office of Great Chamberlain, and resumed his titles as Constable and Admiral. In July he was confirmed as chief steward of the Duchy of Lancaster in the north, and although he was in the same month appointed to a council of administrators for the new Prince of Wales in the Principality, the Duchy of Cornwall and the county of Chester, Richard's chief gains continued to be in the north. A grant first made in June of Warwick's northern heartland, centred on the castles and manors of Middleham and Sheriff Hutton in Yorkshire, and Penrith in Cumberland, was expanded in July to include 'all other lordships, manors and lands in those counties which were entailed to Richard Neville, late earl of Warwick'.[2]

These grants and appointments created a personal power base for Richard and demonstrated his brother the king's trust in him over a vital area of the country. Medieval government depended on regional lords enforcing the king's will. In the north of England, the plain facts of distance from the seat of royal government and difficulties of communication were made even more acute by the border with another sovereign nation. Northern lords had to be relied upon to defend England against Scottish incursion. It says much for Richard's perceived trustworthiness and efficiency that Edward saw him, rather than, say, his elder brother Clarence, as a candidate for this role.

However much faith the king showed in the Duke of Gloucester, Richard's success as a regional magnate depended on his ability to attach the Neville affinity, with its long roots, to himself as a new lord, and to gather new adherents where he could. It also depended on his dealings with the other great powers in the area. The most important of these were the Percys, the Stanleys and the senior branch of the Neville family, whose historic title was the earldom of Westmorland. The retainers who had formerly looked to the Earl of Warwick as their lord were perhaps only to be expected to gravitate towards his replacement. Richard took the sensible course of securing the loyalty of a former Neville loyalist with a wide network in the region, Sir John Conyers. We have encountered Conyers earlier in his career, when he was associated with the rebellion of 'Robin of Redesdale', which became the pretext for Warwick's first break with Edward IV in 1469. If Conyers *had* been Robin, Edward's brother did not hold it against him now. Sir John was appointed Richard's steward and constable of Middleham, and his wages doubled.[3] It was Sir John's brother Thomas (one of a family of 25 children, including 12 sons) who had tried to warn Edward and Richard against entering York on their campaign to retake the throne. This was clearly a useful family loyalty to secure.

Richard's accumulation of land and loyalty in the north began, over the next decade, to take the form of a virtuous circle – certainly for Richard. As the Duke of Gloucester expanded his sphere of influence – acquiring, for example, the castle of Richmond in March 1478 to complete his Yorkshire estates in a swap with Clarence for holdings in Gloucestershire and Wiltshire – so the numbers of those who looked to him for protection, offices and 'good lordship' grew. By the time of Edward's death in 1483, with

Richard using both his local standing and his royal connection to full effect, he had increased his sway over the north of England, into County Durham; and, most strikingly, he had been granted palatine rights in the county of Cumberland – that is, quasi-regal authority.

None of this was inevitable. It depended on the king's backing, on Richard's own capacity to retain followers (which, as we have already seen, he certainly possessed) and how he dealt with potential rivals. If Richard's record of increasing influence and acquisition of a following show that he had the vital attributes of a 'good lord', his dealings with those of a comparable status demonstrate a different side to his character – one in which his refusal to be overawed by men of greater experience and deeper connections can be admired, but which also ran the risk of storing up future enmities. That was not the case, however, with the representative of the senior branch of the Neville family. Richard's securing of the services of Ralph, Lord Neville, heir to the earldom of Westmorland, from 1477, showed that one facet of Warwick's legacy that he could relinquish was the long-running feud between the family's two branches. The senior of the two had remained loyal to the Lancastrians through the civil war, but the real source of their dispute with Warwick's branch was the loss, as they saw it, of the greater part of their inheritance. This had been settled on the first earl's second wife and their descendants, down to Warwick the Kingmaker, from 1440.

By the time that Richard took over that portion of the Neville lands, the Earl of Westmorland was an old man, tired out by years of struggling to regain his lost patrimony. His nephew and heir Ralph Neville is recorded transferring large portions of land in Yorkshire to Richard's chancellor Thomas Barowe, in exchange for £10,000 to be paid by a clutch of Gloucester's adherents, including John Huddleston (brother of Thomas, killed fighting with Richard) and Richard Ratcliffe (an early member of the duke's inner circle, who rose ever higher on Gloucester's ticket, until he achieved the immortality of a pejorative nickname – 'the Rat').[4] The land in question already belonged to Richard, because it was that very disputed Neville land, including Middleham and Sheriff Hutton, which had been Warwick's and granted after his death to the duke. Medieval land transfers were often based on a fictional legal contest. One party agreed to acknowledge the claims of the other in return for a sum of money that was mutually agreed. In a feudal system, where land belonged to a tenant-in-chief, and ultimately, to the Crown, this was a convenient way of buying and selling property, and recording the transaction officially, as the record of the end (the 'Fine') of a 'dispute'. In this case, the fiction was slightly different. Richard's entourage was paying for land that the duke already held, as a way of securing loyalty and drawing a line under a long disagreement. By the time Richard really needed Ralph, in 1483, he could write to him in the most heartfelt of terms, trusting that Neville would come to his side: 'as ever ye love me . . . that ye come to me with that ye may make, defensably arrayde, in all the hast that ys possyble'.[5] The bearer of that plea was one of those who had first taken part in Ralph Neville's introduction to Gloucester's circle, Richard Ratcliffe.

Not all of Richard of Gloucester's dealings with his more influential regional rivals were as smoothly managed as his encounter with Ralph Neville – though before the earthquake of 1483, Richard might have claimed that he had got the better of them. His first clash was with Henry Percy, Earl of Northumberland, and by July 1474 the two lords' interference in each other's spheres of interest had become serious enough to need a formal solution. The indenture drawn up on 28 July that year shows how far Richard, an interloper into a world dominated for centuries by the Percy family, had outstripped his rival. Percy 'Promits and grants unto the said duke to be his faithful servant . . . to do service unto the said duke at all times lawful and convenient'. For his part, as well as promising to be Percy's 'good and faithful Lord', Richard agrees not to 'ask, challenge nor claim any office or offices or fee that the said earl hath of the king's grant'.[6] That, together with a guarantee not to retain Percy's servants, was really a demonstration of how feeble the earl had become. Never before would one of his family have had to resort to such an extraordinary measure to restrain a rival lord. Richard, at least, seems to have stuck to the bargain. Perhaps that was because he had already got what he wanted. Percy, who among other things was warden of the East March towards Scotland as Richard was to the West March, continued to work with Richard while he was Duke of Gloucester; he stood by his side, for example, at the head of a force showing its strength to the citizens of York in 1476. Even after the manoeuvres that became Richard's bid for the throne, Henry Percy remained a reliable ally – right up to August 1485 and Bosworth Field, where the direction of his loyalty was put to the ultimate test.

Richard's relations with the remaining regional magnates, the Stanleys, who held power in the north-west, particularly in Lancashire and Cheshire, were from the beginning far more fraught. We have already seen how the young Duke of Gloucester appears to have supported the Harrington brothers in their dispute with Thomas, Lord Stanley, over Hornby Castle. That dispute played out until January 1475, almost three years after Edward had ruled in Stanley's favour. It seems likely that Richard's continuing support for the Harringtons emboldened them to defy both Stanley and the king for so long. Whether such support was an instance of the duke's credo of fairness, which some supporters have often detected in his actions, is difficult to judge. It seems equally likely that Richard realized he was never likely to persuade Stanley to cooperate in the way Percy and Lord Neville had done, so he threw his support behind Stanley's opponents. In the process, the Harringtons became some of Richard's most reliable adherents, and loyalty was something that the Duke of Gloucester was certainly interested in. That 'motto', 'Loyauté me lie', could also be interpreted as celebrating the support that the loyalty of others – such as the Harringtons – provided, as much as the strong bonds of the duke's own loyalties.

Richard's swelling influence in the north was likely to lead to further confrontations with Stanley, unless one or the other party, probably with firm royal encouragement, could be made to yield. Initially, it looked as if Edward would favour his brother's cause over Stanley's, in the same way that he had across the north. The king appointed Richard to one of Stanley's plum roles, of chief steward of the Duchy of Lancaster in the county palatine of Lancashire (to go with Richard's appointment to Warwick's former role as chief steward of the northern parts of the duchy). He also granted Richard stewardship of other estates that had previously belonged to Stanley, including those of Tottington, Rochdale and Penwortham in Lancashire.[7] Confusingly, those grants came only two weeks after Edward had appointed Stanley to the same roles. The fact that the king followed this up with an admonishment to Stanley not to let his servants obstruct Gloucester's exercise of these offices shows that this was no royal administrative error, of the sort that flourished to general confusion under Henry VI. Edward, unlike Henry, knew what he was doing. He seems simply to have changed his mind, and expected his subjects to change with him. But when it came to Thomas, Lord Stanley, Edward's effectiveness turned out to be more reminiscent of Henry's than he would have liked. Stanley seems to have remained in place in most of the offices that should have gone to Richard, collecting his fee at one estate (Halton) where Richard was officially steward, for example, and continuing to preside over the Lancashire forests of which Richard should also, by royal decree, have had charge.

More direct clashes, Hornby aside, are harder to substantiate between the Duke of Gloucester and Stanley, but a ballad from within the Stanley family tradition, albeit of much later origin, does mention one (which has proved, alas, impossible to corroborate with contemporary evidence). 'The Stanley Poem', found in two manuscripts, including one in the Bodleian Library, where it is entitled 'The Stanleys antiquytyes in englyshe meeter', has been attributed to a later Thomas Stanley, Bishop of Sodor and Man, and dated to around 1562. This Thomas was not above criticizing the family whose name he bore, though he was, in fact, an illegitimate son. Still, he seems to have been proud enough of the Stanleys' Yorkist-defying exploits – 'The valiaunte actes of the stoute Standelais' – to have memorialized them in around 1,200 lines of rhyming couplets.[8] In the poem's 'Third Fytte' we are introduced to King Edward's 'busy brother', very much the Tudor version of Richard, who swears vengeance on Stanley (prematurely promoted to his later earldom of Derby) for 'a fond fray there had benne amongeste their tenantes'. Stanley, who in recorded history had a habit of avoiding armed conflict, is here portrayed as meeting Richard of Gloucester's challenge 'face to face' at Ribble Bridge, beating him back from threatening the Stanley seat at Lathom, and even contriving that one of his followers, 'Jack Moris of Wiggam' (Wigan), should capture Gloucester's banner and keep it on display for forty years at Wigan church. The details of the encounter are surely coloured beyond belief, and a poet who was willing to have Stanley receive his Derby title from Edward IV rather than Henry VII risks having his licence revoked. But the entire episode seems unlikely to have been invented out of nothing, and Stanley's instant following up of his victory with a visit to the king to put his side of the story certainly rings true, based on what we know of Stanley's manoeuvring and Richard's proximity to his brother. What the literary adventure of Ribble Bridge certainly attests to is a tradition of hostility between Richard and Thomas, Lord Stanley. While this may well be a retrospectively conjured episode to flesh out the differences that were known to the poet and his listeners to have played out in Richard III's final hours, the fact that evidence does exist of genuine differences between Gloucester and Stanley makes it at least conceivable. Richard continued to treat Stanley with caution and suspicion. Stanley's second marriage, to Margaret Beaufort, brought him a stepson, Henry Tudor. It would have required supernatural powers of foresight to calculate that Stanley's connection to this obscure exile might be another reason to keep an eye on him. But from his first dealings with Lord Stanley in the north-west, Richard knew that this was not a man to be trusted very far.

Not all Richard's lands, nor all the disputes they engendered, were in the north. One grant led to an episode on which historians have seized for early evidence of Richard's vicious streak: that of the estates of the attainted Earl of Oxford, John de Vere. The Duke of Gloucester received this grant twice, because, having been reinstated, the Earl re-forfeited when he renewed his support for the Lancastrians. It was not, however, these lands that caused controversy in the fifteenth century and today. The earl's mother, the dowager Countess Elizabeth, also had substantial estates in her own name, which had not been made over to Richard. She was able to make arrangements to ensure that these properties in Essex, Cambridgeshire and London would remain hers to dispose of as she wished – even if her son could not inherit them. The record of some proceedings in Chancery of Hilary Term, 1474, however, shows that Richard came to an agreement with the Countess Elizabeth. '[I]t was covenanted, bargayned and agreeed atte desire of the said countesse, and by the advice of hir counseill, bitwene hir and the said duc, that . . . the same feofees [of the countess] to make an estate of all the said manoirs, londez and tentes . . . to the said duc and his his heirs for evermore.' In return Richard promised Elizabeth an annuity of 500 marks, the payment of her (not very substantial) debts, and to find 'competent benefices' for a younger de Vere son, who was studying at Cambridge, and 'p'posing to be a prest'.[9]

The reason that the petition was being heard was that seven of the countess's feofees were refusing to accept the deal. It seems most likely that this was because the deal was a bad one for the countess, and one she was unlikely to have entered into of her own free will. Long after Richard's death, and the reinstatement (once again) of John de Vere to the earldom of Oxford, he brought a case to demonstrate that his mother had indeed been under duress when assigning the estate to Richard. On its own, despite the testimony of six witnesses in support of de Vere's petition, the story that emerges of Richard's threatening the countess, 'under the streight kepyng of the seid dewke' somewhere in London, according to one witness, and giving her to believe 'that he wolde send her to Middleham there to be kept', according to another, might not be very convincing. The case was, after all, being brought by an inveterate enemy of a now thoroughly disgraced (and thoroughly dead) usurper, on whom it was open season. The deponents piled on the details of the aged, frail countess's fears of the 'greate iourney and the grett colde which then was of Frost and snowe', and that 'consideryng her greate age', she 'cowde not endeure to be conueid theder withoute great iopardie of her lyf'. But it is the evidence of Richard's own Chancery petition, with its unlikely account of Countess Elizabeth being 'advised' to accept his less than generous offer, which does more to substantiate the likelihood of the later account. The Chancery proceedings themselves are witness to a dispute rather than an agreement.

The fact that Richard did eventually get his way may well be because of the pressure he brought to bear on the countess. Her son's collection of witnesses may have exaggerated her perception of the danger she was in, but something other than the rather inadequate exchange she was promised must have been behind Elizabeth's decision to make the lands over to Richard. For all that, we should be careful about leaping to any judgement on Richard's character and especially on his future behaviour from this unsavoury episode. It is tendentious to argue, as one reputable historian has done, that 'the man who maltreated the frail old Countess of Oxford was potentially *capable* of murdering the Princes in the Tower'.[10] Yes, and a man who hadn't maltreated her was potentially *capable* of doing so, too. What the case can be conceded to show is that Richard, from the beginning, and like others of his class such as Clarence or Warwick, could be unscrupulous, unyielding and downright ruthless about getting what he wanted. The events of 1483, however peculiar they were, did not fall from a cloudless sky.

A Bride for a Prince

For all his personal qualities, it is clear how much Richard's rise, and his accumulation of land, wealth and power, depended on his royal brother. Richard may have been adept at squeezing the maximum out of his grants, but they were grants nonetheless. There was one way, however, in which a noble in Richard's position could hope to extend his reach on his own account: marriage. The bride he chose was a natural fit, but would come with complications. Anne Neville, the younger of the late Earl of Warwick's two daughters, was a widow after the Battle of Tewkesbury. This in itself was no barrier to the marriage, despite the fact that Richard, if he had not wielded the blade, had been on the side of those who had killed Anne's husband Edward, the Lancastrian Prince of Wales. *Pace* Shakespeare, however, such a match was unlikely to have seemed particularly strange. It is possible, for example, that Richard, whose reading is known to have included chivalric romance, would have known of the story of Yvain and Alundyne. Yvain was one of King Arthur's knights who, having killed his adversary in battle, marries his widow Alundyne. The only extant manuscript of the Middle English version of this story is an early fifteenth-century text in a northern dialect.[11]

Of course, Richard and Anne had met before, sharing a table at George Neville's enthronement feast at the very least. But whether or not Richard had crossed paths with Anne in Warwick's household in his youth – whether, that is, there was any personal attraction between the couple – was probably immaterial. Much more important was what Anne could bring to the marriage. Richard's Neville lands in the north were restricted to those that Richard Neville and his brother John had inherited 'in tail male' from their father, the Earl of Salisbury. In theory, the lands that the Earl of Warwick had held 'in right of his wife' should not have been forfeited, because, though found guilty of treason, Warwick had never been attainted, and his possessions had not automatically reverted to the Crown. Since the Countess of Warwick, Anne Beauchamp, was still alive, all the estates she had inherited that Warwick had enjoyed as her husband should have returned to her. In fact, as a grant of March 1472 makes clear, Edward and Richard's brother George, Duke of Clarence, by virtue of his marriage to Warwick's elder daughter Isabel, had taken possession of these lands. If the Countess of Warwick had apparently forfeited her estates, then they should have been equally shared between her two daughters, Isabel and Anne. The possibility of a half share of these estates was what made Anne an attractive prospect as a wife for the Duke of Gloucester. The desire not to share them was what made Clarence oppose the match. And Anne, aged just fifteen, was now Clarence's ward. Nominally, Richard had to secure his brother's agreement to the union.

Clarence had been more than fairly treated by Edward, considering his repeated disloyalty. Not only had he been granted his wife's inheritance prematurely (and disproportionately), he was also confirmed as Lieutenant of Ireland and holder of Tutbury Castle in Staffordshire. But Richard's proposed marriage seems to have been intolerable to him. He 'therefore had the girl hidden away so that his brother would not know where she was, since he feared a division on the inheritance'. It seems a rather blunt tactic, and it didn't work: 'The Duke of Gloucester, however, was so much the more astute, that having discovered the girl dressed as a kitchen-maid in London, he had her moved into sanctuary in St Martin's.'[12]

If the story isn't an embellishment – and the source is a usually reliable one – we might spare a thought for Richard's future wife. One does not have to subscribe to Shakespeare's contrivance of a widow wooed by her beloved husband's killer to see that Anne Neville's short life cannot have been easy, for all the apparent good fortune of her high birth. Used in the political manoeuvrings of her incorrigibly ambitious father, she had had the prospect of becoming queen consort replaced by that of being an orphan-widow, before the scarcely more dignified fate of becoming the prize in a brothers' game of *cherchez la femme*. Historical novelists have tended to romanticize Richard's rescue of his childhood sweetheart in her maid's disguise.[13] It seems more likely that if the subterfuge really did take place, the discovery of Anne was more a case of retrieving a concealed asset than a lost love. What Anne made of it, no contemporary (and few historians) have bothered to wonder. Clarence would later claim that Richard 'by force had taken to wife the daughter of the earl of Warwick',[14] though this was most likely just one more way of trying to frustrate the marriage, which would have been unlawful if forced. Probably, and as with so many medieval aristocratic marriages, this one was arranged in the ample middle ground between love match and forced union.

Clarence was not the only obstacle to the wedding, though Edward, at least, seems not to have placed any himself. When, eventually, the king brought his two brothers together at Sheen Palace to discuss the marriage, he appears to have taken Richard's side. Sir John Paston reported to his brother on 17 February 1472 that 'the kynge entretyth my Lorde off Clarence for my lorde of Glowcester'.[15] As with Anne's previous marriage, however, there were issues of consanguinity and of affinity. Richard and Anne were both first and second cousins once removed (Anne's grandfather was the brother of Richard's mother Cecily Neville, and her great-great grandfather Edmund of Langley was Richard's great-grandfather). Thus the problem of consanguinity, in the second and third, and third and fourth degrees. Anne's previous marriage to Richard's second cousin Edward (not for nothing has the Wars of the Roses been nicknamed the cousins' war) provided the obstacle of affinity. On such points did canon law turn, and papal dispensation was definitely required to make the marriage legitimate. Recently, the further relation created by Anne's being Richard's sister-in-law (her sister Isabel being married to his brother George) has been put forward as yet another obstacle. According to this interpretation, brother- and sister-in-law could no more marry than could blood brother and sister, and such a connection could not have been dispensed with.

If such an objection did exist, it seems strange that Richard's fiercest contemporary critics, from Clarence down to Henry Tudor, never made it. But the reason for this is that affinity does not arise between the blood relatives of a man who has married and those of his wife. That is, while Clarence could not have married Anne, nor Richard Isabel, if the previous marriage had ended, without dispensation (precisely the 'Great Matter' on which Henry VIII's first marriage to his brother's widow Katherine of Aragon turned), no such obstacle existed between Richard and Anne. On this subject, the Church's teaching had not changed since Gregory the Great wrote to St Augustine after the conversion of the English. In reply to Augustine's question, 'Is it permissible for two brothers to marry two sisters, provided that there be no blood ties between the families?', the pope was unequivocal: 'This is quite permissible. There is nothing in Holy Scripture that seems to forbid it.'[16] If such an affinity had been created, it would have also stood in the way of Anne's first marriage to a cousin of Clarence, her brother-in-law. But in the papal dispensation granted to Anne and Edward in August 1470, there was no mention of such an affinity (the word is actually crossed out); merely of consanguinity in the fourth degree. Richard as 'serial incestor'[17] turns out to be an ingenious modern version of the bottled spider, the duke whose every move conceals a dastardly motive, with as much basis in reality.

Richard and Anne did seek dispensation for the affinity created by her first marriage, the record of which survives in the archive of the Papal Penitentiary, dated 22 April 1472. Why this dispensation did not also refer to the couple's consanguinity is a moot point. Such dispensations were granted, as they had been in the case of Clarence and Isabel (and would be in the case of Henry Tudor and Elizabeth of York). So the idea that Richard and Anne failed to apply for it for fear of being refused is unpersuasive. More convincing is the argument that a dispensation was granted but has been lost. The reason that it wasn't part of the surviving application from 1472, on this argument, is that it could have already been granted as early as 1467, when the Earl of Warwick first contemplated the marriage of his two daughters to the two younger sons of the Duke of York. In the event, only one of these went ahead. But Clarence's dispensation, granted in March 1468, does not survive in the Vatican archives. It is known only from the record of Clarence's own copy (lost in the seventeenth century) and a reference to it by the pope, Paul II, in 1471. Might it be that Richard's dispensation, on which he relied for his marriage when it eventually took place, was lost from the archive just as Clarence's original had been? Like so much with Richard, we can't be sure. And like so much with Richard, very strong arguments are made on the slenderest of evidence, or even in its absence.

Nonetheless, it is more convincing that Richard would not have failed to address the issue of consanguinity if he applied for a dispensation from affinity, than that he cavalierly ignored such impediments to a marriage which Clarence, for one, would have been very happy to see fail. Rarely in Richard's career did he trust to luck when it came to securing his rights to property; and that, of course, is what marriage to Anne implied.[18] It is also worth noting that it would have been unconventional for the consanguinity not to have been mentioned at the time of the wedding ceremony. When Richard attended the wedding of his nephew Richard, Duke of York, a public show was made of the obstacles to the marriage (to Anne Mowbray, the six-year-old heir to the estates of the Duchy of Norfolk), and an 'ample bull of authority' was produced.[19] Could Richard have avoided such a ritual, simply by ignoring the matter? It seems very unlikely.

It was worth picking one's way through this canonical minefield to reach the prize on the other side. Clarence himself was reported as making that clear at the meeting at Sheen, when he declared that Richard 'may weell have my Ladye hys suster in lawe, but they schall parte no lyvlelod [livelihood]'.[20] As that was not an option Richard was prepared to contemplate, the issue festered, and seemed likely to descend into violence, even after the marriage itself had gone ahead. By November of 1473, Sir John Paston was writing nervously to his brother: 'the worlde semyth qweysye heer, fore the most part that be abowt the Kyng haue sende hyddr for ther harneys; and it [is] seyd for serteyn, that the Duke of Claraunce makyth hym bygge in that he kan, schewyng as he wolde but dele with the Duke of Glowcester. But the Kyng ententyth . . . to be as bygge as they bothe, and to be a styffelere atweyen them.'[21] In the event, the royal will prevailed. As another report put it, 'King Edward, their loving brother, intervened and the whole dispute was settled: the duke of Gloucester, once married to the aforesaid Anne, was to have such lands as were agreed upon between them, through arbitrators.'[22] Ultimately, that arbitration was enshrined in an Act of Parliament, in May 1474, which also answered an inconvenient issue raised by the same chronicler: what of 'the countess [of Warwick, Anne's mother], the true lady and heiress of Warwick to whom, during her lifetime, the noble inheritance of Warwick and Despenser belonged'? The Act dealt with that in uncompromising fashion. The countess was passed over, 'as if [she] were naturally dead', so that Clarence and Gloucester, 'in right of their wives', could proceed to the carve-up of 'all the honours, lordships, castles . . . which did or do belong to the said Anne Countess of Warwick'.[23] The lady in question, very much alive, was by this time a guest of her daughter and son-in-law at Middleham Castle. In June 1473 she had been escorted north from her sanctuary at Beaulieu Abbey, where she had remained since the Battle of Tewkesbury, by Richard's servant Sir James Tyrell.

If the countess was a pawn in this game, so too, to some extent, was her daughter. The same Act that declared the countess legally dead provided for the eventuality that Richard and Anne's marriage might, after all, be annulled. In that case, Richard would still hold on to his share of the Warwick lands. This might have been, as has often been argued, because the full papal dispensation had not been obtained; or it might have been to forestall any final play for the whole inheritance by Clarence, who as we have seen made use of the allegation that the marriage was forced. If Richard retained Anne's portion whether he was married to her or not, Clarence's motive for interfering was removed. Whatever lay behind the clause, it was another illustration of Richard's attention to detail and his lack of squeamishness in achieving his ends. If the law stood in the way of Richard securing his 'rights', the law could be changed in Parliament.

The final episode in this part of Richard's career expanded his interests still further. Another Act of Parliament, in February 1475, gave him the remaining Neville lands in the north, which had belonged to Warwick's brother John, Marquess Montagu, as long as a male heir of Montagu lived. Clarence at the same time received Montagu's southern holdings. Later, in 1478, the legitimate heir to these estates, Montagu's son George Neville, who had been made Duke of Bedford when his father was removed from the earldom of Northumberland, was demoted from his title (and all other titles) on the grounds that he did not have enough estates to support 'the same dignity'. Of course, that was because his estates had been given to Clarence and Gloucester. This move made it even less likely that he would ever get them back, removing him from the forum, the House of Lords, where he was most likely to have his case heard. As Clarence was dead by this time, and his heirs prevented from inheriting his estates, the only man who stood to benefit from the demotion of George Neville was Richard. It is very likely that he was behind this cynical gambit.

The wedding that had given rise to all these disputes took place sometime between April and November 1472. No record of the ceremony, or where it happened, remains (a later reference to Westminster as the place cannot be confirmed, and gives an inaccurate date),[24] and it can only be dated even with this degree of accuracy from the two pieces of evidence that Richard and Anne were not married when Clarence disputed the matter in front of the king at Sheen in February 1472, and that Richard's future ally in the north, Ralph Neville, petitioned the parliament that sat between October and November that year about restoring his inheritance 'Provided . . . that this acte extend not nor be prejudiciall ne hurt to the right noble prynces the kynges brethren . . . Richard duke of Gloucestr, and Anne duches of Gloucestr his wyfe'.[25] As the marriage also could not have taken place during Lent, the dates are narrowed further: it must have gone ahead after Easter (29 March), and probably after the papal dispensation of 22 April.

It is difficult to say with any confidence whether there was ever much more to the resulting marriage than Richard's desire to expand his power base – and, if we are prepared to grant Anne any agency in the matter, her desire to attach herself to a man at the centre of power, who could provide her with a measure of security as well as the noble status that she had been brought up to expect. The union produced one son, Edward of Middleham, born there around 1476. For other evidence of the private nature of their marriage we have very little to go on. A manuscript in the British Library of the *Booke of Gostley Grace of Mechtild of Hackeborn*, a devotional treatise detailing the visions of a thirteenth-century German noblewoman, provides a small illustration of marital sharing. It is signed by 'Anne warrewyk' and below that by 'R Gloucestr', on the top of the front flyleaf. Richard has also signed the book at the back. How it came into the couple's possession, whether it belonged to one or other of them first or was presented to them together (less likely, as the manuscript itself is unilluminated, not the sort of copy that would usually be offered to people of the Gloucesters' standing) is unknown. It is also possible that the Anne who signed the book was not Richard's wife but his mother-in-law, Anne Beauchamp, dowager Countess of Warwick and widow of the 'Kingmaker'. But that seems less likely, given that the book is, like all Richard's volumes known to survive, a fairly 'ordinary' copy, not a richly illuminated luxury item. The contents of the book, if they were read by the couple, certainly chime with some of the more pious deeds of both Richard and his wife. Richard was the founder of ten colleges, or chantries, and was responsible as well when king for the re-foundation of Queens' College, Cambridge. (He had also established places when duke, in 1477, for four priests at the college to pray for his own family and his followers who had died by his side at Barnet and Tewkesbury.) His grants to the latter were partially conditional on the Fellows' acceptance of 'our aforesaid consort' as college patron.

Queens' College took its plural name from the fact that Elizabeth Woodville, Edward's queen, had taken up its patronage after the original foundation by Henry VI's queen, Margaret of Anjou. In that sense, Anne was merely adhering to established tradition. But, even allowing for the pious conventions of the age, such acts may point to a shared devotion to the Church. Neither a happy marriage nor a strongly held faith should be thought of as incompatible with Richard's already ruthless pursuit of his own interests in daily life. It seems likely that Richard *was* more than conventionally pious, though as always, we are forced to make deductions from pretty thin evidence. It is also worth noting from what stage of his life some of this evidence comes. Richard's well-known *Book of Hours*, for example (now in Lambeth Palace Library), and the 'personal' prayer it contains, date to the time after he assumed the throne (his birth date is marked as that of 'Ricardus Rex'), whereas several of his foundations pre-date the usurpation, including those at Middlcham and Barnard Castle (1478). It is conventional to think of Henry VI's record as a founder as his one positive and lasting contribution to history. The general public may have a far better notion of who Richard III was when compared to Henry VI, but his name is associated with no British institution as solidly established as Eton College or King's College, Cambridge. Not the least of the differences to the course of history that a victory for Richard at Bosworth would have made would have been the establishment of a mega-chantry at York, with provisions for 100 priests. This would have outstripped anything that had gone before in terms of conspicuous piety. Richard's reputation as a founder, like the rest of his legacy, was abruptly severed in August 1485.

A Bridge on the River Somme

The Parliament at which Gloucester and Clarence's differences were finally settled had a more important task as far as Edward was concerned. For almost two years, the king had been preparing an expedition to France, against his 'auncien and mortall ennemyes'.[26] Parliament had been asked to grant funds for the venture, including an unusual income tax, in sessions from 1472. Launching such an expedition was the most costly thing a medieval king could do – war is never cheap – and Edward meant to spare no expense. The wages for the 13,000 archers promised in the first session of Parliament in 1472 has been calculated as amounting to £118,625 for a year.[27] In today's terms, that is around £60 million. Putting his 'great enterprise' into action was delayed in part because Edward was trying to negotiate an alliance both with Duke Francis of Brittany and with his old host Charles the Bold, Duke of Burgundy. According to the Crowland chronicler, Burgundian support was important enough to be the subject of speeches in Parliament. But equally important were the real difficulties in financing such an ambitious venture. If Edward was to raise enough money, he first had to persuade the House of Commons that the expedition would go ahead. While the involvement of Burgundy and Brittany was clearly an indication that this was a serious project, not a royal whim, it also added more variables to an already complex plan. The Commons made clear that 'if the aforesaid army does not assemble', the 'aforesaid sums' should be returned. They had been stung before, when earlier planned expeditions had not materialized. In the event, the collection was not sufficient to provide for the expedition and Edward moved instead to a concerted round of arm-twisting of his wealthier subjects, raising money from so-called benevolences. This was a hands-on affair. One 'rich widow' in Suffolk received a royal kiss and doubled her contribution to £20.[28] It was a typically Edwardian way of getting the job done, but by June 1475 the king at last had an army to bring to France, and a formal alliance with the Duke of Burgundy to support him (Brittany had long since fallen away).

Richard was one of five dukes who took part in the campaign. With a force of 20,000 men, it was reckoned to be the largest army that any English king had ever brought to France. Richard's contribution, under his banner of the White Boar, was ten knights, 100 lances and 1,000 archers, the same as his brother Clarence. All this was enough to strike fear into any adversary. The Milanese ambassador to the French court, Cristoforo Bollato, reported that Louis XI was 'more discomposed that words can describe, and has almost lost his wits'.[29] Richard could have been forgiven for believing that, as he landed with this great host at Calais, he was about to take part in a glorious new chapter in the Hundred Years War, which had closed so ignominiously during Henry VI's reign.

Any such ambition, however, was about to be disappointed. Although the English army began marching towards the symbolic target of Rheims, where in his more grandiose fantasies Edward planned to be crowned King of France, they had already discovered that the promised Burgundian assistance would not be forthcoming – at least not in anything like the quantity necessary to mount a serious assault on a well-defended opponent. Charles the Bold had exhausted his resources on a fruitless siege of the town of Neuss, which he had only abandoned when Louis attacked his territory. Now he was prepared to offer Edward no more than token help. Worse, he was wary enough of English soldiery to forbid Edward's army entry to Burgundian towns as they made their way through his lands before crossing into France at St Quentin. Forced to retire from the walls of St Quentin when the town unexpectedly put up resistance, Edward and the leaders of his army seem to have realized that a glorious progress through France, sweeping Louis XI's defences aside in alliance with the Duke of Burgundy, was now a very long way off. For his part, Charles now abandoned his English allies and returned to his troops. As if to emphasize the contrast with the storied past, the army had spent two days at Agincourt, where Richard and his brothers' great-uncle, Edward, Duke of York, had been killed fighting for Henry V. It was the closest Richard – or either of his brothers – ever came to the triumphs of sixty years earlier.

Military victory may have been out of the question, but there was still the prospect of diplomatic gains. Louis did not want Edward's army, 'the most numerous, the best disciplined, the best mounted, and the best armed, that ever any king of that nation'[30] had brought to France, to menace his kingdom any longer than necessary. Louis's ambassador Philippe de Commines recalled that Edward had already laid the diplomatic groundwork should his military offensive fail, probably in anticipation of the collapse of the Burgundian alliance. Carefully, and with some subterfuge, the two kings exchanged commitments to a peaceful solution, through intermediaries.

Richard was among the witnesses to the formal instructions to Edward's negotiators, John, Lord Howard, Thomas St Leger and John Morton, the

Master of the Rolls. These set out the English demands, for an immediate payment of 75,000 crowns (£15,000), to be followed by an annual payment, in two instalments, of 50,000 crowns (£10,000). There was also to be a marriage alliance, between the Dauphin and Edward's first or second daughter, with an annual endowment of £60,000. On these conditions, Edward was prepared to withdraw.

Commines describes the English delegates' opening negotiations with rather more vaunted demands ('according to their custom, the crown of France, and by degrees they fell to Normandy and Guienne [Gascony]'). Whether he gives a true picture of the discussion or was merely trying to save face for his master (and his profession), he does report the results which, remarkably, happened to match exactly what the English had set out in their list of demands, including the immediate pay-off, the annual pension for Edward, and the marriage alliance. This was undoubtedly a success for Edward, while his men were bought off with a show of French hospitality. The town of Amiens was thrown open to the English troops, with wine and 'a variety of good dishes of all sorts of food most proper to relish their wine' provided free. For up to four days, as many as 9,000 Englishmen made the most of the entertainment, and 'not a drop of water was drunk'. Eventually, Edward himself cleared his men out of the town, 'much ashamed' of his subjects' behaviour.

Eventually, the two kings formalized their agreement at an elaborate ceremony conducted on a bridge at Picquigny, on the Somme. On 29 August 1475, Louis and Edward agreed what became known as the Treaty of Picquigny. Security was tight, and the two kings communicated only through a screen on the specially constructed bridge. Commines, who had the task of choosing the meeting-point and overseeing the construction of the bridge, explained that the precautions were ordered by Louis, unnerved by the precedent of the murder of John, Duke of Burgundy, by the rival Armagnac faction, on the bridge at Montereau in 1419 at just such a summit.

The whole English army was arrayed one side of the river, and Edward was attended on the bridge by Clarence, Northumberland, Hastings 'and other peers of the realm'. The Duke of Buckingham had already returned home (it is unclear why), but there was one very conspicuous absence from the English royal party among those who remained in France: Richard, Duke of

Gloucester. Commines explains that 'he and some other persons of quality were not present at this interview, as being averse to the treaty'. Richard had attended numerous great ceremonies from childhood onwards, and knew the importance of these public theatricals. He had taken a leading role in one himself during the public reconciliation with Clarence. Considering that he had witnessed the document drawing up English demands, all of which had been met, it is unlikely that he thought Edward had got a bad deal from which he wished to dissociate himself. Staying away from Picquigny was a calculated gesture, but what it was calculated to achieve is hard to say. The implication is that the duke, who inspected the French troops as a guest of the enemy while the meeting was taking place, preferred action to diplomacy. But Richard was not so horrified by this inglorious outbreak of peace that he refused to accept his own offering from Louis. At Amiens, Commines records, after the treaty was agreed, Richard was 'splendidly entertained' by the French king, and accepted his gifts of plate and horses. Nonetheless, as with the episode of Hornby Castle, when Richard appears to have defied his brother, his public spurning of the peace at Picquigny may have sprung from principle.[31]

Richard certainly seems to have had a greater attachment to chivalry than his eldest brother, who in spite of (or perhaps because of) his actual successes on the battlefield, was happy to avoid battle if that seemed the better option. Richard had missed his chance to emulate Ipomedon, the knightly superhero of one of his books, whose exploits had so impressed the duke ('Tant le desieree'). Nor did he get an opportunity to put into practice the sort of generalship advocated by Vegetius, the Roman author of a book of military theory that Richard would later give to his son. The horses and silver plate could not make up for the fact that his experience of the greatest military rivalry of the age was deeply disappointing. Richard was not alone in this. It is possible that Buckingham's abrupt departure was for a similar reason.

There were rumours that the outcome might not be accepted by the wider public at home either, though there seem only to have been minor outbreaks of dissent. In the army itself there was some dissatisfaction. One member of the expeditionary force, Thomas Stonor, writing to his brother from France in July, had 'suppose[d] the kyng wyll go the next way to Pares', and was preparing to meet the French in battle.[32] Two months of kicking his heels was clearly not what this member of the gentry expected. Louis de Breteilles, a Gascon in the service of Anthony, Earl Rivers, the queen's brother, complained that Edward had been cheated by the French, and that 'the ignominy of his returning so soon, after such vast preparations, would be a greater disgrace and stain to his arms than all the honour he had gained in the nine former victories'. Against suggestions that the rank and file more widely might resent the peace, however, we could set the story repeated by Commines that it was widely believed in the English camp that a white pigeon which had settled on the king's tent as he spoke to Louis on the bridge was a manifestation of the Holy Ghost.[33] Edward still had the power, so dramatically witnessed at Mortimer's Cross, to inspire tales of divine intervention. And when the king and his untested army returned to England shortly after Edward had received his pay-off, they were warmly welcomed by the city governors at Blackheath in September. Doubtless they were enthused by the renewed prospects of trade offered as a result of what the English negotiators called the 'intercourse of Merchaundises for their Cuntries and Subjects'. While dissenting voices existed in addition to Richard's silent protest, particularly among professional soldiers who had missed out on the plunder they expected from military success, the Picquigny episode was by no means a humiliation for a king who had nothing to prove on the battlefield.

Richard returned to England with the unblooded, bleary-eyed army and made his way to his northern estates. It was about this time, though no one knows exactly when, that his first and as it turned out only legitimate child, Edward, was born at Middleham. Richard had two illegitimate children, whose birth dates are also unknown: Katherine Plantagenet and John of Gloucester, both of whom are more likely to have been born before his marriage than after, though that cannot be confirmed. He made provision for both when he was king. Arrangements for Edward of Middleham, as he was known, would be far more comprehensive, though initially, like his father as a child, he figures very little in the historical record. Edward was placed in the care of a nurse, Isabel Burgh, after which time he is not heard of again until he was made Earl of Salisbury, in 1478.

If there was a new arrival in Richard's household around this time, it did not stop the business of good lordship being carried on as usual. In January 1476 Richard made an indenture with Elizabeth, Lady Scrope of Masham, who had recently been widowed, and wanted her son, the sixteen-year-old Thomas, the new Lord Scrope, to come under the duke's protection. The Scropes were an ancient northern family, with deep roots in Yorkshire and Northumberland. Although they had begun the 1450s as loyal Lancastrians, their allegiance had gone to the Yorkists once Henry VI's fortunes had become unrevivable. Under Richard's 'Rule and guydyng', Thomas became an extremely loyal follower, although, unusually, he does not seem to have profited materially from the connection. His estates, at least, were protected by the region's most powerful lord. His mother made a commitment to pay Richard an annual fee of 200 marks, in an agreement made six months after the indenture, to make sure of that.[34]

Family Business

Around the time of Thomas Scrope's birth, his father (also Thomas) had, as a loyal servant of the Crown in March 1460, been placed on a commission to 'make inquisition . . . touching the goods and chattels . . . which Richard, duke of York, Richard, earl of Salisbury, and other rebels had . . . forfeit by their rebellion'. This was after York's flight (and abandonment of his wife and younger children) at Ludford Bridge in October 1459. It was to his father's memory, and more specifically his remains, that the Duke of Gloucester and his brothers turned their attention in the year after the French expedition. After his death at Wakefield in 1460, and his posthumous humiliation at Micklegate Bar, Richard of York's body, and that of his son Edmund, Earl of Rutland, had been buried at Pontefract. It was not until Edward's accession in 1461 that the heads had even been reunited with the corpses. Now Edward proposed to honour his father and brother Edmund properly by transferring their remains to the family church (and Richard's birthplace) at Fotheringhay, the Church of the College of the Annunciation and All Saints, where Richard of York's uncle Edward, the duke who had died at Agincourt in 1415, was buried. (York's father, who had died earlier that same year in less propitious circumstances – executed for treason – was buried in Southampton, so the family's mausoleum remained untainted.)

Reburials of great men were not uncommon in the fifteenth century, as posthumous reputations changed or political capital stood to be made.

One of the best attested was that of Richard II, whose body Henry V had disinterred from Langley Abbey and transferred to Westminster Abbey. Thus a Lancastrian king reconnected his claim to the man his father had deposed, by honouring him in death as he had been insulted in life. In the case of Richard of York, the clear aim was retrospectively to make good the father's claim to the throne, and Richard of Gloucester was at the heart of the obsequies. The timing is worth pausing over. Edward had consciously waited until after his French campaign to perform this ritual. His father's own record in France as virtually the last success story for an English commander in the Hundred Years War had been a large part of York's self-image and his claim to a say in national affairs. Perhaps Edward had hoped to rebury his father after he had matched or outstripped his achievements overseas. That was now impossible, but the performance of an act of filial piety on such a grand scale, with all the attendant heraldic symbolism, might have seemed all the more desirable when Edward's chivalric reputation had received a blow from the French venture. On a more practical note, Louis XI's money would have come in useful for an expensive exercise that Edward might otherwise have had difficulty in paying for. That was the view of the Crowland chronicler: 'while the king had . . . been intent upon accumulating these great riches, he spent a great part of them in the ceremonies of the reinterment of his father, Richard'.[35] There is also the important detail that Fotheringhay church was only reglazed around this time so it might not have been deemed ready before. That too, of course, would have cost money, perhaps provided by Edward himself.

When the reburial rituals began with the Duke of York's exhumation, Richard was the chief mourner, mentioned first in the heraldic account of the ceremony preserved in the British Library, among the 'temporal lords' who sat with the body in the elaborately constructed hearse – not a vehicle as today, but a sort of temporary dwelling for the body complete with roof and a special space for the most important mourners.[36] It has been argued that it was Richard himself who was the moving force behind the decision to rebury his father with such honour. The speculation is that Richard's central role was an indication of his particular connection to his father, as guardian of the true bloodline of York, a bloodline ruptured by the supposed eldest son, who Richard believed to be (and may actually have been) illegitimate.[37] This is an ingenious way of reading the events of 1483 back into Richard's earlier life, but it depends on several leaps: not only taking as read Richard's state of mind when he seized the throne, even though, if he ever made the accusation that Edward IV, as against his offspring, was illegitimate, he quickly dropped it; but also discounting the part the king played in ordering and paying for his own father's (and brother Edmund's) reburial, for which he had good enough reasons of his own.

The day after the bodies were exhumed on 21 July 1476, they began their journey, via Doncaster, Blyth, Tuxford-in-the-Clay, Grantham and Stamford, before arriving, on 29 July, at Fotheringhay. The horses that accompanied the coffins were trapped to the ground in black and bore the arms of England and France. The account makes clear that these were the 'whole' arms, meaning that they were displayed as only royalty was permitted to display them. In death, Richard of York at last took his place as a king. At Fotheringhay, the bodies were received by the king and queen, along with Clarence and other senior nobles, as well as ten bishops. Edward was in tears as he kissed his father's body. The remains were placed beneath yet more specially constructed hearses. Lord Ferrers, the son of one of Richard of York's retainers who had been made tutor to the Prince of Wales and sat on his council, was mounted on a magnificently decked-out warhorse, 'an axe held in his hand point downwards'. The king and queen made offerings of cloth of gold, followed by the royal dukes and the rest of the high nobility. A sermon was preached by the Bishop of Lincoln, Thomas Rotherham, and a funeral Mass celebrated.

After the funeral, a great feast was held for as many as 2,000 people, making the statement that this was not an event confined to the royal family or the ranks of the nobility and the prelates. It was a public ceremony to recognize the Yorks' position at the head of the realm. The permanent tombs that replaced the hearses have not survived, and, in fact, Richard of York and Edmund were to be disturbed one more time, when during the reign of Elizabeth I their bodies were uncovered once again in preparation for a replacement of their now dilapidated tombs. That time, they were moved only from a private chapel to the nave of the church. The classical monuments that survive today date not to Edward's filial ritual but to Elizabeth's ancestor veneration in the 1570s, when she preserved the Yorkist connection that her grandfather's marriage to Edward IV's daughter had first established.[38]

For Richard of Gloucester, the prime role he was assigned in the funeral procession made his place of honour in the Yorkist hierarchy clear. Whether that placement meant that he was higher at this time in Edward's estimation than his other brother is impossible to say with conviction. True, Gloucester had always been loyal, in contrast to Clarence, but Clarence's perfidy had been forgiven, and he had received the equal of his brother's grants after Edward's return. Richard was probably chosen to be his family's representative during the funeral procession simply because the route went through Duchy of Lancaster land such as Pontefract and Tickhill, of which Richard was steward, and it would therefore have been pointed to choose Clarence to preside over such a journey. Richard was constable of Pontefract Castle, for example, where the procession began. There is no suggestion that the selection of Gloucester was any comment on the position of Clarence. Clarence after all had been happy to stand with his elder brother on the bridge at Picquigny, when Gloucester stayed away: both brothers could embarrass their king.

More often, however, it had been Clarence who was the source of embarrassment, to the point of exasperation, and six months after the solemn celebrations at Fotheringhay, the 'threefold cord' of the York brothers began to unravel for good. In December 1476, Clarence's wife Isabel died not long after giving birth to a son, Richard, who survived her by only a few days. Shortly after this double blow, which Clarence would soon allege was no accident, news came of another death. The Duke of Burgundy, Charles the Bold, campaigning again against the Swiss, had been killed at Nancy in January 1477. His heir was the unmarried daughter of his first marriage, Mary, whose future husband would become the next duke, with land and power to match a king's. No wonder, then, that when Clarence's sister, Charles's widow Margaret, now dowager Duchess of Burgundy, pressed her younger brother to make a marriage with her step-daughter, Clarence was enthusiastic. Edward, however, was not. The Crowland chronicler makes a personal matter of the dispute, as 'such an exalted destiny for an ungrateful brother was not to the liking of the King'.[39] There were also more practical reasons for opposing the match. Edward had formed an alliance with Louis XI at Picquigny, and implicating his family directly into the affairs of Burgundy, France's most inveterate enemy, would be potentially bloody and indubitably costly.

Such a policy was considered, and could well have involved Richard's participation, if it had gone ahead. In Calais, William, Lord Hastings, arrived in late February 1477 with reinforcements. In London a great council met to discuss Margaret of Burgundy's appeal for help. In the end Edward decided not to take the risk. His decision may have been influenced by a disinclination to waste blood and treasure on a fickle brother, but it was badly received by at least one other sibling, Margaret, who wrote after a French attack on a Burgundian town that she had been abandoned, 'the poorest of widows'. The failure to act may have disappointed another sibling, too. Richard had missed out on military adventure at Picquigny, and would likely have been an enthusiastic commander in any new war party. Writing to his brother John on 14 February 1477, Sir John Paston speculated that 'bothe the Dukys of Clarance and Glowcestre' would be sent across the Channel 'in all hast'.[40]

If both royal dukes were let down by their older brother's reluctance to go to war, for Richard any blow seems to have been easier to accept than for Clarence, for whom it clearly meant rather more: the denial of a chance of a spectacular elevation to rival Edward's own. Old wounds between the king and Clarence may already have been reopened by Edward's decision to take back the lordship of Tutbury after a parliamentary act of resumption. The Staffordshire estate had been Clarence's principal residence, and although he was able to relocate to Warwick Castle, hardly a bad address, it is likely that a man as jealous of his rights and privileges as Clarence had proved to be did not take it lightly. Two incidents into which the duke interposed himself escalated the dispute into something far more serious.

The first saw Clarence take justice somewhat into his own hands. Almost four months after his wife's death, in April 1477 he had two of his men, with an armed party, arrest the former attendant of his wife, Ankarette Twynho, in her house in Somerset. They took her to Warwick Castle, around ninety miles away, before putting her on trial, accused of poisoning Isabel with ale spiked with venom. As the crime was supposed to have been committed in October, and the duchess died towards the end of December, the idea that Ankarette had anything to do with it was preposterous. Only by terrorizing the jury was Clarence able to secure a guilty verdict, and a death sentence. Ankarette was hanged the same day. Clarence also took revenge for the death of his newborn son, for which a Warwick man, another of Clarence's servants, John Thursby, was blamed. He was hanged, too. A third accusation was made against Roger Tocotes, who managed to evade the duke's men.

Clarence's behaviour was cruel and bizarre, characterized by one historian as the product of 'a seriously disturbed mind'.[41] The duke seems to have been trying in a peculiarly vindictive way to regain control of his world after the double loss of his wife and son, and the rebuff over Burgundy. But taking justice into their own hands was not unheard of for some of Edward's most powerful subjects, so it is quite possible that Clarence's latest outrage might have been forgiven, as all his others had been. It was involvement in another case, with more serious public implications, that eventually decided Edward to take steps against him.

On 12 May 1477 a special commission of oyer and terminer was appointed by the king. On it were his stepson Thomas Grey, Marquess of Dorset, and his brother-in-law Anthony Woodville, the second Earl Rivers, as well as three more earls and several eminent knights. The case before them was brought against three men: Thomas Burdet, a retainer of Clarence, and two Oxford men, John Stacey and Thomas Blake. The charges against them were that they had 'falsely and treacherously . . . plotted to encompass the death of the King'. The offence took two forms. The first was supernatural. Burdet had employed the services of Blake and Stacey, the latter described by the Crowland chronicler as 'called the Astronomer though he had rather been a great necromancer', to cast horoscopes for the king and Prince of Wales, 'to calculate and work on . . . the death of the same lord king and prince, to know when the same king and his son Edward shall die'.[42] 'Imagining the King's death' was treated in the same way as plotting it: it was treason, punishable by death. Burdet also made use of more straightforward means of attacking the king. He was accused of having 'composed and made various notes and writing in seditious rhymes and ballads inciting treasonable riots', and distributing them in Holborn and Westminster.

Burdet and Stacey had been previously accused of practising black magic to assist a wealthy woman to get rid of her husband, which is the story on which the Crowland chronicler concentrates when relaying the case. But it was the accusations of treason which were obviously far more serious, and which drew the case into the course of national politics. It has recently been speculated that the Crowland chronicler, who is likely to have been an insider in Edward's government, deliberately obfuscated his account to draw attention away from the matter of Burdet's attack on Edward in his publications. It is difficult to make very much of this, since no record of Burdet's verses survives. But the fact that Burdet had previously been connected to the household of Eleanor Talbot, one of two women with whom Edward IV would later be accused of having contracted a marriage before his union with Elizabeth Woodville, makes it a possibility that this story was the one Burdet was telling – and both Edward and his queen (whose relatives were among those who tried the case) would understandably wish to suppress.[43]

Two more items to add to that argument include the fact that the Bishop of Bath and Wells, Richard Stillington, who came forward after Edward's death with the story of the king's previous marriage, was arrested not long after this trial. Might Edward have thought that he was the source of Burdet's information? The other piece of the jigsaw is the Italian writer Dominic Mancini's reference, in his account written during Richard III's reign, referring to Clarence's fall, to the queen recalling 'the insults to her family and the calumnies with which she was reproached, namely that according to established usage she was not the legitimate wife of the king'. Of course that is a more general reference, which does not explicitly link back to Eleanor Talbot, let alone to Thomas Burdet. Mancini also makes it clear that Clarence was generally opposed, for social reasons, to Edward's marriage, on the grounds that Elizabeth was of 'an obscure family'.[44] But taken together with the other scraps, it offers another reason for Edward to have finally been persuaded to move against Clarence, if he was suspected of sanctioning someone in his household raising doubts over the king's marriage. More has usually been made of another accusation contained in Clarence's eventual indictment before Parliament, that the duke 'said that the king was a bastard'.[45] This was an old tale, which is still entertained in some quarters, and was supposedly part of the challenge that Warwick and Clarence made during their rebellion – though no mention was made of it in their manifesto. That said, either casting doubt on Edward's marriage, and therefore the legitimacy of his successors, or on Edward's own parentage, once again placed Clarence as the legitimate alternative. If that *was* what had happened, it certainly was treason.

Clarence might have been expected to distance himself from his retainer, especially when Burdet and Stacey were found guilty and hanged, drawn and quartered at Tyburn on 20 May 1474. They both 'declared their innocence. Stacey, indeed faintly, but Burdet with great spirit and many words, as though, like Susanna, in the end he was saying, "behold I die, though I have done none of these things".[46] Clarence took this instead as his cue to spring to Burdet's defence. The fact that doing so wouldn't help Burdet much means that Clarence's way of going about it must have been calculated to help himself. The duke came to the King's Council at Westminster, while Edward was at Windsor, the day after the executions and had William Goddard, 'the famous doctor of the order of minors [i.e. a Franciscan]', read out 'the declaration of innocence'. How the declaration had come to be written down we don't know, and the fact that it had makes it likely that this was a prepared manoeuvre, not a response to events. Clarence's 'choice of spokesman' has been called 'tactless to the point of folly',[47] as Dr Goddard was the man who had publicly preached Henry VI's claim to the throne at the Readeption in September 1470. But this, too, is unlikely to have been an accident. Could it have been instead a reasonably clear challenge to Edward's authority, and an attempt to persuade the magnates on the King's Council to transfer their allegiance to a legitimate alternative, that is, the Duke of Clarence? Once again, the Crowland chronicler does not go into the details of the declaration Dr Goddard read out, but it is possible that it contained a repetition of the allegation about the king's marriage – with the defence that Burdet had only been telling the truth.

All this is highly speculative, of course, but some speculation is needed to account for Edward's procedure against his brother at this point. Clarence had long been forgiven for actually having raised arms against the Crown. He had even been rewarded with estates and offices after Edward's return – albeit that his younger brother had been offered more authority. The case of Ankarette Twynho, however shocking it is to modern ears, would have been unlikely to get someone in Clarence's position into serious trouble. The Burdet case was different. It was not just that Clarence was making an 'accusation of injustice'[48] against Edward. Surely more important was the fact that he was publicly defending a convicted traitor, and using a Lancastrian mouthpiece to do so. Edward had shown himself to be a model of tolerance when it came to

Clarence, but siding with a traitor – particularly if that traitor was responsible for circulating such incendiary rumours – could not be ignored. Three weeks after the outburst in the council chamber, Clarence was summoned before the king at Westminster Palace. 'From his own lips', Edward denounced 'the duke's action'. Naturally, Edward would not have wanted to draw attention to the detail of Clarence's apparent backing of a traitor, so he contented himself with referring to his brother's 'great threat to the judges and jurors in the kingdom' – a transgression that could be applied to both the Twynho and the Burdet and Stacey cases. Clarence was arrested and held in the Tower of London. He 'was not found at liberty from that day until his death'.[49]

The delay in launching proceedings that would lead to Clarence's death has been the cause of further speculation. It may simply be accounted for by the lengths to which Edward appears to have gone to pack Parliament, which he had chosen as the instrument of Clarence's demise, with his supporters. Parliament was summoned in November 1477, five months after his brother's arrest: the time might also have been spent in deciding whether to take the final step against Clarence. Edward certainly had the capacity for ruthlessness that observers have more often ascribed to the Duke of Gloucester, but fraternal bonds very obviously counted for something with the king, and we can guess that he was reluctant to proceed. When he made up his mind, however, Edward was coldly calculating in his methods, and made sure to reap the maximum public benefit out of a show of strength – even if the victim was his own brother.

The parliament that met in January 1478 coincided with another very public event. Again, it is tempting to discern a deliberate point being made in the lavish public celebrations that surrounded the marriage of Edward's younger son, the four-year-old Richard, to the five-year-old Anne Mowbray, heiress to the Duchy of Norfolk. Richard of Gloucester attended the ceremony, distributing alms 'amongest the comone people', and leading the new princess, together with the Duke of Buckingham, into the wedding feast. Richard played no such public role in the fall of Clarence, but at this ceremony he would have seen the force of the demonstration that Edward was securing the future of his line with this match. If Clarence had cast doubt on the king's marriage and its issue, here was Edward's answer – which Richard was only too happy to endorse.

The proceedings of the parliamentary trial were not enrolled, but the accusation that Edward made survives. In it he charges Clarence with making 'a conspiracy against him [Edward], the Queen, their son and heir and a great part of the nobility of the land'. He specifically names Clarence's involvement in the Burdet case, accusing Clarence of supporting Burdet as a way of 'turn[ing] his subjects against him'. Finally, the old rumour that 'the King was a bastard' was dusted off.[50] The trial was conducted personally by Edward, and the duke defended himself only by offering to 'uphold his case by personal combat'.[51] The appeal to trial by battle was ignored, and Clarence was formally condemned. The Duke of Buckingham, last seen escorting a five-year-old bride to her wedding feast, was now called upon as newly created Steward of England (an office held previously by the accused) to pronounce a death sentence. There was a further delay, as Edward's nerve apparently faltered, but the Speaker of the House pressed the king, the execution was ordered, and it was carried out at the Tower on 18 February 1478. Clarence's famous end in a butt of malmsey wine (as recorded in Shakespeare) is not in the Crowland account, though the chronicler's vagueness about the method of execution – 'whatever form it took' – leaves room for speculation. The *Great Chronicle of London*, written in Henry VII's reign, is the first to report the drowning story. What lay behind it is now impossible to say. Perhaps it was meant as a form of mercy, avoiding the greater brutalities that usually attended a medieval traitor's death.

Although Richard of Gloucester was among the peers in Parliament, he took no part in the proceedings against his brother, if we follow the Crowland account. Dominic Mancini wrote at the end of 1483 that Gloucester had been 'so overcome with grief for his brother that he could not dissimulate so well, but that he was overheard to say that he would one day avenge his brother's death. Thenceforth he came very rarely to court.'[52] Actually, Richard did continue to appear at court, although campaigning in the north, and Scotland, and running his vast holdings there did keep him away. The story about revenge is also doubtful, written up after Richard's 'revenge' on his brother by usurpation had taken place. Richard had grown up with Clarence, his nearest sibling in age, who had shared the confusing and often terrifying circumstances of his childhood. But Clarence's switch to Warwick's side had created a gulf between them, especially in their relationship with their elder brother. And the evidence of the dispute over Richard's marriage and the Neville inheritance shows that the childhood playmates had long since become rivals. After Richard came to the throne, he implied in a communication with the Irish Earl of Desmond, whose father had been judicially murdered, that he had been powerless to prevent 'the semblable chaunce . . . within this Royaulme of England . . . of his Brother the duc of Clarence'.[53] It would be wrong, however, to read too much into this convenient bout of empathizing. Whatever form Gloucester's grief took, it did not stop him from capitalizing on Clarence's downfall. Richard's son Edward was given Clarence's title of Earl of Salisbury (part of the Neville inheritance). Richard was reappointed Great Chamberlain of England (an office Clarence had made him give up), and he was permitted to vary the terms under which he and Clarence had secured the rights to the Neville estates.

So Gloucester does not seem to have taken his brother's death too hard. The idea that he was, by contrast, somehow responsible for or at least implicated in Clarence's condemnation originates with Thomas More, who still only accuses Richard of 'helping forth his brother Clarence to his death' rather than plotting it, as happens in Shakespeare. Shakespeare's reference to the 'prophecy of "G"' (that someone whose name begins with G, i.e. George, would inherit the throne) is first mentioned by John Rous. It was elaborated by Polydore Vergil, who, again, does not say that Richard was responsible for pinning the prophecy to his brother – merely that as a 'G', Gloucester later fulfilled its terms. The responsibility for Clarence's death clearly lay with Edward, who brought the accusation and set out the case against him – and with Clarence himself, whose behaviour became steadily more provocative – not with Richard.

It is worth noting, as we shall see it again at another time of heightened tension, the swirl of magic, necromancy and prophecy around the episode. This was not the first time that magic had touched the royal family. Edward's mother-in-law, Jaquetta of Luxembourg, dowager Duchess of Bedford, had been accused of sorcery in 1470, and Edward had gone to some lengths to make a public refutation of the charge. In such episodes the medieval world begins to look unfathomably remote from our own, but it is precisely at such moments that observers across the centuries need to take the world they find on its own terms, in this case as displaying an indication of sincerely held beliefs. When people in the Middle Ages accused someone of witchcraft, they did not automatically fall into two categories – the credulous and the manipulative, even if both were represented at times. As the details of the Clarence case make clear, not only had his servant been found guilty of magical practices, Clarence had tried to turn the tables on Edward by saying that 'the king resorted to necromancy'. Whether the 'prophecy of "G"' was current at the time of Clarence's fall or dreamed up in hindsight, the notion that the court was susceptible to magic was not far-fetched in 1478.

Lord of the North

The years between February 1478, when Clarence met his fate, and the end of 1479, when threats from Scotland emerged to provide a real challenge to the Duke of Gloucester in his capacity as 'Lord of the North', were perhaps the least dramatic in Richard's life. It is tempting to pass over them, to hurry towards the duke's next burst of activity as he confronted the Scots. But some of what Richard was up to in these months – as far as we can reconstruct it – gives as much insight into his approach to his position, his self-image and his outlook as those much better-known moments when he was at the mercy of, or trying to control, events. This was a time when the Duke of Gloucester could act the part he was born to play, of a great lord, a loyal prince and a reliable arbiter of disputes, unencumbered by fraternal rivalries, recidivist Lancastrians, or the urgent need to carve out a role for himself. All those challenges lay in the past. The challenges of the future, and in particular his crisis of identity – if that was what 1483 amounted to – were surely inconceivable even a mere five years earlier. In these months, Richard was engaged in the sort of pursuits that would have assured him a relatively minor, but perfectly honourable, place in the nation's history.

Three days after Clarence's execution, Richard received a licence from the king to found two religious colleges, at Middleham in north Yorkshire and at Barnard Castle in County Durham. These were to be chantries staffed by a dean, priests, clerks and choristers, to 'do divyne service there daily', and to pray for the king and queen, for Richard of Gloucester and his family, and for their souls 'after our decesses'. In the statutes of Middleham College, drawn up in July 1478, Richard sets out the pious, practical approach that characterized so much of what he did in public. He describes his own good fortune, that God 'hath called me now unto, to be named, knowed, reputed and called Richard Duc of Gloucestre, and of his infynyte goodnesse not oonly to endewe me with grete possessions and of giftys of His divyne grace, bot also to preserve, kep and deliver me of many grete jeoperd'.[54] He turns to his hopes and expectations, not only for 'such other issue as shal please God to send me', but also for the financial security of the college itself, laying out plans for the eventual removal of the burden of payment for the church that rested on the parishioners of Middleham. The statutes also include fines for slander among the college's priests (2d), for pulling 'violently a knyff' (4d) and for drawing blood (a fine at the discretion of the dean and his colleagues). One wonders what it took to lose your job at a place as holy as Middleham College.

Those looking for a guilty conscience in Richard about the death of Clarence have sometimes detected it in the timing of these two foundations, licensed so soon after the execution. Although Clarence is not excluded from the general round of prayer for Gloucester's deceased relatives in the college statutes, however, he is not singled out in a way that would give any credence to the charge. If anyone had cause to feel guilty about Clarence, it was the granter of the licence, not its recipient. And in March 1478, when Richard returned to his single-minded extension of his northern possessions, moving to secure his final holdings in Yorkshire, including the castle and fee farm at Richmond, all the land in question had belonged to Clarence and passed to the king after his execution. In exchange, Richard gave up Corfe Castle in Dorset, as well as estates in Wiltshire and Gloucestershire.[55] Again, there were no signs here that Richard had not taken the fall of Clarence in his stride. His elder brother had simply become one more great noble, like the Earl of Warwick or the Earl of Oxford, from whose eclipse Richard stood to gain. The thinking behind this final acquisition is easy enough to discern. Although he never became exclusively a northern lord, retaining holdings in East Anglia, for example, Richard was determined to make his northern power base a comprehensive, concentrated whole, with as few anomalous rival holders as possible. One of the ways in which this agglomeration of land operated as a little kingdom was

Richard's use of servants from one part of it in another. Thus the Metcalfe brothers, Thomas and Miles, performed offices for the duke in Richmondshire as well as Durham, in the Duchy of Lancaster as well as the city of York.[56]

In addition to retaining men and finding them offices, the business of being a good lord involved constant travel and the readiness to wear any number of different hats. In July 1478 Richard was named with the Earl of Northumberland and others on a commission *de walliis et fossatis* (concerning walls and ditches) in Yorkshire and Lincolnshire. This was how flood defences were prepared and kept up. (That this took place in the summer could be testament to medieval foresightedness, or a reaction to a wet month.) Here is a reminder that the parcels of lands and estates that Richard and his peers were so eager to acquire were not simple assets, or sources of patronage for their adherents. They were serious responsibilities, and medieval government had no other way to protect and control the land than to turn it over to the stewardship of powerful and reliable men. Richard was placed on another such commission the following year.

More regular than overseeing infrastructure projects was Richard's role as judge and informal arbiter of disputes among his tenants or those who had done homage to him and looked to him for protection. The south porch of the parish church of St Peter, Croft on Tees in north Yorkshire, bears witness to the successful outcome of one such dispute. It was built as a joint venture by the Clervaux and Place families, who came to Richard in April 1478 to settle an argument about encroachment on each other's land and a squabble about who had the right to sit where in church. The disagreement had threatened to become violent, and there had been an armed confrontation one Sunday. Richard ruled that good fences would make better neighbours, and told the complainants to sit where they had always sat, Clervauxes to the south of the nave, Places to the north. He hoped for 'gode concord, frendly suite to be had fro hensfurth between the sayd parties'.[57] The porch, with its carvings of the coats of arms of both families (since removed to the interior of the church), appears to show that the duke's instructions were followed, and his wishes granted.

A rather more combative Duke of Gloucester is on show in a letter written in August 1480 to Sir Robert Claxton. In it the duke takes the part of 'one John Ransdon', who has not been allowed by Claxton to farm a portion of land around Durham. Richard writes that '[we] merveille gretly' that Claxton has neither allowed Ransdon to go about his business, nor bothered to appear before the duke to explain why. There is certainly evidence here of Richard's willingness to back an underdog, 'moved of pite gladly willing him to have according to his right', as he puts it. It is also a reminder of Richard's ever expanding sphere of interest, as this dispute was taking place in an area not strictly under his control. The county palatine of Durham was supposed to be the undisputed purview of the Bishop of Durham, William Dudley, while a reference to Richard's lawyers deliberating in Raby, an estate of the Earls of Westmorland, seems to indicate that here, too, Richard, rather than the lord nominally in power, had the controlling interest.[58]

As a regional dignitary, Richard was also a valued champion of tradesmen and city fathers. In that capacity he could be found securing two four-day fairs and a court of pie-powder (a tribunal to decide disputes arising from the fair) at Middleham. His dealings with the citizens of York are well attested in that city's records.[59] Sometimes this could be as enforcer of the royal will. In March 1476 Richard visited York along with Henry Percy, Earl of Northumberland, and a party numbered at 5,000, to deliver a royal proclamation enjoining the citizens to keep the peace.[60] But Richard could be the citizens' advocate, too. In July the same year he wrote to Lords Hastings and Stanley, asking for their backing for the aldermen of York, who wanted to replace Thomas Yotten, a clerk who had been embezzling city funds. At the end of the year, during which the city's troublemaking had apparently tempted the king to withdraw its privileges, the mayor and council delivered a vote of thanks to their principal protector. 'For his grete labour of now late made unto the kinge's goode grace for the conservacion of the liberites of this Citie', they promised to present Richard on his next visit with six swans and six pike.[61]

Periodically, Richard's involvement with the city of York faced him with that bane of medieval life, the fish garth or fish weir. These were devices set up by enterprising fishermen to trap large numbers of fish, and one indication of how seriously and for how long they concerned people in medieval England is that they were mentioned in Magna Carta. They had to be regulated, as they could disrupt trade and transport, or lead to disputes and shortages. The Duke of Gloucester responded to requests from the mayor and aldermen to have unlicensed examples removed. They were still a nuisance when Richard was king.[62]

The city fathers and the duke were in regular correspondence, too, though we don't always know what about from the records of York, which are apt only to include the information that, for example, letters were taken to the duke by those attending the royal council in London. Richard, for his part, might trust a messenger to deliver his words in person. In November 1478 the *York House Book* records that a 'right trusty servant' of the duke had arrived, but the records only carry his covering letter, with the request that the citizens 'yeve ferme feith and credence' to what he has to tell them, with no clue to what that was.[63] After coming to the throne, Richard would continue to favour York and other northern towns with charters and special privileges. York supported his taking of the crown, and, famously, sent a letter after Richard's death lamenting the passing of 'King Richard late mercifully reigning upon us' ('mercifully' is underlined). It is worth noting that these words form a preamble to a more neutrally worded letter sent to the Earl of Northumberland. In effect the city was looking for the protection of a new lord, once the peculiar situation of their regional protector having also been the king had come to a sudden end. No wonder they were in 'grete hevynesse' at the news from the 'feld of Redemore'.[64]

As the York citizens' letter to the duke attending the royal council in London reminds us, for all the sentimental portrayal of Richard as 'The Northerner',[65] he was always much more than a northern lord. One sign of that was in his appointments, which covered the whole realm. The duke was usually addressed, and signed himself in official correspondence, as 'great Chamberlain' (after 1478), Constable and Admiral. Chamberlain was a ceremonial and honorific role. We have seen a little of what the role of constable entailed, for example in Richard's grim task of dispatching traitors after the Battle of Tewkesbury. His role as admiral did not involve much activity on the high seas. Like the office of constable, it tended towards the judicial. So we find Richard as 'Constable and Admiral', commissioned in March 1477 to enquire into the ransacking of a German merchant ship that had been beached on the Yorkshire coast. While the captain was 'awaiting the flood' to relaunch his vessel, it was allegedly set upon by members of the Lumley family who took off its cargo of '26,000 stockfish [cod], 2,000 staple fish [herring] and 9 tuns of 'trane [oil extracted from the carcass of the right whale, used to make soap]'.[66] Embarrassingly for Richard, this fishy heist had been perpetrated by his retainers. If the allegations had any merit, then Richard the regional lord trumped Richard the national servant on this occasion, as Sir Richard Lumley continued to appear on commissions of the peace in the North and East Ridings after this event, and would attend Richard's coronation in 1483.[67] In December 1477 Richard was tasked with an even more serious case of piracy, kidnap and false imprisonment, when a London merchant, Bartholomew Couper, had been taken prisoner from his ship, *La Mary London*, on his return with 400 Irish pilgrims to Waterford from Santiago de Compostella, and held, it was alleged for three years.[68] It is not known whether the men named as the perpetrators in the commission were ever brought to justice.

'To fight against James, King of Scotland'

Such was the role of a national, rather than a purely regional great lord. It was in Richard's capacity as the holder of a regional office affecting the whole nation that the next period of intense activity occupied him, almost without a break, up to his brother Edward's death in 1483. As warden of the Western Marches towards Scotland, Richard was the obvious appointee to deal with the deterioration in Anglo-Scottish relations, and to offer a military solution should that prove necessary. For centuries, relations between England and Scotland were intertwined with continental politics. England's superior resources would have allowed it comfortably to dominate its northern neighbour if the interests of France and Burgundy had not come into play. The romantic baggage of the 'auld alliance' notwithstanding, it was mostly a French way of keeping the English in check. The spiritual bond between France and Scotland came down to mutual antipathy to England. For their part, English monarchs tended to seek peaceful terms with Scotland when their attentions were turning towards a French venture. No accident, then, that the betrothal of Edward IV's daughter Cecily to James III of Scotland's heir, James, Duke of Rothesay, came in 1474, the year before Edward embarked on the French campaign that ended with the treaty of Picquigny.

Although four years of relative peace between the two neighbours followed, the marriage never materialized, mainly because of the fall-out from another betrothal that set Scotland and England back on a more traditionally hostile footing. In 1478 a marriage was arranged between James III's younger sister Margaret and Edward IV's brother-in-law Anthony, Earl Rivers (yet another favourable Woodville match), and a date was set in October 1479 for the wedding. But the arrangement had to be broken off when it was later revealed that Margaret was pregnant, by a Scottish noble, Lord Crichton, whom she subsequently married. This was an affront to English honour, and might have been enough to turn thoughts to revenge. The brew was made more poisonous, however, by the internal politics of Scotland. In some respects they bear comparison with what had taken place not long before in England, and certainly show that the English were not unique in their capacity for internecine quarrelling in the highest reaches of society.

As with Edward, Clarence and Richard, this was a case of three brothers' bad blood, between James III and his brothers Alexander, Duke of Albany, and John, Earl of Mar. Albany had become disaffected with James following the English alliance, which restricted his room for manoeuvre against the English borderers in his role as warden of the Marches – Gloucester's opposite number. Albany was failing to curb the activities of his followers in the region, threatening the treaty. As with Clarence, there were hints of black magic, too, and a witch predicted that James would be killed by a close relative. James decided to deal with the danger by taking his brother prisoner from his castle in Dunbar, but Albany escaped, first to France, and then to England, where he made common cause with Edward IV. In 1479 James's other brother, the Earl of Mar, also fell foul of the king's suspicions, and was not as lucky as Albany. Accused of consulting 'weches and warloris' (witches and warlocks), he died, not unlike Clarence but rather more like Jean-Paul Marat, when being bled in his bath. There was no official sentence passed against Mar, but his lands were forfeit to the Crown, so his death was clearly no accident either.

It was in such circumstances, with the Scottish king seeing enemies all around him, that fifty Scottish landowners in England took the precaution of making themselves denizens, in other words residents of England, to avoid forfeiting their property south of the border. In the event, however, it was from north of the border that the break came, with an attack on Bamburgh by the Earl of Angus in the spring of 1480. English retaliation was initially carried out by sea, with a fleet led by Lord Howard that attacked the Firth of Forth the following year. The proposal for Edward to follow this up himself with a land invasion never materialized. He later referred to 'adverse turmoil' preventing him from leading an expedition. If this was not an excuse for the king's often suspected indolence, it may well have been because he was unwell. Instead, it was Richard of Gloucester who was appointed to take the initiative, following the sealing of a treaty between his brother and James's exiled brother Albany, at Fotheringhay in 1482. Although ostensibly this was an agreement to assist Albany to recover his Scottish estates, like Bolingbroke and Edward himself when they had returned from enforced exile, Albany's true intention, kept secret for the time being, was to claim the Scottish throne himself and rule as Alexander IV. In return, Alexander would do homage to Edward and return the town of Berwick, the border town that Margaret of Anjou had bartered away, to English hands.

To assist him in this task, the warden of the Western Marches towards Scotland had been given a promotion. In May 1480 Richard was made 'lieutenant-general to fight against James, King of Scotland, who has violated the treaty lately concluded with the king, and his adherents, with power to call out all the king's lieges in the marches towards Scotland and the adjacent counties'.[69] The following month Richard dispatched a letter to Louis XI of France, who had sent him a very useful gift in the circumstances, a demonstration that if England was planning war with Scotland, it would naturally be ensuring peaceful relations with France. The Duke of Gloucester thanked the French king in his own hand for 'the great bombard which you caused to be presented to me, for as I have always taken and still take great pleasure in artillery I assure you it will be a special treasure to me'. This is a rare insight into Richard's personal preferences, if the handwritten response can be taken as an indication of a more than formal expression of gratitude. Not unexpectedly, it reveals a passion for the latest military hardware.[70] It is not known whether Richard ever got a chance to use his new toy, but given the way the later campaign turned out, it is unlikely.

In June 1482, in light of the new agreement with Albany, Richard's appointment as lieutenant-general was renewed. He had already been raiding into Scotland, burning Dumfries, but joining Edward and Albany at Fotheringhay in June, he was about to take on a much larger enterprise. This, the first major command that Richard received, was for nothing less than conquest and regime change. In letters patent issued in June, Edward put his trust in his brother not only because of their blood tie, but also 'propter ejus approbatam in Artibus Bellicosis Militiam caeterasque ejus Virtutes' – 'because of his proven military skill and other virtues'.[71] It should have been a formidable, not to say an impossible task, requiring all Richard's fighting prowess, but, initially at least, James III and his nobility made it surprisingly easy. Despite extensive preparations, when it came to facing Richard's invading army, with the Duke of Albany in his ranks, James's senior subjects instead refused to fight. This decision had very little to do with the external threat, and everything to do with internal politics. James's nobles, like those of Henry VI, realized that their king favoured a small clique and excluded much of the traditional power in the land. 'Alexander IV' might provide a better alternative, and even if James remained, he would be forced to acknowledge that he depended on a wider circle for his country's security and prosperity. The nobles took the king prisoner, hanged some of his followers and confined him to Edinburgh Castle. The way lay open to Richard and Albany not only to retake Berwick but to march unopposed as far as Edinburgh. In a letter to Pope Sixtus IV sent after the campaign in August 1482, Edward referred warmly to his 'very dear brother Richard Duke of Gloucester', and patted him on the back for leaving Scotland's capital in one piece.[72] More material rewards were to follow, and in Parliament in January 1483, Richard was handed the wardenship as a hereditary title, along with carte blanche to take as much border land into his own hands as he could acquire, over which he would then have palatine (i.e. quasi-regal) rights.

What the real achievements of Richard's Scottish campaign were have long been a matter of debate. Berwick was returned to English rule, after its castle surrendered following a short siege, but the duke retreated from Edinburgh and did not force particularly harsh terms on the humiliated James III. In part, he could blame that on the return of James's brother Albany, Clarence's equal in fickleness, to James's side, on the promise of restitution of his original title and estates (perhaps, for Albany, ruling Scotland looked too much like hard work). Richard did not have the authority to continue a campaign once the specific aim of putting Albany on the Scottish throne in James's place had been removed. But Richard didn't wait long for instructions either. Yet the Crowland chronicler may simply have been giving vent to later-confirmed anti-Richard prejudice when he complained that Berwick itself was a 'trifling gain, or perhaps more accurately, loss (for the maintenance of Berwick costs 100,000 marks a year) [which] diminished the substance of the king and the kingdom by more than £100,000 at the time'.[73] Berwick was, after all, one of the stated objectives of the campaign, and Richard could hardly be blamed for achieving it.

In any case, what was good for Richard and what was good for Edward and England didn't always neatly coincide. The Duke of Gloucester had earned his brother's thanks and praise, as well as a licence to create a personal fiefdom out of any further gains. Replacing one Scottish king with another would have made little difference to him, but it was at least part of the original plan. Holding on to Edinburgh long enough to dictate tougher terms to James was not, and there was nothing in it for Richard. With no specific additional orders, Richard could be forgiven for fulfilling as much as possible of what he had been sent to do, and then looking to his own advantage. This was the policy of loyal self-interest that had served him so well over the past decade.

Richard did not celebrate Christmas with Edward at Westminster, where the king disported himself in a robe whose insides were 'lined with such sumptuous fur that, when turned back over the shoulders, they displayed the prince (who always stood out because of his elegant figure) like a new and incomparable spectacle set before the onlookers'.[74] It would have seemed almost unthinkable that this paragon of princely peacocking would be dead a little over four months later. If ill health had caused Edward's absence from the Scottish campaign, his busy preparations for further Scots and French interventions showed that the king did not think he was a dying man. In the New Year of 1483, as well as the awards to Richard, Parliament granted money for the 'hasty and necessarie defence of this youre reame',[75] after a rapprochement between France and Burgundy had led to the terms of the Treaty of Picquigny being violated. Edward's pension from Louis XI had gone unpaid, and the proposed marriage arrangement between his daughter Elizabeth and the Dauphin was overturned by a new arrangement for the Dauphin to marry the infant Margaret of Burgundy, whose mother had died after a fall from her horse in November 1482. This double snub seems to have energized the now normally sedentary Edward into preparing for some sort of revenge. If he had not been taken ill, there is every likelihood that hostilities with France would have been renewed.

The illness that the king contracted at the end of March 1483 has been variously diagnosed as stroke, pneumonia, appendicitis, or (a French contribution, this) a digestive complaint brought on by excessive consumption of fruit and vegetables.[76] The range of options is an indication that, actually, nobody knows what killed Edward IV shortly after a boat trip to undertake the unlikely spectator sport of watching other people fish.[77] Polydore Vergil was the most honest, writing that the king 'repente incipit ex morbo omnibus medicis incognito laborare' – suddenly began to suffer from a disease unknown to all his doctors.[78] Whatever the cause, Edward succumbed on 9 April 1483, at the age of forty. His son and heir, Edward V, was only twelve. Edward IV had one of the most dramatic reigns in English history, and for all the faults that contemporaries and later historians have found with him, he left England far richer, stronger and more united than he found it. It is one of the minor tragedies of the period that the melodrama of the two years that followed have so completely eclipsed Edward's impact on the public imagination.

The council that met in Westminster to discuss arrangements for the new king's arrival from his seat at Ludlow initially disagreed over the size of the retinue young Edward should bring, though they eventually found common ground. What was not in dispute was that 'all who were present keenly desired that this prince should succeed his father in all his glory'.[79] The king's uncle, Richard, Duke of Gloucester, was not present.

The Middleham Jewel, discovered in 1985, now in the Yorkshire Museum.

4

'To Catch the English Crown'

Middleham Castle, which Richard expanded and remodelled on a grand scale when he was Duke of Gloucester, is a roofless ruin today. But it doesn't take much imagination to picture the Great Hall intact at the centre of the keep, rising high to accommodate its three storeys, a palatial space for display and entertainment at the heart of a fortress strengthened with square towers built up at each corner. This was already a place of conspicuous power when the Earl of Warwick lived here. It has been argued that a set of lavish ritual household instructions, in which the head of the estate is raised to almost divine proportions, was created for Warwick, and applies to him living at Middleham.[1] Under Richard, it is likely that there was no reduction in pomp and ceremony surrounding the lord of Middleham.

A find by a metal detectorist in 1985 gives a glimpse of the opulence that might have been on show there. A pendant made in the mid to late fifteenth century – that is, around the time that Richard was in residence – was uncovered a few hundred yards from the castle. This exquisite gold lozenge is engraved with images of the Trinity and saints who offered special protection to women in childbirth, and words of religious and ritual healing power. A sapphire is set into the top. The back could be slid open to store precious objects inside, so the pendant acted as a kind of portable reliquary. When it was found, the Middleham Jewel contained scraps of material that are likely to have had religious significance. No one knows when it was dropped (it doesn't seem to have been buried) or to whom it belonged, though its original owner must have been a wealthy woman.[2] If it was lost about the time when it was first made, it hints at the grandeur of life around the Duke of Gloucester in the 1470s and 1480s. The jewel reminds us that we should see Richard as a mighty rather than a marginal lord at the time of his brother Edward's death in April 1483.

Richard may have lived in grand style in the north, but he has, nonetheless, often been made to cut an isolated figure there. In fact, at this crucial moment, he may have been in the peculiar position of being able to anticipate events in London, rather than trying to keep up with them at a distance, because a rumour of the king's death had actually reached York, and been believed, on 6 April, three days before Edward actually died. It seems likely that this news would have been passed on to Richard, the city's great protector. In any case, four of the central players in the drama that unfolded in the following weeks – Richard, the boy king Edward V, his maternal uncle Earl Rivers, and Richard's cousin the Duke of Buckingham – were away from the capital when the old king died. London was the seat of government, but government itself had to be run by powerful individuals in the localities. Not only Richard in the north, but the household of the young Edward in the Welsh Marches, were a reflection of that. The Prince of Wales's council were responsible for keeping the principality under control, and the education of the prince would have been envisaged as eventually consisting as much in preparing him for that task as in the more formal tutelage that he was also receiving. But now a far bigger task had been thrust upon him. A minority was not something any kingdom would pray for. Moreover, the awkward age of the new king, in a political world where sixteen-year-olds assumed most of the trappings of adulthood, would ensure that any minority government would be short-lived, with little secure long-term advantage to offer those who controlled it. Nevertheless, even though Edward IV's death was unexpected, after twelve years of peace there need not have been too much of a sense of foreboding about the succession. The great dynastic wound from which the Wars of the Roses had grown had not so much been healed as cauterized by the extinction of the House of Lancaster. There was no rush for London, as had happened in earlier, disputed successions. The royal party didn't set out from Ludlow for ten days after hearing the news of Edward IV's death, while Richard took his time, too. And the new king had two uncles to support him: his mother's brother, the sophisticated, cultured, highly experienced Earl Rivers; and his father's, the loyal and reliable Duke of Gloucester, to whom Edward IV had entrusted unprecedented power and vital military command.

How did Richard of Gloucester's fortunes stand on the death of the brother to whom he owed so much? In many ways, they could hardly have been higher. Richard was Lieutenant-General, Constable, Lord Great Chamberlain, Lord High Admiral and hereditary warden of the West March towards Scotland, to name only his most prestigious offices. He had a place at the head of the nobility, as a royal duke, and as uncle of the new king. His holdings were unmatched, too, including the Neville lands in north and west Yorkshire, the recently granted palatinate in Cumberland and the open-ended palatine grant in lands-to-be-conquered in Scotland. In Northumberland, Lancashire and Durham, Richard was a – usually, the – major landholder. And this Lord of the North was not confined to the north, with estates in Abergavenny and Glamorgan, in East Anglia and Essex, in Gloucestershire, Buckinghamshire and Lincolnshire. True, much of this vast agglomeration had initially depended on royal grants, but Richard had long since established himself on these lands, building up a formidable network of loyal servants, by judicious retaining, sensible and fair-minded arbitration, and occasional shows of strength. He was a supporter of the Church, not only in his foundations but also his grants of lands to churches and monasteries.[3] He had proved himself Edward IV's loyal servant, at a time when loyalty was anything but assured, even from those closest to the king. Richard had shown, too, that he was a reliable soldier, from his earliest exploits at Barnet and Tewkesbury to his recent campaigning in Scotland culminating in the successful recapture of Berwick-upon-Tweed. On the face of it, as things stood in April 1483, Richard might have been envisaged as the ideal figure to steer the young king through his early years, and into government, being a powerful, experienced and trustworthy figure on the model of William Marshal, the great thirteenth-century knight who had shepherded Henry III through his minority.

So where did it all go wrong? Put another way, given this position of apparently supreme strength and security, why did Richard risk everything for a tilt at the Crown? One way of answering that is to look again at Richard's position in April 1483. Take those prestigious appointments first. Richard knew, having been the beneficiary of confiscations from previous holders including his own brother, that even the highest offices of state depended on royal will. No matter if they were granted for life or even as hereditary awards: if the king, or those who had his ear, wanted to remove them, he could and would. Then there were Richard's estates. The Neville inheritance, which was at their core, was never entirely secure, owing to the peculiar circumstances in which Richard had acquired it, and despite his best efforts to shore up his position through parliamentary confirmation and personal legal action. The latter included his arrangements with other potential claimants to the central portion of the inheritance, including Middleham and Sheriff Hutton, who were generously compensated to quit their claims. From 1475, the Act of Parliament that granted the part of the Neville lands which had belonged to Warwick's brother Marquess Montagu, had set out the unusual arrangement that Gloucester and his heirs should retain their claim only as long as the surviving Neville heir, Montagu's son George Neville, or any male issue, were alive. If the Montagu–Neville line was extinguished, Richard's title reverted to a life interest, and other members of the Neville family – who, we surmise, were not deemed to be tainted by Montagu's treachery – could lay claim.

George Neville, who had been demoted from his dukedom in 1478, and not even compensated with a barony (probably, as we have seen, so that he had no forum in the Lords to plead his case to overturn the arrangement of 1475), was still a minor in 1483. His survival, and successful production of a male heir, were in Richard's interests, but the duke, who had acquired Neville's wardship in 1480, had not yet managed to marry him off. In fact, George Neville died unmarried less than a month after Edward IV, on 4 May 1483. But by that date Richard had already made his first move (though we should allow that, as George was in Richard's care, he may have realized he had a life-threatening illness some time before). It is possible that news of George Neville's death, and thus the threat to his estates, part of which would now by right pass to Richard, Lord Latimer, on the Duke of Gloucester's death, turned the duke's thoughts to aiming higher. But before Neville's death, and even, perhaps, for some considerable time after it, Richard's moves should not necessarily be interpreted as designs on the throne. The unsatisfactory situation of the potential loss of part (an important and to Richard highly valued part, admittedly) of his inheritable estate would still not, of itself, have given the duke reason to gamble everything. Would it not have made more sense for Richard to calculate that he might use his influence over the new king, and his likely role of Protector, to change the Neville arrangement to his advantage? If we are looking for sources of insecurity, or even perceived insecurity, in Richard's position, we should surely look elsewhere.

It is possible Richard was worried about money. Acquiring his lands had at times been an expensive business (the quitclaim to Ralph, Lord Neville, alone had cost £10,000). Retaining them could be costly, too (all those mouths to feed, purses to fill and positions to find). The recent campaign in Scotland is likely to have left the duke out of pocket, despite generous recompense from the king, including a grant of 10,000 marks in 1483. Further military ventures to secure those palatine rights north of the border would continue to drain his resources. Certainly, Richard had made his priority the acquisition of power, not of cash, and even his great holdings were employed more as a vehicle for political advancement or consolidation than a source of wealth. At the time of Edward IV's death, the duke may well have felt financially exposed, and unsure of the extent of royal backing for any future venture.

Richard's shaky finances and complex territorial arrangements should certainly adjust the picture of a supremely powerful and secure noble. But if there was one overriding source of insecurity that the Duke of Gloucester really feared in the changed circumstances of the new reign, it was – as his behaviour over the coming weeks demonstrated – the obvious one: the new king's maternal family, the Woodvilles. Future political security depended on control of the king, who would remain underage for at least four years, whether or not he was crowned immediately. Whatever arrangements had been or would be made for his minority government, the people with the most influence over Edward V could expect to benefit. In April 1483 the Woodvilles occupied that position. The king's maternal uncle, who was also his governor and tutor, Earl Rivers, was with Edward V at Ludlow when his father died. Naturally, Rivers took charge of arrangements to conduct his nephew to London for his coronation. If Rivers had been alone, the Duke of Gloucester might have anticipated that he could cooperate with him, or dominate him. Yet he was anything but alone. Other members of his clan who could be expected to wield influence included: Rivers' sister, the queen mother; his brother Sir Edward Woodville; his sister's sons by her first marriage, Thomas Grey, Marquess of Dorset, and Richard Grey, who was with the Ludlow party; as well as the queen's other brother, Lionel Woodville, Bishop of Salisbury.

To say that Richard feared the Woodvilles is not to allege that there was any deep or long-standing enmity between them. Too often, the Woodvilles are portrayed as a grasping, hated cabal who had to be stopped, and against whom Richard had long borne a grudge. The groundswell of opinion against them, however, was surely much weakened since the time when the Nevilles and Clarence had exploited it for their own ends more than a decade before. For his part, Richard had recently campaigned with Rivers in Scotland, and the earl had asked the duke to arbitrate in a dispute in March 1483, a month before Edward IV's death. While his brother was on the throne, Richard had no reason to resent the Woodvilles, who had never stood in his way. Other nobles certainly did dislike them, including Lord Hastings, whom Edward tried to reconcile with his wife's people on his deathbed, and the Duke of Buckingham, who was later alleged to have 'his own reasons for detesting the queen's kin: for, when he was younger, he had been forced to marry the queen's sister, whom he scorned to wed on account of her humble origin.'[4] (One presumes that this revulsion had not existed when the match was made, when Buckingham was about ten years old.) The unexpected death of Richard's brother, however, had changed everything. Although Rivers does not seem to have realized it, Gloucester now saw him and his family as a threat. It was not fundamental insecurity, but an abrupt change in circumstances, that led Richard to make his first move. There is no need to believe that Richard already had the Crown in mind. Each step in these weeks made turning back less likely, but nothing was inevitable or irreversible.

Up to this point in Richard's life, reconstructing his day-to-day movements is often difficult. It can be a constant source of frustration, with the earlier part of Richard's story, that while evidence is not exactly minimal, it is glaringly incomplete. We know details of quite minor incidents (and have therefore to avoid the temptation to inflate their importance merely because we know something about them), but lack concrete evidence for much larger ones. We don't know, for example, when Richard's son Edward was born. (This is unique among Princes of Wales; for every other holder of that title from 1301 to the present day, we have an attested date of birth. For Edward of Middleham there isn't even an agreed year.) From April 1483 to Richard's death in 1485, there is very much more to go on. But we still can't read Richard's mind, and he left no diary to help us. The facts, mostly agreed upon (with a few very significant exceptions), bear almost diametrically opposed interpretations. The last years of Richard's life are the most interesting, and the most mysterious (which, of course, partly accounts for their interest). They began – and ended – with a series of journeys.

The first was undertaken by Edward IV's corpse. After lying in state at Westminster Palace for a week, then being carried to a service in the abbey, the king's remains were conveyed on the night of 16 April with great ceremony westwards out of the city, via Syon church, to St George's chapel at Windsor. This was the 'new chirche' constructed by Edward's master mason Henry Janyns from 1475, a glorious, fan-vaulted, late-Perpendicular pocket cathedral that is perhaps the most eloquent testimony to the peace dividends of Edward's 'second reign'. There, eminent lords spiritual and temporal, and a 'great press' of knights and esquires of the body celebrated a last Mass for the king. His giant master of horse, the six-foot-eight Sir John Cheyne, led in a mounted, armed, but bare-headed knight, Sir William Parr, carrying 'an axe in his hand, the pomel downward', to indicate that the king's fighting days were over, just as Lord Ferrers had done at the reinterment of Edward's father and brother in 1476.[5] Parr, brother of Thomas, whom Richard had remembered as a fallen comrade that same year, was a councillor of the Duke of Gloucester as well as a royal servant, one of the commissioners of the duke's office of constable, appointed in 1482. Richard may have been away in the north when Edward was buried, but as Parr's role hints, the duke intended no snub to his brother's memory. The need to bury Edward with reasonable speed accounts too for most of the other notable absentees, including the new king Edward V and his uncle Earl Rivers, as well as the Duke of Buckingham and the aged Thomas Bourchier, Archbishop of Canterbury. If the Seventy-two-year-old archbishop, who had already appointed a suffragan to carry out most of the duties of a role that could not be resigned, had hoped to have retired from public affairs, the melodrama that followed would disabuse him of the notion.

As well as paying their respects to their dead king, the peers who assembled at Westminster and Windsor gathered to decide what happened next. If Edward himself had left specific instructions, they have not survived and were, in any case, not binding on his successor. The two nearest to contemporary accounts of this period – the *Crowland Chronicle* and Dominic Mancini's *Usurpation of Richard the Third*, both written in Latin, give slightly different versions of what the councillors discussed, and the tensions that lay behind the discussions. Mancini was an Italian visitor to England who wrote up his account of the 'machinations [by which] Richard the third, now reigning in Britain, attained the high degree of kingship', for his patron Angelo Cato, Archbishop of Vienne, by November 1483.

The identity of the author of the section of the *Crowland Chronicle* that covers these years, by contrast, has never been securely proved. There is no doubt, however, that the Crowland 'continuator', as he is also known (he was the third such to take up the abbey's story, in the fifteenth century), was nearer to the heart of power than Mancini. Writing in the spring of 1486, he describes himself at one point as a royal councillor and doctor of canon law who was sent to Burgundy on a diplomatic mission for Edward IV in 1471. He was not a key player in the events he describes, but in his 'Whitehall kind of history'[6] he displays a civil servant's inside knowledge. He is the writer who tells us that the councillors who gathered before Edward's funeral, including the queen, concentrated on the issue of the size of armed retinue that should accompany the new king as he made his way from Ludlow to London: 'Some suggested more, some less . . . The more foresighted members of the Council, however, thought that the uncles and brothers on the mother's side should be absolutely forbidden to have control of the person of the young man until he came of age. They believed that this could not be easily achieved if those of the queen's relatives who were most influential with the prince were allowed to bring his person to the ceremonies with an immoderate number of horse.'[7]

Like the Crowland chronicler, Mancini names Lord Hastings, who as Lieutenant of Calais had almost a private army to call upon, as the main voice of opposition to the Woodvilles. But Mancini's account casts the scope of the discussion much wider, to include the form of government that should operate during the king's minority and, most importantly, who should be in charge of it. Mancini writes that Richard was put forward by some on the council as the lawful head of government under Edward V, in part 'because Edward [IV] in his will had so directed'. But, he reports, the opposing view prevailed, that Richard should merely be one among 'many persons' who would form a government. 'All who favoured the queen's family voted for this proposal.'[8] Mancini's explanation for this decision – 'they were afraid that, if Richard took unto himself the crown or even governed alone, they, who bore the blame of Clarence's death, would suffer death or at least be ejected from their high estate' – may smack deafeningly of hindsight, but the Crowland chronicler's account of the squabble over retinue size alludes in essence to the same concern. Who would take charge? If a Protectorate had been rejected, in favour of a swift coronation and an advisory council, then Richard's proposed role was definitely more restricted than he would have envisaged. If Hastings, as Mancini alleges, did communicate to Richard that the Woodville group had made a move to reduce his influence, this may have persuaded the duke that he needed to redress the balance.

That there was some wider concern and uncertainty over the future of the kingdom emerges from a letter sent around the time of Edward IV's funeral. On 19 April John Gigur, warden of Tattershall College, Lincolnshire, wrote that 'we wete . . . not hoo schal be oure lord nor hoo schale haue the reule aboute us'.[9] That could be taken as a sign that even at this early stage some observers feared a full-scale coup. But it could simply refer to the anticipated power struggle *around* Edward V, between the Woodvilles, the Duke of Gloucester – and not forgetting other powerful men with a vested interest in maintaining influence over government, such as the Duke of Buckingham, the Stanley family, the Earl of Northumberland and Lord Hastings. Gigur's fears, moreover, specifically refer to the future of his college. Until it was clear who would take charge of a minority government, the college warden thought his institution was in 'jeopardy'. This certainly can't be taken as 'proof' that a struggle for the Crown itself, based around still live rumours of the illegitimacy of Edward IV or his children, was widely anticipated.

Uncle and Protector

Richard stayed in Yorkshire long enough to hold a funeral ceremony for his brother at York Minster, and to swear fealty, along with his principal followers, to the new king. He also sent a condolence letter to the queen and council, and reminded them, according to Mancini, of his unimpeachable loyalty, and his 'deserts . . . when disposing of the government, to which he was entitled by law, and his brother's ordinance'.[10] The coronation date was set for 4 May, so Richard began to make his way south around 23 April, while Rivers and Edward V set out around the same time from Ludlow, with a retinue, as agreed by the council, of 2,000. The Duke of Buckingham was also on the move from his estates in Wales. Mancini writes that the two dukes corresponded about their fear and loathing of the Woodvilles, and agreed to make common cause.[11] Later accounts detail the secret movements of Buckingham's trusted servant Persivall, who told Richard about Edward IV's death, offered his master's assistance, and arranged for the two to meet outside Northampton.[12] By this time Edward V and Rivers had arrived at Stony Stratford, about thirteen miles south of Northampton, but Rivers turned north to meet the dukes, apparently unaware of any threat. On 29 April Rivers was 'greeted with a particularly cheerful and merry face and, sitting at the duke's [Richard's] table for dinner, they passed the whole time in very pleasant conversation'.[13] In the morning all three set out for Stony Stratford, but as they approached the town, Gloucester and Buckingham suddenly arrested Rivers, along with Sir Richard Grey, his nephew (the king's half-brother), Sir Thomas Vaughan, 'an aged knight, the prince's chamberlain',[14] and unnamed other attendants. They were sent north under armed guard.

When news of this frightening development reached London, the queen and her adult son, another of Edward V's half-brothers, the Marquess of Dorset, first attempted to muster an armed response, but when it appeared that public opinion had been swayed by Richard's messages of peace, they fled to the sanctuary of Westminster Abbey, with the king's younger brother Richard, Duke of York, and his older sisters. Richard entered London with Edward V and the Duke of Buckingham on 4 May, to be greeted by all the major representatives of the City and their followers, finely turned out in scarlet, *pied de lyon* (an orange colour) and murrey (a purple-red cloth). To show what the Woodvilles had been plotting, Gloucester and Buckingham displayed four cartloads of weapons 'bearing the devices of the queen's brothers and sons', and appointed 'criers to make generally known throughout the crowded places by whatsoever way they passed, that these arms had been collected by the duke's enemies and stored at convenient spots outside the capital, so as to attack and slay the duke of

Gloucester coming from the country'. Mancini tells us that this plan backfired: 'Since many knew these charges to be false, because the arms in question had been placed there long before the late king's death for an altogether different purpose, when war was being waged against the Scots, mistrust both of his accusation and designs upon the throne was exceedingly augmented.'[15]

Richard had also told Edward that he had been forced to make the arrests because he had learned that Rivers's party were plotting to attack him. It is possible that this was the content of the letters that Mancini says Hastings had sent to Richard after the decision of the council went against him. Even if it was a complete fabrication on Richard's (and Buckingham's) part, this does not mean that his professions of loyalty to the young king were insincere. Richard may have suspected (or realized) that the Woodville party would freeze him out of the minority government, with all the negative consequences that would entail for the duke's now accustomed place as the mightiest noble in the country. He may have heard that the queen had gained access to the treasury; that the Marquess of Dorset was becoming the chief voice on the council (Mancini reports him as saying 'We are so important, that even without the King's uncle we can make and enforce decisions'[16]); and that the queen's brother Sir Edward Woodville had been ordered to put to sea with a fleet (only totalling four ships, two of which were hired help crewed by Genoese), ostensibly to deal with French pirates – who, under Philippe de Crèvecoeur, 'Lord Cordes' as the English called him, had been carrying out raids on English shipping since Edward IV's death – but apparently with authority to take a portion of the royal treasure with him. Sir Edward left the day of the arrests, which Richard cannot have known, but his appointment was made earlier. Faced with such a strong alliance of forces that certainly appeared to be opposed to him, Richard needed something on his side to tip the scales back towards him. That something was the new king. This is why we do not need to look for evidence of a long-term feud between Richard and Rivers and the other Woodvilles. Rivers had control of Edward V. If Richard wanted to retain his place at the heart of government, he had to wrest power over the king away from his maternal uncle. It was nothing personal.

Was Richard at this point aiming at anything beyond establishing himself as Protector? Since all the accounts of these days were written by authors who knew that Richard did become king, their judgements are not especially to be relied upon. Mancini implies that Richard was looking further than the protectorship straight after Stony Stratford: 'Some, however, who understood his ambition and deceit, always suspected whither his enterprises would lead.'[17] The Crowland chronicler is more circumspect, but he still builds up a menacing picture of, on the one hand, the Duke of Gloucester's professions of total loyalty to his nephew and, on the other, a methodical clearing of his own path to power: first, the issue of orders that no one from the king's household should 'come near any places where the King might go, on pain of death'; next, the faintly sinister description of the councillors' agreement that, after his arrival in London, Edward should be moved from the Bishop of London's palace at St Paul's to the Tower of London, an 'opinion verbally accepted by all, even by those who did not wish it'; finally, after Gloucester's official assumption of the protectorship, his ambivalent conduct, by turns 'exercis[ing] this authority with the consent and the good-will of all the lords', and 'commanding and forbidding everything like another king'.[18] The implication is clear: Richard was dissembling, biding his time until he could strike.

This picture of Richard taking steps to consolidate his position before launching the ruthless assault that would land him on the throne is one on which all subsequent chroniclers built. For motivation, Tudor historians such as Polydore Vergil, Thomas More, Edward Hall and even Shakespeare offered a concoction of insatiable ambition, bad character and resentment. An evil deed is all the more evil if the result of long contemplation, and Shakespeare, by backdating Richard's royal ambitions not just to Edward IV's reign, but to near its beginning (to a time when Richard was, in fact, around twelve years old), merely completed the work begun by Mancini and the Crowland chronicler. We can discount the more extreme retrospective projections of Richard's ultimate ambition. Even the queen's seeking sanctuary is not proof that she and Dorset thought Richard wanted to be king in her son's place. They may simply have feared their fate at Richard's hands as Protector. But had Richard decided by the time of the arrests to take the throne?

Not necessarily. Attempts to argue that Richard made his final decision at a later date partly depend on emphasizing the amount of time that elapsed between 30 April, when Richard and Buckingham moved against Rivers and company, and 10 June, when Richard sent a letter to York seeking armed assistance against an apparent revival of Woodville ambitions – a move that is generally, if not universally, accepted as marking a definite intention to seize power. During those five weeks, Richard set about confirming the fall of the Woodvilles, removing them from positions of authority, and replacing one of their most vocal allies, Thomas Rotherham, Archbishop of York, as chancellor with John Russell, Bishop of Lincoln. Rotherham had, according to later writers, given the Great Seal to the queen, presumably so that Richard of York could issue commands under it in the event of his brother's deposition or death. Rotherham thought better of it, and went to retrieve the seal the next day. But on 2 May, Edward V sent Thomas Bourchier, the Archbishop of Canterbury, a letter, which was by this time written under the Duke of Gloucester's eyes, instructing the archbishop to 'see fro the saufegarde and sure keping of the gret seale of this our realme unto our comyng to our cite of London'.[19]

Archbishop Bourchier took the seal into his custody five days later. He did so in the presence of Richard, Duke of Gloucester, several fellow bishops, Richard's mother Cecily, and other great lords such as Buckingham, Hastings and Stanley. This took place at Baynard's Castle, the Yorks' London residence, and was combined with a sequestration of Edward IV's goods and jewels, because the executors of his will had not taken them into custody. This has been interpreted as the 'beginning of the formal setting aside of Edward IV's authority and legitimacy', as if it necessarily meant that his will was not to be carried out, and implied that his still legitimate offspring were also to be cut out. It seems unlikely that this is what was happening. If Richard was moving towards a usurpation but anxious not to reveal his hand yet, why allow such a suspicious demonstration to occur? Its importance would only have been symbolic, but the symbolism of Edward V being delegitimized was not evident yet in Richard's other acts. It seems more likely that this was a practical way of securing Edward IV's chattels at an uncertain time, when his wife and younger son, who were bound to be beneficiaries, were still in sanctuary.[20]

Richard also launched a partially successful attempt to neutralize Edward Woodville at sea. (Two large ships were captured when their Genoese crews defected to the government's side, but Woodville himself, along with £10,201 he had acquired from a vessel in Southampton on 14 May, as well as any money he had extracted from the Treasury, got away, ending up in Brittany, where

Henry Tudor was still exiled.)[21] Finally, the duke tried to persuade the queen and her family to come out of sanctuary. For the time being, he was rebuffed.

The chief beneficiary of the degrading of the Woodvilles was the Duke of Buckingham, who was certainly made far more powerful, particularly in Wales. A grant enrolled at Westminster on 16 May details dozens of lordships and castles that passed to the duke, as well as the offices of chief justice and chamberlain of north and south Wales and, the grant concludes matter-of-factly, 'the governance and supervision of all the king's subjects in South and North Wales and the marches'.[22] Never before had one man received so vast an increase in his powers at a stroke. Many other appointments, however, were made of loyal servants of Edward IV. This, combined with ongoing preparations for the coronation of Edward V, which had been postponed to 22 June, make it credible that Richard was not thinking yet of usurpation. In his draft sermon for the parliament that was scheduled to follow the coronation, Bishop Russell makes it clear that the protectorate was expected to continue afterwards, so that Richard's position was not immediately affected. If we accept that Richard wasn't planning to usurp all along, then what changed his mind? Perhaps it was that he realized the limits of his power as Protector, and what that implied once the protectorate was over. Edward V was twelve years old, and as his reportedly bold defiance of his uncle and Buckingham after the arrest of Rivers indicated, he was precocious. He could not be expected to wait much more than four years to take up the reins of power. After all, his own father had come to the throne aged nineteen, but he had been a very active Earl of March from the age of seventeen.

The main issue on which Richard was thwarted as Protector was the matter of the fate of Rivers, Grey and Vaughan. After failing to convince the general public about Woodville plots against them, Gloucester and Buckingham made equally little headway in convincing the council to sentence the leaders of these plots to death. This failure did not merely frustrate some perverse blood lust in Richard. It went to the heart of his reasons for arresting Rivers and company in the first place. Unless he effectively removed Woodville influence from the political scene, Richard could expect it in due course to eclipse his own. He had seen how Edward IV's attempts to rehabilitate his opponents, from Warwick to Clarence, had failed. Further back in recent history, the last Protector during a minority and also a Duke of Gloucester, Humphrey, who had presided over Henry VI's minority, had been forced into retirement by hostile factions led by Cardinal Beaufort and then the Earl of Suffolk. Richard seems to have concluded that the only effective way to ensure his own future was to remove such opposition. When that proved impossible as Protector, he made up his mind to aim higher.

We can only ever make educated guesses at Richard's state of mind, but the final possibility is that he kept both courses of action open. It cannot have failed to occur to him that he *could* launch an attempt on the throne after Stony Stratford. After all, his father and brother Edward had done so, with different results. His father's experiences as Protector, though under very different circumstances, may also have formed part of his thinking. Richard had been a child when his father's unsuccessful attempts to fulfil the role of Protector had taken place, but the story would have survived not just in official records but as a family tale of family honour thwarted. Richard's own insecurities came from different sources. Not long after he had entered London with Edward V, he would have learned that George Neville, former Duke of Bedford, had died the same day, leaving Richard with no legitimate heritable claim to a swathe of his northern estates. If he had not felt insecure before, he might have begun to by now. But perhaps he decided to see how the protectorship played out rather than viewing it from the beginning either as a mere staging-post to the ultimate prize, or as the prize itself, from which he was only diverted by force of circumstance. Historians tend to enjoy demolishing other historians' cases to make their own. With Richard's usurpation, it seems likely that more than one side of the argument is valid.

Friday the Thirteenth

Whatever Richard's true intentions, and at whatever pace they developed, his actions on 13 June marked a definite break, and left no one in doubt of his ruthlessness. On that Friday, Richard divided the King's Council between Westminster and the Tower, and attended the latter. The other members of that party included Lord Hastings, Thomas Rotherham, Archbishop of York, and John Morton, Bishop of Ely. Suddenly, these 'three strongest supports of the new King' were arrested. The Crowland chronicler gives the facts without adornment: 'on the authority of the Protector, Lord Hastings was beheaded'.

Mancini writes that Hastings was 'cut down' when Richard gave a pre-arranged signal that he, the Protector, was being ambushed. The latter scenario at least accounts for the shocking absence of anything even vaguely resembling due process. The prelates were spared death, 'out of respect for their order', but were sent to 'different castles in Wales'.[23] Morton came under the charge of the Duke of Buckingham in Brecon by July. Lord Stanley, who was also arrested, managed to avoid either death or extended captivity, but was probably under some suspicion for the rest of Richard's life.

Why did Richard have Hastings killed? The Protector's own suspicions, or those he affected, were given in the letter he had sent three days before, summoning troops from York. 'We hertely pray you to come unto us in London in all the diligence ye can possible . . . with as mony as ye can make defensibly arraied, their to eide and assiste us ayanst the Quiene, hir blod adherentts and affinitie, which have entended and daly doith intend, to murder and utterly distroy us and our cousyn, the duc of Bukkyngham, and the old royall blode of this realme, and as it is now openly knowen, by their subtill and dampnabill wais forcasted the same . . .'[24] One possibly contemporary witness, an annalist whose notes were copied later by a herald in the College of Arms, wrote that 'dyvers imagenyd the deyth of the duke of Gloceter, and hit was asspiyd and the Lord Hastinges was takyn in the Towur and byhedyd forthwith'.[25] Mancini says that Hastings, Rotherham and Morton sometimes 'forgathered in each other's houses'.[26] Might these accounts show Hastings plotting the Protector's downfall? Perhaps, but if this was supposed to be part of a Woodville plot, it seems extremely unlikely that Hastings would have been implicated. He had a long-standing dislike of the Woodvilles, mentioned by Mancini and implied by the Crowland chronicler, and had been 'bursting with joy' over their ejection. While loyalty may not have been the signature virtue of the age, it is difficult to see why, in pragmatic terms, someone who had just assisted in the removal of the queen's family from influence would conspire with them for their reinstatement. As for the Woodvilles, they were not at this time very promising co-conspirators. They were either under arrest, in sanctuary or had fled the country. If Hastings was part of a plot against Gloucester, it is unlikely that the Woodvilles were involved.

There was, however, one Woodville to whom Hastings seems to have offered unswerving loyalty: Elizabeth's son, Edward V. One possible indication of that is the beautiful illuminated manuscript in the British Library known as the *Hastings Hours*. It has been speculated that this volume, with its whimsical illustrations of battling monsters or a tournament between tears and kisses, its full-page depiction of the patron saint of Wales, St David, and its picture of the royal barge dwarfed by a pennant bearing the Garter motto, might have originally been given to Edward V when he was Prince of Wales, as all these embellishments were appropriate to his age and station. If it was subsequently passed to Hastings, that is most likely to have happened when the new king saw his father's loyal retainer in the Tower.[27] Here is a suggestion of a bond between the young king and Lord Chamberlain that would have been hard to break.

While duty to the king and duty to the Protector coincided, Hastings was safe. But had Hastings realized they were about to diverge? If Edward and Hastings did have any private conversation, the king might have shared his apprehension about his uncle's plans. Contemporaries indicate, however, that Hastings got his information from a different source. Mancini has Buckingham sounding out Hastings's 'loyalty' (he leaves it open as to whether to the king or to the Protector) and that of the two prelates; and the story told by Thomas More, in which William Catesby, a lawyer who was a member of Buckingham's affinity, does the sounding out, makes clear that Hastings was reported to be 'so fast' against Richard's 'purpose', in other words usurping the Crown.[28] Catesby is a plausible go-between because, through his uncle Sir John Catesby, one of Hastings's councillors, William had also worked for Hastings. Buckingham himself may have had reasons to want Hastings removed, in order to increase his influence in the north Midlands, where Hastings was the dominant landowner.[29] The Crowland chronicler, on the other hand, while seeing Hastings and the prelates as obstacles to Richard's plans, also reckons that once these three 'were removed, and with all the rest of his [Edward V's] faithful men expecting something similar, these two dukes thereafter did whatever they wanted'. That is, Hastings was an example, whose brutal treatment was intended as a clear message to any other putative opponents. In all these scenarios, the speed of Hastings's execution gave him no time to deny the accusation, which could only add to the atmosphere of terror. But it also gave him no chance to publicize Richard's intentions, if they had been revealed to him. The main point against this interpretation of events is why then Hastings felt secure enough to attend a council in the Tower with

Richard at its head. More says it was because Hastings trusted Catesby to bring any machinations against him to his attention, which is certainly possible. But perhaps he had not fully grasped the Protector's intentions, merely revealed his own hostility to such a move, discussed obliquely without attribution. Or perhaps he had underestimated Richard's capacity for swift and brutal action. By the time the blade fell, Hastings must have realized what Richard planned to do.

One other potential puzzle is why Richard acted *before* he had the backing of the troops he had summoned from the north in his letter to the city of York. It has been argued that this was because his hand was forced. Hastings found out, and Richard had to act, taking his chances. But it could also be because Richard thought that while a show of armed strength would be needed once he revealed his intention to take the throne, an earlier display might spook Hastings, and he could rely instead on the weakness of any opposition in the shock after Hastings's death. And if the Woodville–Hastings conspiracy was a fiction, Richard had no need to wait for a large force to overawe a few isolated individuals. It should be remembered, too, that he had arrived with an armed retinue at the end of April. It is unlikely that all those soldiers had returned home. Thomas More, in his lurid version of the fatal council meeting, has 'rushing men in harneys, as many as ye chambre might hold', surrounding the victims. If Richard had been forced to call on armed support, he was not alone.[30]

In terms of how Richard has been judged by history, it may seem odd that the murder of Hastings – for that is what it was, whether or not you believe Richard had reasons to fear him – has ranked so low. Partly that is because even worse has so long been alleged of Richard III. But if other charges brought against Richard are weak, difficult to substantiate, or on occasion entirely unbelievable, the death of Hastings is not. Richard ordered the killing without trial of a fellow subject, 'without justice or judgement', as the Crowland chronicler puts it.[31] Even if he had been king already, this was a grave crime. When popular books and television programmes absolve Richard of murder on the grounds that the available evidence would not stand up to modern scrutiny, they are trying the wrong case. Any competent prosecutor could secure a conviction of Richard for murder in the case of Lord Hastings.

The reaction to the events of Friday 13 June was, initially, one of terror. Mancini writes that 'the townsmen, who had heard the uproar but were uncertain of the cause, became panic-stricken, and each one seized his weapons. But, to calm the multitude, the duke instantly sent a herald to proclaim that a plot had been detected in the citadel, and Hastings, the originator of the plot, had paid the penalty.'[32] More says that the proclamation was so polished that it had obviously been prepared before, but if there were doubts, no one seemed ready to act on them. Eight days later Simon Stallworth, a canon and servant of Bishop Russell, the new chancellor, wrote the second of two letters to his contact Sir William Stonor, a member of the Oxfordshire gentry. The first, written on 9 June, before the execution of Hastings but after Gloucester had taken up the protectorship, had been cautiously optimistic. The queen and her younger son may have been in sanctuary, but Stallworth confirmed that the 'coronacion ... schalbe this day fortnyght as we say', in other words 22 June.[33] When Stallworth wrote to Stonor again, on 21 June, everything had changed. Stallworth himself was ill and employed an amanuensis to write the first part of the letter, which gave news of Hastings's beheading, the appearance at Westminster of 'gret plentye of harnest mene', and the predictable result that 'ther was the dylyveraunce of the Dewke of Yorke to my lord Cardenale ... my lorde Protectour recevynge hyme at the Starre Chambere dore with many lovynge wordys and so departede with my lorde Cardenale to the Toure where he is, blessid be Jhesu Mery'.[34]

Stallworth took up his own pen to finish off the account of more arrests, seizure of property, and general uncertainty. He is the only contemporary witness to mention 'Mistress Shore', Elizabeth Shore, whose part in an alleged plot with Hastings was given prominence by Thomas More. What her involvement was is impossible to know. As she had been Edward IV's lover before possibly becoming Hastings's, she was, as More says, an unlikely go-between for a rapprochement between Hastings and the queen in sanctuary. Nevertheless, the fact that Shore was arrested shows that Richard suspected her of some involvement or threat to his plans. She remained in captivity, imprisoned at Ludgate until after Richard became king, when she was made to do public penance, and was linked to yet another adulterous liaison, with Thomas Grey, Marquess of Dorset. She was not the only 'collateral' victim of these paranoid days. Stallworth mentions Oliver King, who had been Edward IV's secretary and performed the same function for Edward V, and 'Foster', who 'is in holde and mene fer hys lyffe'. John Foster, or Forster, was a Hertfordshire lawyer with connections to Elizabeth Woodville,

Hastings and Morton. He petitioned Parliament in Henry VII's reign, when he revealed that he had been seized from his home in Hertfordshire and imprisoned in the Tower for the next ten months. Starved for the first three days of his imprisonment, he was then subjected to extortion, to the tune of 1,000 marks, on pain of death and forfeiture of his property.[35] The round of arrests and imprisonments was backed up by the threat of a northern army, which the feverish Stallworth put at 'xx thousand of my lord protector and my lord of Bukyngham'. This was far bigger than the force that actually arrived. York's own response, for example, was to muster 200 men to go to Pontefract to the Earl of Northumberland, who was playing his usual game of waiting as long as possible to commit his loyalties.[36] But if Gloucester and Buckingham's plan was to overawe potential resistance, it had worked.

The removal of the Duke of York, Edward V's eight-year-old brother, from sanctuary on 16 June, negotiated by Archbishop Bourchier, was presented as further preparation for the delayed coronation. Writs were issued the same day postponing the ceremony and the parliament to accompany it once again, this time until 9 November. But slowly, Richard and his supporters were beginning to reveal what by now must have been their true intentions, to postpone the coronation of Edward V permanently, and to begin arrangements for the elevation of Richard himself. He had now made too many enemies to turn back. Even if the initial plan had not been to seek the throne, it had become the only seat in the country that could offer him some protection. Mancini tells us that one sign of this public alteration was Gloucester's decision to stop wearing mourning black – which he had maintained in the face of others, such as the gaudily clad party of aldermen and representatives of the London City companies who had greeted Edward V's arrival with his paternal uncle. Now, Richard assumed a kingly purple, and appeared in public with a bigger entourage.

At some point he moved his household from Crosby's Place, in Bishopsgate, the residence built by a rich wool-trader and warden of the Grocers' Company, Sir John Crosby, to the Yorks' family residence in London, where his mother lived by the Thames, Baynard's Castle.[37] Mancini says that Richard had a thousand followers, which is certainly an exaggeration, and that he also began to entertain on a more lavish scale.[38] The archaeologists who studied Richard's femur and ribs and discovered a marked alteration in Richard's diet around the time he became king – evidence of 'consumption of high trophic level, terrestrial foods, such as freshwater fish and wildfowl . . . [which] corresponds to an increase in these "luxury foods" in the last 2–5 years of his life' – may have uncovered material remains of a lifestyle change that began as a conscious effort to appear more regal.[39] The date range given, however, also allows for a switch while Edward IV was still alive, which would give the lie to the image later cultivated by Richard of his more ascetic way of life compared to the dissipations of Edward's court. Behind the scenes, away from the world of conspicuous consumption, there was a 'shut down' of the business of government: grants and appointments that passed through the various tendrils of royal bureaucracy – the signet office (the king's personal seal), the offices of the great and privy seals – slowed, and then ceased altogether by 15 June.[40]

'Ordeigned to Reigne upon the people'

Despite all these signals, when the ailing Simon Stallworth sent his second letter, on 21 June, he was still in the dark, if filled with foreboding: 'what schall happyne hyr I knowe nott'. The activities of the next day, Sunday 22 June, made plain what was going to happen. At St Paul's Cross, and throughout the city, sermons were preached alleging either that Edward V and his brother were bastards, because their parents had never been properly married in the eyes of the Church, or that Edward IV had been illegitimate – 'conceived in adultery and in every way . . . unlike the Duke of York [his father]'.[41] There are no contemporary records of the content of the sermons, or who gave them – the identification of Ralph Shaa, or Shaw, the mayor's brother and a prebendary of St Paul's, is made by the London chroniclers and More, but no earlier. But the story of Edward IV's alleged bastardy was an old one. It was used by the Duke of Clarence, according to Edward himself in his parliamentary indictment of his brother in 1478, and even, Mancini says, proffered by Edward and Richard's own mother, Cecily, apparently because Edward's marriage to Elizabeth Woodville had put his mother into a 'frenzy'.[42] The story had been adopted by Charles the Bold, who had begun in 1475 to refer to Edward as 'Blayborgne', supposedly the name of the French archer who was his real father.[43] This was the kind of persistent tittle-tattle that had lost all force of revelation by being so frequently rehearsed, and openly dismissed. What was new, if it had not already leaked out during the Burdet case around the time of the fall of Clarence, was a credible enough case against Edward's marriage. If that could be shown to be invalid, then its offspring would be illegitimate, with the added advantage that Richard's own mother would not have to suffer further assaults on her reputation – something which, even if we are not prepared to grant Richard sensitivities over his mother's feelings, would hardly do if she were about to resume the role of queen mother.

At the crucial moment, Richard was apparently vouchsafed just such an authority. The Crowland chronicler writes: 'It was put forward, by means of a supplication contained in a certain parchment, that King Edward's sons were bastards, by submitting that he had been pre-contracted to a certain Lady Eleanor Boteler [Butler] before he married Elizabeth [Woodville].'[44] Mancini had heard the pre-contract story, too, but associated it with a different marriage – one arranged for Edward by the Earl of Warwick (with Bona of Savoy). That contemporaries differed on such crucial details does not add to the credibility of Richard's case. Nor, on the face of it, does the timing of the announcement. If Edward's children were illegitimate, why did it emerge only now, when his brother had removed all opposition with violent efficiency? It is the French diplomat Philippe de Commines who first named Bishop Stillington of Bath and Wells as the source of the pre-contract story. Referring to Stillington as 'this malicious prelate', Commines describes how the bishop alleged that he had married Edward and the unnamed Eleanor Butler so that the king 'Could enjoy her person'. Although Commines called Stillington's intervention 'revenge', kept 'in his heart' for almost twenty years, he does not, in fact, dismiss it as a fabrication. He comments instead, of Edward's roving eye, that 'such games are dangerous'.[45]

The suspiciously convenient timing of the revelation need not make us discount it altogether, if we allow that Stillington was in control of the information. While Edward IV was alive, and even while Edward V was strongly supported, this was a secret with potentially lethal implications for its keeper. But once support had begun to be removed from Edward V, the information suddenly became extraordinarily valuable. Whether this interpretation puts Richard in a more sympathetic light, however, is still open to question. It relies on the fact that he had already decided to claim the throne, rather than feeling obliged to do so, as he later protested, by the revelation of his nephews' illegitimacy. It also makes no allowance for any potential solution to the problem that might have re-legitimized Edward V and his siblings. These included securing a retrospective canonical or papal judgement of the invalidity of the pre-contract; an Act of Parliament legitimizing the children of Edward and Elizabeth Woodville's marriage, as happened to Henry VIII's variously tainted offspring; or even ignoring the issue and proceeding to the coronation of Edward V, which would legitimize him by making him the Lord's anointed, and render allegations of his bastardy as newer versions of the old tittle-tattle about his father. That Richard took none of these courses was because he had no interest in doing so. His staunchest defenders ask us to take the pre-contract story at face value, but even if we do, it does not absolve Richard of already having plotted to usurp the Crown. If Stillington did play the part ascribed to him honestly, that was because he understood this, too.

One difficulty of being sure of precisely how and on what grounds Richard claimed the throne – let alone what he really believed himself – is that the most detailed statement about it was only published by Richard himself in Parliament in January 1484, half a year after he had seized power. This was the Bill called Titulus Regius, the royal title, which purported to reproduce the text of the petition offered to Richard as Duke of Gloucester requesting him to take the Crown. There, Richard's supporters set out the case that the pre-contract between Edward and Eleanor Butler had rendered the marriage of Edward and Elizabeth Woodville invalid, 'as the common opinion of the people and the public voice and fame is throughout the land'. The fact that Edward's 'official' marriage had been conducted clandestinely (and it will be recalled that its announcement came as a shock to most of his courtiers) meant that any notion that the pre-contract had been expunged by the subsequent marriage could not stand. There were ways in which Richard's use of the bastardy allegation did not follow established precedent, principally in not giving the children in question, or their mother, any opportunity to reply. It was true, too, that Parliament, although it could act as a court, could not usurp the jurisdiction of an ecclesiastical court, as it was, under the terms of Titulus Regius, being asked to do. But, contrary to some later arguments, if true, the case presented in the Bill, and possibly in the petition first made to Richard as Protector, certainly could have sufficed as a legal case for excluding Edward IV's sons from the succession.[46] Whether the Bill did reproduce the substance of the petition is a moot point. Before the parliamentary declaration of his legal claim, as surviving copies of instructions sent out to Calais at the time of the seizure of power indicate, Richard was content to make a bald statement of national support, but without specific details of his title: 'every good true englissheman is bounde upon knowlage . . . to make his outhe of newe and owe his service and fidelite to him that good lawe reason and the concorde assent of lordes & Comons of the Royaulme have ordeigned to Reigne upon the people'. Without going into any more details, the letter makes reference to a 'bille of peticione' presented to Richard on 26 June.[47] That was the first day of Richard III's reign.

In the days leading up to it, following the preaching of sermons in his favour, two processes had been brought to conclusion. The first was the removal of threats and alternatives. Earl Rivers, Sir Richard Grey and Sir Thomas Vaughan were executed on 25 June, at Pontefract: more deaths ordered by a Protector prematurely assuming the status of a king. One later writer says that the men were tried under the jurisdiction of the Earl of Northumberland, Richard's erstwhile rival in the north with whom he had built up a successful working relationship, and who had now decided to jump to Richard's side.[48] But the more nearly contemporary Mancini and the Crowland chronicler make it clear that they died 'without any form of trial', dealt with by 'dependable officers', under the command of Sir Richard Ratcliffe, the bearer of the 10 June letter to York who was now returning southwards at the head of a formidable 'multitude'.[49] Alternative claimants were now in Richard's hands, both the 'Princes in the Tower' and his other nephew, Clarence's son, Edward, Earl of Warwick, who was placed in his wife Anne's care, despite the fact that the boy's father had been attainted and Edward was, in the words later promulgated by Titulus Regius, 'disabled and barred from all right and claim to the crown'. Richard, Mancini writes, 'feared that if the entire progeny of King Edward were extinct, yet this child, who was also of royal blood, would still embarrass him'.[50]

The second process was to ensure that Richard had the necessary backing to take power. Ultimately, that was far more important than any legal argument in his favour. Richard might have had childhood memories of the time when his father had botched his attempt to claim the Crown in frankly more justifiable circumstances. In 1460, when Richard was just eight, the Duke of York had failed to garner enough support, even from his own followers, to push through his attempt. The Duke of Gloucester did not make the same mistake. On 25 June Richard's high-born stooge the Duke of Buckingham addressed an assembly of London worthies in the Guildhall, or one of lords elsewhere in the city – or both – to set out Richard's claim and his nephews' unfitness. Persuaded by the arguments, or the fait accompli with which they had been presented, Buckingham's audience fell into line. The following day, at Baynard's Castle, a deputation asked Richard to 'assume his lawful rights': this is likely to have been when the petition was delivered. Mancini tells us that Buckingham had warned his audience that Richard would be reluctant but could be persuaded. The Crowland chronicler makes no mention of any reluctance, calls the petition a pretext and says that Richard 'claimed for himself the government of the kingdom with the name and title of king'. He also writes that the roll containing the 'supplication . . . originated in the North whence so many people came to London although there was no-one who did not know the identity of the author (who was in London all the time)'.[51] The little drama created by More and rendered unforgettably by Shakespeare, of a mock-reluctant, mock-pious Gloucester surrendering to an overawed, sycophantic crowd may not have taken place at all. There were, at least, no remaining signs of hesitancy when Richard proceeded to Westminster the same day, 26 June, his saddle of crimson cloth of gold furred with lettice (the white fur of the winter weasel, powdered to resemble the more regal ermine), preceded by a sword bearer.[52] Richard entered Westminster Hall as Duke of Gloucester and Protector. He left it as King Richard III.

Such were the practical steps Richard took to lead him to the throne. There is no doubt that he was in many respects a supreme pragmatist, a risk-taker, a man who by now had proved that he was capable of decisive action in pursuit of his goal, even if we can debate how much that action had been premeditated and how much stemmed from panic. But it is important, too, to remember that Richard was a man of his time, and the mental world he inhabited allowed for influences that are alien to modern sensibilities. It may be difficult to detect much sign of Richard's often invoked piety in the weeks between April and June 1483, unless it can be located in his aversion to the consequences of his brother Edward's alleged immorality. In a period of around ten weeks, Richard had arrested bishops, threatened to violate sanctuary and shed innocent blood – or dispensed with the formalities of establishing guilt before proceeding to execution. (Although even the unwaveringly hostile Thomas More allows that Richard permitted Hastings to make a 'short shrift' before execution, suggesting that he was prepared to kill his brother's Lord Chamberlain, but not to damn him.) Formal religion, however, was not the only manifestation of the metaphysical in the fifteenth century. This was also a world of prophecy, curses and witchcraft, and there are signs that Richard felt these influences powerfully in the weeks leading up to the usurpation. It should come as no surprise if he did. Edward IV, after all, had himself claimed the Crown in an atmosphere of supernatural and alchemical fervour, as an Arthurian hero ready to heal the nation after its decline under the maimed Fisher-King Henry VI. Edward's way to the throne had been eased by a military victory at which an astronomical miracle had been observed – the treble suns at Mortimer's Cross. During his reign 'A Prophecy of Merlin Concerning Henry VI' was written, setting out Edward's status as a man of destiny.[53]

Richard's path, by contrast, was strewn with magical as well as political obstacles. In his letter to York of 10 June, for example, when Richard accused the queen and her family and followers of plotting his and Buckingham's death, he added the information that they had, 'as it is now openly knowen, by their subtill and dampnabill wais forcasted the same'.[54] It is difficult today to recapture the genuine sense of menace that could arise from 'forecasting' someone's death, usually by commissioning an astrologer to compile a horoscope. In 1441 Eleanor Cobham, wife of another Duke of Gloucester (and uncle to the king), Humphrey, had been sentenced to life imprisonment on the Isle of Man after being found guilty of treasonable necromancy. Her crime was to have had a horoscope of Henry VI drawn up, showing when he might fall ill, which was interpreted as conspiring the king's death. Of course, the fact that medieval people took such matters seriously does not mean that they were incapable of using such fears for their own ends. But it is also possible that Richard convinced himself that the Woodvilles – whom we have seen he had neutralized politically – still posed a threat, and that news or rumours ('as it is now known') had reached him of Elizabeth Woodville's optimistic invocation of supernatural means to accomplish what was now impossible by any other. In the College of Arms annals, the reference to 'dyvers [who] imagenyd the deyth of the duke of Gloceter' has also been read as 'divined' (the word seems to be written as 'diuagenyd', which could be interpreted either way); this has a similar connotation to the forecasting of Gloucester's letter.[55]

Both Elizabeth and her mother had been accused of sorcery before, around the time of Elizabeth's marriage to Edward and, in her mother Jaquetta's case, as the Earl of Warwick turned against his protégé in 1470. They would be again in Titulus Regius, which mentions the 'sorcerie and witchcrafte committed by . . . Elizabeth and hir mother Jaquet, duchess of Bedford'.[56] Elizabeth's doctor Lewis Caerleon, who certainly visited her in sanctuary, was also an astrologer and astronomer (the modern distinction did not really apply). Among his papers, in a set of lunar eclipse predictions for 1483, he wrote a note to explain that he had rewritten them after his originals had been lost 'per exspoliationem regis Ricardi, ego existens incarceratus in turre Londoniarum' – 'through the pillaging of King Richard, while I was imprisoned in the Tower of London'.[57] If Richard had been going through Caerleon's papers, he may well have been seeking evidence of supernatural meddling.

The best-known witchcraft accusation around the usurpation, first introduced by Thomas More, is the hardest to substantiate as having actually taken place. More describes how, during the dramatic council meeting of 13 June at which Hastings was arrested, Richard accused 'Shoris wife', long after known as Jane (her real name was Elizabeth), of casting a spell to wither his arm, which all 'wel knew . . . was euer such since his birth'.[58] As noted earlier, Elizabeth Shore had been Edward IV's mistress, and then possibly the mistress of Hastings and/or the Marquess of Dorset. She was a rare example of an independent woman who apparently did not rely on marriage to secure her place in society. Although More calls her 'Shore's wife', she had in fact been unmarried since 1476, when her marriage to William Shore was dissolved on the grounds of his impotence, and remained so until at least 1483. Such an unusually self-sufficient woman was vulnerable to accusations of witchcraft. Buckingham's view of the queen mother, reported by Mancini, that 'it was not the business of women but of men to govern kingdoms',[59] reflected more general prejudices.

We don't know, however, whether the specific accusation was ever made against Elizabeth Shore. It forms no part of the Crowland or Mancini versions of the downfall of Hastings. Unlike More, we now know that Richard's arm was not withered. In the words of the authors of the medical report on his rediscovered skeleton, 'The physical disfigurement from Richard's scoliosis was probably slight since he had a well balanced curve. His trunk would have been short relative to the length of his limbs, and his right shoulder a little higher than the left. However, a good tailor and custom-made armour could have minimised the visual impact of this.'[60] Ingenious explanations that Richard might have been suffering an allergic reaction to a 'mess of strawberries', which More tells us he ordered from the Bishop of Ely's garden that day, are only required if we take More at his word that Richard did make the specific accusation against Elizabeth Shore, rather than viewing it as one more brushstroke in a high-coloured production.[61] What is known is that after Richard came to power, Shore was imprisoned in Ludgate. This is just as likely, however, to have been connected to the new king's morality campaign, introduced to contrast his rule to his brother's, and directed against a woman whose notoriously loose lifestyle could be linked directly to the king whom Richard was now working to discredit.[62]

As well as magical impediments, there may have been prophetic encouragements behind Richard's project. Most prophecies that survive from the period are, unsurprisingly, retrospective, composed after the events they 'predict'. This makes them hard to date. The 'Prophecy of "G"', for example, first discussed in connection with the fall of Clarence, is probably a Tudor invention, but it is also possible that it was current around the time of the usurpation, adding to the impression of inevitability about Richard's succession as he took the Crown. Another prophecy, 'In the yere of our lorde', specifically referring to 1483, survives in an early sixteenth-century manuscript, but contains enough mistaken predictions that it might be contemporary. This prophecy invokes the 'trew R' who can crown 'E', so it may reflect a different strand of prophetic thinking, in which Richard's role as Protector is valued – unless it was written early enough for R to mean Rivers. There is also a prophecy of Robert Nixon of Cheshire, which again survives in later versions, but may be contemporary with the 'Richard, son of Richard' whose reign it welcomes ('Thrice happy he who sees this time to come,/When England shall know rest and peace again').

Again, the prophecy's mistakes make it more likely to be contemporary: if it was written after Richard III's time on the throne, why would it predict a 'happy reign' when the very opposite had come to pass?[63]

What effect such prophecies had on Richard's thinking is impossible to say, but it is likely nevertheless that they reflected a far larger current of oral rumour. For a glimpse of the confusion and enervated spread of gossip of these days, there is the nine-line note to be found in the correspondence of the Cely family of wool merchants, but probably written by or for Sir John Weston, prior of St John's and a councillor to Edward IV. 'Ther ys grett romber in the Reme', the note tells us, and passes on news of Scottish invasion, the death of the 'Schamberlayne' (Lord Hastings), the removal of the chancellor, and the death of the Bishop of Ely. It ends with a series of conditionals, including 'Yf the Kyng [Edward V], God ssaffe his lyffe, wher dessett [deceased]/The Dewke of Glossetter wher in any parell.' One of the statements was certainly wrong: the Bishop of Ely had been arrested, but survived into Henry VII's reign. Among the 'ifs', fears for Gloucester and Lord Howard, who was emerging as one of his most loyal supporters, were misplaced, but indicate, perhaps, how rumours originating with Richard's camp about the threat he and his affinity were under mixed with rumours about his enemies.[64] Such talk was clearly having an effect on the populace at large, and we should not dismiss out of hand the idea that its influence extended to Richard himself, persuading him that these were perilous times, in which more than pure politics was pushing him towards the Crown. At the very least, Richard was obviously willing to make use of such rumours to advance his claim and discredit his opponents. In his letter to York and in Titulus Regius, Richard builds his case that he is not simply a better, more legitimate candidate to be king. He is the only candidate whose rights are 'grounded in the laws of God and nature'. Like Edward IV before him, Richard had to work to establish his rights to a disputed title, by appealing to spiritual as well as legal precedent, even after he had begun his reign.

Richard had achieved his goal by a mixture of luck and ruthlessness, and if he made it appear, or even believed himself, that destiny played a part, this only made him a man in step with his times. Modern historians have no time for destiny, but sometimes the more 'structuralist' interpretations of the events surrounding the usurpation can come close to it. When we read that 'The chances of preserving an unchallenged succession were . . . weakened by the estrangement of many of the rank-and-file nobility from . . . high politics, which was partly a consequence of the Wars of the Roses and partly of Edward IV's own policies', it is hard not to conclude that an unforeseeable turn of events is being recast as a predictable one. But without one overriding factor – the actions of Richard, Duke of Gloucester after he took the decision to make himself King Richard III – none of this could have happened. That is, when the same author concedes 'Nor can we discount Richard's own forceful character', he is pitching it rather low.[65]

Edward IV had not left behind a factional fault line waiting to be shaken apart. Richard of Gloucester's decision to usurp was a political earthquake that could not have been forecast on 9 April, when Edward died. After all, Simon Stallworth did not even anticipate it on 21 June, the day before Richard went public. We should be wary of allowing hindsight to give us more clairvoyance than the well-informed contemporary who had no idea 'what schall happyne'. This is not to argue that Richard's will alone allowed him to take the Crown. Clearly, the circumstances of a minority, the existence of powerful magnates with access to private forces, and the reasonably recent examples of resorts to violence and deposition of kings, made Richard's path a more conceivable one. But Richard's own tactics, his arrest of Rivers, Vaughan and Grey, the rounding up of Hastings and the bishops, relied on surprise. If men as close as these to the workings of high politics at a delicate juncture had no inkling of what might happen, the least historians can do is to reflect that uncertainty, and grant that what took place between April and June 1483 may have been conceivable, but was very far from predictable.

The same note of caution should be sounded about the rest of the drama. The fact that Richard's rise was followed by an equally spectacular fall is what made his story such a pleasing subject for tragedians. Not only Shakespeare, but also Thomas More and less well-remembered practitioners such as Thomas Legge in his *Richardus Tertiu*, approached Richard's reign as a moral tale following the familiar arc of hubris and nemesis. It has been argued that 'with the probable exception of Julius Caesar and his contemporaries, Richard III appeared on the Elizabethan stage more often than any other historical or legendary figure'.[66] The facts are undeniable, but that does not give us an excuse to render them as unalterable by those who lived through them. As always with Richard, as from almost his first breath, the most likely turn of events was not the one that came to pass.

5

'Her comyth Richard the third'

In 2005 the Parliamentary Estates directorate commissioned works to make a new visitor reception at Westminster Palace. Investigations began on the great flight of stone steps at the south end of Westminster Hall, which had settled by more than 6 inches. Beneath the steps, workers discovered the elaborately carved and arched marble remains of the legs of the King's Table, behind which the King's Bench, in fact a throne, was placed in the Middle Ages. The table had been broken up during the Commonwealth, though how it came to form part of the fabric of the room it once dominated remains a mystery. The throne itself has not been found, but the discovery of the remains of the table – which, when it sat at the south end of the Hall, was a 12-foot-long marble slab – was a reminder of the significance since the reign of Henry III of this most venerated piece of royal furniture. The model for the throne, fifty years older and far more important than St Edward's chair in Westminster Abbey, was the throne of Solomon. Like the biblical chair, it was carved with lions. It was a permanent demonstration that, like Charlemagne and the emperors of Byzantium, who also had carved marble thrones, the English king was a sovereign judge. From this chair, the king dispensed justice and displayed himself wearing his crown at the coronation banquet and other formal 'crown-wearings'. When the Lord Chancellor sat there with the Great Seal in the king's absence, he had the authority to seal writs and charters. As Richard III took his place there on 26 June 1483, his reign began.[1] The hostile Crowland chronicler describes the way he 'thrust himself into the marble chair', but there was no need for that. Richard had nearly always displayed a proper reverence for and understanding of the importance of the ceremonial. At the moment of proclaiming his royal estate, he could act with all the decorum required.

Sitting where his father had not dared to sit when Richard was eight years old, the new king gave a speech appealing to all classes of his new subjects, 'but speciall the Lawyers of this realme',[2] not only because he spoke from the place that represented the king as supreme legal authority but also, one suspects, because he wished from the outset to emphasize his own legitimacy. According to Thomas More, Richard backed up the spirit of reconciliation with a special gesture to Sir John Fogge, one of Edward IV's leading councillors and treasurer to the royal household, who had married a cousin of Elizabeth Woodville, and had recently taken sanctuary. 'In the sight of the people, [Richard] tooke him by the hand.'[3] The gesture, if More is to be trusted (and Fogge was appointed a Justice of the Peace in Kent soon afterwards), marks the beginning of a concerted effort to put the ship of state back on an even keel after the storms of the past two months. Richard named the date of his coronation, too, the ceremony that he expected to set the seal on his actions, and to impress all his subjects into obedience to their new ruler. How much harder it would have been to 'exclude' Edward V if he had already been crowned and anointed? The significance of the ceremony is difficult to overestimate. Not only was it a public confirmation of a king's right to rule. It was, through the ceremony of anointing, a confirmation of God's blessing. Accordingly, Richard lost no time. He was to be crowned on 6 July, only ten days away. Although some preparations would already have been in train for the much postponed coronation of Edward V, getting such a lavish ceremony ready at such short notice was extraordinarily demanding, not least for the keeper of the Great Wardrobe, Peter Courteys, who had even less time to provide the necessary robes, by 3 July. An added complication was that this was to be a double coronation, of Queen Anne as well as King Richard, the first such since 1308, when Edward II and Queen Isabella were crowned: not, perhaps, the most auspicious precedent.

On 3 July the force Richard had summoned from the north as Protector arrived at London, to be greeted on Finsbury Fields by a king. Although some Londoners mocked the shabby turnout of these soldiers, they were left in no doubt that Richard had the muscle to back up the audacity of his assumption of power. The next day Richard and Anne took the short trip, probably by barge, from Baynard's Castle to the Tower of London, the traditional residence of kings before their coronation. The fact that Richard adhered to this precedent is a reminder that there was nothing sinister – on the face of it – about Edward V's having been moved to the same royal palace in anticipation of the same ritual. In the days after the delivery of Richard of York there, the brothers had been 'seen shotyng and playyng In the Gardyn of the Towyr by sundry tymys'.[4] But not long afterwards, as Mancini writes, they had been withdrawn to 'the inner apartments of the Tower proper, and day by day began to be seen more rarely behind the bars and windows, till at length they cease to appear altogether'. The 'last of his attendants whose services the king [Edward] enjoyed' was his personal physician, John Argentine, who had studied in Italy and seems to have communicated directly with Mancini. Argentine reported that 'the young king, like a victim prepared for sacrifice, sought remission of his sins by daily confession and penance, because he believed that death was facing him'.[5] A note of 18 July from Richard's signet records confirms payments to servants 'for theire services doone to oure derrest Brothere late king whoome god absoille and to Edward Bastard late called king Edward the Vth'.[6] By that time, Edward V had no more need of the fourteen men named. It seems extremely unlikely, too, that Richard would have allowed his path to cross with his nephew's as they briefly occupied the same palace premises. Their trajectories were now set in firmly opposite directions.

While the blameless Edward confessed his sins, perhaps dwelling anxiously on the words of the penitential psalm, *quia defecerunt sicut fumus dies mei et ossa mea sicut gremium aruerunt* ('for my days have failed like smoke, and my bones have dried like firewood'),[7] he cannot have failed to notice the signs of other, more public and elaborate rituals being performed within the same walls in anticipation of his uncle's coronation in his place. Just as Richard himself had done in 1461 as a boy before his brother Edward IV's coronation, a group of esquires chosen to be made Knights of the Bath went through the solemn process of ritual shaving, cleansing and robing, before being presented to the new king in their red, black and white garments, to be dubbed knights and given their spurs.

Two banquets were held in the two days before the whole coronation party set out from the Tower on 5 July in a great procession towards Westminster

Abbey. This was the most public part of the whole sequence of events, and as well as the Knights of the Bath, the king and queen were attended by London aldermen, heralds, the holders of the great ceremonial offices of Earl Marshal (the new Duke of Norfolk, Lord Howard, already in possession of the title that had been one of Prince Richard of York's), Lord Great Chamberlain (the Duke of Buckingham), and the bearer of the king's sword (most likely the Earl of Surrey, Howard's son). The king walked under a canopy made of red and green baldachin – silk embroidered with gold thread – carried by three groups of four knights in a relay, changing over at several stopping points on the route through the City. The slow pace gave observers the chance to see the procession, and there were presentations along the way. For all his hostility, Mancini gives no impression that there was any public show of dissent towards Richard: 'with bared head he greeted all onlookers, who stood along the streets, and himself received their acclamations'.[8] Sixty knights and 100 esquires followed the king, preceding the queen's section of the procession, which was similarly attended. When they arrived at Westminster, they participated in more presentations, with the lords and household officers, before taking supper at Westminster Hall. The king took a ritual bath before retiring. The coronation day itself would start early, the first order of business at 7 a.m. in the Great Hall, when the fully attired king and queen would receive a delegation of clergy.

Richard then joined a great procession into Westminster Abbey, preceded by three ceremonial swords: Curtana (the squared-off Sword of Mercy) and the two swords of temporal and spiritual justice, carried unsheathed. The king was dressed in the prescribed finery – including satin surcoat and mantle, the latter lined with miniver and ermine – but unshod. The coronation included not only ceremonies of crowning and anointing but also one of vestment. By the time he left the abbey, Richard was many pounds heavier, weighed down not only with the imperial crown, the orb and the sceptre, but, in his third set of clothes for the day (his coronation robes were put on and removed in the abbey), dressed in 15 yards of purple velvet, a cap of estate under the crown, lined with ermine and the fur from lambs' legs ('bogy shanks'), and sandalled. The queen's costume was even more lavish, calling for 56 yards of cloth.[9]

The most important parts of the ceremony itself were carried out by the aged Thomas Bourchier, Cardinal Archbishop of Canterbury – 'unwillingly', according to Mancini.[10] It was the archbishop's duty to present the king to the people, and to receive their assent in the time-honoured manner: 'whereunto the people shall say with a great voice Kinge Richard, Kynge Richard, Kinge Richard ye ye ye soo be it'.[11] Bourchier may in fact not have been up to that task, leaving it to the Bishop of St Asaph, Richard Redman, but he did put the coronation oath to Richard – spoken for the first time in English – anointed him with the holy oil of St Thomas Becket, and set the crown on his head, before doing the same for Queen Anne. For all the awe-inspiring display of wealth and power, there was almost equal emphasis on duty, obligation and humility before God. The swords were reminders of the administration of justice tempered with mercy, the oath of the king's duty to his subjects. Richard spent a period 'grovelyng' before the altar while the archbishop read a prayer, *Deus humilium visitator*, 'God who visits the humble'.

The newly crowned couple returned to their chambers in Westminster Hall, taking breakfast, before appearing again at a lavish banquet. Each course was greeted with trumpets. The most striking ritual of this part of the day was when the king's champion Sir Robert Dymmok – serving in a role first claimed by his great-great grandfather in 1377 – rode into the Hall on a horse trapped to the ground in red and white silk. A herald announced that Sir Robert was ready to 'maintain with his body' King Richard's claim against anyone who dared dispute it. The assembled company shouted for King Richard and the champion threw down his gauntlet three times before making his obeisance and departing. No one challenged the king that day.

Celebrations continued for the following week, including, if custom were followed in this as it was in the other parts of the ceremonial, a series of jousts in Westminster Abbey Sanctuary (where Elizabeth Woodville and her daughters, apparently passed over by the turn of events, remained). It was a week, too, of feasting and most likely of dancing. After three months of uncertainty, fear and violence, of arrests, shocking claims and rumours, the observation of every letter of established royal procedure for the coronation was Richard's clearest way of demonstrating that the kingdom was returned to safe hands. He made sure, too, that the air of celebration, and of open-handed hospitality, was maintained. The accession of Richard was presented as the answer to the nation's prayers, the rescue of a kingdom from the ignominy of an illegitimate ruler. Perhaps Richard really believed that was what he had achieved. It was certainly important for him to persuade his new subjects that he had. To make the same point to the realm at large, the king set out on a royal progress, beginning in Greenwich, before making his way via Windsor and Oxford through the Cotswolds to Gloucester, into the Midlands where he visited Coventry and Leicester, then northwards, to Nottingham and York.

This extended tour, lasting from July until late September, when Richard made his way back from York, is worth comparing with the earliest days of Edward IVs reign, if only to emphasize how much more tranquil it appeared to be. While Edward had mustered an army shortly after his accession, and marched north to fight the Lancastrians in the greatest battle of the Wars of the Roses, at Towton, Richard was able to disband his armed retinue and make an untroubled progress around a newly claimed realm. He was greeted by pageants as he travelled, and gave grants to the towns he passed through.[12] At Oxford he heard learned disputations at Magdalen College, rewarding the participants with money and venison, and gave a 50-mark annuity to the Franciscans.[13] There was further largesse at Gloucester, Tewkesbury and York, among other stops. Richard had utterly thrown off the mourning clothes and attitudes of two months ago, spending £180 on 'silks and other goods . . . to the use of the said lord King and the lady Queen Anne his consort'.[14]

Richard made sure to refuse all gifts, which was good publicity and was one way in which he would try to differentiate himself from his brother, whose 'unlawful invencions and inordinate covetise, ayenst the lawe of this roialme' he would later denounce in an Act of Parliament.[15] Actually, Edward had managed to set royal finances back on an even keel after the disastrous waste and inefficiency of Henry VI. Richard was, initially, the beneficiary of the better practice instituted by Edward, though it is true that expenditure towards the end of Edward's reign had outstripped income. But that expenditure was hardly frivolous. It included the outgoings on maintaining Berwick (£700 a month recorded by the exchequer), the fleet against Crèvecoeur (£3,670), and the cost of other preparations for resuming a French war; and after Edward's death, there was his funeral, the next king's coronation (that the identity of the king changed didn't affect the expense of the ceremony, which would only have become greater when a queen's coronation was added to the bill), and the cost of Richard's progress and the crown-wearing and investiture for the Prince of Wales at York that followed. There was nothing frivolous about spending so much money on display, either. It was a vital part of medieval kingship. And for the time being, all Richard's references to Edward were still to a lamented brother, not a licentious spendthrift. In grants issued on Richard's progress, Edward is 'the famous prince of moost noble memorie . . . our brothere whom god assoylle [absolve]'.[16]

The words of one of the king's councillors, Bishop Thomas Langton of St David's, who was with his master at this time, have often been taken as an indication of Richard's popularity in the first months of his reign. In the course of a letter to the prior of Christ Church, Canterbury, principally concerned with advice on the importation of claret, Langton remarked that Richard 'contents the people wher he goys best that ever did prince; for many a poor man that suffred wrong many days have be relevyd and helpyd by hym and his commands in his progress'. Langton was likely to be well disposed towards the king. He had been a trusted servant of Edward IV, but when Edward died, the bishop threw in his lot with Richard rather than Edward V. Langton had been made a bishop two days before Richard's coronation, at Richard's request. He revealed in the same letter that he already had hopes for a more prestigious post: 'I trust to God ye shal here such tythings in hast that I shalbe an Ynglish man and no more Walshe – Sit hoc clam omnes [mum's the word]'.[17] His faith was rewarded, though not as quickly as the bishop seems to have anticipated. He was translated to the see of Salisbury in 1485, and stood by Richard to the end, initially incurring the displeasure of Henry VII. But Langton was a survivor, of the type regularly thrown up in these years of transferable loyalties. He died in 1501, five days after Henry had promoted him to the pinnacle of an ambitious churchman's career, the archbishopric of Canterbury.

So it might not surprise us that someone who had already gained from Richard's patronage, and whose career shows him to have been a discerning trimmer to prevailing political winds, should declare 'On my trouth I lykyd never the condicions of ony prince so wel as his; God hath sent hym for the wele of us al'. This is not to say that it was not Langton's honest opinion, written in a private letter: merely that, as someone close to the king who had clearly not been put off by the manner in which he claimed the throne, Langton was likely to approve of his master's showing on his progress, during which Richard without question demonstrated all the generosity and munificence expected of a Renaissance prince.[18] More intriguing is the bishop's reference, for which he breaks again into Latin, directly following this encomium, only portions of which survive (they appear from the manuscript to have faded rather than being deliberately excised), 'al neque . . . voluptas aliquis regnat'.[19] This has plausibly been reconstructed as 'sensual pleasure holds sway to an increasing extent . . .',[20] a glimpse, perhaps, of a less strait-laced court than Richard's later attacks on the immorality of his brother Edward's household and those connected with it might give us to expect. There is a sense from these days that Richard was revelling in his new position, and it would not be a surprise if his courtiers reflected that exuberance in their own conduct.

'The Princes in the Tower'

The revels were bound to end. It was while the king and queen were on their triumphal progress that the first indications of resistance to the new regime emerged. On 29 July Richard was staying at Minster Lovell in Oxfordshire, the manor of his old companion Francis Lovell, who had been made viscount at the beginning of the year, chief butler of England by Richard when he was Protector, and chamberlain when Richard became king. That day Richard wrote to the chancellor, John Russell, Bishop of Lincoln: 'We understande that certaine personnes of such as of late had taken upon thaym the fact of an enterpruise as We doubte nat ye have herd, bee attached, and in warde. We desire and wol you that ye doo make our lettres of commission to such personnes as by you and our counsaill shalbee advised forto sitt upon thaym and to procede to the due execucion of our lawes in that behalve. Faille ye nat hereof as our perfacte trust is in you.'[21] This perhaps deliberately vague letter has been linked to a London conspiracy to free the 'Princes in the Tower' – and, less convincingly, to the murder of the princes themselves.[22] If it were the latter, this would make Richard more cynical than even Shakespeare portrayed him, ordering the dispatch of the princes (the deed characterized as 'the fact of an enterpruise') and then abandoning the perpetrators to their fate, or rather, consigning them to it ('the due execucion of our lawes'). Even if such a move were not beyond Richard, the needless complication and risk involved in exposing his assassins to some form of trial would surely have dissuaded him from such a course of action. Byzantine complexity governed by the need to base theories on the only extant evidence is the hallmark of most detailed explanations of the murder – or survival – of the princes. Most of them have the virtue of not being capable of being disproved, but that puts them in the class of theories known to philosophers as 'Bertrand Russell's teapot'.[23]

Much more likely is that these were participants in a rising in the capital, as described by the Elizabethan antiquary John Stow and the contemporary French chronicler Thomas Basin. Stow seems to have seen an indictment that no longer survives, and names four men who were executed for their part in the plot. Of the accused, the two best connected were John Smith, groom of the stirrup to Edward IV (whose commander, Sir John Cheyne, had been master of the king's horse), and Stephen Ireland, wardrober in the Tower. The conspirators' plan, Stow writes, was to create a diversion by setting fires in 'divers parts of London, which fire, whilest men had beene stanching, they would have stolen out of the Tower, the prince Edward, and his brother the Duke of Yorke'.[24] Stow also tells us that the ringleaders had written letters to gather support, and names the Earls of Richmond and Pembroke, that is Henry Tudor and his uncle Jasper, which if correct must mean that the Tudor involvement was initially envisaged as part of a Yorkist restoration, though it may be a misdating of a later appeal. According to Basin, fifty Londoners were involved in the diversion. Neither Basin nor Stow say why the rebellion failed. It is impossible to be certain that Richard's letter relates to this conspiracy – just as with the disappearance or otherwise of the princes, because a document survives that *could* be applicable to the case, this does not mean it is – or how much support the plot really gathered. But any such manoeuvre would have concentrated the king's mind on the unfinished business of his nephews. While they lived they would, like Henry VI before them, be the focus of potential rebellion. Richard had experienced at first hand the consequences of allowing a deposed king to live. He had been involved alongside his brother Edward in the loss of a kingdom, exile, two bloody battles and subsequent reprisals to overturn the 'Readeption' of Henry VI. Who can doubt that if Edward IV, and indeed his younger brother, had fallen into Lancastrian hands at this time, they would have been killed themselves? The lessons of 1471 were clear.

So did Richard order his nephews' death? The short answer is that we don't know. All the ingenious theorizing and posthumous mudslinging that have made the fate of the 'Princes in the Tower' a historical cause célèbre depend on the lack of concrete evidence. The passage of time is not the only reason for this uncertainty. Contemporaries did not know what had happened to the sons of Edward IV either. Mancini's hesitancy, following his description of the preparations he had heard Edward V had been making for his own death – 'whether, however, he has been done away with, and by what manner of death, so far I have not at all discovered' – is echoed in the account of the Silesian diplomat, Niclas Von Popplau, who visited Richard's court in 1484. Von Popplau makes one apparently unequivocal remark – 'King Richard has killed King Edward his brother's sons, so that not they, but he was crowned' – before contradicting himself: 'However, many people say – and I agree with them – that they are still alive and are kept in a very dark cellar.'[25] Whenever a new scrap of 'evidence' comes to light, it is almost always an addition to this hearsay material. The statement in the College of Heralds annals that 'this yer King Edward the vth, late callyd Preince Walys, and Richard duke of Yourke hys brother, Kyng Edward the iiij sonys, wer put to deyth in the Towur of London be the vise [on the advice] of the duke of Buckingham' gives us another suspect for the crime, but it is only evidence of what 'an earlier tradition' might have preserved of the rumours of the period. That is, if we grant that this manuscript is based on a contemporary commonplace book (as suggested by its editor), then this is what a 'London citizen' *thought* had happened to the boys, and who *might* have been behind it. It is no more evidence of what did happen than is today's gossip about royal parentage or the whereabouts of Lord Lucan. The same can be said about the records of Edward V's death date as reported in a Colchester Oath Book or the princes' fate as discussed in a fifteenth-century genealogy probably written in 1485, where the king's nephews are described as 'snatched from the light of this world', again 'with the advice of the duke of Buckingham'.[26]

In January 1484 such rumours had already crossed the Channel, where the French chancellor, Guillaume de Rochefort, warned the Estates General at Tours, faced with their own minority in the form of the thirteen-year-old Charles VIII, who had succeeded Louis XI, that the French nobility must not follow the example of England: 'Think, I beg you, what happened in that land after the death of king Edward, that his children already grown up and remarkable, were killed with impunity, and the royal crown was passed, with the people's blessing, to their killer.'[27] The fact that only rumour convicted Richard of the murders at the time might have been the result of a deliberate policy. Richard had proved himself a consummate manipulator of public opinion already, from his dissemination of Woodville plots to the promotion of apparently varying reasons to exclude Edward V and his brother from the succession. After displacing Edward, Richard found himself in a unique position. Previous usurpers had made a point of producing the corpse of the deposed king to prove that he was dead and head off rumours of survival behind which new rebellions could take shape. In some cases it frankly hadn't worked. Richard II was reincarnated in the person of one Thomas Trumpington, who took the role in abortive attempts to rally support against Henry IV. Even Edward II was persistently rumoured to have survived the indignities of Berkeley Castle – a story persuasive enough still to be given credence in some quarters today.[28] But generally, a dead body, openly displayed as Henry VI's had been, made a strong case.

As has been pointed out many times, however, Richard never produced his nephews alive to scotch rumours of their death, or dead to scotch rumours of their survival. In this case, however, the benefits of displaying the corpses would have been outweighed by the horror at confirmation that the new king had done away with them. Previous victims after deposition had been convincingly portrayed as tyrannical, or at least ineffectual to the point of endangering the realm (and it had taken an awfully long time for Henry VI to fall victim to that, fairly accurate, characterization). It had also been publicly alleged that earlier deposed kings had died of natural causes. None of those strategies would work against a minor who had been afforded no chance to reign, let alone rule, and his even younger brother (one 'natural' death might have been believed, but two would stretch credibility). This is the strongest circumstantial argument that, despite the absence of securely identified bodies, then or subsequently, they were dead by 1484. While producing the boys alive might have given succour to potential rebels, once the rebellion turned its focus to Henry Tudor, it could have been an effective way to torpedo his candidature. The conclusion seems difficult to avoid, that Richard didn't show that the princes were alive, because they weren't. Richard's most effective strategy in the circumstances was for the princes to disappear and for his subjects to be unsure what had happened to them. That would explain why foreigners, beyond Richard's reach, are the only contemporary source of stories of their death. Richard's own subjects could not risk making their fears public. Richard never denied killing the princes because no one, as far as we know, ever asked him directly if he had. How could they? Here is another example of the likelihood that 'intolerance to uncertainty syndrome' is a misdiagnosis for Richard III. In the case of his nephews, he seems to have thrived on it.

It is likely that no literary or documentary discovery will convincingly settle the case of Edward V and Richard of York. Certainly, the balance of probabilities is very firmly for the princes' premature death, and against Richard III as their murderer (or rather director of their murder). The London conspiracy had given him the motive to remove permanently candidates who, despite being excluded in law, would clearly continue to command support. (The fact that the princes' cousin, Clarence's son the Earl of Warwick, did not command such support, at least in Richard's lifetime, is sufficient argument against the question of why, if Richard did away with Edward and Richard of York, he let Warwick, like the princes excluded in law but with a plausible blood claim, remain alive in his hands.)[29] The princes were under lock and key by Richard's command, and guarded by his men (Edward's own servants having been dismissed). Despite the suggestion that the Duke of Buckingham was involved, which is perfectly plausible given his record of support and ruthlessness in the usurpation, it is just as unbelievable that the duke would take responsibility for ordering the murder of the children against the king's wishes – or even in spite of his ignorance – as that Richard himself should have been personally responsible, without the permission of Edward IV, for the death of Henry VI in similar circumstances.

None of the written evidence that has been uncovered to this day 'proves' that the princes died at this time, or that Richard ordered their deaths. But nothing exists to contradict the very strong likelihood that this is what happened. For those who see their task as exonerating or condemning Richard there is enough ammunition for either argument. To historians used to dealing with shades of grey, the evidence has, time and again, pointed overwhelmingly at the princes' death before the end of 1483, and to Richard's guilt. It is not simply professional jealousy that seems to have made the case for Richard's responsibility for the murders (as distinct from his all-round evil à la Shakespeare and Thomas More) the province of academic historians from James Gairdner to Charles Ross – and the case for clearing him that of gifted amateurs from Horace Walpole to Josephine Tey. It may just be a matter of habit. Academic historians, too, are tolerant of uncertainty.

There is something other than literary evidence potentially available, which has come to seem all the more tantalizing in the light of the science so effectively brought to bear on the rediscovered remains of Richard himself in Leicester. These are the bones contained in a sarcophagus in Westminster Abbey, with the Latin inscription translated as: 'Here lie the relics of Edward V, King of England, and Richard, Duke of York. These brothers being confined in the Tower of London, and there stifled with pillows, were privately and meanly buried, by the order of their perfidious uncle Richard the Usurper; whose bones, long enquired after and wished for, after 191 years in the rubbish of the stairs (those lately leading to the Chapel of the White Tower) were on the 17th day of July 1674, by undoubted proofs discovered, being buried deep in that place. Charles II, a most compassionate prince, pitying their severe fate, ordered these unhappy Princes to be laid amongst the monuments of their predecessors, 1678, in the 30th year of his reign.'

The story behind the discovery is actually more complicated. To begin with, this was one of several discoveries of the alleged remains of Edward V and Richard of York. For example, Sir George Buck, one of Richard III's earliest rehabilitators, wrote in 1619 that 'there were certain bones, like to the bones of a child being found lately in a high desolate turret in the Tower. And they suppose that *these* bones were the bones of one of these young princes. But others are of opinion *that* this was the carcase and bones of an ape which was kept in the Tower.'[30] There were also two separate finds, by some accounts, of skeletons walled up in secret chambers in the Tower – one, reportedly, during the incarceration of Sir Walter Raleigh. The discovery made in 1674, however, which ended up in the royally commissioned monument, designed by Sir Christopher Wren, is the most promising of an undistinguished sample. The location of the discovery 'in the rubbish of the stairs . . . leading to the Chapel' (St John's) poses problems if it is to be squared with Thomas More's account, the most detailed of those written at least within living memory of the events, though not of course by a contemporary. More writes that the boys' remains, while indeed initially buried 'at the stairyre foot . . . vnder a great heape of stones' (though giving no indication as to which stair), were subsequently dug up and moved by a priest, on Richard's orders ('Loe the honorable corage of a kynge'), who wished to give them a more fitting burial. The priest 'secretly entered them in such place as by the occasion of his deathe, whiche onely knew it, could neuer synce come to light'.[31] If that was nearer, or within, consecrated ground, then the location of the discovery in 1674 is unhelpful. It may be worth noting in connection with this story that an ambassador to Burgundy after Richard's death told Margaret of York that he could show her servant the chapel where the princes were buried, though as she was busily promoting Perkin Warbeck as the surviving younger prince, Richard of York, at the time, the story is, like all others in this matter, not to be relied on very strongly. None the less, if More's account was being used as corroboration for the bones being found at the bottom of a staircase, his second point – admittedly based on hearsay – was conveniently ignored.

It might be hoped that the rigours of modern science would throw a little more light on the subject of the remains in the abbey. Only once have scientists been permitted to disinter the remains, when, in 1933, the Professor of Anatomy William Wright and the abbey's archivist Lawrence Tanner were given six days to examine the contents of the sarcophagus. Their conclusions, published in 1935, were that the skeletons belonged to two boys, of the correct ages, one of whose skulls showed evidence of a bloodstain, which 'together with the complete separation of the facial skeleton, lends support to the traditional account of the manner of the brothers' death, suffocated "under a feather bed and pillows, kept down by force hard into their mouths"'.[32]

Perhaps unsurprisingly, these astonishingly confident and convenient conclusions have been questioned in subsequent discussion of the scientific evidence. A thorough review of the study, first published in 1987, pointed out that Professor Wright had failed to establish the sex of the skeletons (he assumed they were male) and was far too blasé about their age given the parameters of the techniques available to him. As for the 'bloodstain', not only did Wright offer no firm evidence that the stain actually was blood (it may have been caused by a rusty nail), the idea that suffocation causes staining of the skull in this way 'is not borne out by experience'.[33] Not long after this damning conclusion, however, another scientist, Dr Theya Molleson, offered a contrary view, based on the dental and skeletal evidence discernible from the photographs taken for Wright and Tanner's investigation. Molleson did feel able to conclude that the skeletons were male, related, and of the correct age range. In this she was assisted by the excavation and examination of Anne Mowbray's body in Stepney in 1965, Richard of York's cousin and child bride. Molleson also argued for a time of death for the princes 'some time in the year 1484', which is a little late by most historians' reckoning, but still very much on Richard's watch.

Without further investigation, DNA testing or radiocarbon analysis, of the sort to which Richard III's own bones have now been subjected, it seems unlikely that scientists will be able to provide a firmer answer than historians to the question of whether the remains in Westminster Abbey do belong to the 'Princes', let alone who was responsible for their deaths. For understandable reasons, the abbey authorities have repeatedly rejected requests for another disinterment. A spokeswoman explained in 2013 that 'The recent discovery of Richard III does not change the abbey's position, which is that the mortal remains of two young children, widely believed since the 17th century to be the princes in tower, should not be disturbed.'[34] The most we can say is that the possibilities that they are the remains of Edward V and Richard of York, and that they died while Richard was king (which, as both their sovereign and the man entrusted with their care, at least makes him partly culpable for their deaths), have not been discounted by the various scientific attempts to make the bones speak.

It is tempting to hive off the 'Mystery of the Princes in the Tower' as just that, a historical whodunnit that is a distraction ('a vexed question that has received too much attention' in the words of one eminent historian)[35] from the more 'serious' business of the high politics of the final phase of the Wars of the Roses. But apart from the offensiveness of dismissing the murder of children as a distraction, this would be a serious misreading of history. The fate of Edward V and Richard of York mattered to contemporaries very much, and if we want to understand Richard and his time, it should therefore matter to us. This was not just because many believed that Richard had killed the legitimate king and the heir presumptive. It was also because they were children, and 'innocents', as both the compiler of the *Great Chronicle* and a Welsh bard writing shortly after Bosworth called them. This was a violent age, though until 1483 the level of political violence, in Edward IV's 'second reign', had decreased dramatically. Nonetheless, killing children was no more 'acceptable' in Richard's day than it is in ours. The Feast of the Holy Innocents was not only a holy day in the Church (also known as Childermas), the biblical episode which inspired it formed one of the most dramatic scenes in mystery plays performed throughout the country, from East Anglia to York. Richard's alleged crime was the crime of Herod. Nor did the high incidence of child mortality make medieval adults more sanguine about individual deaths; the reports of Richard and Queen Anne's own grief at the death of their son, Edward of Middleham, in 1484, is demonstration enough of that. Richard's short reign was dominated by a struggle to prove his legitimacy. If it was a crisis of legitimacy that eventually brought about his downfall, its origins surely lie in the alleged murder of Edward V, aged twelve, and his brother Richard of York, aged nine.

'To shine as a king'

Whatever fate awaited Edward V and Richard of York, Richard III was not sufficiently disturbed by the rising in their favour to cut short his progress. A plot had been foiled, and the deluded diehards behind it were being dealt with. Perhaps the bastard sons of his eldest brother were being dealt with, too, or perhaps they had a little more time. There were other indications of disaffection. John Welles, who had been part of the force sent to confront Edward Woodville's fleet, rebelled, and on 13 August the 'guyding & oversighte' of his lands were granted to Lord Scrope of Bolton, with instructions to his tenants to cooperate 'As ye wolle advoid our high displeasure at youre perilles'.[36] While at Leicester on 18 August, the king suddenly sent to his armoury for 2,000 Welsh bills 'in all haste'. But this did not stop Richard from continuing the other serious business of kingship, not only showing himself and his family to the people but carrying out the wider duties of his office. It was while on his progress that he began to

formulate a foreign policy. The first continental contacts the king made were
with France and Brittany, initially to deal with an outbreak of piracy on all
sides – in part a sign of the breakdown in international relations that resulted
from England's domestic troubles, though some acts of piracy, after a period of
abeyance during Edward IV's reign, had started up again in the Channel before
his death. Richard sent deputations to Francis, Duke of Brittany, and to Philippe
de Crèvecoeur, 'Lord Cordes', who had been preying on English shipping, and
was himself the victim of English retaliation. Crèvecoeur's career shows that
protean loyalties were not the sole preserve of the English aristocracy. He is
unusual in having been awarded the highest chivalric orders of Burgundy and
France – the Golden Fleece and the Ordre de Saint-Michel – in each case, in
recognition of his service against the other. One constant in his life, however,
whether in the cause of Burgundy or France, was his hostility to the English. In
ordinary circumstances, Richard is more likely to have exacted retribution for
Crèvecoeur's attacks; that was the mission with which Sir Edward Woodville's
fleet had been entrusted before Richard's moves against the Woodvilles had
turned it into a rebel fleet and its admiral into an outlaw. Now, however, was
not a good time to open hostilities with foreign powers, and it was a delegation
with instructions to negotiate that was dispatched to Boulogne in July. The
offer was both the restitution of two impounded ships, lying at Sandwich, and
a discussion of any further 'damages and interesse'.[37]

Richard made similar approaches to the Duke of Brittany, offering to convene
a conference to discuss attacks on shipping since Edward IV's death, an event
that seemed to have persuaded 'diverse folkes of simple disposicion' that all
treaties between the two powers no longer applied. In the case of Brittany,
there were two further complicating factors, though the relative importance
Richard apparently assigned to them may surprise us at first. Duke Francis had
taken in Sir Edward Woodville when he had escaped from Portsmouth with
two ships and a large amount of cash. Richard's envoy to Francis, Dr Thomas
Hutton, was instructed to 'fele and understand the mynde and disposicion of
the duc anempst [towards] Sir Edward Wodevile', and whether he was planning
any 'enterprise out of land upon any part of this realme'.[38]

Another long-term guest of the duke, however, who for a time had been put
under the fifteenth-century equivalent of a control order after negotiation with

Edward IV, was not mentioned in the instructions passed to Dr Hutton that July. Henry Tudor, the dispossessed Earl of Richmond, had been in Brittany with his uncle Jasper, former Earl of Pembroke, since their escape from Tenby in Wales in September 1471. Henry was not so much a king over the water as a trifling noble of at best the second rank, who had struggled vainly to gain recognition of his right to an earldom and succession to his mother's estates, never mind any grander ambitions. True, Edward had tried to get custody of Henry and Jasper, but that may have been as much because Louis XI was also trying to secure them, and could have used them as a way of interfering in English politics, as for any threat they posed on their own. At the time of Edward's death, Henry's mother, Margaret Beaufort's lobbying had begun to work on the king, and it seemed likely that Henry would have at least been able to return and enter into his inheritance. By the time Duke Francis replied to Richard on 26 August, however, after Hutton's visit, the Earl of Richmond had moved up the agenda. Louis XI's attempt to compel Francis to give him up and Francis's appeal for support to resist Louis, take up most of the letter.[39] The request for 4,000 English archers could not be answered lightly, as it would be tantamount to declaring war on France. Nevertheless, it demonstrated how Richard's accession had made Henry Tudor a more valuable commodity, even if he was not yet a pretender to the throne.

Richard did have an exchange with Louis himself at the beginning of his reign. Edward had been making serious preparations for reopening hostilities with France before his death. Richard could not know that Louis, too, had little time to live, and that his death would put the French monarchy into its own minority crisis. Richard's correspondence with Louis in August reads like a feeling-out exercise that did not have time to yield results; in response to Louis's informal offer of friendship, Richard mentions the threats made by the French to English merchant shipping, and asks what Louis's intentions are. The fact that this letter was conveyed not by a liveried herald, as the first of Richard's letters had been, but by 'one of the grooms of my stable', was likely a calculated insult. It has been described as a unique surviving example of Richard's sense of humour.[40] Certainly, it strikes a rather different note from the breathless enthusiasm of the then Duke of Gloucester's thank-you letter to Louis for the artillery piece. The model for the joke was possibly the famous exchange between Henry V and the Dauphin Louis before the Agincourt campaign.[41] Whereas that grim joshing about tennis balls and cannon balls was occasioned by a firm intention to wage war, however, what Richard needed was peace. He had neither the resources nor, most likely, the domestic backing, to emulate his (Lancastrian) predecessor. If he did mean to offend Louis, it was not a well-timed joke. What would have been gained if Louis *had* taken offence? A more consistent diplomat than Richard would have continued the pleasantries while preparing an alternative policy (in fact what Richard himself did in the case of Scotland). Anyone who had read the letter containing the jibe would not have been surprised when Richard sent a fleet to Calais to confront French piracy.[42] Richard, too, seems to have had second thoughts. Two days after the facetious letter, he sent another, this time via his herald Blanc Sanglier, to plead with Louis not to interfere with a consignment of wine destined for the royal table.[43]

Because personality so rarely flashes through official correspondence, it is tempting to read too much into this moment. But if we compare it to Richard's earlier dealings with the King of France, when he had pointedly stayed away from the ceremony at Picquigny and then accepted royal hospitality, we begin to see the actions of a man with an acute sense of honour and personal dignity – but not the light touch that served subtler rulers, such as Louis XI himself and to an extent Edward IV (not to mention Henry VII) so well. When Richard descended to gesture politics, he does not always seem to have figured out the consequences of the gesture. Few would accuse Louis, the 'Spider King', of a similar fault. Such moments may be rare, but they give us an alternative picture of Richard to the scheming Machiavellian of Shakespeare, Polydore Vergil and Thomas More. Richard had shown himself more than capable of dissembling, but his pretence had tended to conceal imminent bold action, and to operate over the short term. As we have seen with the events surrounding the usurpation, his actions do not necessarily fit into an overall scheme, and make more sense as a series of reactions to circumstances, among which those of Richard's *amour propre* being threatened should not be discounted. When the pioneer printer William Caxton decided to shed his Woodville connections and seek the king's patronage in 1484, his translation of *The Ordre of Chyvalry* or *Knyghthode* was an extremely appropriate choice. An earlier translation, *The Game and Playe of the Chesse*, might have taught Richard more.[44]

In the event, Louis is unlikely to have seen either letter, as he died at the end of August. He was succeeded by his thirteen-year-old son Charles, and France was governed by a regency until the young king turned twenty-one. For the time being, this allowed Richard to rest easy about prospects of war with France, though it would not take long for the regency government to resume Louis's schemes. The respite was a stroke of luck, not a tactical triumph.

Richard's other continental contacts were with Burgundy and Spain. Philip of Austria (the titular Duke of Burgundy, but in fact a minor, under the regency of Maximilian I) wrote to complain about English piracy and murder perpetrated against his merchants trading out of Nieuwpoort, Ostend and Dunkirk. Isabella of Castile, on the other hand, was the only unequivocally supportive continental contact Richard received, her letter on 8 August outlining her hopes for a 'good and firm' peace between Castile and England, and offering to form an alliance to attack Louis XI. Isabella gave an unexpectedly personal view of her motives in an oral message delivered by her ambassador, Jofre de Sasiola, duly recorded by Richard's secretaries. She had been insulted by Edward IV, who had rejected her offer of marriage 'and taking to his wiff a wedowe of England'. With Edward dead, Isabella finds herself 'retournyng to her naturall kinde disposicion'.[45] Although Richard knighted Sasiola in September, nothing came of the proposal for an alliance. Two years after this, Isabella gave birth to her youngest daughter, Catalina, by her husband and fellow monarch Ferdinand of Aragon. We know her better as Katherine of Aragon, later the bride of two sons of Richard's nemesis, Henry Tudor. Sasiola was appointed to negotiate the first match in 1492, though in the event he was too ill to travel. On the wider stage of European dynastic politics, the eruptions of 1483–5 in England did not change time-honoured ways of doing business for long.

All these contacts in effect left Richard's position unaltered. He could hope to reduce piracy, but any alliance offered would only provoke opposition from other powers. Still, stasis was preferable to too much activity for the time being. It is noticeable that none of Richard's correspondents offered a direct challenge or threat. None seemed disturbed enough by the circumstances of Richard's rise to power to voice any objection to it. All addressed him with the usual formal and cousinly royal courtesies, as 'treshault et trespuissant' or 'illustrissimo atque potentissimo'. Richard would have been under no illusions that the King of France and the Dukes of Burgundy and Brittany were all potential threats, but none of them, for the moment, was an immediate one. He trod carefully with Francis of Brittany's request for armed assistance, for despite his flirtation with offending the French king, he did not seek confrontation with France from the beginning.

Scotland was different. Hostilities had not really ceased since Richard's campaign with Albany in 1482, and, as we have seen, one of Edward's final pieces of legislation was to grant Richard palatine rights over new acquisitions in the Scottish borders. Rather than attempt to take advantage of potential uncertainty in England by launching an assault, however, James III of Scotland was keen to restore peace. He wrote to his 'righte trusty and welbeloved Cousing' in August 1483, proposing 'abstinence of werre' for eight months, leading to 'peas in tyme commyng'.[46] Richard replied encouragingly, and arrangements were made for a peace conference that was eventually held in Nottingham Castle in August 1484. But by that time Richard had already supported a renewed attempt by Albany and the Earl of Douglas on the Scottish throne. It was only after that venture had failed that Richard's actions caught up with his diplomatic gestures. In most respects, this can be seen as the conventional play of power politics between two kingdoms that were never at peace for long, particularly when continental alliances were brought into play. The consequences for Richard were by no means catastrophic, though it is noticeable that there was a Scottish contingent in the Earl of Richmond's invading army in 1485. By a combination of bad luck, bad timing and bad judgement, Richard eventually faced a formidable coalition of foreign powers gathered against him. Although domestic opposition would remain important, it was Richard's unsuccessful handling of foreign policy – his inability to inhabit the role of European as well as English monarch effectively – that turned out to be the most serious failure in his short reign. But looking at the opening moves he made in the flurry of diplomacy while on his progress in summer 1483, it is hard, without the benefit of hindsight, to spot any glaring errors in Richard's approach. It didn't work in the end, but this is not to say it is obvious that he could have done anything differently to better effect.

A coronation, a royal progress, a clutch of letters to the crowned heads of Europe: Richard was doing what medieval kings did, and as kings needed their heirs to be recognized, it was to his son Edward of Middleham, aged between nine and eleven (around the same age as Richard of York), that he turned his mind next. He summoned the boy from Middleham, in a 'chariot' with two men paid 6s 8d to run alongside him, according to the royal accounts.[47] When Edward arrived at Nottingham, he was proclaimed on 24 August as Prince of Wales and Earl of Chester. There was nothing precipitate about this, or about the fact that Edward was still a minor. Edward IV had waited even less time to proclaim his son as Prince of Wales – a son born in sanctuary in Westminster while his father was in exile – when the child was only seven months old. But Richard's decision to hold a ceremony of investiture in York, the culmination of his northern progress, seems to have been made fairly late. It wasn't until a week after Edward's arrival that Richard sent for the necessary robes for the ceremony to the long-suffering Peter Courteys. The keeper of the Great Wardrobe obliged, sending up yards of velvet, satin and cloth of gold, together with banners and pennons in their hundreds, and 13,000 'Quynysans' (cognizances, in other words badges, with Richard's white-boar device – a striking indication of the expected turnout for the ceremony).[48]

For those who wish to follow Thomas More's account of Richard, and who see in almost every transaction of the early part of the reign a hint of what they take to be its most important event – the disappearance of the princes – the Great Wardrobe accounts for this period provide another bone to chew over. Specifically, they mention that 'the parcels of stuff noted' found their way to Sir James Tyrell, Richard's Master of Horse. Tyrell is the man whom More writes confessed to the murder of the princes in Henry VII's reign, shortly before being executed for different offences. Whether or not any credence should be given to this private confession reported by hearsay, the Wardrobe Accounts do not assist us to come to a conclusion. Sir James was with Richard in York, and while it is just possible that he made the extremely long round trip in person to collect these goods in the very short time available – and therefore might have been in London around the time of the princes' disappearance and thus to have had a hand in it – it is extremely unlikely. As the modern editors of the Wardrobe Accounts put it, the clothing and other stuff 'could have been delivered by a menial', and John Frisley, 'clerc of thoffice of the Stable', is named in the Wardrobe Accounts as the man who actually handled the material. They do not allow that sending the Master of the Horse as an errand boy might have been a cover story, but that may be because the errand would have struck contemporary observers, as it has struck later ones, as a very odd one, more likely to draw attention to the journey than explain it away. If Tyrell had anything to do with the disappearance of the princes, he almost certainly did not manage the deed while acting as the king's personal shopper.[49]

There can have been almost no time to dole out and fit all this finery before, on 8 September, the feast of the Nativity of the Blessed Virgin, following a service at York Minster, Edward of Middleham 'was created Prince by the Lord King in the presence of all'[50] during a ceremony and banquet at the Archbishop of York's palace lasting more than four hours. Added to Edward's traditional spheres of influence in Wales and the Marches was the Lieutenancy of Ireland. A deputy, the Earl of Kildare, was appointed for at least a year.

The York ceremony, at which the king and queen wore their crowns, came at the end of a week of civic receptions, solemn processions and pageants. Richard's secretary John Kendall, who wrote to York on 23 August, was confident that the citizens would more than match the welcome parties of other towns and cities that Richard and Anne had passed through, and so it proved. The Crowland chronicler did not doubt that Richard was at home in the north, 'where he had spent most of his time previously'.[51] On his progress he had seen only displays of loyalty and celebrations of his majesty, which he had answered with gracious words, grants and charters, while refusing offers of money and gifts himself. The 'fact of an enterpruise' attempted in London had been tidied up and had barely broken his stride. In retrospect, these days in York would have seemed the high point of his reign, less than three months old. Richard had some successes after York, not least in the way he dealt with the next challenge to his authority. But did he ever recapture the optimism of those days, the sense that here was a prince among his people, able 'to shine as a king in the midst of his nobles and to adorn the greater and lesser stars in the whole court of heaven with his outstanding light' – as he put it himself?[52]

A facsimile of Richard's own addition to a letter to the Lord Chancellor, 12 October 1483, in which he describes the Duke of Buckingham (in the penultimate line) as a 'falsse traytor'.

'The most untrewe creature lyvyng'

Richard left York on 20 September and began to travel south, via Pontefract, Gainsborough and Lincoln. He had known even before he arrived in York that there were disturbances in some southern counties, and on 28 August he had appointed the Duke of Buckingham and the Duke of Norfolk to a commission of oyer and terminer into treasons and felonies in London and the surrounding counties.[53] The initial focus for these risings seems to have been the same as for the London rising described by Basin and Stow: the liberation of Edward V and Richard of York. But from around mid-September the rebels had a new champion: Henry, Earl of Richmond. This 'false traitor and rebel' – in the words of the Act of Attainder published in Richard's parliament in January 1484 – was the son of Edmund Tudor, Henry VI's half-brother (who died before Henry was born), and Margaret Beaufort, now married to Lord Stanley. Margaret was a descendant of John of Gaunt, Edward III's son, by his mistress Katherine Swynford, whom Gaunt only married after their four children had been born. The children were legitimated in 1396–7, though when this was confirmed by Henry IV, he had spelt out that this did not mean they stood in the line of succession – *excepta dignitate regali*. This connection, however, was the extent of Henry Tudor's blood claim to the throne. That was why his supporters, among whom numbered many loyal servants of Edward IV, were encouraged by his pledge to marry Edward's eldest daughter Elizabeth of York, still in sanctuary with her mother at Westminster. When rumours spread that Edward IV's daughters might escape sanctuary and flee the country in disguise, 'the sacred church of the monks of Westminster and the whole neighbourhood took on the appearance of a castle and a fortress and men of the greatest strictness were appointed as keepers there by King Richard'.[54]

Henry Tudor himself was still in Brittany, where he had been for the past twelve years. The reason that the rebels turned to such an unlikely figurehead was clear to those who wrote about it afterwards: 'a rumour arose that King Edward's sons, by some unknown manner of violent destruction, had met their fate. For this reason, all those who had begun this agitation, realising that if they could not find someone new at their head for their conquest it would soon be all over with them, remembered Henry, earl of Richmond, who had already spent many years in exile in Brittany'.[55] The London chronicles, also written after Richard's reign, agree that the rebellion took place because the king had 'put to silence' his brother's children, though they do not mention the Earl of Richmond at this point. Henry's mother, Margaret Beaufort, had long campaigned for her son to be allowed to return from exile, and to take up his earldom, but it was only in the circumstances of August to September 1483 that she and those around her seem to have conceived that a greater prize was now available. If Richard III's rise to the throne was one governed as much by luck as calculation, the contingent rise of the man who became his nemesis was a dual forecast of the longest odds.

It is not clear when Richard was made aware that the Earl of Richmond had decided to claim the Crown. On 12 October, at Lincoln, the king sent a letter to his chancellor requesting the Great Seal, which he would need to issue summons to raise an army against the spreading rebellion. There was a different surprise in this letter: the 'rebelle and traytoure' whom the king now had to meet was the Duke of Buckingham. The man who had been instrumental in clearing Richard's path to power, and who had benefited most materially from it, had betrayed him. The letter was dictated to a secretary, but the king wrote a bitter postscript himself, scrawling up the side of the manuscript: '. . . Here loved be god ys all well & trewly determyned & for to resyste the malysse of hym that hadde best cawse to be trewe the duc of Bokyngham the most untrewe creature lyvyng whom with Godes grace we shall not be long tyll we wyll be in that partyes & subdewe hys malys. We assure you was never falss traytor better purvayde for . . .'.[56]

The last phrase shows how deeply Richard felt the sense of betrayal, and Buckingham has not been treated kindly by history. Richard may have suffered a more comprehensive blackening of his reputation, but for the man who was among the first to resist him, there has been no equivalent rehabilitation. Subscriptions to a Duke of Buckingham society would not, one suspects, raise enough for a dinner, let alone an excavation. But as in the case of Richard himself, and in the same way without requiring the duke to be exonerated of his crimes, there is another way of looking at Buckingham than the quintessentially self-interested late-medieval aristocrat, insanely ambitious and totally disloyal, the 'most untrewe creature lyvyng'. In those weeks between August and October 1483, what were the choices open to Buckingham, as he began to receive intelligence of a growing movement against the man he had helped to put on the throne, and darker rumours of the fate of the boy whom Richard had displaced? Buckingham was in Brecon on the Welsh border, so the news of the southern risings would have taken some time to get to him, and the apparent extent of the rebellion would have given him pause. The composition of the rebel numbers has been comprehensively analysed, from the Act of Attainder published after the rising in 1484 as well as other sources. As with any large-scale rebellion, the discernible motives for joining were not the same for all. Some were Woodville supporters – and in the case of Lionel, Bishop of Salisbury, Thomas Grey, Marquess of Dorset and (more circuitously) Thomas St Leger, whose daughter was married to Grey's son, they had family connections. A very small minority had never been reconciled to the Yorkist regime, so might have been expected to join a sizeable rebellion to unseat a Yorkist king. An example was Edward Courtenay, heir to the Lancastrian Earldom of Devon. Men like these were either already known opponents, or were so closely related to the Woodvilles that they would have been under suspicion already.

Of much more concern to Richard were the large numbers of former servants of Edward IV who joined the rebellion. These were the very people whom Richard appears to have hoped, by keeping them in place both as royal servants and men of local influence, would ensure stability through continuity. Sir William Stonor, for example, had been one of Edward IV's knights of the body, and his brother had been on the French campaign that ended in the Treaty of Picquigny. Stonor was the man who had received Simon Stallworth's anxious letters in June, but he had remained a trusted local leader in the Thames Valley. He was well known to another landowner in the same region, Richard's companion Viscount Lovell, who addressed him as 'cousin' and who had exchanged 'tokens' with his wife as long ago as 1478. As Richard was writing to his chancellor from Lincoln in October, Lovell sent a letter to Stonor. He asked him not only to respond to the king's general call to arms, but to meet up with Lovell's own men at Banbury and bring them to him at Leicester. Instead, Stonor joined the rebels. Lovell's letter is the last in the collection that was preserved when it fell into Crown hands, possibly as a result of legal proceedings caused by Stonor's rebellion.[57]

The cause of men like these – a hitherto unthinkable coalition of arch-Yorkists and arch-Lancastrians – was, surely, what it appeared to be: they believed Richard to be an illegitimate king. All his efforts to establish himself as rightful king, from the moment he sat in Solomonic splendour on the King's Bench, had not convinced them. As Richard's progress had shown, he knew how to be popular, especially but not exclusively in those areas where he was a familiar lord. But he could not will himself into being legitimate. To some, not only was Edward IV's heir preferable despite his tender age and the aspersions cast on his birth. Once Edward V appeared to have been removed, even a candidate as remote as Henry, Earl of Richmond – specifically discounted from the succession, a man whose family were supporters of Henry VI, against whom many of the rebels and their families had fought – was more desirable. There may well have been some revulsion at Richard's apparent murder of innocents, but it is clear that even before the rumours of that crime spread, a significant portion of the ruling members of society across the south had come to the conclusion that Richard was not their rightful king.

While it seems unlikely that Buckingham had a crisis of conscience inspired by such reasoning, the scale and spread of the defections, together with the rumour of the princes' demise, gave him a decision to make. Unlike Lovell, he was not by the king's side, nor did he have a very long-standing bond with Richard. The high price of his loyalty had only recently been paid. Finally, Richard had asked Buckingham to act as jailer to a man who, later writers such as Thomas More and Polydore Vergil allege, was able to persuade him that Henry Tudor was a viable alternative to Richard: John Morton, Bishop of Ely, whom Richard had put under Buckingham's guard after the arrests in the Tower on 13 June. It has been suggested that Buckingham's own royal blood persuaded him that he could aim for the throne himself. (He could trace his descent from two of Edward III's sons, John of Gaunt and Thomas of Woodstock, whose royal arms he had borne since 1474, though Thomas had been attainted as a traitor.) But, even allowing for the questionable judgement of a man who had been conspicuously excluded from Edward IV's inner circle, this seems less plausible, if not impossible. If that was Buckingham's plan, it would have been a long-term one, involving the unseating of not one king, but two (Richard and Henry VII); no rebel proclaimed Buckingham as king in Richard's place, as was specifically done for Henry. The idea popularized by Shakespeare that Buckingham's acquisitive streak had been denied by Richard over a particular inheritance is weakened by the fact that Richard had in fact granted him that inheritance.[58] The most plausible explanation for Buckingham's decision to rebel, therefore, is that he thought he was joining a winning cause. Buckingham did not instigate the rebellion of 1483, and led it only in the sense that he was the senior noble who took up arms. Rather, he appears to have decided that he had no choice but to follow it.

With his apparently vast sources of manpower both from his own family estates and those lands granted to him since the usurpation, Buckingham's involvement might have proved overwhelming to Richard. If the duke had managed to lead a force from the Western Marches to challenge the king on a third front, together with the attacks from the east and south, he could have been instrumental in putting a second usurper on the throne within six months. Buckingham's involvement, however, was one of the factors that led to the rebellion's failure. That was because, for all his resources, he was unable to muster any significant force, and may have convinced those who did not join him to resist the rebellion. He seems to have been an unpopular landlord ('a sore, hard-dealing man', according to Polydore Vergil), and the powers of persuasion that had served him so well in convincing eminent Londoners to back the Duke of Gloucester seem to have deserted him when it came to getting Welshmen and the people of the Welsh Marches to take up arms. Buckingham also failed to persuade the other important landowners in the region, Lord Stanley and Sir Gilbert Talbot, who had control of the lands of the earldom of Shrewsbury, to join him. That Stanley refused to help Buckingham may be surprising, considering his wife was Margaret Beaufort, who had devoted her life to promoting the son of her first marriage, who now had a realistic chance of success. But Stanley was able to wait longer than Buckingham to decide which way to jump (a tactic he would famously continue to employ up to and including the Battle of Bosworth). A letter survives, written on 18 October, from a connection of Stanley's son Lord Strange, giving the information that Strange had 10,000 men ready to march, but the writer didn't know where. It is likely that Strange and his father were biding their time. The Stanleys had not put Richard on the throne, so if a rebellion did succeed in making Henry Tudor king, he did not have to expect to be an enemy of the new regime if he hadn't actively supported it, unlike Buckingham.[59]

The Earl of Richmond did put to sea, backed by money from the Duke of Brittany, who had not been offered the help he requested from Richard and consequently decided to support his rival. But the timing was all wrong. Henry only launched his would-be invasion on 30 October. By that time, both in the south and the west, the rebels were on the run. In the west, Buckingham's element had never really got off the ground. He marched out from Brecon, either north, straight towards Weobley, or first in an easterly direction, towards Monmouth and the Forest of Dean. But whichever route he chose, he was unable to gather enough support. The weather also took a hand, with torrential downpours making the Rivers Severn and Avon impassable. Realizing he had failed, Buckingham entrusted his son to a nurse, and fled north. He was betrayed in Wem, Shropshire, by a retainer, Ralph Banastre, whom Richard later rewarded. On 1 November he was brought to Salisbury, where the king was staying, overseeing the operation against the western rebels. Richard refused to see a man whose disloyalty seems to have shocked him deeply. On 2 November, in the market square, the Duke of Buckingham was beheaded.

The parts of the rebellion that had looked better supported also began to fail. One reason for that was the efforts of Thomas Howard, the new Duke of Norfolk, and his son, the Earl of Surrey, in London, Kent, East Anglia and Sussex. Howard held London, always the key to any ultimately successful rebellion. He had written to John Paston about 'the Kentysshmen [who] be up in the weld [Weald] and say that they wol come and robbe the cite, which I shall lett [prevent] yf I may'. Whether Paston's provision at Howard's request of 'six talle felaws in harnesse' helped deter the rebels we cannot say, but the duke held out.[60]

Richard, too, brought the fight to the rebels. He issued a proclamation from Leicester on 23 October against the ringleaders, including Buckingham, Dorset, and the two bishops John Morton (Ely) and Lionel Woodville (Salisbury). This document also contained the first sign of what would become a theme in Richard's public pronouncements for the rest of his reign. His opponents, he announced, were not only 'rebelles and traytours', but morally degenerate, 'orible adultres and bawdes'. Thomas Grey, Marquess of Dorset, 'hath many and sundry maydes, wydowes and wifes dampnably and without shame devoured, defloured and defouled, holding the unshampfull and myschevous woman called Shore's wife in adultery'.[61] As with self-appointed guardians of the nation's morals through the ages, Richard denounced depravity with a peculiar relish. Whether this was a true reflection of his own character or merely a political decision to stake his claim on the moral high ground is difficult to say. Richard's own illegitimate offspring show that he was not a puritanical exception to the behaviour of his class, but it may be he had convinced himself that his enemies really were morally suspect. Certainly he decided that it was worth trying to convince his subjects that they were. He marched out of Leicester the following day and headed westwards, via Oxford, Salisbury, Dorchester and Bridport, arriving in Exeter on 8 November, and scattering rebels in Dorset and Wiltshire.

Henry Tudor turned back at the beginning of November, around the same time that one group of rebels proclaimed him as their king at Bodmin in Cornwall. By the time Richard himself arrived in Exeter, the rebels knew they had failed. Henry Tudor wasn't coming, Buckingham had been executed, and the rebels in the south and east were being steadily reduced by the Duke of Norfolk and his son, the Earl of Surrey. In Sussex, some resisted for a few days at Bodiam Castle, which belonged to Thomas Lewkenore, who had been made a Knight of the Bath at Richard's coronation, but further west, large numbers of rebel leaders had already taken flight. For many, unlike previous rebellions, there seems to have been no desire for pardon and reconciliation – or perhaps no hope of them. This was a rising aimed at overthrowing the king, not the traditional medieval protest movement aimed at 'evil counsellors'. Of course, the civil war had made such events more common, but a spontaneous agglomeration of different parties gathering behind the standard of a largely unknown pretender was a new thing. It was a coalition created by the unique circumstances of Richard's rise to power, which struck enough constituencies as manifestly wrong to coalesce a group with varying reasons for disaffection, ranging from outraged loyalists to calculators of the main chance.

For any leading rebels who fell into Richard's hands, and for those who refused to give in when they had an opportunity, there was no mercy. Thomas St Leger was executed at Exeter on 13 November. Six more men were condemned to death when Bodiam finally fell. Of those who escaped, 'as many of them as could find ships in readiness', salvation lay in Brittany.[62] Among those who made the crossing were the Marquess of Dorset, the Bishops of Exeter, Ely and Salisbury, as well as numerous members of the gentry, former servants of Edward IV whose fortunes rose under Henry, such as Giles Daubeney (made Baron Daubeney in 1486), John Cheyne (Baron Cheyne, 1487) and Robert Willoughby (Baron Willoughby de Broke, 1488). The figure of 500 men fetching up at Henry Tudor's court in exile may be high, but it was certainly in the hundreds.[63]

For all his febrile rhetoric, Richard's response to the rebellion was not especially harsh, though there surely would have been a higher death toll if some of those who escaped had been captured, among them men named in the Leicester proclamation. But that proclamation contained the seeds of royal mercy, too, promising that 'no yoman nor commoner thus abused and blynded . . . shall not be hurte in their bodies ne goodes if they withdrawe them self from their false company and medell no ferther with theym'. When the dust had settled, more prominent rebels also received pardons, even ones as intransigent as Thomas Lewkenore, though he, like many 'repentaunt subgetts' who returned to Richard's favour, did so on the basis of sureties offered by his friends for his good behaviour, of 1,000 marks.[64] The quality of Richard's mercy was weighed out in silver. Sir John Fogge, the royal servant whom Richard had gone out of his way to conciliate right at the beginning of his reign, had been a rebel leader in Kent. Although Fogge was attainted and his lands were confiscated in 1484, by the beginning of 1485 he, too, managed to obtain a royal pardon. These were in essence attempts to ensure good behaviour from men in whom the king no longer felt able to place his trust. This reaction to the rebellion does not speak of a thirst for revenge, and compared to the 'harvest of heads' that had attended previous rebellions, it was relatively restrained, but Richard still had a problem to solve. There was now, if not a vacuum, then a significant void, in the arrangement of local government. Local landowners who had rebelled had been instrumental in running the country around them on behalf of the king. Richard needed to fill the void quickly.

Some have argued that Richard acted too quickly, redistributing rebel lands before any act of attainder had been passed to deprive the holders formally.[65] In November and December 1483 a series of commissions were given authority to assess rebel holdings, which were rapidly reassigned. This was not unprecedented. Richard himself had benefited from similar royal dispensing with formality when he was granted portions of Warwick's and Montagu's estates years before either was formally attainted. Warwick and Montagu, however, had committed manifest treason, 'appearing against the king in arms when the king himself was present with his banner displayed' at Barnet.[66] The same could not be said of all the rebels whose land Richard redistributed in 1483. When John, Lord Scrope of Bolton, received his commission to 'arrest and imprison all rebels in the counties of Devon and Cornwall, to take their castles, lordships, manors, lands, chattels and possessions into the king's hands' on 13 November 1483, while similar orders were concurrently issued for Somerset, Dorset, Southampton, Wiltshire, Oxfordshire and Berkshire, this gave notice of a far more sweeping confiscation policy than had been put in place before formal legal proceedings hitherto.[67] There was no way that all those who had joined the rebellion throughout these counties would fall under the definition of manifest treason. In fact, Richard had not had to confront rebels himself at all, despite summoning an army to do so. His mere presence at Salisbury and Exeter had had the desired effect.

There were sensible reasons for proceeding more formally. If the party who had been dispossessed, or their relatives, wanted to challenge the confiscation, they would usually have to wait until after an act of attainder had been passed, with its proviso for such challenges. Equally, any new landholder would prefer to have undisputed title, not a temporary claim. Richard's policy certainly did cause problems. Take the case of his solicitor, Thomas Lynom, to whom Richard granted a manor in Bedfordshire forfeited by the rebel Sir Roger Tocotes. The manor was seized at the end of January 1484 and granted to Lynom at the beginning of March. That left no time for due diligence, and in this case, the manor turned out to be the property not of Tocotes but of his widow, Lady St Amand, who had come into it through her first husband. The manor should not therefore have been forfeited and Lynom was not able to secure it.[68] The fact that Richard decided to act first and tidy up later does not mean he had a cavalier attitude to due process. Of course his usurpation had been a series of unforeseeable legal transgressions – from the arrest of Rivers's party, to his demand for their execution, to the killing of Hastings. But, as has been observed many times before, Richard was in more normal circumstances a scrupulous upholder of the law; that was what made the events of April to June 1483 so shocking. The elaborate legal buttressing he had constructed for his claim to the throne, with its emphasis on right rather than might, only had force if the law itself was shown to be more than a rubber stamp on royal prerogative. After the rebellion of 1483, however, such large numbers of office-holders in a vital area – especially along the south coast, in Kent, Sussex, Hampshire, Dorset, Devon and Cornwall, from which Richard could expect any renewed invasion attempt – had forfeited their roles that the king felt the need to re-establish his authority quickly through trusted lieutenants, if his success in seeing off the rebellion was to last.

What exercised some contemporaries more than the legal precedents for Richard's behaviour were the people he chose to do his bidding. The rebellion showed that his attempt to maintain continuity with Edward IV's reign, to keep large numbers of local office-holders in place, had manifestly failed south of the Thames. It is estimated that as many as half of the ninety-eight rebels attainted in 1484 were former servants of Edward IV. After the redistribution of land and offices, more than two-thirds of new sheriffs, to take an example of one vital arm of royal government, were new appointments. The replacements would be men whom Richard could trust but, crucially, they would struggle to command local support. That was because they were not local men themselves. Overwhelmingly, they came from the north, and those estates where Richard had built up his power and affinity as Duke of Gloucester. As far as the Crowland chronicler was concerned, the policy didn't work: 'what great numbers of estates and inheritances were amassed in the king's treasury . . . ! He distributed all these amongst his northerners whom he planted in every part of his dominions, to the shame of the southern people who murmured ceaselessly and longed more each day for the return of the old lords in place of the tyranny of the present ones.'[69]

Northerners were by nature no more 'tyrannical' than southerners, though it is possible that some treated unfamiliar tenants more peremptorily than those they had known for generations. Magnates were reallocated estates with some frequency in the fifteenth century: Richard's own case of being moved from Wales to the north was not exceptional; compare the experience of William Herbert, the Earl of Pembroke, whom Edward IV not only erased as a Welsh landowner, providing him with a dozen Somerset manors and a single manor in Dorset in compensation, but whose title was removed, too. In 1479 Herbert became the Earl of Huntingdon. Yet lower down the social hierarchy, where the new men would be expected to conduct local business regularly, a 'plantation' of outsiders on such a scale, in a volatile political situation, was almost bound to be resented. It is to this divisive policy that many modern historians have traced Richard's own tyranny: not to the cruelty and savagery of Shakespeare's monster, but to the exclusion of a whole swathe of society from their traditional place. Tradition, as Richard knew, counted for almost everything in his world. A king who was willing to ride roughshod over it, on this view, was a tyrant.[70]

A comparison with Richard's policy in Wales and the Marches shows that where he could draw on local influence, he did. The level of forfeiture in the region was much lower, and principally affected major estates and offices because of the Duke of Buckingham's involvement. Despite having ancestral holdings in the region, the massive expansion granted to Buckingham during the protectorate and into Richard's reign made him the interloper. His failure to draw support either from the local gentry or neighbouring magnates for the rebellion probably demonstrated that fact. After Buckingham's death, Richard reintroduced William Herbert as a major land- and office-holder in the region. Herbert's surrender of the earldom of Pembroke (in turn taken from Jasper Tudor), during Edward IV's reign, had been made so that Edward could build up the power of the Prince of Wales's council. Herbert's reintroduction partially re-established a family with strong regional roots – even if Richard did not allow the Earl of Huntingdon to reclaim his Pembroke title. Herbert, who also married Richard's illegitimate daughter Katherine (his first wife, Mary Woodville, had died in 1481), stayed loyal, despite the approaches of Henry Tudor, and the fact that their connections dated far enough back that a match had once been mooted between Henry and Herbert's sister, Maud. Another beneficiary of Buckingham's fall was the Stanley family. Sir William Stanley was made chief justice of north Wales, and his brother Thomas, Lord Stanley, took Buckingham's office of Constable of England (he was also made Knight of the Garter), and they received extensive lands in Wales and along the Welsh border. That this policy turned out to be less effective in ensuring Stanley's loyalty had more to do with the Stanley trademark equivocation (and the fact of Lord Stanley being Henry Tudor's stepfather) than with their being outsiders in their newly extended holdings.

Elsewhere, Richard likewise did not favour 'northerners' out of some regional prejudice. The list of his other major supporters who benefited after the rebellion shows this. Richard granted lands to the Howards, Duke of Norfolk and Earl of Surrey, to his nephew John, Earl of Lincoln, to the Earl of Nottingham, and to three men who had risen with him and served him well on the way: Francis Lovell, James Tyrell and William Catesby. These were not northerners, and where their established interests coincided with the estates at his disposal, Richard matched them up. Relying on men with regional connections where that was possible did not necessarily solve Richard's problems. But the Stanley example is another warning against reading Richard's reign backwards, from its known end at Bosworth. The Crowland chronicler's judgement about the failure of the northern 'plantation' was the first to do so, and just because later research to a great extent bears him out in showing how southern gentry society began to resent the post-rebellion settlement, it does not make it any clearer how Richard might better have dealt with the issue.[71] He needed trustworthy servants in a vital area of the country from which many local candidates had discounted themselves by their own conduct. Given time, some at least of the 'planted' northerners could have established themselves and become accepted figures in local southern society, though in the long term there would still have been a difficulty with men whose holdings were split between north and south. But magnates like Richard himself as Duke of Gloucester had addressed that, by consolidating holdings in one region through swapping distant estates for ones nearer a power base. On a smaller scale, with royal backing, such a solution could have been effected for some, at least, of the planted northerners. From

Christmas 1483 to around July the following year, during which time no new threat emerged, most importantly from across the Channel, the 'failure' of the northern plantation could not have been predicted with any certainty.

This was also the period in which the outlines of Richard's overall approach to being king begin to emerge. In essence, these months show what sort of king Richard might have been if the threat to his monarchy had receded – or more plausibly, given the unlikelihood of that threat simply disappearing, how Richard might have continued to rule if he had been victorious at Bosworth. After the events of August to December 1483, Richard's regime was already likely to be much altered from what he seems to have envisaged at the time of his coronation. He would not simply be able to rule through his brother Edward's personnel bar a few, mostly Woodvilles, whose antipathy could be predicted. The overwhelming fact of Richard's reign remained that it was threatened almost from the beginning, because of the way he had seized the throne. This means that all his actions as king can be seen through the prism of wanting to attract support. But he knew that there was more to being king than clinging on to power. Richard did have a vision of kingship. In the first half of 1484, before the net began to close, he showed most clearly what that vision was.

6

'In one body there are many members'

In the book that William Caxton chose to reprint in 1483, before he had managed to secure the new king's patronage, there were some appropriate lines for Richard, now returning to his capital in triumph. In Caxton's own translation of this Latin work by an Italian friar, *The Game and Playe of the Chesse*, we read: 'for as moche as the kynge holdeth the dygnyté above alle other and the seignorye royall, therfore hit apperteyneth not that he absente hym long, ne wythdrawe hym ferre by space of tyme from the maister siege of his royame'. If the king acted in the prescribed manner, he could reap the benefits: 'and is attributed to hym the victorye of the knyghtes, the prudence of the juges, the auctorité of the vycayrs or legates, the contynence of the quene, the concorde and unyté of the people. So ben alle thise thynges ascribed unto the honour and worshyp of the kyng in his yssue, whan he mevyth first'.[1]

The fortunes of the new king's attempt to re-establish 'concord and unity' must have been keenly followed at Westminster, not only by Elizabeth Woodville and her daughters, who remained in the abbey sanctuary, but by Caxton himself, who lived and worked at the sign of the Red Pale in the abbey precincts. We know as much because Caxton sued Richard for pardon afterwards. The capital had, after the initial failed attempt to rescue the princes, not risen against the king, and it is unlikely that Caxton had been actively involved in the rebellion. But his decision to add his name to the lists of those petitioners (numbering 1,100) who wished to emphasize their loyalty to the king shows how suspicion could fall on anyone connected, as Caxton had been, with the previous regime. Richard had won, but his triumph had altered assumptions about loyalty on both the king's and his subjects' sides. It certainly could not be taken for granted.[2]

None the less, on 25 November 1483, like his brother Edward after the Battle of Towton, and with rather less bloodshed, Richard returned to his capital not only a crowned king but a victorious one. He 'came to London triumphant over the enemy without a battle'.[3] The Crowland chronicler contrives to make the absence of war sound like cheating, but Richard could be content with the outcome, if not with the escape of so many rebels. He arrived to official fanfare. The Journal of the City of London's Court of Common Council itemizes groups of city guildsmen over 400 strong in total, from haberdashers to goldsmiths, decked out in murrey, who gave him a reception, just as they had for Edward V and his uncle when they entered the capital earlier in the year. York may have counted on a special bond with Richard, but London tried to maintain its relationship no matter who was on the throne. Over the coming months, they would loan or grant the king more than £4,000 for the defence of the realm. Yet, when that proved unsuccessful, they greeted the new king Henry VII with equal pomp and offered him 1,000 marks when they met him in Shoreditch, fresh from his victory at Bosworth Field.[4]

In time, Richard's solution to the question of governing the south beyond London would be put to the test. But for now, the king could resume the business of ruling, which he had been carrying on with such apparent success before he was so rudely interrupted by those who questioned his right to do so. Richard and Anne celebrated their first Christmas and Epiphany as king and queen at Westminster, during which the king ran up a huge bill for silver plate (given as gifts) and jewellery (for their own use) of £764.[5] In January 1484, Richard travelled into Kent, visiting Canterbury and Sandwich. It has been suggested that Richard's choice of resting place outside Canterbury, at Harbledown in a tented pavilion (known as 'le Hale in le Blean'), on the pilgrims' route, might indicate that he was doing penance for the murder of his nephews. But as Edward IV is recorded as having stayed in the same place on numerous occasions, this is not persuasive: Richard, despite numerous ingenious attempts to prove otherwise, does not seem to have gone in for subconscious admissions of his guilt. He did refuse a gift of 50 marks from the city authorities, but didn't say no to 'four large fatted boars, twenty fatted rams, and twenty of the fattest capons'. The purse in which the money was offered was given instead to Thomas Langton, which no doubt made the king rise even further in that bishop's estimation.

If the king's immortal soul had been on his mind at St Thomas's shrine at Canterbury, by the time he went to the cinque port of Sandwich he had returned to more earthly considerations. There he bought 164 suits of armour from a Breton and a Genoese merchant, at 5 marks apiece.[6] He would have heard by now that Henry Tudor, Earl of Richmond, had on Christmas Day sworn to seek the hand in marriage of Edward IV's eldest daughter, Elizabeth of York. This would be Henry's way of strengthening his tenuous claim to the throne by associating himself with the House of York, to which many of his supporters were attached. Elizabeth was still in sanctuary at Westminster. Henry's move gave Richard a decision to make, but there were more pressing matters of state to deal with first.

On 9 December writs of summons had been issued for a parliament to be held on 23 January 1484. The recipients in towns and boroughs could have been forgiven for treating them with scepticism. This was the third parliament to be summoned since Edward IV's death, but the first that actually went ahead. As the proceedings of Richard's only parliament proved, he needed it, not so much for the reason that most of his predecessors had called parliaments, to raise money – though that was not neglected – as for the stamp of authority it could offer a monarch whose claim had been openly challenged months after his accession. The chancellor, John Russell, Bishop of Lincoln, at last got his chance to deliver a sermon he had written three times. In the painted chamber of the Palace of Westminster, in front of the king seated on his throne, Russell 'memorably declared and announced the reasons for summoning the aforesaid parliament, taking as his theme: "In the body there are many limbs, but not all have the same function". In which words he gravely and very astutely explained the fealty which subjects of the king and the functions individual members owe to the principal member, asserting that there are three kinds of body, namely the natural, the aggregate and the politic, and going on to suggest that one coin, the tenth, had been lost from the most precious fabric of the body politic of England and that to hunt for it and find it would require the king and all the lords spiritual and temporal to be very assiduous and diligent during this parliament'; the missing coin, of course, was the rebellious element that would be attainted later in the proceedings.[7] The House of Commons demonstrated their loyal intentions in their first act, electing William Catesby as their Speaker. Catesby had become Richard's trusted servant, his chamberlain and chancellor of the exchequer, as well as an esquire of the body, but he had never before been elected to Parliament.

Richard used his parliament to establish his right to rule in the popular consciousness. The most obvious ways in which he did so were by publishing his title, the Titulus Regius, as well as the Bill of Attainder against the defeated rebels. As we have seen, the grounds on which Richard based his claim, if accepted as true, were broadly legitimate, and the king made sure that his case was publicized even further, for example in April, when London City livery companies were gathered to hear Richard's 'tytylle & right' read out.[8]

One new development was that, in contrast to his policy before the rebellion, Richard no longer modelled his actions explicitly on those of his brother Edward. Previously, his official pronouncements had tied his actions seamlessly to those of his predecessor: 'in the same place, time, and manner as they were in the time of our brother, the lord Edward IV, late King of England', in the words of Richard's charter to Gloucester, which begins by rehearsing his predecessor's letters patent of 1462.[9] Now he cut the cord. Instead of offering the only protection against frittering away Edward's achievements, Richard now presented himself as the only man to right his brother's wrongs. The Titulus Regius, which ostensibly enrolled the petition made to Richard before he took the throne, but was certainly redrafted, if not wholly rewritten, for the occasion, spoke of how, in 'the tyme of the reigne of Kyng Edward the iiij.th, late decessed . . . the ordre of all poletique rule was perverted, the lawes of God and of Goddes church, and also the lawes of nature and of Englond, and also the laudable customes and liberties of the same, wherin every Englisshman is inherite, broken, subverted and contempned, ayenst all reason and justice'.[10] Thus, and in the same vein for several more sentences, did Richard in essence make the traditional case for deposition of a predecessor – the danger to the realm posed by the bad government of the present monarch – while conveniently glossing over the fact that the accused party was already dead and had been succeeded by someone whose record, as against his title, could hardly be questioned. Although Edward IV's own parliamentary statement of his title in 1461 displayed rather more self-confidence (Edward 'toke upon him hym to use his right and title to the seid reame'), the 'highly coloured and vituperative' language that has sometimes been detected in Richard's assertion of his title was not exceptional.[11] The Commons in Edward's time reserved their most colourful phrases for the deeds of another dead king, Henry IV, responsible for Richard II's 'moost vyle, heynous and lamentable deth . . . therfore [England] hath suffred the charge of intollerable persecucion, punicion and tribulacion, wherof the lyke hath not been seen or herde in any other Cristen reame, by any memorie or recorde'.[12] If the (nameless) Woodvilles were the target of similar calumny in Richard's parliament, it is unlikely that many listeners would have been shocked by an outbreak of unparliamentary language.

Richard made a more practical statement of his intent to break with Edwardian precedent when abolishing the innovation of 'benevolences'. This had been Edward's not particularly subtle way of taxing his subjects without appearing to tax them, by 'persuading' them to give up money for such ventures as the expedition to France in 1475. Thus the Commons, 'by newe and unlawfull invencions and inordinate covetise, ageynst the lawe of this roialme have be put to gret thraldome and inportable charges and exaccions'.[13] In rejecting benevolences, Richard was undoubtedly attempting a populist move. It is by no means obvious, however, that benevolences were the universally hated innovation that Richard's bill made them out to be. The general taxes known as parliamentary subsidies were definitely unpopular, as John Paston had complained ('I prey God send yow the Holy Gost amonge yow in the parlement howse, and rather the devyll, we sey, then ye shold grante eny more taskys [taxes]').[14] After 1475, Edward had avoided such general levies on the laity (a new subsidy had been granted in Edward's last parliament in 1483, for renewing the war with France, but never collected). The lengths to which both Edward and Richard went to avoid requesting subsidies give the impression that these were the really unpopular tax. The poorest were exempt, but subsidies extended far further into the population than selective taxation.

The fact that benevolences could, by contrast, be 'targeted' made them the lesser of two evils in broader terms. As one historian has put it, 'in effect, [the benevolence] was a national tax on incomes over £10 and movables of the value of £40 and upwards'.[15] Then there was the fact that Edward's own charisma seems to have been responsible for some, at least, of the sums raised (flirting with widows to extract more money, for example), which might anyway have made the benevolence a less attractive strategy to Richard, a king struggling for that sort of popularity in some areas of his kingdom – and who was taking a stand against such lewd royal behaviour in any case. The chronicler who described Edward's own charm as being responsible for raising 'more money by those meanys than he shuld have hadd by two ffyfftenys' (i.e. two taxes of a fifteenth on movable property, the rural rate charged in a subsidy) may have been exaggerating.[16] But Richard's attempts to cast his brother as a widely mistrusted monarch doesn't ring true in the sphere of royal finances. Ultimately, the appeal of abolishing benevolences probably rested on the fact that the classes represented in Parliament – a fraction of those subject to more general taxation – were exactly those who paid them.

Richard did have money problems, which wouldn't be solved by abjuring taxation in whatever form. The Crowland chronicler thought that the rebellion had already put a strain on royal finances. Historians don't agree about the state in which Edward left the Treasury, but its resources would certainly have been stretched by the fact that Sir Edward Woodville and the Marquess of Dorset had taken at least a portion of it away at the time of Edward V's accession, apart from any demands made on it after Richard's reign began. The king addressed the shortfall in Parliament by confirming conventional revenues from commercial activity – the 'tonage and poundage' raised from merchants – and by collecting a subsidy on aliens. He did not institute a national lay subsidy, nor did he try to collect the subsidy granted in Edward IV's last parliament. Perhaps unsurprisingly, given the strain put on the economy by the need to resist rebellion or the threat of it, this wasn't enough. The same chronicler exulted at describing how, later in his reign, the king who had made a point of rejecting benevolences was forced to take out loans from his subjects, 'the exactions of King Edward which he had himself condemned in Parliament, only avoiding in every case the word "benevolence"'.[17] In fact, these loans were at least formally requested and recorded, with specific promise of a repayment time.[18] Richard could justifiably plead that the circumstances were exceptional – 'great and excessive costes' were being generated – and once the threat had passed, the loans could be paid back. Only if we begin from a position of settled hostility to Richard (like the Crowland chronicler) does it follow that this measure was a rank hypocrisy.

Other bills passed in this parliament have also suffered from the fact that they form the total of the sample on which we can judge Richard's legislative track record. But, just as with his coronation and the progress at the beginning of the reign, Richard showed his suitability for his role by doing what kings were supposed to do. In the case of the king in Parliament, he would demonstrate his commitment to justice and the 'common weal'. In general, it should be conceded that there is no reason to make an exception of Richard and dismiss all his measures as merely directed at winning support. If they were popular, that can equally be because they were good laws. But by the same token, we do not have to raise Richard into a reincarnation of Henry II or Edward I just because he passed some laws that were not immediately rejected by his successor. It is impossible, too, to know how much legislation was Richard's idea, and how much the idea of his royal councillors – most importantly John Russell, his chancellor. Again, however, we shouldn't make too much of that distinction. Medieval kings took credit or blame for the legislation they passed because they were directly involved in its creation. The urge for observers to make an exception of Richard surely stems from the need to find clues to his character – or conversely to dismiss those who would draw such inferences – in his every public act. So often with Richard the most convincing explanation of his behaviour is that he took a conventional course (again it was when he didn't that he shocked contemporaries and puzzled posterity). If his legislation is held to give an insight into his character, it probably confirms that he sought conventional ways of ruling well.

Richard's attempts to deal with two causes of land disputes, in statutes on 'Uses' and on 'Fines', are a case in point. Both of these have to do with the complex arrangements for landholding that existed during a period when the formal operation of feudal tenure had been relaxed, but had not yet been replaced by anything like a modern property market. Thus the bill on Uses attempted to simplify the operation of what we know as trusts, and make it clearer who had claims on property. As for Fines, we have encountered

these in Richard's own dealings as Duke of Gloucester. Because these were the
method by which property was conveyed, it was desirable for the transaction
to be as public as possible. Richard's parliament legislated to widen the
proclamation of fines in the courts of assize and of the justices of the peace
in the relevant county. It is possible to detect here Richard putting to use his
own experience as a magnate deeply involved in property dealings, but this
was simply an area of the law that hadn't been working very satisfactorily.
Historians have debated the effectiveness of Richard's response, but there is
no doubt that the intentions behind them were sensible and just: these were
no mere populist gestures.

The measures establishing bail for those accused of felony, raising the
qualification levels for jurymen, and reforming the punishment of corrupt
officials at courts that presided over markets (pie-powder courts), were
all directed at improving the lot of less powerful members of society. It is
possible to exaggerate how innovative these bills were. Bail, for example, had
been a feature of the English legal system since before the Norman Conquest,
though Richard's legislation extended its scope, while jury empanelment had
been under discussion since the 1470s. Nonetheless, there is no question that
these were benevolent innovations, aimed at improving subjects' lives. The
enrolments of Acts of Parliament in English, which began with Richard, has
also been interpreted as a move to bring government closer to the people.
That may be so, although it was a development that built on steadily greater
use of English in Parliament throughout the fifteenth century, rather than
being a complete revolution, and one wonders how much statute law formed
the reading matter of the average English subject, then as now. Richard had
also been the first king to take his coronation oath in English, and he made
capital out of the fact that, unlike Edward IV (or Henry Tudor), he had
been born in England. Taking all such gestures together, this might amount
to a concerted attempt to 'anglicize' – and one assumes, popularize – his
government. The same instincts also apply to Richard's more nakedly populist
decision to reverse the ruling of the previous parliament that allowed royal
rights of wardship in the Duchy of Lancaster, even over those lands that had
been enfeoffed (i.e. were under the care of a third party, who would normally
receive the profits from wardships). Although these measures would have

benefited the king, Richard made clear that he, 'havyng more affeccion to the commen wele of this his realme and of his subgiettes then to his owne singler profit, hath ordeigned, enacted and stablisshed that the forseid actes, and every of theym, be adnulled, repeled and of no force ne effect'.[19] If those who stood to profit from such measures gave the king who enacted these laws their loyalty, so much the better.

The case for Richard as a disinterested legislator is more difficult to make with his measures against foreigners, the less palatable side of his pro-English agenda. Richard not only collected a subsidy on aliens raised in Edward's last parliament; he also granted petitions against an impressively long list of 'merchauntes straungiers' ('gurdelers, poyntmakers, pynners, pursers, glovers, cutlers, bladsmythes, blaksmythes, sporiours, goldebeters, peyntours, sadelers, lorymers, founders, cardemakers, hurers, wiremongers, wevers, horners, botelmakers and copersmythes'), and against the 'subtile meanes' of Lombard importers of bow staves. This was straightforward protectionism, obviously meant to appeal to the interests of the merchants and craftsmen behind it. It had some precedent in the 1460s, though not through Edward's reign. Edward had probably avoided such interference to maintain good relations with foreign trading powers. It was not a sign of Richard's strength that he didn't follow suit. Rather, these bills recognized the need to cultivate domestic support, at the potential cost of making enemies overseas. The fate of the realm may not have depended on the correct measure for a butt of malmsey wine or the price of a batch of bow staves. But Richard's need to reward supporters at home does point to a wider problem, that the king was manoeuvred into isolationism. Eventually, Richard's inability to find friends abroad would cost him as much as, perhaps more than, his struggle to keep them at home.

Parliament was by no means the only arena in which the king could demonstrate his desire to rule well – or alternatively, his need to find support wherever it could be secured. Those in search of a more benign Richard – one who lives up to the unexpectedly positive characterization by Sir Francis Bacon as a 'good law-maker, for ease and solace of the common people'[20] – have lit on the role of John Harington as administrator of 'bills, requests, and supplications of poor persons'.[21] This was the origin of the Tudor Court of

Requests, although, as there is no evidence of how much or how effectively it worked in practice (other than Richard's gratitude to its administrator), we probably shouldn't call this arrangement 'legal aid'.[22]

Early in 1484 Richard gave royal charters to two bodies, the Company of Wax Chandlers and the College of Heralds. The Wax Chandlers were the body responsible for producing one of the most important of medieval commodities – beeswax. Although ordinary candles were made from tallow (animal fat – Edward IV had granted a charter to the Tallow Chandlers), beeswax candles were used in church services. Beeswax was also used in seals on documents and letters, for wax writing tablets, as well as wax 'images', such as the vast image of her sick son that Agnes Paston ordered for the shrine at Walsingham in 1443. The body responsible for this was clearly an important part of the world of medieval business, but it is questionable whether we should read much more into the incorporation, or draw a significant contrast between the 'carnally given' Edward's royal approval for the Tallow Chandlers as against Richard's for the purveyors of 'sweeter and slower burning' wax.[23] Admittedly, there were indications during this year of a growing emphasis on morality in Richard's public pronouncements. Not only had he denounced in Parliament those around Edward as 'led by sensuality and concupiscence'. In March he sent a circular to his bishops expressing 'our principalle entent and fervent desire . . . to see vertue and clennesse of lyvyng to be avunced encresed and multiplied'.[24] But it may be a stretch to include the incorporation of the Wax Chandlers as part of this moral regeneration programme.

Richard's second incorporation is more easily seen as a personal choice. It was the grant of a charter to the heralds, who became the College of Arms, and received a riverside mansion, Cold Harbour on Upper Thames Street, from which to conduct their business. It is natural to detect Richard's martial and chivalric preoccupations in this grant to a body of men who celebrated and safeguarded the display of knightly virtues. But most medieval kings relied on heralds and wished to be seen as representing the highest standards of chivalry. Edward III, Henry V or indeed Edward IV (whose Household Black Book makes provision for the treatment of heralds) could all be imagined making such a foundation. If there is any particular significance to attach to the fact that Richard, and not his predecessors, gave the grant, on 2 March 1484, it may be that the new king realized that he needed to be able to rely on a group who existed partially to confirm or confer legitimacy. Grants of arms, and the right to bear particular arms, were a conspicuous stamp of fifteenth-century approval. The grant could also have been the expression of a more personal favour. The chief herald, Garter King of Arms John Writhe, was a faithful servant of Edward IV who had transferred his loyalty to Richard, officiating at both Edward's funeral and Richard's coronation, and was employed by Richard on diplomatic missions. By giving Writhe and his fellow heralds official status, and a prestigious address from which to exercise it, Richard was, once again, repaying the loyalty offered him.

At the end of February 1484, Richard summoned a group of senior subjects to offer an oath of allegiance to his son, Edward, Prince of Wales, recognizing him as his father's heir. This, the Crowland chronicler alleges, was a 'Certain new oath, drawn up by persons unknown to me', which casts Richard's actions in that writer's usual suspect light. But getting the most important men in the kingdom to promise their support to his heir was a minimum insurance measure, which was very far from unprecedented. It was what Edward IV had done when he was newly re-established on the throne and his son, the future Edward V, was less than a year old. Richard probably knew, as Henry I probably did when obliging his nobles to make a similar promise about his daughter Matilda, that such oaths might well not be treated as binding after the king's death. If the succession was disputed, more pragmatic considerations would come into play. But it was as well for Richard to have his followers publicly committed to the succession. Anything that made his position look more permanent was desirable.

The king himself took a public oath a few days later, in front of 'my lordes spirituelle & temporelle and you Maire & Aldermen of my Cite of London'. What Richard promised exposed the fiction of business as usual. What the promise secured was that on 1 March 1484, Elizabeth Woodville and her daughters at last emerged from sanctuary at Westminster, where they had been living since 30 April the previous year. The Crowland chronicler says that Elizabeth had been 'urged by frequent intercessions and dire threats', and there is no suggestion that she had been reassured that her sons by

Edward IV were alive, as has sometimes been argued. On the contrary, without them her position looked extremely weak, compounded by the deaths of her executed brother Earl Rivers and her son Sir Richard Grey, and the absence of another son, Thomas, Marquess of Dorset, and two other brothers, Lionel and Edward Woodville, in exile with Richard's enemy Henry Tudor. Richard was apparently secure on the throne, and the emergence of Henry as a pretender, who had promised to marry Elizabeth of York, left Elizabeth Woodville with little option but to demonstrate that she and her family accepted Richard's regime, if they were not to be treated as traitors, like the other Woodvilles. For his part, Richard guaranteed that Elizabeth's five daughters 'shalbe in suretie of their lyffes and also not suffre any maner hurt by any maner persone or persones to theim or any of theim in their bodies and persones to be done by wey of Ravisshement or defouling contrarie their willes'. To this he added that he would not imprison them 'within the Toure of London or other prisone'.[25]

It is hard to read all this as anything other than the promise of a man who had already done great harm to a family not to do any more. The mention of the last place Elizabeth's sons had been seen alive is particularly suggestive. Kings did not normally have to promise that individual subjects wouldn't suffer at their hands. Normally, as the sureties Richard extracted from pardoned rebels demonstrate, it was the other way round. Richard went on to set out plans to provide suitable husbands for the girls of marriageable age, with dowries, and for Elizabeth Woodville herself a generous stipend of 700 marks a year. In the case of the eldest daughter, Elizabeth of York, of course, the marriage plan had a practical purpose, as it would remove the prospect of her legitimizing Henry Tudor's claim by becoming his wife. For the Woodvilles' part, no promises of good behaviour were expected, and if the king heard 'evylle report' of them, he assured them that he would not give it credence without hearing their side of the story first. The oath – less its content than the fact that Richard felt the need to swear it – goes to the heart of the questions that hung over his short reign: Did he deserve to be king, and what had he done to become one? That such questions were asked did not in itself doom Richard's reign to failure. Other kings had been asked similar questions before, and one, Henry IV, had founded a dynasty that only the incompetence of his grandson had endangered. But it did make Richard's task of holding on to power, and passing it to a successor, all the more difficult.[26]

Castle of Care

Richard's contemporaries were conscious of the importance of a king doing right not only by his earthly duties, but also by his spiritual and moral ones. It was with this in mind that, a week after swearing the oath, Richard and Anne set out for Cambridge. There, Anne endowed Queens' College, with which Richard had already been associated, despite its foundation by one queen he opposed – Margaret of Anjou – and having another, Elizabeth Woodville, as patroness. Richard also gave 'not a little money' for building King's College chapel, the foundation of Henry VI. Unlike rulers of later ages, late-medieval English kings seem to have been happy to adapt their opponents' legacies to their own ends and their own glory.

From Cambridge the royal party travelled north, via Huntingdon, Stamford and Grantham, arriving at Nottingham Castle on 17 March. They stayed there, with brief visits to Derby and Burton, for the next six weeks. While at Nottingham they received the devastating news that their only son, Edward of Middleham, had died 'after a short illness'. The Crowland chronicler would surely not have been alone among contemporaries in thinking that this was a divine judgement: 'they learned how vain are the attempts of man to regulate his affairs without God'.[27] Richard and Anne, he wrote, were 'almost out of their minds for a long time when faced with the sudden grief'. Edward was the couple's only child. There is no sign that he had been sickly before Richard's very public presentation of him, investing him with such ceremony in York as Prince of Wales. Edward had also been appointed Lieutenant of Ireland, and it seems probable that he was being lined up for a similar role as nominal head of the newly created Council of the North. All this public exposure points to the likelihood that Edward had been a healthy child who was deliberately being shown to the nobility and the commons to establish him as the rightful heir and natural successor. The Crowland chronicler gives an unusually sympathetic glimpse of Richard's inconsolable personal grief at losing his only (legitimate) son. But it was, of course, a loss of great political significance, too. The fact that Anne had only successfully given birth to one child in twelve years of marriage made it unlikely that she would bear another.

Up to this point, though Richard's rule had been tested, he had shown himself capable of seeing off the challenges thrown at him. We do not know how much he was prey to self-doubt, and his public pronouncements continued to display his customary self-assuredness. But it would be strange if a man as apparently genuinely pious as Richard had not reflected on the blow that fate had struck. The king's *Book of Hours*, preserved in Lambeth Palace Library, famously contains a prayer copied in – one of sixty additional pages of additional prayers – that was once argued to be personal to Richard. In fact, though it contains his name, the prayer is based on a text used throughout western Europe. We do not know exactly when Richard acquired the book, and attempts to make the prayer – which was entered when he was already king – reveal something about the fate of the princes in the Tower are doomed to failure.[28] But it seems very likely that, when his only son Edward died, Richard found consolation in the words (originally in Latin) reflecting how Christ was sent 'into the world to deliver the sinful from their transgressions, comfort the afflicted . . . comfort the sad, and to console those in grief and distress'.[29]

Nottingham, according to local tradition, became known to Richard ever after his son's death as his 'Castle of Care' – the place, perhaps, where he first began to doubt the dream of kingship and its inseparable correlative, a dynasty to preserve his legacy. But for all his grief, the demands of ruling could not be ignored. Around July, he established the Council of the North, with at its head John de la Pole, Earl of Lincoln and Richard's nephew (by his sister Elizabeth, Duchess of Suffolk). In time, Richard would confirm Lincoln as his designated heir. The Council was given authority to keep the peace and resolve disputes 'in the North parties' – essentially the same area over which Richard himself had had control as Lieutenant of the North, except for the parts that had been retained directly by him, such as the Cumberland palatinate. The Council has been described as 'Richard's most enduring monument', because it was adopted by the Tudors, at first fairly informally, but more permanently by Henry VIII after the Pilgrimage of Grace, and lasted until just before the Civil War.[30] It was certainly a more formal and less personal arrangement than Edward IV had instituted after 1472, when he had essentially divided the north between Richard and Henry Percy, Earl of Northumberland, before Richard assumed overall authority.

Under Richard III the Council had a permanent home, at Sandal Castle, from where the Duke of York, Richard's father, had made his last sally, and there were even building works to accommodate the new arrangements there. But Richard's policy of appointing the young and inexperienced Earl of Lincoln rather than his old rival the Earl of Northumberland to the head of the Council was a risk, and maybe a simple mistake. Lincoln's loyalty could presumably be relied upon whether he had received the office or not, but what would Percy have made of the fact that, even after Richard had left the north for higher things, he was still not trusted to take control? Instead, as with the 'plantation' so resented by some in the south, Richard introduced an outsider. John, Earl of Lincoln, had no lands or connections in the north. Percy never rebelled against Richard, but he hardly proved the staunchest of allies either. In fact, in the crisis of August 1485, the earl did the bare minimum, and at the crucial moment reverted to his time-honoured tactic of doing nothing, though why is still debated.[31] We have seen how limited was Richard's room for manoeuvre when he had to restore order after Buckingham's rebellion. In the case of the Council of the North, Richard did have a choice to make, and he probably made the wrong one.

The problems facing Richard were in some respects the opposite of the ones traditionally faced by England's kings in the Middle Ages. So often, his predecessors had struggled to deal with the peripheries of the kingdom while the more prosperous, better-governed south stayed biddable – with the exceptions of the popular uprisings of 1381 and 1450. For Richard, the Council of the North solved a problem that his own knowledge of and affinity to the region had already made manageable. Meanwhile, the loyalty of the south was open to question.

The king's ability to deal with external threats was tested in 1484 in two confrontations with Scotland. On land, Richard tacitly backed a renewed assault by James III's brother the Duke of Albany, who had fallen foul of his king again and fled to England for support in 1483. Albany and the Earl of Douglas led a small army of Scottish and English cavalry, which was defeated at Lochmaben in Dumfries on 22 July. Albany fled, but Douglas was captured. The Crowland chronicler, however – usually so ill-disposed to Richard and therefore perhaps more trustworthy on this point – relates that at sea, Richard 'had remarkable success against the Scots'.[32] Certainly the outcome was that, on 7 September, England and Scotland agreed a three-year truce, sealed at Nottingham Castle, to which Richard had returned after a tour of the north and a brief stay in London in August. The treaty also arranged a marriage between James III's son the Duke of Rothesay, the future James IV, and Ann de la Pole, Richard's niece and the Earl of Lincoln's sister. For a time, there was a prospect of a de la Pole on the throne of England and of Scotland. Richard's fall reverberated beyond his own borders.

It was while on his northern tour, at Middleham in May 1484, that Richard met Niclas Von Popplau, who left a brief account of his visit. Von Popplau's original has been lost, but a German translation was made and is preserved in a nineteenth-century publication. For years Von Popplau's description of Richard as 'three fingers taller, a little thinner and not so thickset [as himself], also much more lean; he had delicate arms and legs also a great heart', has been used as a scrap of evidence on which to base a discussion of Richard's physical appearance. The discovery of Richard's skeleton and the conclusions drawn from its secrets have made much of that discussion otiose. Apologists for Richard used to note that Von Popplau made no mention of any deformity – and argued therefore that later writers, including Polydore Vergil and Thomas More, who claimed to be drawing on contemporary testimony of Richard's 'uneven shoulders', were clearly unreliable propagandists. The findings that Richard suffered from quite severe scoliosis, which would indeed have made his shoulders appear uneven, point to something different about Von Popplau's remarks. He clearly noticed something unusual about the king's appearance, with the contrast of delicacy and strength that he pointed out. But, well concealed by clothing, Richard's actual condition was difficult to recognize.

We don't need to take the fact that Von Popplau doesn't mention Richard's symptoms as casting doubt on his account – though the fact he mentioned that their meeting took place in Pontefract rather than Middleham, where Richard was known to have been staying on 1 May, is a sign that he wasn't a stickler for detail. Perhaps most revealing is Richard's apparent outburst when Von Popplau told him about the King of Hungary's victory against the Turks (probably referring to the defeat by Croatian forces of an Ottoman army, which Matthias Corvinus, King of Hungary, reported to the pope in November 1483): 'I wish that my kingdom lay upon the confines of Turkey: with my own people alone and without the help of other princes I should like to drive away not only the Turks, but all my foes.' To a conventional expression of crusading zeal Richard adds a dose of personal enthusiasm, as well as a convincingly embattled note. The king knew that it was not Turks but enemies much closer to home whom he would have to defeat.[33]

Von Popplau stayed with Richard for ten days, during which time he seems to have been treated as an honoured guest. Richard gave him a gold necklace 'retrieved from a certain Lord'. As so often, we must be cautious about reading too much into one of the rare informal glimpses of Richard as king. We have seen that neither Von Popplau's references to the fate of Richard's nephews nor his physical description of the king can be relied upon to provide us with dependable insights. But the flashes of personality in his narrative – of a generous formal host, a would-be victorious crusader and a man acutely conscious of the threats to his position – all ring true.

'All Engeland, undyr an hogge'

After the departure of Richard's welcome guest, the king remained in the north. He travelled around Yorkshire and into Durham, also visiting Scarborough where in July 1484 he issued orders for the protection of merchant shipping from attack at sea. At the beginning of the year French ships had attacked an English fleet off Scarborough and captured two of Richard's sea captains, Sir Thomas Everingham and John Nesfield. By July, however, internal as well as external threats had begun to resurface. John, Lord Scrope of Bolton, to whom Richard had given the task of mopping up rebellion in Devon and Cornwall, received two appointments against rebels in that region: James Newenham (who 'with others' was accused of 'certain treasons and other offences') and a group of unnamed Cornishmen who had arranged for £52 to be sent to other

West Country rebels, Robert Willoughby and Peter Courtenay, the attainted Bishop of Exeter, in exile with Henry Tudor in Brittany.[34]

It was another West Country rebel, William Collingbourne, who achieved the most lasting fame for his defiance in this year, though only the culmination of it has remained in the popular consciousness. Collingbourne had been a loyal servant of Edward IV, serving at different times as sheriff of Wiltshire, Somerset and Devon. He seems to have stayed loyal to the Crown through Buckingham's rebellion, or at least avoided punishment for any suspected involvement, and had even been appointed to a position in the household of Cecily Neville, Richard's mother. But in June 1484 Richard wrote to her (the only surviving example of their correspondence), offering 'my lord, my Chambreleyn [Viscount Lovell] to be youre officer in Wiltshire in such as Colingbourne had'.[35] The reason Collingbourne could no longer occupy the post was revealed almost five months later, on 29 November, in the appointment of a commission at Westminster packed with two dukes, two earls, two viscounts (including Lovell), a selection of distinguished knights, and the mayor of London, to try him and John Turburvyle 'touching certain treasons and other offences'. The indictment, which the Tudor historian Raphael Holinshed claimed to have seen, accused Collingbourne of paying one Thomas Yate £8 on 10 July to go to Henry Tudor in Brittany and encourage him to invade, landing at Poole in Dorset, 'before the feast of Saint Luke' (18 October). Yate was also supposed to get Henry's trusted officer Sir John Cheyney to go to the French court and say that Richard was merely stalling French ambassadors who were in England, and was in fact preparing to invade France.

Eight days later, on 18 July, Collingbourne posted up a bill on the door of St Paul's and 'other places of the Cyte', which read: 'The Catt, the Ratt, and lovell our dogge Rulyn all Engeland, undyr an hogge'.[36] William Catesby, Richard Ratcliffe and Francis Lovell were the nicknamed followers of the king whose badge of the white boar identified him as the hog. Although Lovell was indeed one of Richard's most trusted servants, it may be that his inclusion stemmed from Collingbourne's personal animus against the man who had taken his post in Cecily Neville's household. Lovell was the only one of the three named who sat in judgement on the accused. They made an example of Collingbourne. He was hanged, drawn and quartered, the extreme fate of the traitor that most rebels had hitherto avoided. Historians from Holinshed onwards have argued that Collingbourne was taken so seriously not because of the rhyme, but because of his more active plotting with the enemy.[37] That may be so, but Richard was acutely aware of the importance of words in the battle to hold on to power. Throughout his short reign, he tried to stamp out expressions of dissent before they spread. Richard understood that if he was to succeed as king, he had to be in command of the narrative of his reign. He was right, as other oppressive regimes have discovered across the ages. Satire is a powerful tool for undermining legitimacy. For that reason alone, it is perfectly possible that Collingbourne died as much for his memorable rhyme as his more active scheming.

As for those schemes, if the dates given in the account of the indictment are correct, Collingbourne seems to have been at large for a long time after suspicion first fell on him. He was evidently already under a cloud when Richard wrote the letter at the beginning of June, and Collingbourne revealed his hand in mid-July with the poster campaign. But it was not until the end of November that he was tried, presumably shortly after he had fallen into government hands. We don't know whether Yate made the journey to Brittany – or, indeed, whether it was Yate's evidence that convicted Collingbourne. It is not clear either why Cheyne was instructed to say that Richard was stalling the French ambassadors 'to drive off the time till the winter season were past' when the message was being relayed in summer: that would require an awful lot of stalling before spring.[38] However, taken with the disturbances in Devon and Cornwall that Scrope had tackled, these amount to a significant if still low-level pattern of resistance. By the time of the trial, the threatened invasion date had passed without incident. Nonetheless, when Richard requested of his mother 'youre daly blissing to my Synguler comfort & defence in my nede', the words had a resonance beyond the conventional. Henry Tudor remained a genuine threat, who was apparently in communication with disaffected subjects back in England. What is more, all interested parties knew that if Henry secured French backing, as well as or instead of Breton, the threat he posed to Richard took on a whole new complexion.

Richard was aware, too, of one more potential threat across the Channel. This was John de Vere, the attainted Earl of Oxford, a portion of whose patrimony

Richard had, as Duke of Gloucester, prised away from his aged mother. As king, he rewarded one of his most steadfast supporters, John Howard, Duke of Norfolk, with more de Vere lands in East Anglia. De Vere had personal reasons enough for antipathy to Richard, but he was also a rare case in this period of a man who stuck to his cause, even the forlorn cause of the Lancastrians. Edward IV had imprisoned him at Hammes Castle near Calais, which probably seemed like a good way of avoiding his prison becoming the focus of disaffection in England. But after Henry Tudor had emerged as a serious threat in France, albeit in Brittany, and the nearest a Lancastrian was going to get to a plausible candidate, de Vere suddenly looked as if he were too far away – or too near the pretender – for comfort. On 28 October 1484 Richard sent for him to be brought back to England, but it was too late. In another indication that the king's grip on formerly trusted servants was loosening, the celebrated prisoner managed to persuade two of his guards, the captain of the castle Sir James Blount, and John Fortescue, to escape with him to the French court. Worse, on 2 November several former servants of Edward IV who had connections to de Vere took ship from Essex to join Henry Tudor, before a charge of treason could be brought against them.

Just over a month later, on 7 December 1484, Richard made a proclamation under the Great Seal to be distributed to sheriffs throughout the kingdom. For the first time, 'John late Erle of Oxenford' was named among Henry, Earl of Richmond's principal supporters, along with Henry's uncle Jasper, the Bishop of Exeter, and the two Woodville exiles, Sir Edward Woodville and Thomas Grey, who had been stripped of his title of Marquess of Dorset.[39] By this time de Vere, a veteran of the Battle of Barnet and a consistent raider against Edward IV's regime, had already managed to relieve the garrison of Hammes, which had gone over to Richmond's side and had been besieged by Richard's servant Lord Dinham. The garrison provided more welcome reinforcements for Henry's party. De Vere himself, whose military experience was not in fact an unblemished record of success, was nevertheless an intrepid and imperturbable opponent, and was duly given strategic command of Henry's forces.

As the proclamation makes clear, these forces were now being assembled not under the relatively unthreatening protection of the aged Duke of Brittany, but that of Charles VIII, King of France. The flight of Henry Tudor to France was another story, as far as Richard was concerned, of bad luck. He had throughout the year been negotiating with the Breton treasurer Pierre Landais, who controlled the government of the duchy on behalf of the frail Duke Francis. Landais and Maximilian of Austria, who wished to reclaim his Burgundian lands forfeited by the Treaty of Arras, in 1482, attempted to form a grand alliance with Richard against France. What they had to offer was Henry Tudor. By June 1484 all appeared agreed. A formal truce was sealed at Pontefract between Richard and Francis, negotiated by a Burgundian-backed go-between, Juan de Salazar (later to be found fighting alongside Richard at Bosworth). Richard promised 1,000 English archers to the duke; handing over Henry in exchange could not form part of the formal proceedings, as such a clause would have tipped off Henry. But probably as a result of Henry's stepfather Thomas Stanley, word did get out anyway.

Meanwhile, at the French court, the regent, Charles VIII's elder sister Anne of Beaujeu, had given sanctuary to a group of rebel Breton nobles. They, too, saw Henry as a potentially useful piece in the power game with Pierre Landais. Henry was not entirely at the mercy of events, but when the exiled Bishop of Ely, John Morton, sent his envoy Christopher Urswick to Henry at Vannes, with news that the Breton government planned to hand him over to the English king, he realized he must escape. Urswick was immediately sent to the French court to ask whether they would receive Henry, a request that Anne of Beaujeu enthusiastically accepted. Although Richard's new ally Landais attempted to secure his prisoner, as with the Earl of Oxford, it was too late. Henry managed to escape over the border, and was welcomed into the regency court. More remarkably, the Duke of Brittany seems to have decided that Landais had exceeded his authority by attempting to arrest Henry. He allowed Henry's followers, who had in any case been putting a strain on Breton finances, to make their way to their master at the court of the King of France.

That was how, by late 1484, Richard III found himself threatened not by an upstart backed by the forces of a decrepit French duke whose duchy was beset by infighting, but by France itself. Admittedly the French were not united at the time either, but the prospect of French support for Henry was a major setback for Richard. Rather than extinguishing the threat of Henry, he appeared to have increased it. In late November 1484 letters sent by Henry arrived in England. In them he no longer described himself as the Earl of Richmond, but signed himself, if the manuscript copy made in the seventeenth century is to be trusted, with the regal initials HR and wrote of his preparation for the 'furtherance of my rightful claim due and lineal inheritance of the crown'. Richard, on the other hand, he described as 'that homicide and unnatural tyrant'.[40]

To grasp the importance of this moment, it is worth considering what might have happened if Henry Tudor had fallen into Richard's hands. He would no doubt have been executed, as a rebel who had proclaimed himself as king. It is difficult to imagine who might have emerged as an alternative candidate. Without one, and despite the difficulties that Richard's lack of support in the south might cause, it seems very unlikely that a viable challenge to his rule would have arisen. The obscurity of Henry Tudor is often used as a stick with which to beat Richard. It is offered as proof that the king was so unpopular, his crimes so heinous, that almost anyone would have commanded support in his place. But Richard had shown that he could be a strong and just king. If the twin obstacles of his dubious legitimacy and the horror of his alleged murder of the princes began to recede into the past, it is perfectly possible that he would have been a success. It was not misrule that threatened Richard. It was a challenge to his right to rule, and a credible challenger to make such a claim. Granted, Henry Tudor was made credible by the support he drew from disaffected Yorkists, by his promise to marry Edward IV's eldest daughter – and, not least, by the fact that his extremely active mother occupied a position near to the heart of power at home. But if Henry had been removed, it is difficult to imagine that such a constellation of support, including the crucial continental backing, could have been confected for a newly promoted alternative.

With French support the Duke of Clarence and Warwick the Kingmaker had managed to chase the far better established Edward IV off the throne. Henry's growing band could by no means lay claim to the sort of domestic popularity from which Warwick had benefited. France, too, was less powerful than it had been, with a regency government ruling for an underage king. And as before, it is important not to look at the English situation in isolation. The French were interested in backing Henry as a way of tying down the English and preventing them from making anything of their alliance with Brittany.

If the French, on the other hand, came to an agreement with the Bretons (as they did, temporarily, shortly after Henry's invasion in 1485), they would have had much less interest in involving themselves in cross-Channel politics. For his part, Richard, despite sending an embassy under Thomas Langton in March 1484, had been unable to negotiate French neutrality. Richard had various internal troubles to deal with in the coming months. Indeed, news that the English 'were greatly and wondrously divided amongst themselves' had reached the French court.[41] But the prospect of an invasion launched from the continent became from this moment his overriding priority. If up to this point Richard had been concentrating on legitimizing his regime to the widest circle of subjects, by now he must have known that there was a substantial and determined enemy preparing to test that legitimacy in armed combat.

Evil Reports

By November 1484 Richard was back in Westminster, where he stayed, apart from a brief visit to Canterbury, until 12 January 1485. In Richard's time, Christmas did not come at the end of the year, which was reckoned to begin on Lady Day, 25 March, but if he was in reflective mood on his return to the capital, he can have had little to cheer him. To the personal and political blow of the loss of his only son was added the strengthening of his rival's position across the Channel, and signs that at home his regime was still far from universally accepted. The Earl of Oxford had fled to his enemies, and the king's finances were even less healthy after campaigns against the Scots on land and sea, and the promise of armed support to Brittany. On the other hand, the Scots had been pacified, Richard had presided over a parliament in which his legitimacy had been shored up, and he had been able to demonstrate a positive programme of legislation. He had established the Council of the North and throughout the year had drawn his more reliable supporters closer to him with grants and offices.

It was also in 1484 that Richard had set in motion plans to establish a huge chantry of 100 priests at York, to be paid for out of the revenues of the

Duchy of Lancaster.[42] As this foundation was 'to sing there in the worship of god oure lady seint George & seint Nynyan . . ', there is no direct evidence, contrary to some arguments put forward around the time of the rediscovery of Richard's remains, that this was to be the king's own final resting place. He had buried his son Edward, it is thought, either in Middleham or in Sheriff Hutton (where the remains of an alabaster effigy, with a piece of stained glass showing the Yorkist sun in splendour above it, can still be seen). It is possible that Edward would have been moved to York if the chantry chapel had ever been built. What is clear is that Richard, in spite, or perhaps in recognition, of all the threats to his security, found time to reflect on eternity as well as the everyday. And at Westminster for Christmas he was also, apparently, in high enough spirits to celebrate with some gusto, to the disapproval of the Crowland chronicler, who complained that 'during the Christmas feast too much attention was paid to singing and dancing and to vain exchanges of dress between Queen Anne and Lady Elizabeth, eldest daughter of the dead king, who were alike in complexion and figure'.[43] It was after this conspicuous display that rumours began to spread that Richard meant to marry his niece, 'either after the death of the queen, or by means of a divorce for which he believed he had sufficient grounds'.

As the Crowland author knew that in the following year the path was indeed cleared for Richard's potential remarriage, this remark, like so many of his, was deliberately pregnant with meaning. On 16 March 1484, after an illness that apparently began shortly after Christmas, Queen Anne died. On the same day, just after half past two in the afternoon, the sun began to darken. By a quarter to three it was almost entirely obscured in an eclipse. Edward IV's reign had been presaged by the appearance of three suns in the sky. In Richard's, the sun disappeared. Did some contemporaries wonder whether the sun of York was about to be eclipsed, too?

Anne was buried at Westminster. This could be taken as another indication that Richard was not planning York as a royal mausoleum: it would be one thing to remove a son's remains from the relative obscurity of a parish church to a more honoured place, quite another to do so after interment at the epicentre of English monarchical ceremony, 'with honours no less than befitted the burial of a queen'. Soon afterwards, there is contemporary evidence for the rumours of Richard's intention to marry his niece. It would be easy to dismiss this as the malicious invention of his enemies, but several points make it quite possible that Richard did contemplate such a controversial match. The controversy lay not only in the likelihood, according to the king's opponents at least, that Richard had murdered his would-be bride's brothers. In any case, a man was forbidden from marrying his niece (he still can't in the United Kingdom, though he can in France). Papal dispensations could be secured, as happened later in the century for Joanna of Naples and her nephew Ferrante, who were related in the same degree (she was his aunt). But to a king who wished to avoid controversy, these were not negligible obstacles. On the other hand, marrying Elizabeth would remove her as a potentially legitimizing bride for Henry Tudor – a prospect, Polydore Vergil writes, that 'pinched [him] by the very stomach'. The fact that, by Richard's own Act of Parliament, Elizabeth was not herself legitimate would surely have mattered less than the advantage of removing a prop from Henry's claim, which appeared to have secured Yorkist support for a cause otherwise based on a broadly Lancastrian foundation.

Two pieces of evidence apart from the Crowland chronicler's references suggest that the marriage was contemplated. The first is that Richard was forced to deny it in public, apparently at the insistence of his loyal supporters Sir Richard Ratcliffe and William Catesby. Thus, as recorded in the Mercers' Company records, on 30 March, Richard, 'in the presens of many of his lordes & of much other peple shewde his grefe and displeasure afforsaid & said it newer came in his thought or mynde to marry in such maner wise'.[44] He was also at pains to deny the accompanying rumour, that he had poisoned Anne to clear his path to Elizabeth. For the second time in a little over a year, the anointed king had been forced to make a public declaration of his good intentions towards the offspring of his brother, first not to harm them, and then not to marry one of them.

The other clue that Richard really did contemplate the marriage to Elizabeth of York is less reliable than the first, but can't be entirely dismissed. If it is to be believed, it originally dates from before the public disavowal and shows that Richard apparently felt confident enough of carrying public opinion with him. It is the letter reported by one of Richard's earliest posthumous defenders, the Elizabethan Master of Revels Sir George Buck, from Elizabeth of York herself to John Howard, Duke of Norfolk, Richard's most loyal magnate supporter. In it, Buck claims, Elizabeth – in late February, before Anne's death – pleads with Howard to intercede on her behalf. 'She prayed him as before to be a mediator for her in the cause of the marriage to the king, who, as she wrote, was her only joy in the world, and that she was his in heart and in thoughts, in body and in all.' Buck claimed to have seen this letter in Howard's descendant's 'cabinet, among precious jewels and rare monuments', but it no longer survives (if it ever existed).[45] It would be easy to discount this evidence, but, as Buck's modern editor points out, 'he was careful about his documentation and sharply critical of writers who "deliver all . . . upon their own bare and worthless word".'[46] As his *History of King Richard III* was dedicated to this descendant of the first Howard, Duke of Norfolk, namely the Earl of Arundel, it seems unlikely that Buck made the letter up, though he and the family could have been taken in by a forgery. Whatever the reality behind the account, Richard's declaration put paid to any prospect of the marriage.[47] It can also be seen as the moment when his bid for legitimacy began to look like a losing hand.

Richard's second public declaration of innocence adds to the substantial evidence that the king was increasingly subject to rumours and 'evil reports'. The combination of a genuine threat from outside and an apparently growing tide of hostile innuendo at home was difficult to resist. Richard's proclamations understandably don't go into specifics about what was being said against him. Even Collingbourne's rhyme is known from a posthumous account rather than a contemporary record (the *Great Chronicle* of Robert Fabyan). But in April 1485 the king issued a letter that was read to councils in towns as far apart as York and Southampton, warning of the 'daily . . . noise and disclaundre agayenst our persone'. Responsible citizens were enjoined to arrest anyone suspected of spreading such 'false and contrived invencions' and to tear down 'without reding or shewing the same to any othre person' any bill posted, or similar material.[48] The idea that rumours could be suppressed by such measures may sound optimistic, but Richard could hardly tolerate them either. The fact that he tried so hard to quash them is an indication of the threat he thought they posed to this regime. Since he had spent as much time and energy in trying to convince his subjects at large of his right to rule as he had in taking practical steps to make himself secure on the throne, this was a sobering development. Rumours of the king's crimes might not of themselves threaten Richard. But they must have played a part in the decision-making process of those expected to support him, especially in arms. As with any contest to win support, the decision to back a potential victor can become self-reinforcing. If enough people think one candidate is going to win (or lose), they make that outcome all the more likely by their support (or lack of it). That is the importance of rumour in the reign of Richard III: less whether it concealed a truth about what the king had done, or what his body looked like, than whether enough people believed it did to make ruling impossible.

As Richard knew, one big thing could puncture the rumours, possibly for good: defeating Henry Tudor in battle. Again, the model is Edward IV. Richard's brother had been acclaimed as king in March 1461, but until he defeated his Lancastrian enemy on that freezing Palm Sunday at the end of the month, he could not feel secure. Edward's coronation came after the result of Towton had made him king in deed as well as by right. Edward had had the disadvantage that his opponent wouldn't or couldn't take the field in person, but Henry Tudor was a man in his prime, who would be sure to lead his army himself. Thus the chances were that if Richard met his opponent in battle, the issue might be settled by the death of one or the other. It is not surprising that when Richard received intelligence to expect an invasion 'as soon as summer came . . . he wanted nothing better than this, since it might well be thought that it would put an end to all his doubts and misfortunes'.[49] In the months leading up to that summer, the doubts would only increase, but success on the battlefield could have dealt with them for good.

Not since 1066 had an English king spent so much time anticipating a foreign invasion. England had been invaded on numerous occasions since William the Conqueror, twice within Richard's lifetime (and by his own brothers). But no king since Harold had faced the threat over months of a well-supported pretender whose landing place could not be reliably predicted. In facing it, the last Plantagenet encountered many of the same problems as the last Anglo-Saxon. Without knowing when and where the blow might fall, how was he to keep an armed response ready? Of course, four centuries had witnessed wholesale changes in the ways armies (and fleets) were summoned, equipped and commanded. But ultimately, Richard depended on shire and town levies, and on the followings of great lords. He had no standing army. Richard tried to prepare his subjects to be ready to respond quickly to a call to arms. In December 1484 and again in June 1485 he issued commissions of array to 'every shire in England', exhorting the commissioners to command 'alle knightes Squiers and gentilmen to prepaire and arredy theimself in theire propre persones to doo the king service upon an houre warnyng'. He also reissued the proclamation against 'Henry tydder Son of Edmond Tydder' and his followers, emphasizing their French backing, and the fact that even the Bretons had rejected their cause as 'to gretely unnaturalle and abhomynable for theim to graunt'.[50]

It is not clear from the surviving records of the long-anticipated clash between Richard and Henry that came in August whether the shire levies or many town and city forces did in the end turn out. There is some evidence from Buckinghamshire that some did, but even the famously loyal city of York may not have been represented on Bosworth Field.[51] Equally, for all his preparations, and the threats of sanctions that accompanied summons to arms, 'upon peyne of forfaicture unto us of all that ye may forfait and loose', Richard could not know which of his more powerful subjects would stand by him (would Percy? would the Stanleys? to name only two of the more questionably loyal great families).[52] He could not know either whether those lords' retainers would stand by *them*. The recent experience of the Duke of Buckingham had demonstrated that, but the phenomenon of unresponsive retainers, let alone vacillating nobility, was not restricted to Richard's reign in the fifteenth century. Marquess Montagu had been unable to raise a force to resist the returning Edward IV in 1471, for example, and Percy could only show his support by 'sitting still' (though that might have been a deliberate tactic on the earl's part, rather than all that he could do).

There were two options for meeting an invasion. The first was to beat it away before ships made landfall or before they established a beachhead. The second was to wait for the invaders, trusting that their numbers would not swell unduly, and meet them at a place of the defender's choosing. The second option allowed the defender time enough to gather his forces, and should give him the advantage of terrain. The advantages of the first were self-evident, but it was much more difficult to achieve. In the long wait for Henry's second attempt, Richard appears to have tried both approaches. In 1484 he had adapted Edward's system, set up for the Scottish campaign, 'of allocating one mounted courier to every 20 miles; riding with the utmost skill and not crossing their bounds, these men carried messages 200 miles within two days without fail by letters passed from hand to hand.'[53] He had also been recruiting 'spies overseas, at whatever price he could get them, from whom he learned almost all the movements of his enemies'. That 'almost', as it turned out, was doing a lot of work. In theory, if Richard knew when and where the invasion was coming, he could prepare forces to meet it. In practice, when Henry's invasion came, despite the fact that he landed five miles from his birthplace in Pembrokeshire, hardly an unimaginable choice, Richard had no one anywhere nearby to resist it.

If that was due to lack of intelligence, the reason may well have been money. The Crowland chronicler's reference to the courier system and the spies is from 1484, around the time of Edward of Middleham's death, when 'the king was better prepared to resist . . . than he would have been at any time afterwards'. One of the reasons for that is 'the treasure which he had in hand'. By the summer of 1485, and despite Richard's resort to more or less forced loans from his subjects, the high cost of maintaining an early-warning system and a network of spies may have become too much to bear. Similarly, the other way of forestalling an invasion – at sea – was expensive and technically demanding. Richard had had some naval success against the Scots, but preventing an invasion fleet from reaching shore was a matter of luck rather than judgement. As Edward IV had shown in 1471, even if a fleet was prevented from landing in one place there were unlikely to be enough resources to stop it landing altogether. Sir George Neville was put at the head of 'a force which the king has ordered to go to sea to resist his enemies' in April 1485, a commission that was scheduled to last until August. But if a significant fleet was put together, it proved unable to stop Henry getting through.[54]

Richard's orders of June 1485 were issued from Nottingham Castle, an indication that he had by this time settled on the second strategy, of meeting an invasion at the time and place of his choosing. From a central position, but near enough to his likely sources of strength in the north, Richard waited between early June and 11 August, when news of Henry's landing at Angle, near Milford Haven, finally came. Richard would get the battle he desired. If he had some idea of where he would fight it, the king could only wait and see which of his subjects would fight beside him. In some cases, that is what his subjects would do, too, from very eminent men like Lord Stanley and the Earl of Northumberland, to people lower down the social scale, including those whose names happen to have come down to us, such as John Paston, to those whom history has forgotten altogether. Paston was summoned by Richard's trustworthy Duke of Norfolk, in a letter 'delyveryd in hast', written around 12 August, asking him to meet at Bury St Edmunds with 'seche company of tall men as ye may goodly make at my cost and charge'.[55] There also survives a single letter sent by Richard himself at this time, to an esquire of the body, Henry Vernon, summoning him 'with such nombre as ye have promysed unto us sufficently horsed and harneised'.[56] In neither Vernon's nor Paston's case can it be shown that they did fight on Richard's side at Bosworth. Vernon later fought for Henry VII, at Stoke, which may mean that he did not turn out for Richard, but as Henry didn't pursue all those who fought against him after Bosworth, we can't be sure.

Throughout the Wars of the Roses, the reliability of armies from top to bottom was not very great. Bosworth was not exceptional in men failing to respond to summons, refusing to fight when there, or even changing sides. From Ludford Bridge, where Andrew Trollope's men had switched sides, to 'Losecote Field', where Sir Robert Welles's rebels turned tail, self-preservation often trumped blind loyalty. For all that, Richard probably had the larger army in the field against Henry when they finally clashed on 22 August. It has been argued that it 'was a measure of Richard's failure' that he didn't manage 'to make new friends' between his coronation and his final examination at Bosworth.[57] But not making new friends, or not keeping old ones, was not a uniquely Ricardian failing. His brother Edward had been far more comprehensively abandoned, betrayed by his closest ally Warwick and his sibling Clarence. Richard's inability to persuade overwhelming numbers to join him, and actually fight, at Bosworth certainly made Henry's chances greater. But the outcome on that day could not have been predicted with any certainty. Hastings and Bosworth are the two most famous battles fought on English soil. They have something else in common, too: the favourite lost.

A replica of the 'Bosworth Boar' badge found at the battlefield in 2009, as sold by the Bosworth Battlefield Heritage Centre, where the original is on display.

7

'Tant le desieree'

On 1 March 2009 a lead ball 3 centimetres across – smaller than a golf ball – was dug up in a field south of the village of Upton, in Leicestershire. By December of the following year, 33 more lead projectiles had been uncovered. All dated from the late fifteenth century, and together they accounted for more material evidence of guns and artillery 'than from all other archaeological surveys on battlefields of the fifteenth century put together'.[1] All this shot could only have come from the encounter we know as Bosworth, but which had been assigned twelve different names in the five centuries since it took place. The archaeologists from the Battlefields Trust had securely located a battlefield that had been as good as lost for around 300 years, since it had slipped from an oral tradition that could be traced back to living memory. They had also reminded us that an encounter often (and wrongly) seen as the last medieval battle in England was one in which gunpowder played a crucial role.

Subsequent discoveries, including the extraordinary find of a silver-gilt boar badge, very likely worn by a high-status member of Richard's personal retinue, have helped to flesh out the details of a battle that has always resisted simple explanation. By no means all the mysteries of Bosworth Field have been solved by archaeology, though further light on Richard's last moments has been shed by the detailed examination of the king's skeleton. But combining these newest finds with the narrative accounts that date from between five and about fifty years after the battle, we can begin to build a much clearer picture.

We certainly need to. One of the earliest Tudor histories that mentions the battle, written within living memory around fifteen years afterwards by a French biographer of Henry VII, Bernard André, took a uniquely honest approach. Faced with the confusion of oral accounts of the engagement, André was reduced to silence: 'Rather than affirm anything rashly, therefore, I pass over the date, place and order of battle, for as I have said I lack the illumination of eye-witnesses. Until I am fully instructed, for this field of battle I shall leave a blank space as broad * * * * * *.'[2] Not all historians, of the time or afterwards, have been so circumspect, but reconciling their accounts has proved impossible. Taking the latest archaeology into consideration, however, we can make more informed suggestions about what to accept and what to reject.

The numbers of the opposing armies and the way they arrived at the battlefield outside Leicester are the first stumbling blocks. Of course, the two opponents had very different journeys to make, and different obstacles to recruitment. Henry Tudor, having arrived in west Wales on 11 August, began to march north, up the Cardigan coast as far as Aberystwyth, attempting to gather support as he went. According to Polydore Vergil, Henry landed with around 2,000 men, which is a much more credible figure than the exaggerations of, for example, the French chronicler Jean Molinet, who gives a figure of 20,000. To this force, about half of which was English, with the remainder made up by a party of Scottish archers and a larger group of French mercenaries, Henry added as many as another 3,000 Welsh troops on his journey. He was backed not only by French manpower but also by French money. It may not be true that Henry was able to spend the 40,000 livres tournois (around £4,400) loaned to him by a combination of the French government and private lenders, on 'well-trained and drilled' Swiss pikemen, who happened to be in Normandy after a campaign in Flanders (they had almost certainly dispersed some time before).[3] But his army is likely to have included hard-bitten professional soldiers in its ranks.

The additional recruits that Henry made on his progress through Wales were not the result of a spontaneous flocking to his colours. Like Richard, Henry had sent letters to potential supporters, and continued to do so as he marched. Henry's uncle, Jasper Tudor, who still claimed the title of Earl of Pembroke, is likely to have been important in this process, appealing to former loyalties. And, as the Crowland chronicler pointed out, the 'lord steward and chamberlain of North Wales, in sole command' was Sir William Stanley (the brother of Thomas Stanley, Henry's stepfather), whose loyalty, along with that of his family, was still in the balance.[4] Among those who responded to the rebel summons, Polydore Vergil tells us, were Rhys ap Thomas, the Carmarthenshire landholder memorialized in a descendant's biography, whose grandfather had died fighting for Jasper Tudor at Mortimer's Cross. Rhys had been given an annuity of 40 marks by Richard in 1484,[5] and had apparently not joined Buckingham's rebellion. But the reappearance of the former Earl of Pembroke must have been powerfully persuasive. When Henry finally turned towards England, Sir John Savage came to him in Cheshire. Sir John was the nephew of Lord Stanley, and the connection suggested another reason for Henry to hope that his stepfather would eventually follow suit.

Richard might have expected that, as Henry entered England, he would begin to face stiffer resistance. But Shrewsbury, for example, was 'delivered unto your hands' by the actions of one Richard Crompe, though that, too, might also have something to do with William Stanley's influence.[6] At the next town on his march east, Newport, Henry was joined by Sir Gilbert Talbot, with 500 men. This was a particularly significant defection. Talbot was another of those who in 1483 had declined to support Buckingham (and by implication, Henry, Earl of Richmond). Now that Henry had arrived in person, and was unequivocally claiming the throne, Talbot like Rhys chose to throw in his lot with him.

Henry's route had been taking him on a collision course to Nottingham, where Richard was waiting. At Stafford, however, Henry changed direction, heading south-east, on the route towards London. We cannot tell whether he was aiming for the capital, which was well defended. Richard would not have known either, and when he set out from Nottingham, marching south to cut off Henry's advance, probably on 19 or 20 August, it was in haste: the king's forces, we are told, 'were not yet fully assembled'.[7] For all his lengthy preparations, and the knowledge for several days of Henry's arrival and advance, Richard was still hurried in his response. More troops joined him at Leicester when he arrived from Nottingham on 20 August. Two of the largest expected contingents, those of Thomas Stanley and Northumberland, certainly never made it to Nottingham. Northumberland may not have joined up with Richard's army until it had left Leicester for the battlefield itself on 21 August. Stanley, who had excused himself from coming to the king earlier on grounds of sickness, held aloof even longer. His army was present at Bosworth, but no one knew which side, if any, it would fight for.

It is tempting to see all this uncertainty as the reality behind the chaos of battle that reaches its apogee in Shakespeare. Richard had definitely been let down by some whose support he might have hoped for, and as surely had expectations of another defection from his opponent's stepfather. That much we know, because Richard kept Stanley's son Lord Strange a hostage, in much the same way as Edward IV had attempted to guarantee Sir Robert Welles's good behaviour by threatening (and ultimately executing) his father fifteen years earlier. Nevertheless, Richard was at the head of an army of perhaps 7,000 men, including the well-equipped soldiers brought by the Duke of Norfolk and the Earl of Northumberland, as he camped overnight on 21 August. The royal army was probably at Ambion Hill, once thought to be the location of the battle itself (and the place where the Bosworth Battlefield Visitor Centre was constructed in 1975). With the re-siting of the engagement about three miles to the west, Ambion can be logically suggested as the royal encampment, a relatively secure stopping place. The discovery of the most impressive artefact of all those associated with the battle, the 'Bosworth Cross', in the vicinity in the eighteenth century also makes more sense if this was a camp rather than a battlefield. This beautiful gilded crucifix, almost 2 feet high, was carried as a processional cross mounted on a staff, and decorated on the back with what are probably Yorkist 'sun in splendour' roundels. It seems unlikely that such an object would have been carried into battle. For a Mass before the battle, however, it is entirely appropriate.[8] The picture painted by the Crowland chronicler of Richard unable to celebrate Mass, because his chaplains weren't ready, which is supported by an oral tradition attributed to the king's carver, Bigod, has been challenged more recently as a Tudor smear. If Richard didn't hear divine office or was interrupted – and there is evidence that the crucifix was abandoned before it had been properly stored – he still had time to deploy his artillery, which even a man of his reputed piety might have thought more important.

There are no eyewitness accounts of the actual fighting at Bosworth, so Richard's state of mind can only be guessed at. In recent years the traditional Tudor picture of a king descending into paranoia following a fitful night's sleep has been contested. The evidence of substantial artillery fire points to a more deliberate approach than is suggested by such accounts. On the other hand, it seems unlikely that one recent historian of Bosworth is correct to have Richard rising in time to present himself to his troops wearing the 'precious crown of Edward the Confessor'. That puts a lot of strain on the words of the Crowland chronicler, 'diadema portans in capite' – 'wearing the diadem on his head'. This could refer to any form of crown, and in any case is specifically dated to the king's riding out of Leicester on 21 August, not to the morning of the battle itself. It is the Crowland author who says that Richard couldn't hear Mass and missed breakfast on the morning of the battle. He also tells us that 'the king, so it was reported, had seen that night, in a terrible dream, a multitude of demons apparently surrounding him'.[9] The origins of Shakespeare's nightmare scene are here. We are at liberty to dismiss all this as the posthumous account of a hostile source, but it won't really do to interpret the same author as apparently telling the opposite story of a measured, ceremonious preparation for battle.[10] It is quite plausible that Richard was interrupted as he got ready to hear Mass (which would have preceded his breakfast) by the arrival of Henry's troops on the battlefield. But if he was hurried, he was not panicked. He was ready for Henry. He had been waiting for more than a year.

How the two armies lined up against each other is still not agreed upon, in part because the hand-to-hand melee, which usually leaves an archaeological signature, has not yet been found to have done so at Bosworth. So we know that the two sides fired at each other, but cannot be certain where or exactly how their deployments clashed. Added to this are two almost insuperable mysteries about the roles played, or not played, by the Stanleys and the Earl of Northumberland. Sir William Stanley may have shown his hand earlier for Henry, but it is impossible to be sure. Northumberland seems to have played little part, but whether that was by accident or design – whether the mob who turned on him four years after the battle 'ffor the dysapoyntyng of kyng Rychard at Bosworth ffeeld' had a point – is equally difficult to decide.[11] Given these uncertainties, what follows is one plausible version of the events of 22 August 1485, not the final word.

The two vanguards, behind which the two commanders placed their own, smaller 'battles', were led by the Duke of Norfolk on Richard's side and the Earl of Oxford on Henry's. Northumberland's battle was placed on the left wing of

Richard's army, with Norfolk on the right. Richard had the advantage of terrain, with his troops and guns taking up position on the ridge below Ambion Hill, from which they could see Henry's army's advance. They were protected by an area of marsh, either in front of the whole line, or on Northumberland's left, protecting his flank. If this is how the armies were drawn up, it reflects Richard's reputation as an experienced commander, well versed in military theory. If Northumberland had a marsh to his side, for example, that was following the letter of Vegetius, the classic military theorist, a copy of whose work Richard had commissioned for his son.[12]

The king was certainly more experienced than his opponent. He had demonstrated bravery and dependability at Barnet and Tewkesbury, and had seen through the Scottish campaign with aplomb. Henry, by contrast, had attended the Battle of Edgecote as a twelve-year-old and had escaped a siege of Pembroke Castle two years later. But this shouldn't make us exaggerate Richard's qualities as a general. He had been following orders at the earlier battles, and in the Scottish campaign he faced an enemy that was disinclined to fight. For all the evidence that Richard was a keener soldier than his predecessor, and disappointed by Edward IV's reluctance to reopen the Hundred Years War, it was Edward who had the more impressive military record. At Mortimer's Cross and Towton, Edward seems to have inspired his followers to endure extraordinarily harsh conditions and savage hand-to-hand fighting. The discoveries from a mass grave at Towton show evidence of the horrific injuries that could result. Tewkesbury, on the other hand, was a tactical triumph. Richard's military record could not compare with his brother's, and as both inspirational commander and tactician he was tested at Bosworth.

Richard's failure at Bosworth has usually been interpreted as a failure to inspire enough support, both before the battle started and as it progressed. It has been calculated that only 6 out of 40 noblemen summoned for service by Richard fought for him at Bosworth.[13] He could not command loyalty, in other words, as a king or as a general in the field, despite the fact that, as even his enemies later admitted, he was himself a model of personal courage. The lack of support before Bosworth can be conceded, though the short time between Henry's landing and the battle could account for many absences. But on the field, it may be a tactical miscalculation rather than a failure of moral leadership that really let Richard down. As Oxford's vanguard advanced along the Roman road known as Fenn Lane, aiming for the left wing of Richard's army, it was met with a volley of long-range gunfire. Richard had summoned Sir Robert Brackenbury, constable of the Tower of London, who had been given the slip by two prisoners whom he was escorting as he made his way north, but it is likely that he did arrive with ordnance from the Tower arsenal. Richard had a long-standing interest in gunnery, as we know from his enthusiastic letter to Louis XI. In March 1484 he had ordered the authorities in Southampton to reimburse his clerk of ships, Thomas Rogers, for £24 spent on 20 new guns and 2 serpentines (a cannon that could be used on land and on board ship).[14] Although Henry had been supplied with some French artillery, and may have acquired more pieces on his march, he was outgunned.

From just over half a mile away, Richard's larger guns fired from their slightly elevated position. Lead shot up to 10 centimetres in diameter bounced into Oxford's line. Richard had a minimum of ten heavier guns, but probably many more. The survivors of the first onslaught continued their advance, but had to endure another volley of smaller arms fire, which is likely to have been far more deadly, as they closed on the enemy's position, perhaps still 200 yards away. They were now well within bowshot, and there was an exchange of arrows. Whether at a preordained signal, or simply in reaction to the artillery onslaught, Oxford now turned his army towards his opponent's right, where Norfolk was stationed. As Norfolk's battle moved in response, it is possible that it left no room for Northumberland to manoeuvre to engage Oxford's flank, hemmed in by the marsh. If this interpretation is right, then Northumberland's contingent, likely populated by just the sort of northerners who Richard would have expected to fight loyally, were not held back by the duplicity of their leader. They were stymied by the position they had taken up, which would have been on the king's instruction. In which case, tactics, not treachery, turned the battle against Richard III.[15]

All was not yet lost. Oxford's advance to engage with Norfolk had left Henry himself relatively exposed, protected by a small lifeguard of perhaps a few hundred men. Richard, decisive and impetuous in equal measure – and undoubtedly courageous – resolved to launch a cavalry charge across the ground that separated the two leaders. Accompanied by heavily armed mounted knights, he galloped over several hundred yards, and almost reached Henry himself. Polydore Vergil leaves us in no doubt about the sheer bravado of Richard's move: 'In the first charge Richard killed several men; toppled Henry's standard, along with the standard bearer William Brandon, contended with John Cheyney, a man of surpassing bravery who stood in his way, and thrust him to the ground with great force and made a path for himself through the press of steel.'[16]

All this time, Lord Stanley had apparently been holding back, possibly observing from the high ground that would later become known as Crown Hill, to the south of the battlefield. The Crowland chronicler writes that Richard had ordered the execution of his son, but it had not been carried out. It seems likely that this was because, like Stanley himself, those given the orders wanted to wait to see the outcome of the battle, now 'at a very critical stage'.[17] Stanley's intervention has traditionally been seen as the turning point in the battle, and the culminating act of treachery against a king beset by disloyalty. But it is just as likely that Stanley, true to form, was still waiting to join the winning side. From his vantage point he would have been able to witness the moment when Richard was cut down, and only then to make his choice.

The king had not battered his way through to Henry. He was knocked from his horse, but the evidence of the eleven 'perimortem' injuries to his skeleton and particularly to his skull makes it very unlikely that he had time to call for another. The testimony of the Spanish soldier Juan de Salazar, fighting on Richard's side, that he encouraged the king to flee (as Salazar did himself), is probably, if genuine, to be timed before Richard's fatal charge, but when the battle was already slipping from his grasp.[18] As he fell, Richard lost his helmet. He took a dagger thrust to the jaw, where he was cut or stabbed three times. His right cheek was pierced, the knife exiting on the other side of his face. There was a blow to the back of his head, and three times a sharp blade was aimed at the top of his skull, shaving off some of the bone. Despite this sustained assault, from several different attackers, he was still alive. Even the rondel driven into his head from above was not the death blow. There were two of those, also aimed from above, and behind the skull, probably with a halberd spike. Richard was on his knees, or even lying flat, face down, on the ground. The blows penetrated deep into his brain, and he died instantly.[19] Like his father and his brother Edmund, Richard went down fighting, overwhelmed by sheer numbers. The family of Rhys ap Thomas later claimed that he had delivered the fatal blow. Rhys was certainly knighted on the battlefield.

The focus on who fought or failed to fight for Richard, and in particular on the contribution of the Stanleys, obscures a simple truth about Bosworth, and perhaps about Richard III. It was one that the Tudor historian Polydore Vergil recognized. 'The report is that Richard could have saved himself by flight.' He could have left the battlefield, as others had done before (including the father he venerated), to fight another day. He would have lost Bosworth, and survived. Edward IV had been more bereft of support than Richard ever was, both after Edgecote and at the Readeption, yet had managed to return. There were still men loyal to Richard, as the actions of Francis Lovell, the spontaneous grief of the citizens of York and those protesters who turned on the Earl of Northumberland in 1489 all make clear. The otherwise complete capitulation of the Ricardian establishment was not a demonstration that they had been under the heel of a tyrant. Richard's cause died with him. Staying loyal to it was an act of desperation only likely to be embraced by those, not very numerous, to whom Henry Tudor refused a pardon – but that hard core could have formed the basis for a fightback, as Edward's had for him.

Edward's valour, however, had been diluted with discretion, and that was not a virtue that Richard had prized, as his actions from Picquigny onwards had made clear. Richard's final charge was a gamble, but still a calculated one. He had made many such bets before, and he had won most of them. In the gamble for the Crown itself, he had certainly risked his life. If he had failed then, it was treason, and he could have expected the same ultimate fate as Clarence. At Bosworth, he risked his life again, realizing that if he killed Henry he would not only win the day, but, probably, establish himself as undisputed king. In the end, of the two mottoes associated with Richard, it was not 'Loyauté me lie' (Loyalty binds me) that proved to be his undoing. It was 'Tant le desirée' (I have longed for it – for glory, for the rewards of chivalry – so much) that led him to death. This was the sentiment of an adolescent preserved by a man who, for all his intelligent grasp of realpolitik, retained a sense of naivety. Much of Richard's life and career were spent in a cool and entirely unromantic devotion to improving his status and laying up treasures on earth. But what happened at Bosworth is the perfect illustration of the complexity at the heart of his character, a complexity that, paradoxically, made him more representative of his time than any king since Henry V. He was ambitious, ruthless and occasionally impulsive. He was also a pious man of destiny, who retained a faith in the code of chivalry. He may – at least by August 1485 if not already in June 1483 – have convinced himself of the rightness of his cause. Such a conviction gave a man the courage to launch an attack head on at his opponent. Richard was in that way the opposite of Shakespeare's double-dealer. Richard III believed in his own publicity. Very likely he also died believing in it.

With Richard's death, and the rout of Howard's vanguard, during which the Duke of Norfolk was killed and his son taken prisoner, the battle ended abruptly. One of the Stanleys (both William and Thomas have been credited) apparently found Richard's crown (the 'battle crown' from his helmet, one assumes) and placed it on Henry's head. This ad hoc ceremony might well have taken place on the hill that shortly afterwards acquired the name Crown Hill – which was possibly where Lord Stanley had been all along.

As for Richard, it was important that he was known to have died, and for his corpse to be seen by as many people as possible. That was the only sure way to scotch rumours of his survival. 'Many other insults were offered' to Richard's body as it was carried back to Leicester.[20] One at least is recorded on his bones: a stab to the buttock, probably as his near-naked corpse passed, slung over a horse, or was dragged by a halter round his neck. When it reached the Grey Friars church in Leicester, the body was 'exposed [for] three days to universal gaze'.[21] Most sources agree that he was naked or nearly naked, which would have revealed for the first time to the public the extent of Richard's scoliosis.

The blackening of Richard's reputation had begun, of course, well before his death. It was one of the more intractable enemies the king faced during his short reign. Before the rediscovery of Richard's remains in Leicester in 2012, pro-Ricardians had always been at pains to point out that no reference to any 'deformity' could be dated to before his death. This could be taken as an indication that much of what was written about him was simply made up, posthumous 'propaganda', or victors' history. Now that we know Richard *did* suffer from an altered body shape, and one which was severe enough that it is likely to have suggested a concomitant twisting of personality to contemporaries, once they saw it or heard about it, it is remarkable to observe how quickly the news of the disability spread. The Welsh bard Dafydd Llwyd's poem celebrating Henry Tudor's victory was written shortly afterwards, while the outcome was still unconfirmed. Daffyd begins: 'The crown is on the eagle's [Henry's] brow,/If it is true the mole [Richard] and his men are slain.' The poem's most recent commentator found no evidence that Dafydd believed Richard to be deformed, but this seems to ignore the accumulation of physically insulting references to him, not only as a mole, but also as 'little R . . . /Pallid, cruel letter,/Forked . . ', with 'A pale leg where was a mighty thigh', 'little boar', guilty of 'monstrous deceit', 'the little caterpillar of London/Was to be curled up in a knot of thorns', 'A little ape with a magpie's leash./A curse on the twisted crown upon him . . '. Dafydd's poem was based on hearsay, about Henry's victory, about Richard's crimes (the murders of both Henry VI and the princes are conditionally pinned on him) – and about his physique. The build-up of twisted, monstrous imagery suggests that Dafydd has heard that there was something 'unnatural' about Richard, but he didn't know quite what.[22]

The intimations of physical deformity and what that meant about Richard were among the first influences on his posthumous reputation. As for his body, it was buried hastily, uncoffined and unshrouded, in the choir at Grey Friars in Leicester. The grave appears to have been hastily dug, and Richard's body was crammed into a space too small to accommodate it, dropped feet first. His hands may have been tied.[23] There, despite rumours that it had been dug up and the bones scattered in the River Soar, his corpse remained, through the dissolution of the monasteries, the destruction of the church above it, and of the private house and garden that succeeded that, until its extraordinary rediscovery, under the most famous car park in Britain.

8

'My shadow as I pass'

A strange, formless patch of shadow falls across a palace door, moves over a stone pavement and is at length seen in profile, revealed as that of a stooped man, leaning in intimate conversation with the crowned figure of a king. The first lumpen shade is Laurence Olivier's, in his 1955 film of Shakespeare's *Richard III* (the second is Cedric Hardwicke's Edward IV, who 'cannot live long'). It is worth acknowledging at the beginning of any attempt to think about Richard's afterlife the shadow cast not just by Shakespeare himself, but by Olivier. It is his simpering, wink-tipping portrayal of the king, shifting the play's balance between black comedy and horror decidedly towards the former, that still dominates the popular imagination sixty years later. When a television presenter of a documentary in 2014 about the excavation of Richard III's remains wishes to summon up the spirit of the king as he wanders through the ruins of Middleham Castle, it is Olivier's Richard – exaggerated limp, 'envious mountain on my back', and strangulated RSC tones – that he cannot resist adopting.[1] Anyone who admits to an interest in, let alone to writing a book about, Richard III, consigns himself to a bombardment of Olivier impersonations. Nobody offers an Ian McKellen (filmed in 1995), an Al Pacino (filmed in 1996), let alone one of the celebrated theatrical performances, from Antony Sher to Kevin Spacey. For most of us, Richard III *is* Laurence Olivier.

The interpretation of Richard that Olivier offers is at the limits of coldness and gleeful calculation, without a glimmer of humanity – if not so exaggerated in its portrayal of the physical deformity of Shakespeare's king as some renditions. It might therefore be assumed to be the culmination of five centuries of the blackening of Richard's name, the refinement of 'Tudor propaganda' to its purest, least balanced form. But if it can be argued that Shakespeare was aiming to present at least a version of history, coloured by the need to celebrate the Tudor dynasty, that is emphatically not what Olivier was doing. The opening credits of his film, which in any case admit to including 'some interpolations' by two eighteenth-century actor-managers, Colley Cibber and David Garrick, also volunteer that what follows is not history, but 'legend', without which, we are told, history is 'like letters without poetry, [or] flowers without perfume'. Just in case the viewer misses the point, it is repeated and amplified, in capital letters: 'HERE NOW BEGINS ONE OF THE MOST FAMOUS AND AT THE SAME TIME INFAMOUS OF THE LEGENDS THAT ARE ATTACHED TO . . . THE CROWN OF ENGLAND.'

Olivier knew that Shakespeare's Richard could no longer be justified as history, and he expected his audience to understand the distinction, too. Historians had long argued over and redrawn the king's portrait, particularly in the twentieth century. Olivier's film was, moreover, released into a culture that had eagerly assimilated the most successful example of pro-Ricardianism ever printed: Josephine Tey's novel, *The Daughter of Time* (1951). Tey's book, usually described as a work of historical fiction, but in fact a detective novel taking a historical subject as its case, has never been out of print, and was voted the top crime novel of all time in 1990 by the Crime Writers' Association in Britain (the US equivalent made it number 4). John Gielgud, one of four theatrical knights cast by Olivier in his film, was a friend of Tey's (whose real name was Elizabeth MacKintosh, though she preferred to be known by yet another pseudonym, Gordon Daviot), and Olivier had played Bothwell in her play *Queen of Scots* before the Second World War. We can be sure that both Olivier and Gielgud had read her novel, and were therefore persuaded that Shakespeare's version of Richard was something other than history, whether or not they bought into the novel's wholesale rehabilitation of the king.

If Olivier's Richard is merely the king made into a story, is Shakespeare's Richard nevertheless visible as a would-be historical portrayal on a Tudor continuum that begins in Henry VII's time? There were historians under Henry who did begin to write about Richard as the murderous dissembler with whom Shakespeare made us all familiar. But right at the beginning of Henry VII's reign the approach to his predecessor was different. The initial plan, if there was one, was not to blacken Richard so much as to erase him entirely.

That process began shortly after Bosworth when, following the period of exposure to ensure that Richard was widely known to have been killed, his body was quickly, and it would seem unceremoniously, buried. Then, when Henry called his first parliament, he initiated a more considered policy of erasure. A day was lopped off the last king's reign, so that those who fought for Richard at Bosworth were deemed already to have been in rebellion. More radically, Richard III's parliamentary claim to the throne, Titulus Regius, was not only overturned, but the record of it was directed to be 'avoided out of the rolle and recordes of the seid parlement of the seid late kyng, [and to be] brent and utterly destroyed'.[2] Contrary to the more febrile claims of Ricardians, it seems unlikely that Henry did this because he thought Titulus Regius contained a ticking time bomb in the form of the truth about the illegitimacy of Edward IV's offspring (which would shortly include Henry's wife). To begin with, Henry would surely have realized that, even if all copies were burnt, their contents, like those of the bills that Richard had ordered to be destroyed unread, would be hard to forget. The inclusion of the burden of Titulus Regius by the Crowland chronicler, writing in April 1486, more than five months after Henry's parliament, is testimony to that. And what about the record of the order to destroy the Act, in Henry's own parliamentary rolls? While this text did not reproduce any more than the opening lines of Richard's Act, it made it very clear what was being referred to. As we have seen, Titulus Regius was not only enacted in Parliament, but was more widely promulgated (and a copy did survive, on the Parliament Rolls, available at the National Archives as item C 65/114).

The wording of Henry's expunging seems therefore to draw attention to the very thing it ostensibly wants to erase. If the new king was engaged in a suspicious cover-up, he was going about it in rather public fashion. It seems far more probable that this was part of a wider process of wiping official memory of the reign of a king referred to as 'in dede and not of right kyng of England' in Henry's parliament rolls. The accusation contained in Titulus Regius against Henry's future queen was of course unconscionable – but just because Henry didn't want it to be repeated doesn't mean he thought it was true, or thought that he could entirely manipulate his subjects' own memories. Late-medieval kings, even ones credited with the sophistication of Henry VII, were not yet in the business of brainwashing their people, for which neither the techniques, the bureaucracy – nor, most likely the inclination – yet existed.

In some ways, Henry followed Richard's own lead in the manner in which he dealt with an inconvenient predecessor. Like Richard, Henry did his best to ignore the last incumbent. Whereas Richard went about effacing the few weeks' reign of a boy-king declared illegitimate, however, Henry had to contend with the two-year reign of a king who had had a profound effect on his kingdom, not least in prompting subjects in unprecedented numbers to decide whether to be loyal to him or not. This was why Henry had to make a greater effort to obliterate the traces of Richard's time on the throne. But if we compare the official language that Richard used to describe not Edward V, but Edward IV, with Henry's official descriptions of Richard, the former seem far more vituperative, after Richard had changed tack and decide to excoriate his brother. If anyone indulged in propaganda with a view to actively blackening a predecessor's reputation, it was Richard, not Henry. Compare Henry's bland proclamation shortly after Bosworth (fresh enough that it contained the erroneous information that the Earls of Surrey and Lincoln, as well as Viscount Lovell, had all been killed there) with Richard's damning references to Edward. Henry refers to 'Richard duke of Gloucester, late called King Richard', but gives us no further description, either of the king or his rule.[3] Richard, by contrast, happily went into details about Edward IV in Parliament, with references to Edward's 'ungraciouse pretensed mariage' and the result that 'all poletique rule was perverted'.[4]

'By broken faith'

This is not to argue that, shortly after Bosworth, Richard was not criticized or defamed, merely that Henry himself doesn't seem to have been directing any such moves. Perhaps, of course, he didn't feel the need. Court flattery was a thriving art and men at all levels of society knew that the establishment of a new regime would smile on the damning of the old. The Italian poet Pietro Carmeliano, for example, had dedicated verses to Edwards IV and V and then to Richard, whom he described in a preface to a Life of St Catherine in glowing terms: 'If we look for truth of soul, for wisdom, for loftiness of mind united with modesty, who stands before our King Richard?'[5] But in 1486, with a new patron to flatter, Carmeliano played a new tune, celebrating the birth of Henry's heir, Prince Arthur, in a poem that portrayed Richard as a tyrant and murderer of Henry VI and his own nephews. For Carmeliano, the tactic worked. He was made Henry's Latin secretary, by 1490 at the latest. Born a year before Richard, Carmeliano lived well into Henry VIII's reign and grew rich with ecclesiastical preferments. Only literary fashion – harder, perhaps, to adapt to than political changes – finally excluded him from the highest social circles. Despite all the risk and unpredictability for which the life of Richard and so many of his contemporaries are evidence, there were ways of living through, and profiting from, the political storms of the late fifteenth century. When considering Richard's reputation, we must always bear in mind that those who formed it were working under contemporary constraints.

The Warwick priest and antiquary John Rous was another who needed no official prompt to trim his literary sails. As we have seen, Rous took the opportunity of revising one version (though not all) of his history of the Earls of Warwick to change his description of Richard, while his royal history, completed in 1486, contained an all-out attack on a monstrous tyrant. From a little later, Polydore Vergil's treatment of Richard, in his *Anglica Historia*, which was encouraged by Henry VII but not completed until after his death, bears more of the hallmarks of what we would recognize as the Tudor version of the last Plantagenet. Vergil's Richard is not physically impaired, but he is a consummate schemer, who plans to take the throne from the moment of his brother's death, and is constantly 'gnawed' ('moredebatur') by his conscience, while nonetheless plunging on with his crimes. The personal distaste of the Crowland chronicler has developed in Vergil into a more rounded picture of a tyrant in action.

Reflections on Richard's record and character were not confined to literary works. After years of effacing and ignoring his memory, Henry VII apparently returned to the subject. In 1494, Henry had seen off the initial threats to his rule by Richard's diehard supporters, including Francis Lovell, as well as the first of two impostors, Lambert Simnel. Backed by Richard's nephew the Earl of Lincoln (and once again, by Lovell), Simnel had attempted an invasion, masquerading as 'Edward VI', Clarence's son, the Earl of Warwick (who was in fact in Henry's custody). That force had been defeated at Stoke in 1487 (a serious affair that has a better claim to being the last battle of the Wars of the Roses than Bosworth). But in 1493 a new impostor emerged, backed by Richard's sister Margaret, the dowager Duchess of Burgundy. Margaret claimed that a man later identified as Perkin Warbeck was in fact her nephew Richard, Duke of York, Edward V's younger brother and one of the princes in the Tower. This Richard, it was alleged, had miraculously escaped death and was now gathering support to make an attempt to regain the Crown for the Plantagenet dynasty. It was as these preparations were being made that Henry commissioned an alabaster tomb for Richard III, along with an epitaph. Although Richard's was hardly the sort of lavish monument that Henry had envisaged for his own memorial, neither the tomb nor the accompanying inscription insulted Richard's memory. The epitaph, in the text that survives to us from the sixteenth century, does describe Richard as holding the throne 'by broken faith', but there are no further accusations, other than that Richard was 'deserted by the English' before encountering Henry at Bosworth.[6] We can't say whether the political circumstances of Henry's reign dictated this surprisingly benign, if belated, treatment of his predecessor. But it certainly shows that he felt no urge towards a concerted dismantling of his reputation.

Voices that continued to speak up for Richard were, unsurprisingly, rare and marginal. If his tomb and epitaph represented a qualified official seal of approval, it was very much the exception. The York councillors' lament for Richard ('late mercifully reigning upon us') on the news of his death in battle was shortly followed by overtures to his successor. The only difference between this and the literary about-turns of Carmeliano or Rous was the admittedly important one of timing. York took a risk by allowing their pro-Richard views to be recorded after his death. But again, we should be wary of imposing on this period later notions of what could safely be voiced. Henry would have been under no illusions that York had been Richard's most loyal civic supporter – though, as we have also seen, London was hardly a reluctant follower. If the new king was ever made aware of the citizens of York's grief at losing a royal protector, it surely wouldn't have surprised him. Medieval kings had often been compelled to deal with formerly rebellious subjects, and expected most to shift their allegiance to the new realities. Even Thomas Howard – son of one of Richard's most reliable supporters, John, Duke of Norfolk, who had been killed fighting against Henry at Bosworth – managed to manoeuvre his way into Henry's affections, and, after three years' imprisonment, was restored to his title and rose to a prominent position at the Tudor court. The wholesale exclusion of political enemies had not happened in Richard's reign, and it would not happen in Henry's. It was Henry VII's successor who introduced a level of political paranoia that would have seemed a departure to either of his two predecessors.

Equally well, the fact of York's posthumous praise for Richard should not sway us too much into believing that they spoke for a loyalist Ricardian majority, who 'knew' that Richard had been a good king, if only they had been permitted to say so. Consider the evidence of a case heard by the councillors of York in 1491. In the course of a drunken argument about the merits of the Earl of Northumberland (killed in 1489 by a mob who may have resented his equivocal performance at Bosworth and support for Henry afterwards), one William Burton, a schoolmaster, presumably defending the earl's questionable loyalty to Richard III, said 'Kyng Richgard was an ypocryte, a crochebake, and beried in a dike like a dogge'. Interestingly, the reason this brawl came to official attention was more to do with the criticism of Northumberland and the implied slander of *Henry*, who, the loyal deponents pointed out, had actually made sure that Richard was buried 'like a noble gentilman' (even before his tomb had been commissioned) than with any aspersions against Richard. Still, it demonstrates that even in York, within living memory, Richard's reputation was a contested one, as well as that the two principal charges against him, hypocrisy and physical deformity, were not the exclusive property of a literary elite.[7]

The first tour de force of anti-Ricardian prose, Thomas More's *History of King Richard III* (c. 1513–18), was a private enterprise rather than an official commission. With More's *History*, drawing on Rous and Vergil, the essential elements of the wicked uncle Richard, the perfect combination of cruelty and hypocrisy, are in place. The result has been described as an exercise in humanistic rhetoric on the subject of tyranny (though More abruptly ended his history when he reached the point of Buckingham's rebellion, so the exercise is actually more focused on the act of usurpation, rather than what succeeds it). It has also been called a 'masterpiece of sardonic wit and drama'.[8] More loads nearly all the charges that he can on to Richard, including the murder of Henry VI and a secret working to the same end for Richard's brother Clarence, as well as the killings of Hastings, Rivers, Vaughan and Grey – and the two princes (though he does not accuse Richard of killing Henry VI's son Edward, as some writers did). He also gives us a deformed Richard, 'little of stature, ill fetured of limmes, croke backed, his left shoulder much higher than his right, hard fauoured of visage'.[9] He leaves us in no doubt that these marks of nature were the outward stamp of an evil character.

This line of exaggerated versions of Richard can be followed from Rous and Vergil, via More, through to the later Tudor writers such as Edward Hall, Raphael Holinshed and thus on to Shakespeare. All follow the same trend, which gives us a portrait of consummate evil and scheming hypocrisy contained in a deformed frame. Richard's quintessence of wickedness is contrasted less with a faultless Henry VII than with the prospect of peace itself. In Shakespeare, for example, the telescoping of Edward IV's second reign, the period when 'Our bruisèd arms [are] hung up for monuments' and 'Grim-visaged war hath smoothed his wrinkled front', so that it is almost immediately superseded by Richard's bloody march to power, is reflected in Henry's final speech: 'Enrich the time to come with smooth-faced peace,/With smiling plenty and fair prosperous days!'[10] Peace happens offstage, war and skulduggery happen in plain sight.

Perhaps it isn't surprising that this version of Richard began to be challenged fairly early. In 1617, William Cornwallis printed the tract 'In Praise of King Richard the Third', though its authorship is still disputed. This work challenged all of the crimes attributed to Richard, either absolving him of them or justifying them. Some of the justifications strike a modern reader, at least, as so rhetorical as perhaps to be tongue in cheek. How seriously should we take an author who commends the murder of the princes as an act motivated by the public good, which 'freed the people from dissension', and asking 'how could he demonstrate his love more amply, than to adventure his soul for their [the people's] quiet?'[11] If that reads like the sort of justification that Shakespeare himself would have been happy to put in Richard's mouth (compare 'Simple, plain Clarence! I do love thee so,/That I will shortly send thy soul to heaven'),[12] then George Buck offered a rather more plausible defence of Richard, in his very capacious *History* written around the same time as the Cornwallis tract. Buck was the first writer to use the Crowland chronicle continuation openly and extensively, though not without manipulation when its tenor didn't suit his argument. Defences of Richard, or at least challenges to the 'Tudor' version, continued to be written, most famously by Horace Walpole, whose *Historic Doubts* were published in 1768. The details of the cases these authors put forward are less important than the fact that they were being written at all. Every generation, it seems, has taken upon itself the need to right the eternal wrong of Richard's reputation. Unsurprisingly, elements of the arguments proffered by the likes of Walpole have been successfully challenged. Famously, Walpole himself challenged them, changing his mind about Richard in the aftermath of the French Revolution. But no one writing history in the twenty-first century would expect to place much credence in an eighteenth-century version of the late Middle Ages, long before modern historical standards of source treatment had been established. The case of Richard III should be no exception.

The trouble defenders of Richard have had in establishing their case has less to do with its merits than the fact that they were fighting an unequal battle. Some historians did reply to specific arguments put forward by pro-Ricardians. The turn of the twentieth century, for example, saw champions from both sides, James Gairdner and Clements Markham, argue their case in the pages of the *English Historical Review* and subsequent editions of their books on Richard. Historians in the later twentieth century have moved the study of Richard into new territory. Perhaps the first signal of a more rounded approach was given by the National Portrait Gallery's exhibition devoted to Richard in 1973, curated by Pamela Tudor-Craig. This put Richard in a European context, as part of 'a country hovering . . . on the edge of international trade' (though, as always, present concerns were evident: the UK had joined the European Common Market at the beginning of that year). Tudor-Craig also pointed out that, for all the frustrating gaps in the evidence for the life and reign of King Richard, there was still a lot to sift through: 'Some may feel . . . that there are too many documents, though they only represent a tenth of the bulk which do survive from those months'.[13] The work of Charles Ross and Rosemary Horrox, among others, that followed, was all written in the same spirit, attempting to move Richard's story on from what Tudor-Craig called 'the central mystery' and to see Richard in comparison to other nobles, and other kings, of his time.

These modern works support some of the Ricardians' arguments about the lack of evidence for Richard's guilt in at least some of the crimes attributed to him. As neutral historians, however, none of them was making 'a case for the defence' (or, indeed, the prosecution). But from a Ricardian point of view that was not the problem. What Ricardians have never had is an equivalent weapon to the constant revival of the most eloquently stated, if also most exaggerated, attack on their man. That is, only anti-Ricardians have Shakespeare, and it is actually the emotional pull of Shakespeare's assault, rather than disputes over facts, against which Ricardians have contended for so many years. Although a few controversialists still cling to Shakespeare's picture as mostly true, the majority of historians have long since rejected it. And yet in popular terms the 'debate' around Richard III still focuses on the question 'was he really the psychopath of Shakespeare's play?' Were it not for the peculiar circumstance of a 500-year-old play still being regularly performed around the world, the Ricardians could be said to have long since won their battle to clear Richard's name, in popular opinion at least. It would be a brave historical novelist who offered a fictionalized version of the 'black legend' of Richard today.

'To secure a reassessment'

The reason for that is not confined to individual historians, or to individual novelists, even ones as successful as Josephine Tey. In 1924 a tiny group of friends led by a Liverpudlian obstetrician, Samuel Saxon Barton, finding a shared interest in Richard III, and persuaded that his recent defenders had a point that needed to be more widely advertised, founded the Fellowship of the White Boar. It didn't do very much, at least in public, during the 1920s. In the 1930s, Saxon Barton began a correspondence in the *Yorkshire Herald* on the subject of the identification of a monument in Sheriff Hutton church, which he argued was that of Edward of Middleham. This set a precedent for much of the unshowy work of what became the Richard III Society over the coming decades. Membership was a self-selecting group of Ricardians (the Fellowship's third member joined once he had 'qualified himself by a study of [the late Victorian uber-Ricardian, Clements] Markham').[14] Most of what they actually engaged in was more narrowly focused on antiquarian detail rather than wholesale rehabilitation. This had the advantage of gaining respectability: the Fellowship and then the Society's efforts to conserve or repair sites of Ricardian interest from Fotheringhay to Bosworth were both praiseworthy and fitted in with the growing interest in 'heritage'. It is only when you consider that all this was done in part to set the record straight (in the words of the Society's mission statement, 'to promote in every possible way, research into the life and times of Richard III, and to secure a reassessment of the . . . role of this monarch in English history') that such projects begin to take on a slightly stranger tinge. Why should tidying up the site of 'King Richard's Well' at Bosworth, or putting up a plaque to his memory at Fotheringhay, show Richard in a more favourable light?

The extraordinary success of the Society in the twenty-first century, in spearheading a project that led to the recovery of the king's remains, has only emphasized this discrepancy. While academics – some of them closely involved with the Society – have continued to attempt to broaden the way Richard is seen in the context of his time, the Society itself depends on a far more elemental level of 'enthusiasm' for Richard, characterized by commemoration and re-enactment more than analysis and debate. The tension has to some extent been internalized, and is nicely illustrated in the two separate publications the Society produces. The first, *The Ricardian*, is a scholarly journal, edited by a leading expert in the field (since 1979, by Anne F. Sutton; previous editors include Peter and Carolyn Hammond), and carrying articles on an extraordinarily wide variety of fifteenth-century subjects, by no means exclusively focused on Richard himself. *The Ricardian* happily prints articles from respected scholars, such as Colin Richmond and Michael Hicks, who are rather less than full-blooded Ricardians themselves. The Society's other publication, the *Ricardian Bulletin*, is a much lighter affair. Although it does print some articles containing discussions or discoveries to do with 'the man himself', as Richard is usually described, it is more focused on the business of meetings and outreach ('Morning refreshments included boar-shaped ginger biscuits made by Mandy Ford'), and carries a faintly obsessive collation of mentions of Richard in recent local and national print media.

The Richard III Society has performed this balancing act for years. When the 'Looking for Richard' project found their man, the assumption that the discovery, and the attendant excitement about what should happen to the remains, would cast Richard in a new light, was often taken for granted. As we have learned, some specific aspects of the king, especially his health and his final hours, have been revealed by the evidence of his bones. But Richard's skeleton can't tell us what sort of man, let alone what sort of king, he was. It has been hard to resist the implication that because Ricardians 'found' Richard, Ricardianism as a whole is 'right'. Remarkably, in the first stages after the discovery, the University of Leicester, while scrupulously controlling the scientific and archaeological investigation, seem to have ceded the writing of the history of the king to the Richard III Society. Even now, the university's webpage on Richard III presents a broadly Ricardian view. In its account of Richard's rise to power, 'a long-standing popular belief that Richard had his nephews murdered in order to remove any competing claim to the throne' is conceded but no mention of the reputable, and widely accepted, historical arguments for Richard's responsibility for the murder is made. Other victims of Richard's rise, from Hastings to Rivers, are conspicuously absent. The summary moves swiftly on to the Richard III Society's promotion of the 'inarguably good works of this popular King', among which are included the introduction of the presumption of innocence, which stretches still further the already tendentious idea that Richard 'introduced' the notion of bail.[15]

Despite this concession of the historiographical ground to Ricardianism, there have been predictable strains between the academics of Leicester and the representatives of the Richard III Society. Philippa Langley, the driving force behind and fundraiser for the Looking for Richard project, has complained that the university has tried to 'suppress the role of Ricardians and their funding', by alleging that the decision to excavate the remains found on the first day of the Grey Friars dig on 25 August 2012, which turned out to be Richard's, was taken on purely archaeological grounds, rather than made possible by an additional provision of Richard III Society cash.[16] Whatever the truth of that particular spat, it demonstrates how hard professionals find it when amateurs are proved right. The internet has, inevitably, both widened and thinned debate about Richard. While numerous sites affiliated to the Society have sprung up over the past decade, and proved invaluable for raising funds on the Looking for Richard project, the wilder reaches of pro- and (occasionally) anti-Richard III theorizing, and decidedly unacademic discourse, is given full rein.[17]

The next chapter in Richard's story centred on an even less edifying contest. The representatives of a hastily assembled body called the Plantagenet Alliance mounted a legal challenge in 2014 to the decision of the Secretary of State for Justice that allowed the University of Leicester to arrange for the disposal of Richard's remains as they saw fit. The Alliance, who claimed descent from Richard (a broad category when collateral descendants are included), argued that York was a more appropriate place, and that, given the unusual circumstances of finding the bones of an anointed king, the usual procedure of a licence granted to archaeologists to authorize them to dispose properly of human remains did not apply. The legal case centred on whether the Secretary of State had a 'duty to consult' on the matter. Despite the narrow basis of the case, and the rather dry piling up of legal precedent that the government's counsel performed when it came to Judicial Review, the challenge gave an excuse for an outbreak of opinionating on where the bones should be reinterred. Arguments were put forward for York, as a sort of spiritual home for Richard (and where, more relevantly, he had planned his great chantry, though that didn't necessarily mean he wanted to be buried there); for Westminster Abbey, where his queen is buried; for Fotheringhay, where he was born. Wags even suggested Australia or outer space. The debate petered out, but did not entirely cease, when the court's unequivocal judgement, that there was no duty to consult, and Leicester could therefore go ahead with their arrangements, was handed down in May 2014.

As the date for the reinterment ceremonies for Richard's body approached in March 2015, there were signs that Ricardians would not completely control the narrative. The university and Leicester Cathedral's plans for Richard occasionally clashed with what Ricardians thought was appropriate (including proposals for the design of the tomb). Not only that, but, a little belatedly, commentators began to wonder why so much attention was being paid to a king of such debatable character, though some writers didn't quite put it like that ('It's mad to make this child killer a national hero: Richard III was one of the most evil, detestable tyrants ever to walk this earth, says Michael Thornton').[18] Intriguingly, by the time the ceremonies began on 22 March, when Richard's coffin was taken around the sites of his final hours, and then brought to Leicester Cathedral, public opinion about the king seemed to have settled on a version of the remark made by the aldermen of London to Cardinal Wolsey: 'although he did evill, yet in his tyme wer many good actes made, not by hym onely, but by the consent of the body of the whole realme, whiche is the parliament'.[19]

Richard's popular reputation thus might be said to have come full circle, to a position before Shakespeare's charming monster took the stage. That may be convenient for those who have invested such an enormous amount of energy and resources in the project of 'dignity and honour' for his remains. Whether it is fair to the historical record is another matter. As we have seen, the case for Richard's involvement in some of the notorious acts ascribed to him varies in strength. The case for his own benign record has also certainly been exaggerated. But the wider question of whether he was a 'good king', as his contemporaries might have understood the phrase, has been rather obscured by constantly being conflated with the moral arguments. Fundamentally, the first duty of a king was to command loyalty. It had taken Henry VI around twenty years of incompetence and eventually incapability to lose the support of a significant proportion, though by no means all, of his senior nobility. Richard did it in just two years. That was not because he was incompetent, nor because his rule was so tyrannical as to be intolerable. It was because he never established his legitimacy to the satisfaction of enough of his subjects, particularly the most powerful. We cannot know the exact reasons for that, but the way Richard came to power, and the strong likelihood (at the very least, the widespread belief) that on seizing power he had caused his two young nephews to be killed, must have played their part. That is not to say that, with a bit more luck and perhaps one more loyal magnate, Richard could not have resisted the challenge of Henry Tudor. But Richard's failure meant that he had no chance to redeem his kingship. His supporters have attempted to redeem him ever since, but his record of failure cannot be overturned. Whether or not Richard was a bad man, he was a bad king. His actions led not only to his own destruction, but that of his dynasty. Can there be a blacker mark against a medieval king's name than that?

If a more sophisticated view of Richard the man, somewhere between Shakespeare and Josephine Tey, has taken hold, the perception of the age he lived in and how he fitted into it has been harder to shift. The Wars of the

Roses are still seen as a time of almost constant fighting, concentrated virtually exclusively on dynastic power games and lust for power. The long period of peace under Edward IV, of which Richard, Duke of Gloucester, was perhaps the greatest beneficiary, is still too easily skated over à la Shakespeare. The idea that what we call the Wars of the Roses were initiated not by dynastic politics but issues of fundamental competence and the breakdown of the body politic is even less widely accepted. Shakespeare, and our natural preference for 'personalities' over 'issues', may only be partly to blame. Richard tried to present his own bid for power as motivated by concerns for the 'commonweal'. But, whatever he did to prove that by his actions as king, his actions as Protector had revealed the opposite. If anyone should be blamed for the caricature of his era as a naked fight for power, it is Richard III.

Richard is still routinely described as England's last medieval monarch. But the Middle Ages did not end at Bosworth, and Henry VII drew quietly on the precedents of his Yorkist predecessors as he established his rule. Henry VIII, too, was as much a medieval monarch as a Renaissance prince, whose savage manipulation of judicial revenge was a match for the bloodiest moments of Richard's rise, and far outstripped those of his short reign. And if Richard's successors were sometimes medieval, Richard and his contemporaries could be surprisingly 'modern'. The reassessment of Bosworth Field as a place of gunfire and ordnance as much as sword and plate armour is one facet of that picture. The sophistication of the court of Edward IV, and to some extent of Richard III, too, with its Italian poets and talented musicians, is another. Refining our picture of the age Richard lived in helps us to see the full complexity of the choices he made, and to see that his choices were not governed by his time, even if they were influenced by it.

Richard at Rest

At 11.30 a.m. on Thursday, 26 March 2015, to the strains of Henry Purcell, the 'Service of Reinterment of the Remains of Richard III by the grace of God King of England and France and Lord of Ireland' began at Leicester Cathedral. The decision of the High Court had given Leicester control of Richard's last rites, and the events of the weeks leading up to the service had demonstrated that Leicester was going to make the most of it. This was not a state funeral, but members of the royal family were present. The Queen offered a message, printed in the Order of Service, recognizing a 'King who lived through turbulent times and whose Christian faith sustained him in life and death'. Richard's indisputable piety seemed a suitably uncontroversial quality on which to focus. His *Book of Hours* was incorporated into the service, which was based on one for the reinterment of the Earl of Warwick, probably in 1475; a copy of the manuscript for that rite was found only in 2009 by Dr Alexandra Buckle.[20] As some of the musical choices demonstrated, however, as well as the inclusion of a new poem by the poet laureate Carol Ann Duffy, this was not a re-enacted medieval rite, but a contemporary service with medieval elements. The television cameras prowling quietly around the aisles, and the familiar faces of actors, including one with a newly discovered familial connection to the king, Benedict Cumberbatch (a second cousin sixteen times removed), were our own age's most conspicuous contribution.

Outside, the crowds were not quite as thick as they had been earlier in the week, when Richard's coffin was taken through the streets of Leicester before being placed on public view in the cathedral on Monday, 23 March. If there was a medieval precedent for that in the sort of journey that the body of Richard's father took from Pontefract to Fotheringhay, the twenty-first-century version went by a rather more circuitous route. Although King Richard's body was found only yards from the cathedral, it had resided ever since at the university, about two miles away. Over the weekend before the reinterment, Richard's remains were taken on a repeat of his final journey, out of Leicester, to Bosworth, Dadlington and Sutton Cheney, and back again. There were no fewer than seven ceremonies and services on this royal progress, which included the gathering of soil from significant places in Richard's life (Fotheringhay, Middleham and Fenn Lane, for Bosworth) and the wrapping of a garland of roses around Bow Bridge post (white roses only, of course). Several thousands turned out for this unique and slightly bizarre occasion, lining the route, many dressed in replica costumes. (Leicester must be the only city in Britain where a full suit of armour is advertised for sale in the window of the local department store, along with toasters and tights.)[21]

Queues stretched beyond the cathedral precincts, as people waited to glimpse the simple coffin made by Richard's female-line descendant Michael Ibsen, whose DNA had helped prove the body's identity.[22]

On the day of the reinterment, some of those who stood behind barriers in the rain had dressed for the occasion in medieval wimples and snoods, but the mounted knights who had accompanied the coffin to the cathedral on its arrival were replaced by invited guests in suits and ties and, mostly, funereal black. (Impressively, the man who had first traced Richard's DNA, among other contributions to Ricardianism, Dr John Ashdown-Hill, wore a white suit, as if he was the only person who had really understood that this was not a funeral, but something rather different.) The fondness for pageantry that we ascribe to the Middle Ages showed no signs of having faded in the twenty-first century, however, as the British love of uniforms was indulged to the full (naval, army and air force, academic gowns, Lord Lieutenant, Yeoman of the Guard, all manner of clergy, and a riot of hats, fascinators, mortar-boards, wigs, boots, spurs and webbing).

Inside the cathedral, Richard was given every mark of respect, not just as a deserving Christian but as a king. In the eulogy offered by the Orator of Leicester University, Gordon Campbell, and the sermon by the Bishop of Leicester, Tim Stevens, Richard's piety continued to be emphasized, along with the idea that as a Christian he deserved a decent burial. But there was barely a hint that any of this might be controversial. Few would deny a Christian burial to a man who lived and died a Christian (and, of course, had already had a Christian burial, and a tomb, paid for by his successor). But this was very much more. It was not only an international media event, but one with very clear stamps of official approval, in the presence not only of royalty and a royal message, but of the Archbishop of Canterbury, who led the ceremony of reinterment itself.

For months we had been hearing how unique an event the reinterment was. It cannot be denied that this is the first time in modern memory that science had conclusively confirmed that the body of a lost English king had been rediscovered. No one can blame the university or the city of Leicester for making the most of this extraordinary piece of luck, which members of their own community had done so much to bring about. The very clear public interest and excitement about Richard and the reinterment ceremonies in a sense proved them right in their approach. But this was not the first time that the remains of a king of England had been rediscovered after centuries, and accepted, according to prevailing authorities, as genuine. That was what happened in 1674, when the remains of two children were discovered in the Tower, and 'upon the Presumptions that these were the bones of the said Princes, His Majesty King Charles II, was graciously pleased to command that the said Bones should be put into a Marble Urn, and deposited among the Reliques of the Royal Family in the Chapel of king Henry the Seventh, in Westminster Abbey'.[23] The fact that this simple command took four years to fulfil is difficult to explain. Christopher Wren's urn, in which were interred what he and his contemporaries assumed were the remains of Edward V and Richard of York, is an impressive object, but there is no record of any public event, or even a church service, attending the transfer. In making the comparison, I am not seeking to cast any doubt on the scientific identification of Richard III, which is clearly very much more secure than that for Edward V. Rather, it seems worth reflecting on the fact that the blameless Edward V and his brother were quietly dealt with, while the man accused of their murder was offered a farewell tour and a dozen church services. We do things very differently now.

It will be interesting to see whether the extraordinary surge of interest in all things Ricardian has any lasting effect. The history has not changed very much as a consequence of the discovery, but the perception of Richard may have done. It is possible that the very publicity of Leicester 2015 may come to be seen as an aberration, a little like the readjustment of public mood in the years after the funeral of Princess Diana, when it seemed as if a faint sense of embarrassment had taken hold, that so many people could get *that* carried away about somebody they hadn't known. The Richard effect may simply be a version of the British love affair with royalty. Perhaps it didn't really matter to those queuing to see Richard what sort of man or king he had been. He was king once, and that is all that counts. In which case, perhaps Richard himself was right all along. Nobody would have made this much fuss about a loyal uncle who had gone to his death as Richard, Duke of Gloucester.

Acknowledgements

R obin Baird-Smith is an exemplary editor who convinced me that I could write this book, and made sure I did so, with good humour and unfailing encouragement. Being published by Bloomsbury has been a pleasure: the professionalism of Jamie Birkett, Jude Drake and the eagle-eyed Richard Mason made my life much easier. At Rogers, Coleridge and White, Peter Straus, Emma Paterson and Matt Turner have always been on hand.

To write a book about Richard III is to tread over well-worn and often treacherous terrain. The assistance of the Richard III Society is now indispensable for such a task, and, in particular, I have been lucky to be able to call on Marie Barnfield and Keith Horry, the Society's librarians, for advice and expertise as well as back copies and books. The librarians of the British, London and Stoke Newington Libraries made research a pleasure, as did archivists in Canterbury, Finsbury and Norwich. I have tried not to bore most of my friends too much with my fifteenth-century obsessions, but some have been extraordinarily patient and (apparently) interested. Mark Bostridge generously offered excellent advice and expert suggestions from the very beginning. Harry Mount made me a card-carrying 'Ricardian'. Toby Clements has always been ready to swap Middle Aged anecdotage. Thomas Penn made me think again about Warwick the Kingmaker. Chris Skidmore gave me a copy of his speech and shared thoughts about Ricardianism. Amy Licence let me in on her thinking about the whereabouts of Cecily Neville. Ros Smith shared her findings about floods and Buckingham's rebellion.

At the *TLS* my editor Peter Stothard has, as before, enabled me to hold down a day job and try to be an author, and done so with great generosity. Rupert Shortt has always been ready to discuss English history with great insight, and went out of his way to help me secure entrance to the reinterment of the king in Leicester. Catharine Morris, Adrian Tahourdin, Robert Potts and Mika Ross-Southall have affected not to notice when Richard intruded on *TLS* business.

My biggest slice of good fortune has been the opportunity to draw on the generosity of Helen Castor, who knows so much more about the Middle Ages than I do and was happy to share that knowledge and intelligence, reading the whole text of the book and making numerous suggestions to improve it and save me from error. Those errors that remain are, of course, all my fault. Helen also introduced me to Dr Richard Beadle, whose patient explanation of a Paston Letter conundrum made me feel as though Thomas Edison had showed me how to change a light bulb.

I have written most of this book at home: without my family, I simply could not have managed. Jules constantly juggled her own much busier life to make space for Richard. She also helped me improve the book, and gave me the self-belief to write it in the first place. Her help means everything to me. My sons Jude and Johan have lived patiently with Richard 'one hundred and eleven', too: thank you, boys. My mother, brother and family, and my mother- and father-in-law all deserve my thanks for their support and good humour.

My father lived to see me begin work on the book, but not to end it. I owe to him my first interest in history, and I am proud to dedicate the finished product to his memory.

List of Abbreviations

CC Nicholas Pronay and John Cox, eds, *The Crowland Chronicle Continuations, 1459–1486*

CPR
Calendar of the Patent Rolls preserved in the Public Record Office: Henry VI vol. VI 1452–1461
Calendar of the Patent Rolls preserved in the Public Record Office: Edward IV 1461–1467
Calendar of the Patent Rolls preserved in the Public Record Office: Edward IV, Henry VI 1467–1477
Calendar of the Patent Rolls in the Public Record Office: Edward IV, Edward V, Richard III 1476—1485

CSP Milan Allen B. Hinds, ed., *Calendar of State Papers and Manuscripts in the Archives and Collections of Milan: 1385–1618* (online at www.british-history.ac.uk.)

Harley MS 433 Rosemary Horrox and P.W. Hammond, eds, *British Library Harleian Manuscript 433*, 4 vols (London: Richard III Society, 1979–83)

ODNB Oxford Dictionary of National Biography

PROME Chris Given-Wilson et al., eds, *Parliament Rolls of Medieval England* (Woodbridge: Boydell and Brewer, and online at www.british-history.ac.uk)

Notes

Introduction

1 NPG website, and see discussion of the twin portraits of Edward IV and Richard III in the collection of the Society of Antiquaries, dated to 'soon after 1510', in David Gaimster, Sarah McCarthy and Bernard Nurse, eds, *Making History: Antiquaries in Britain, 1707–2007* (London: Royal Academy of Arts, 2007), p. 84.

2 'The old pun has meaning: the White Boar really is a bit of a bore.' G. R. Elton, reviewing Charles Ross's biography, *The Times Literary Supplement* (London), 22 January 1982, p. 70.

3 James Gairdner, *History of the Life and Reign of Richard III, to which is added the story of Perkin Warbeck* (Cambridge: Cambridge University Press, 1898, revised edn), p. xi.

4 Clements E. Markham, *Richard III: His Life and Character Reviewed in the Light of Recent Research* (London: Smith, Elder and Co., 1906), p. 187.

5 Quoted in Charles Ross, *Richard III* (London: Yale University Press, 1981), p. 225.

6 http://www.brad.ac.uk/life-sciences/research/archaeological-sciences/biological-anthropology-research-centre/previous-projects/towton-mass-grave-project/

Chapter 1

1 See Alec J. Green, 'Fotheringhay castle', *The Ricardian* 3, no. 45 (June 1974), pp. 2–5.

2 William Shakespeare, *Richard III*, Act I, scene i.

3 Richard Buckley et al., 'The king in the car park: New light on the death and burial of Richard III in the Grey Friars church, Leicester, in 1485', *Antiquity* 87 (2013), p. 536.

4 John Rous, 'History of the kings of England', in Keith Dockray, *Richard III: A Source Book* (Stroud: Sutton Publishing, 1997), p. 11. In fact, Rous wrote about Richard on three occasions: in the Latin and English versions of a history of the Earls of

Warwick, the Rous rolls (it is the unrevised English version that retains his original complimentary words about the still-living Richard III); and in the *Historia regum Angliae*, completed in 1486, dedicated to Henry VII, and therefore unsurprisingly hostile to Henry's predecessor.

5   James Gairdner, *History of the Life and Reign of Richard III, to which is added the story of Perkin Warbeck* (Cambridge: Cambridge University Press, 1898), pp. 5–6.

6   Quoted in K. W. Barnardiston, *Clare Priory: Seven Centuries of a Suffolk House* (Cambridge: W. Heffer), p. 68.

7   T. Hoccleve, *The Regiment of Princes* (1411–12), ed. Charles R. Blyth (Kalamazoo, MI: Medieval Institute Publications), vol. l, lines 2,514 and 2,488–9.

8   J. Huizinga, *The Waning of the Middle Ages* (Harmondsworth: Penguin, 1924; trans. F. Hopman, 1955), p. 18.

9   K. B. McFarlane, 'The Wars of the Roses', *Proceedings of the British Academy* 1 (1964), in G. L. Harriss, ed., *England in the Fifteenth Century* (London: Hambledon, 1981), p. 238.

10   Lionel is often described as Edward III's second son, John of Gaunt his third son, and Edmund of Langley his fourth son, but this leaves out Edward's actual second son, William of Hatfield, who died as a four-month-old baby. Contemporaries didn't forget William: he was mentioned in the parliamentary discussion of Edward IV's title in 1461, for example.

11   'Historical memoranda of John Stowe: On Cade's rebellion (1450)', *Three Fifteenth-Century Chronicles: With Historical Memoranda by John Stowe* (London: Camden Society, 1880), pp. 94–103.

12   See e.g. E. F. Jacob, *The Fifteenth Century, 1399–1485* (Oxford: Oxford University Press, 1961), p. 499; G. Harriss, *Shaping the Nation: England 1360–1461* (Oxford: Oxford University Press, 2005), p. 623.

13   LM/COR/1/19, discussed in R. Griffiths, 'Richard Duke of York and the crisis of Henry VI's household in 1450–51', *Journal of Medieval History* 38 (2012), from which the quotations from York and Henry are taken.

14   R. A. Griffiths, 'Duke Richard of York's intentions in 1450 and the origins of the Wars of the Roses', *Journal of Medieval History* 1 (1975), pp. 203–5.

15   Chris Given-Wilson, Paul Brand, Seymour Phillips, Mark Ormrod, Geoffrey Martin, Anne Curry and Rosemary Horrox, eds, *Parliament Rolls of Medieval England* (Woodbridge: Boydell and Brewer, 2005), accessed online at http://www.british-history.ac.uk/no-series/parliament-rolls-medieval (*PROME* hereafter); Henry VI July 1455 Appendix 14 (Thomas Young) and 26 (William Oldhall).

16   A. H. Thomas and I. D. Thornley, eds, *The Great Chronicle of London* (London: George Jones, 1938), p. 186; this is often attributed to the author of *The Newe Cronycles of England and Fraunce* (also known as *Fabyan's Chronicle*), the London draper (and alderman) Robert Fabyan, who died in 1511.

17 MS Rawlinson B.355, in Ralph Flenley, ed., *Six Town Chronicles of England* (Oxford: Oxford University Press, 1911), p. 107; trans. J. R. Lander, *The Wars of the Roses* (London: Secker and Warburg, 1965), p. 69.

18 For the suggestion that he did, see P. W. Hammond and Anne F. Sutton, *Richard III: The Road to Bosworth Field* (London: Constable, 1985), p. 25.

19 See Anne F. Sutton and Livia Visser-Fuchs, *Richard III's Books: Ideals and Reality in the Life and Library of a Medieval Prince* (Stroud: Sutton Publishing, 1997), p. 5.

20 Bale's Chronicle, in Flenley, *Six Town Chronicles of England*, p. 140.

21 Latin in J. A. Giles, ed., *Incerti Scriptoris Chronicon Angliae* (London: D. Nutt, 1848), p. 44, trans. in Wendy Turner, ed., *Madness in Medieval Law and Custom* (Leiden: Brill, 2010), p. 186.

22 *PROME* Henry VI March 1453, 32.

23 York's letter to the burgesses of Salisbury, 1452, in Lander, *The Wars of the Roses*, p. 66.

24 *PROME* Henry VI March 1453, 35.

25 'The Dijon Relation', trans. in Lander, *The Wars of the Roses*, pp. 77–8.

26 William Shakespeare, *Henry VI: Part Two*, Act 5, scene ii, line 67.

27 John Silvester Davies, ed., *An English Chronicle of the Reigns of Richard II, Henry IV, Henry V, and Henry VI Written before the Year 1471* (London: Camden Society, 1856), p. 79.

28 Thomas Gascoigne, *Loci e Libro Veritatum*, ed. J. E. T. Rodgers (Oxford: Clarendon Press, 1881), p. 205; quoted in Helen Maurer, *Margaret of Anjou: Queenship and Power in Late Medieval England* (Woodbridge: Boydell and Brewer, 2003), p. 115.

29 Maurer, *Margaret of Anjou*, p. 113.

30 James Gairdner, ed., *Historical Collections of a Citizen of London in the Fifteenth Century* (London: Camden Society, 1876), pp. 196–210; a sermon of William Ive before Henry VI at Coventry in 1458.

31 Davies, ed., *English Chronicle*, p. 79.

32 *CPR* 1452–61, p. 542.

33 Gregory's Chronicle, 1459, in Gairdner, ed., *Historical Collections*.

34 Davies, ed., *English Chronicle*, p. 83.

35 D. A. L. Morgan, 'Hearne's "Fragment" and the long prehistory of English memoirs', *English Historical Review* 124, no. 509 (August 2009), which also argues the case for Howard's authorship

36 Gregory's Chronicle, 1459, in Gairdner, ed., *Historical Collections*.

37 See *PROME* Henry VI November 1459, Introduction.

38 Gregory's Chronicle, 1459, in Gairdner, ed., *Historical Collections.*

39 Paston Letters, William Worcester to John Berney, January 1460. '[R]eceved' is in James Gairdner's edition (vol. III, p. 203), where the reference to the duchess is glossed as referring to the Duchess of York. In his modern edition, Norman Davis reads 'returned', not 'receved', and notes that the duchess in question is the dowager Duchess of Bedford, Lord Rivers's wife (Davis, ed., *Paston Letters and Papers of the Fifteenth Century* [Oxford: Clarendon Press, 1971–6], vol. II, pp. 538–40), which seems much more likely. Checking the original letter would certainly seem to confirm Davis's reading, though it cannot, of course, confirm whether he is right about the duchess in question being of Bedford or of York (BL Add. MS 43488 f.49).

40 For Tonbridge, see e.g. Philippa Langley and Michael Jones, *The King's Grave: The Search for Richard III* (London: John Murray, 2013), p. 73; for Writtle, see Hannes Kleineke, 'Alice Martyn, widow of London: An episode from Richard's youth', *The Ricardian* 14 (2004), pp. 32–6.

41 Davies, ed., *English Chronicle*, p. 93.

42 Davies, ed., *English Chronicle*, p. 96.

43 Nicholas Pronay and John Cox, eds, *The Crowland Chronicle Continuations: 1459–1486* (Langley, Berkshire: Richard III Society and Yorkist History Trust, 1986), p. 111.

44 Davis, ed., *Paston Letters*, II, pp. 216–17. My thanks to Richard Beadle and Helen Castor for clearing up a confusion about this letter's date. The reference to a receipt on 25 September at the bottom of the letter seems to be an accounting note, nothing to do with the original letter that was sent in October.

45 Gregory's Chronicle, 1460, in Gairdner, ed., *Historical Collections.*

46 *Registrum Abbatiae Johannis Whetamstede Abbatis Sancti Albani*, vol. I, pp. 376–8, trans Lander, *The Wars of the Roses*, p. 108.

47 A. H. Thomas and I. D. Thornley, eds, *The Great Chronicle of London* (London: George Jones, 1938), p. 195; quoted in L. Vissa-Fuchs, 'Richard in Holland, 1461', *The Ricardian* 6, no. 81 (1983).

48 TNA 1/23/1247B quoted in Kleineke, 'Alice Martyn, widow of London'.

49 Letter of Bishop David to Edward IV, quoted in Visser-Fuchs, 'Richard in Holland, 1461'.

50 Davies, ed., *English Chronicle.*

51 Gregory's Chronicle, 1455, in Gairdner, ed., *Historical Collections.*

52 Gregory's Chronicle, 1461, in Gairdner, ed., *Historical Collections.*

53 Calendar of State Papers and Manuscripts in the Archives and Collections of Milan: 1385–1618, no. 71.

54 Crowland Chronicle, second continuation, quoted in Lander, *The Wars of the Roses*, pp. 118–19.

55 H. T. Riley, ed., *Registrum Abbatiae Johannis Whethamstede* (London: Longman, 1872–3), p. 390.

56 Davis, ed., *Paston Letters*, I, p. 198.

57 Davies, ed., *English Chronicle*.

58 Nicholas O'Flanagan, Bishop of Elphin, to Francesco Coppino, Bishop of Terni, Legate of the Apostolic See Calendar of State Papers and Manuscripts in the Archives and Collections of Milan: 1385–1618, 10 April 1461 (no. 82).

59 Veronica Fiorato, Anthea Boylston and Christopher Knusel, eds, *Blood Red Roses: The Archaeology of a Mass Grave from the Battle of Towton AD 1461* (Oxford: Oxbow, 2001), p. 101.

60 In 2013 the Towton Battlefield Society's annual Palm Sunday commemoration and re-enactment event at Towton was cancelled due to bad weather.

61 Fiorato et al., *Blood Red Roses*, p. 99.

62 Fiorato et al., *Blood Red Roses*, p. 186.

63 *CSP Milan*, 18 April 1461 (no. 91).

64 See Anne F. Sutton, 'The return to England of Richard of Gloucester after his first exile', *The Ricardian* 3, no. 50 (1975).

65 See, e.g., Edward's letter of protection granted to Eton College in 1461, quoted in C. A. J. Armstrong, 'Inauguration ceremonies of the Yorkist kings', *TRHS*, Fourth Series, vol. 30 (1948), p. 53.

66 'Hearne's Fragment', Chapter 5, in *Chronicles of the White Rose of York* (London: James Bohn, 1845), p. 10.

67 *CPR 1467–77*, pp. 295–6 (10 December 1471).

68 *CPR 1461–7*, p. 214 (12 October 1462).

69 *CPR 1461–7*, p. 197 (12 August 1462).

70 Letter of March 1464, in Charles Ross, *Edward IV* (London: Yale University Press, 1983), p. 63 n. 2.

71 See Jonathan Hughes, *Arthurian Myths and Alchemy: The Kingship of Edward IV* (Stroud: Sutton Publishing, 2002), pp. 114–59, for a discussion of these points.

72 A. R. Myers, ed., *The Household of Edward IV: The Black Book and the Ordinance of 1478* (Manchester: Manchester University Press, 1959), pp. 126–7.

73 Lorraine Attreed, ed., *The York House Books, 1461–1490* (Stroud: Sutton Publishing, 1991), vol. 2, 4f 169v.

74 The children were his brother, George, Duke of Clarence's son and daughter, whose father had been attainted but for whom a claim could have plausibly been made; Richard's own illegitimate daughter, Katherine, and another nephew, John de la Pole,

were also resident there. See Anne Sutton, Livia Visser-Fuchs and Hannes Kleineke, 'The children in the care of Richard III: New references. A lawsuit between Peter Courteys, keeper of Richard III's Great Wardrobe, and Thomas Lynom, solicitor of Richard III 1495–1501', *The Ricardian* 24 (2014), pp. 31–62.

75 P. M. Kendall, *Richard III* (London: Allen and Unwin, 1955), p. 106.

76 *CPR 1467–77*, p. 51.

77 C. Ross, 'Some servants and lovers of Richard in his youth', *The Ricardian* 4, no. 55 (December 1976).

78 See Jordi Sánchez Martí, 'Longleat House MS 257 – a description', *Atlantis* 27, no. 1 (June 2005): pp. 79–89; and Visser-Fuchs and Sutton, *Richard III's Books*.

79 L. Visser-Fuchs, 'He hardly touched his food: what Niclas Von Popplau really wrote about Richard III', *The Ricardian* 11, no. 145 (1999).

80 Quoting the Roman poet Statius: 'Numquam tantum animum natura minori / corpore, nec tantas nisa est includare vir[es]', as rendered by George Buck, *The History of King Richard III* (1619), ed. A. N. Kincaid (Gloucester: Alan Sutton, 1979), p. 206; it is not often remarked that the Latin description was applied to the mythical hero Tydeus, who as well as being associated, like Richard, with the boar, was portrayed as monstrously violent, eating the brains of one of his victims: perhaps the diplomat's remark was not an unalloyed compliment.

81 William Shakespeare, *Henry VI: Part 3*, Act 3, scene ii; *Richard III*, Act 4, scene iv.

82 John Rous, *Historia Regum Angliae*, quoted in Alison Hanham, *Richard III and His Early Historians, 1483–1535* (Oxford: Clarendon Press, 1975), p. 123.

83 William Shakespeare, *Richard III*, Act 1, scene iii.

84 J. Stevenson, ed., *Letters and Papers Illustrative of the Wars of the English in France during the Reign of Henry the Sixth, King of England* (London: Longman, 1861–4), vol. 2, part 2, p. 785 (*Annales rerum angicarum* formerly attributed to William of Worcester).

85 The feast is very commonly located at Cawood Castle, the archbishop's residence outside York (not least by the present owners, who advertise the 'fact' to prospective tenants), but Leland makes no mention of Cawood, and refers specifically to the Close as the site of the celebration.

86 Joannis Lelandi Antiquarii, *De Rebus Britannicis Collectanea* (London, 1770), vol. 6, pp. 2–14; for calculations of the duration of the feast, etc., see C. M. Woolgar, 'Conspicuous consumption and the nobility', in M. A. Hicks, ed., *The Fifteenth Century V: Revolution and Consumption* (Woodbridge: Boydell and Brewer, 2001), p. 23.

87 Richard Buckley et al., 'The king in the car park', p. 536.

88 Henry Ellis, ed., *The New Chronicles of England and France, in Two Parts by Robert Fabyan* (London: Rivington, 1811), p. 654; private, even clandestine marriages, were not unheard of, even in Edward's own family. His father's parents had been married in secret.

89 Richard S. Sylvester, ed., *The Complete Works of St Thomas More*. Volume II, *The History of King Richard III* (London: Yale University Press, 1961).

90 Ellis, ed., *The New Chronicles of England and France*, p. 654.

91 David MacGibbon, *Elizabeth Woodville: A Life* (1938) (Stroud: Amberley, 2013), p. 201 n. 67.

92 *CPR* 1467–77, p. 190.

93 *Annales rerum anglicarum*, p. 783, quoted in Ross, *Edward IV*, p. 93.

94 Sir John Howard to Lord Rivers, in B. Botfield, ed., *Manners and Household Expenses of England in the Thirteenth and Fifteenth Centuries Illustrated by Original Records* (London: W. Nicol, 1841), p. 197; Calendar of State Papers and Manuscripts in the Archives and Collections of Milan: 1385–1618, p. 114.

95 Message of Queen Isabella of Castile, Harley MS 433 III, p. 24.

96 Pronay and Cox, eds, *The Crowland Chronicle Continuations: 1459–1486*, p. 115; for a discussion of authorship of this continuation, and the suggestion that it was Dr Henry Sharp, not Bishop John Russell, see ibid., pp. 78–95; for an alternative candidate, Master Richard Langport, see Michael Hicks, 'The second anonymous Continuation of the Crowland Abbey Chronicle 1459–86 revisited', *English Historical Review* 122, no. 496 (2007), pp. 349–70.

97 S. Bentley, ed., *Excerpta historica, or Illustrations of English History* (London: n.p., 1831), p. 227.

Chapter 2

1 P. W. Hammond and Anne F. Sutton, *Richard III: The Road to Bosworth Field* (London: Constable, 1985), p. 184.

2 Charles Ross, *Edward IV* (London: Yale University Press, 1983), p. 123, ref to KB 9/320 (in the National Archives).

3 MS Ashmole 1160, in John Warkworth, ed. J. O. Halliwell-Phillips, *A Chronicle of the First Thirteen Years of the Reign of King Edward the Fourth* (London: Camden Society, 1839), p. 46.

4 In John Nichols, *A Collection of ordinances and regulations for the government of the royal household, made in divers reigns from King Edward III to King William and Queen Mary* (London: Society of Antiquaries, 1790), pp. 87–105.

5 Warkworth, *Chronicle*, p. 47.

6 Hammond and Sutton, *Richard III*, p. 36. The editors read the postscript 'Sir I say . . ', but the correction is widely accepted.

7   According to Warkworth, 2,000 out of a force of 14,000 were killed. While most chroniclers exaggerate numbers, the loss of life was clearly significant.

8   Warkworth, *Chronicle*, p. 7.

9   For a discussion of William of Worcester's and John Warkworth's differing lists of the dead, see Howell T. Evans, *Wales and the Wars of the Roses* (Cambridge: Cambridge University Press, 1915), pp. 184–5, where the author remarks that 'It is easy to understand why the defeat was regarded in Wales as a national calamity.'

10 CC, p. 117.

11 Warkworth, *Chronicle*, p. 7.

12 *CPR* 1467–77, p. 178.

13 *CPR* 1467–77, p. 195.

14 *CPR* 1467–77, pp. 180–1.

15 *CPR* 1467–77, pp. 179–80; p. 185.

16 *CPR* 1467–77, p. 179.

17 R. A. Griffiths, 'William Herbert, second earl of Pembroke', in *ODNB*.

18 Chronicle of the rebellion in Lincolnshire, in J. R. Lander, *The Wars of the Roses* (London: Secker and Warburg, 1965), pp. 166–7.

19 *CCR* 1468–76, pp. 135–7.

20 Wenlock's career is an example of how difficult it was to maintain loyalties in the Wars of the Roses. He began as a soldier in Henry V's French campaigns, and remained a trusted Lancastrian servant until he went over to the Yorkists at Ludlow. Ennobled by Edward after his succession, Wenlock subsequently came into Warwick's orbit. Although he stuck by Edward when refusing Warwick entry to Calais, the king seems to have lost trust in him, and eventually he returned to the Lancastrian cause with Warwick.

21 Reproduced in *Archaeologia Cambrensis* 9, 3rd series 1863, p. 55 (article by W. W. E. W[ynne]). Interestingly, this was a grant to one of Richard's Welsh retainers (Reginald ap Sir Gruffyd Vaghan), showing that he was carrying out his Welsh duties even as he inserted himself into English northern disputes.

22 Norman Davis, ed., *Paston Letters and Papers of the Fifteenth Century* (Oxford: Clarendon Press, 1971–6), vol. II, pp. 432–3.

23 It might be granted as an 'astonishing volte face' for Margaret though. See Ralph A. Griffiths, *The Reign of King Henry VI: The Exercise of Royal Authority, 1422–1461* (London: Benn, 1981), p. 890; quoted in Peter D. Clarke, 'English royal marriages and the papal penitentiary', *English Historical Review* 120, no. 488 (2005), p. 1,020.

24   Clarke, 'English royal marriages', pp. 1,020–1.

25   BM Harleian MS 543 f.169b, in Lander, *Wars of the Roses*, p. 170.

26   *CSP Milan* 29 June 1470; 24 July 1470.

27   '[Q]uia quarto consanguinitatis gradu invicem sunt sunt [sic] coniuncti'. ASV PA
     Reg. 19, fo. 42r, quoted in Clarke, 'English royal marriages', p. 1,021 n. 33 (John of
     Gaunt was the couple's great-grandfather). The betrothal was witnessed by Louis's
     brother, the Duke of Guienne, who also agreed to help Warwick against Edward IV
     (BL Cotton MS Vespasian F 111 32).

28   Lander, *Wars of the Roses*, p. 172.

29   For the office of warden, see R. R. Reid, 'The office of warden of the Marches: Its
     origin and early history', *English Historical Review* 32, no. 128 (1917), pp. 479–96, and
     R. L. Storey, 'The wardens of the Marches of England towards Scotland, 1377–1489',
     English Historical Review 72, no. 285 (1957), pp. 593–615.

30   *CPR* 167–77, p. 206.

31   *CSP Milan* 12 October 1470.

32   Warkworth's *Chronicle*, in Lander, *Wars of the Roses*, p. 173.

33   Lynn Hall Book, 1470, Norfolk Record Office KL/C7/4 p. 284, and see W. I. Haward,
     'Economic aspects of the Wars of the Roses in East Anglia', *English Historical Review*
     41, no. 162 (April 1926), pp. 170–89; my thanks to Marie Barnfield for her help in
     deciphering these records.

34   Philippe de Commines, *Memoirs*, in Hammond and Sutton, *Richard III*, p. 38.

35   Two articles by Livia Visser-Fuchs discuss the evidence and possible movements of
     Richard in Holland: 'Richard in Holland, 1471–2', *The Ricardian* 6, no. 82
     (September 1983), pp. 220–8; and 'Richard was late', *The Ricardian* 11, no. 147
     (December 1999), pp. 616–19.

36   Warkworth's *Chronicle*, in Lander, *Wars of the Roses*, p. 174.

37   *CSP Milan* 9 April 1471.

38   John Bruce, ed., *Historie of the Arrivall of Edward IV in England and the Finall
     Recouverye of His Kingdomes from Henry VI AD. M. CCCC. LXXI* (London: Camden
     Society, 1838), p. 10.

39   M. Jones, ed. Philippe de Commines, *Memoirs*, 1972, p. 185, in John Ashdown-
     Hill, *The Third Plantagenet: George, Duke of Clarence, Richard III's Brother* (Stroud:
     History Press, 2014), p. 120.

40   See Rosemary Horrox, *Richard III: A Study of Service* (Cambridge: Cambridge
     University Press, 1989), pp. 40–3, and Horrox, 'Preparations for Edward's return
     from exile', *The Ricardian* 6, no. 79 (December 1982), pp. 124–7.

41 Adrian de But, quoted in Visser-Fuchs, 'Richard was late'.

42 L. M. E. Dupont, ed., *Anchiennes Croniques d'Engleterre par Jehan de Wavrin: Choix de chapitres inédits* (Paris: Renouard, 1858–63), vol. 3, pp. 106–7; British Library Royal MS 15 E IV, vol. I, illumination at f.14.

43 The identification was made by the artist Joseph Strutt. For a discussion, and of Richard's possible fashion choices, see Anne F. Sutton, 'Richard III as a fop: A foolish myth', *The Ricardian* 18 (2008), pp. 58–65.

44 Bruce, ed., *Historie of the Arrivall*, p. 5.

45 Bruce, ed., *Historie of the Arrivall*, pp. 6–7.

46 Bruce, ed., *Historie of the Arrivall*, p. 11.

47 Lettre de Marguerite d'York . . . à la duchesse douairière de Bourgogne, in Dupont, *Anchiennes Croniques d'Engleterre par Jehan de Wavrin*, vol. 3, p. 210.

48 Polydore Vergil, *Historie of England*, ed. Henry Ellis (1844), p. 141.

49 For Henry's confidence in Edward, see Margaret of Burgundy's letter in Dupont, vol. 3, p. 211.

50 *Great Chronicle of London*, in Hammond and Sutton, *Richard III*, p. 43.

51 John Adair, 'The newsletter of Gerhard von Wesel, 17 April 1471', *Journal of Army Historical Research* (Summer 1968), pp. 65–9, and discussion in Livia Visser-Fuchs, 'A Ricardian riddle: The casualty list of the Battle of Barnet', *The Ricardian* 8, no. 100 (March 1988), pp. 9–12.

52 Bruce, ed., *Historie of the Arrivall*, pp. 27–9.

53 Bruce, ed., *Historie of the Arrivall*, p. 30.

54 Bruce, ed., *Historie of the Arrivall*, p. 30.

55 *Great Chronicle of London*, in Keith Dockray, *Richard III: A Source Book*, p. 20.

56 In *Richard III*, Act I, scene ii, Richard says that Prince Edward was 'slain by [King] Edward's hands' (in *3 Henry VI*, Edward is indeed one of the three who stabs the prince), but Anne replies: 'In thy foul throat thou liest: Queen Margaret saw/Thy murd'rous falchion smoking in his blood.' The audience, in no doubt as to who is the more trustworthy of the two, is clearly meant to believe that Richard and only Richard is the culprit.

57 The mayor of London's reply to Fauconberg, referring to this self-description, quoted in C. F. Richmond, 'Fauconberg's Kentish Rising of May 1471', *English Historical Review* 85, no. 337 (1970), p. 675.

58 'In crastino Dux Gloucester cum primo exercitu Regis intravit Canciam; quem sequitur dominus Rex in die Ascensionis cum residuo exercitu, viz xxiii die dicti mensis Maii'; 'Yorkist notes, 1471', in C. L. Kingsford, ed., *English Historical Literature in the Fifteenth Century* (Oxford: Clarendon Press, 1913), p. 375.

59 'Yorkist notes', p. 375.

60 Bruce, ed., *Historie of the Arrivall*, p. 38.

61 Entry on Close Roll 1471, in I. D. Thornley, ed., *England Under the Yorkists, 1460–85* (London: Longman, 1920), p. 80.

Chapter 3

1 BL Cotton MS Julius BXIII, ff. 108–316: for a discussion of this document, see 'Richard III's cartulary in the British Library', in M. A. Hicks, *Richard III and His Rivals: Magnates and their Motives in the Wars of the Roses* (London: Hambledon, 1991), pp. 281–9.

2 *CPR 1467–77*, p. 266.

3 Rosemary Horrox, *Richard III: A Study in Service* (Cambridge: Cambridge University Press, 1989), p. 49.

4 Feet of Fines C.P. 25/1/281/164/32 (on http://medievalgenealogy.org.uk/fines).

5 P. W. Hammond and Anne F. Sutton, *Richard III: The Road to Bosworth Field* (London: Constable, 1985), p. 104.

6 Quoted in M. A. Hicks, 'The fourth earl of Northumberland, 1470–89', in *Richard III and His Rivals*, p. 370.

7 Horrox, *Richard III*, p. 68.

8 The manuscript is Bodl Oxf MS Rawl. poet. 143, ff. 12–27; the poem is printed from it in J. O. Halliwell, ed., *Palatine Anthology: A Collection of Ancient Poems and Ballads Relating to Lancashire and Cheshire* (London: n.p., 1850), pp. 208–71.

9 John Bayley, ed., *Calendars of the Proceedings in Chancery, in the Reign of Queen Elizabeth*, (London: Eyre and Strahan, 1827), vol. I, p. xc; and see M. A. Hicks, 'The last days of Elizabeth Countess of Oxford', in *Richard III and His Rivals*.

10 Hicks, 'Last days', p. 298.

11 BL Cotton Galba E. ix, discussed in Mary Flowers Braswell, ed., *Sir Perceval of Galles and Ywain and Gawain* (Kalamazoo, MI: Medieval Institute Publications, 1995).

12 *CC*, p. 133.

13 See e.g. Sharon Penman, *The Sunne in Splendour* (London: Macmillan, 1982).

14 Cristoforo Bollato to Galeazzo Sforza, 7 February 1474, *CSP Milan* p. 177.

15 Norman Davis, ed., *Paston Letters and Papers of the Fifteenth Century* (Oxford: Clarendon Press, 1971), vol. I, p. 447.

16 Bede, *A History of the English Church and People*, trans. L. Shirley-Price, rev. R. E. Latham (Harmondsworth: Penguin, 1968), p. 74 (I.27).

17 M. A. Hicks, *Anne Neville: Queen to Richard III* (Stroud: History Press, 2006).

18 For Richard's marriage, the case 'against' is made by Michael Hicks in his biography of Anne Neville. The 'incest' accusation is convincingly refuted by Marie Barnfield, 'Beyond the papal pale or simply the wrong sort of affinity?', *Ricardian Bulletin* 6 (2006), pp. 55–7; and 'Only if it may stand with the law of the Church', *Ricardian Bulletin* 9 (2006), pp. 55–7, with a further elaboration in 'Diriment impediments, dispensations and divorce: Richard III and matrimony', *The Ricardian* 17 (2007). The surviving dispensation appears in Peter D. Clarke, 'English royal marriages and the papal penitentiary', *English Historical Review* 120, no. 488 (2005), pp. 1,014–29. For definitions of affinity, see John P. Beal, James A. Coriden, and Thomas J. Green, eds, *New Commentary on the Code of Canon Law* (New York: Paulist Press, 1999), pp. 1,293–4.

19 Hammond and Sutton, *Richard III*, 'The Narrative of the Marriage of Richard Duke of York with Anne of Norfolk, 1477', p. 69.

20 Davis, ed., *Paston Letters*, I, p. 447.

21 Davis, ed., *Paston Letters*, I, p. 468.

22 *CC*, p. 133.

23 *PROME* Edward IV May 1474 (*RP* VI 100).

24 Hearne's Fragment, 'in the yere of our Lorde M.CCCC.LXXIIII [1474] att Westmonstre', in Hammond and Sutton, *Richard III*, p. 58.

25 *PROME* Edward IV October 1472: First Roll, 24

26 *PROME* Edward IV October 1472: First Roll, 8.

27 *PROME* Edward IV October 1472: Introduction.

28 Charles Ross, *Edward IV* (London: Yale University Press, 1983), p. 217; the story is told in the *Great Chronicle*.

29 *CSP Milan* 1475, 275 (undated).

30 *The memoirs of Philip de Commines, Lord of Argenton: containing the histories of Louis XI and Charles VIII, King of France and of Charles the Bold, Duke of Burgundy; to which is added, The scandalous chronicle of the secret history of Louis XI*, trans. Andrew R. Scoble (London: George Bell, 1896–1900), vol. I, pp. 251–80, for the quotations that follow.

31 *The memoirs of Philip de Commines*, I, p. 277.

32 C. L. Kingsford, ed., *The Stonor Letters and Papers, 1290–1483* (London: Royal Historical Society, 1919), vol. I, p. 158.

33 *The memoirs of Philip de Commines*, I, p. 279. Ever the man of the world, Commines also reports that the pigeon might just have been trying to dry its feathers after a rain shower.

34 See Lorraine Attreed, 'An indenture between Richard Duke of Gloucester and the Scrope family of Masham and Upsall', *Speculum* 58, no. 4 (October 1983), pp. 1,018–25.

35 *CC*, p. 139.

36 For discussion of the reburial and the texts of the nearest to contemporary documents with translations, see 'The reburial of the Duke of York' by P. W. Hammond, Anne F. Sutton and Livia Visser-Fuchs, *The Ricardian* 10, no. 127 (December 1994), pp. 122–65.

37 See Michael K. Jones, *Bosworth 1485: Psychology of a Battle* (Stroud: Tempus, 2002), pp. 48–53.

38 See Sofija Matich and Jennifer S. Alexander, 'Creating and recreating the Yorkist tombs in Fotheringhay church (Northants)', *Church Monuments* 26 (2011), pp. 82–103.

39 *CC*, p. 143.

40 Davis, ed., *Paston Letters*, I, p. 498; see Michael K. Jones, '1477 – The expedition that never was: Chivalric expectation in late Yorkist England', *The Ricardian* 12, no. 153 (June 2001), pp. 275–2.

41 J. R. Lander, 'The treason and death of the Duke of Clarence: A reinterpretation', *Canadian Journal of History* 2, no. 2 (1967), pp. 1–28.

42 H. Grimstone and T. Leach, eds, *Reports of Sir George Croke, Knight, of Select Cases*, trans. John Ashdown-Hill in *The Third Plantagenet: George, Duke of Clarence, Richard III's Brother* (Stroud: History Press, 2014), pp. 143–4.

43 See the chapter 'Thomas Burdet's secrets', in Ashdown-Hill, *Third Plantagenet*, pp. 138–48, for the details of this argument.

44 C. A. J. Armstrong, ed., *The Usurpation of Richard the Third: Dominicus Mancinus ad Angelum Catonem De occupatione regni Anglie per Ricardum Tercium libellus* (Oxford: Oxford University Press, 1936), pp. 75–7.

45 *PROME* Edward IV January 1478, Appendix 1478, 1. For a discussion of the allegation of Edward's bastardy, see Jones, *Bosworth*, pp. 73–8, which only suggests that Clarence and his mother 'toyed with the prospect of a formal declaration of Edward IV's illegitimacy', rather than actually made one. For the case for (and against) Edward's actual illegitimacy, see Josephine Wilkinson, *Richard: The Young King to Be* (Stroud: Amberley, 2009), pp. 156–9.

46 *CC*, p. 145.

47 Lander, 'Treason and death', p. 9.

48 Lander, 'Treason and death', p. 9.

49 *CC*, p. 145.

50 *PROME* Edward IV January 1478, Appendix 1478, 1.

51 *CC*, p. 147.

52 Armstrong, ed., *Dominicus Mancinus*, p. 77.

53 Hammond and Sutton, *Richard III*, p. 133.

54 Statutes of the College of Middleham, Hammond and Sutton, *Richard III*, pp. 75–6.

55 *CPR* 1476–85, p. 90.

56 Horrox, *Richard III*, pp. 57–8.

57 A. J. Pollard, 'Richard Clervaux of Croft', *Yorkshire Archaeological Journal* 50, no. 9 (1978), p. 162; in Hammond and Sutton, *Richard III*, p. 74.

58 Letter, Library of Congress Thatcher 1004 reproduced in A. J. Pollard, *Richard III and the Princes in the Tower* (Stroud: Sutton Publishing, 1995), p. 237; see also Pollard, 'St Cuthbert and the Hog', in Ralph A. Griffiths and James Sherborne, eds, *Kings and Nobles in the Later Middle Ages* (Stroud: Sutton Publishing, 1995).

59 See L. Attreed, *The York House Books, 1461–1490* (Stroud: Sutton Publishing), vol. I, e.g. f.42b, 76; vol. II/4 f.56b.

60 Attreed, *The York House Books*, I, f.2v. pp. 8–9.

61 Attreed, *The York House Books*, I, f.42b; see also D. M. Palliser, *Medieval York: 600–1540* (Oxford: Oxford University Press), pp. 246–8; and Palliser in Horrox, ed., *Richard III and the North* (Hull: University of Hull, 1986).

62 Attreed, *The York House Books*, I, 10 f.35v, 128 f.75, 130 f.76, 311–12 f.123v.

63 Attreed, *The York House Books*, I, 215 f.5, 171 f.98v.

64 Attreed, *The York House Books*, II/4, f.169v.

65 See e.g. P. M. Kendall's chapter of that name in his *Richard III* (London: Allen and Unwin, 1955).

66 *CPR* 1476–85, p. 49.

67 See entry and refs in http://www.girders.net, database compiled by Ian Rogers.

68 *CPR* 1476–85, p. 79.

69 *CPR* 1476–85, p. 205.

70 Anne Sutton and Livia Visser-Fuchs, 'Richard of Gloucester and La Grosse Bombarde', *The Ricardian* 10, no. 134 (1996), pp. 461–5; MS français 2908 f.13 item 1; for other references to Richard's interest in guns and artillery, see Rosemary Horrox and P. W. Harmmond, eds, *British Library Harleian Manuscript 433*, vol. II, pp. 72, 103, 223.

71 Thomas Rymer, *Foedera* (The Hague: J. Neulme, 1739–45), vol. 12, p. 157.

72 Hammond and Sutton, *Richard III*, pp. 86–7.

73 *CC*, p. 149.

74   *CC*, p. 149.

75   *PROME* Edward IV January 1483.

76   Stroke, P. M. Kendall; pneumonia, John Rae; appendicitis, Winston Churchill; deadly fruit and veg., Thomas Basin (1412–1491).

77   Armstrong, ed., *Dominicus Mancinus*, p. 73.

78   Polydore Vergil, *Anglica Historia*, ed. and trans. Denys Hays (London: Royal Historical Society), vol. 24, ch. 28.

79   *CC*, p. 153.

Chapter 4

1   Kim M. Philipps, 'The invisible man: body and ritual in a fifteenth-century noble household', referring to BL Harley MS 6815, *Journal of Medieval History* 31, no. 2 (2005), pp. 143–62.

2   Peter Murray Jones and Lea T. Olson, 'Middleham jewel: Ritual, power, devotion', *Viator* 31 (2000), pp. 249–90.

3   See Hicks, *Richard III and His Rivals: Magnates and their Motives in the Wars of the Roses* (London: Hambledon, 1991), p. 277.

4   C. A. J. Armstrong, ed., *The Usurpation of Richard the Third: Dominicus Mancinus ad Angelum Catonem De occupatione regni Anglie per Ricardum Tercium libellus* (Oxford: Oxford University Press, 1936), p. 91.

5   'The funeral of Edward IV' (College of Arms MS I.7.f.7), in J. Gairdner, ed., *Letters and Papers Illustrative of the Reigns of Henry VII and Richard III* (London: Longman, 1861–3), vol. I, pp. 3–10.

6   *CC*, p. 78; see Chapter 1 n. 96 for reference to discussions of the *Continuation*'s authorship.

7   *CC*, pp. 153–5.

8   Armstrong, ed., *Dominicus Mancinus*, p. 87.

9   See Colin Richmond, '1483: The year of decision', in John Gillingham, ed., *Richard III: A Medieval Kingship* (London: Collins and Brown, 1993), p. 43; for the argument that a struggle *was* anticipated, see Michael K. Jones, *Bosworth 1485: Psychology of a Battle* (Stroud: Tempus, 2002), p. 83.

10   Armstrong, ed., *Dominicus Mancinus*, p. 89.

11   Armstrong, ed., *Dominicus Mancinus*, p. 91.

12 John Hardyng, *The Chronicle of John Hardyng . . . Together with the continuation by R. Grafton*, ed. H. Ellis (1812), p. 475; discussed by Armstrong in *Dominicus Mancinus*, pp. 140–1 n. 42.

13 *CC*, p. 155.

14 *CC*, p. 157.

15 Armstrong, ed., *Dominicus Mancinus*, p. 103.

16 Armstrong, ed., *Dominicus Mancinus*, p. 91.

17 Armstrong, ed., *Dominicus Mancinus*, p. 101.

18 *CC*, p. 157.

19 Letter quoted by Armstrong in *Dominicus Mancinus*, pp. 145–6.

20 Jones, *Bosworth 1485*, pp. 85–6, for 'setting aside'; Sequestration in *Registrum Thome Bourgchier Cantuariensis Archiepiscopi*, ed. F. R. H. Du Boulay (Oxford: Oxford University Press, 1957), pp. 52–3.

21 Christopher Wilkins, *The Last Knight Errant: Sir Edward Woodville and the Age of Chivalry* (London: I. B. Tauris, 2010), p. 177, for indenture between an unnamed patron and Edward V's government; Armstrong, ed., *Dominicus Mancinus*, pp. 105–6.

22 *CPR* 1476–85, p. 350.

23 *CC*, p. 159.

24 York Civic Records, quoted in P. W. Hammond and Anne F. Sutton, *Richard III: The Road to Bosworth Field* (London: Constable, 1985), p. 103.

25 Richard Firth Green, 'Historical notes of a London citizen, 1483–1488', *English Historical Review* 96, no. 380 (July 1981), p. 588.

26 Armstrong, ed., *Dominicus Mancinus*, p. 111.

27 See Pamela Tudor-Craig, ed., *Richard III*, catalogue to the National Portrait Gallery exhibition (London: National Portrait Gallery, 1973), p. 9.

28 Richard S. Sylvester, ed., *The Complete Works of St Thomas More*. Volume II, *The History of King Richard III* (London: Yale University Press, 1961), p. 46.

29 See Rosemary Horrox, *Richard III: A Study of Service* (Cambridge: Cambridge University Press, 1989), p. 134.

30 Sylvester, ed., *St Thomas More*, p. 48.

31 *CC*, p. 159.

32 Armstrong, ed., *Dominicus Mancinus*, pp. 112–13.

33 Hammond and Sutton, *Richard III*, p. 102.

34 Hammond and Sutton, *Richard III*, p. 109.

35   Geoffrey Wheeler, 'Who is Foster', *The Ricardian* 2, no. 40 (1973), and Lorraine
     Attreed, 'Hanham redivivus – A salvage operation', *The Ricardian* 5, no. 65 (1979),
     pp. 41–50; *PROME* Henry VII November 1487 part 1.

36   York civic records, in Anne F. Sutton and P. W. Hammond, eds, *The Coronation of
     Richard III: The Extant Documents* (Gloucester: Alan Sutton, 1983), p. 22.

37   Crosby Place itself has a fascinating afterlife. Thomas More, who mentions it in
     his *History*, actually bought the house, the tallest in London, in 1523, for £150.
     Shakespeare, who mentions the residence three times in *Richard III*, lived for a time
     in Bishopsgate and would have worshipped in the church where Sir John and Lady
     Crosby were buried, St Helen's Bishopsgate. The Hall was a rare survival into the
     twentieth century, but was dismantled in 1909 to make way for the Bank of India
     and moved west. It was reconstructed in Cheyne Walk, Chelsea, where it is once
     again a private residence, now in the process of a painstaking 're-contextualization'
     supervised by the owner and a team of experts.

38   Armstrong, ed., *Dominicus Mancinus*, p. 115.

39   A. L. Lamb et al., 'Multi-isotope analysis demonstrates significant lifestyle changes
     in King Richard III', *Journal of Archaeological Science* (2014), http://dx.doi.
     org/10.1016/j.jas.2014.06.021.

40   Harley MS 433 I, p. xxii.

41   Armstrong, ed., *Dominicus Mancinus*, p. 117.

42   *PROME* Edward IV: January 1478, Appendix 1; Armstrong, ed., *Dominicus
     Mancinus*, p. 75.

43   *The memoirs of Philip de Commines, Lord of Argenton: containing the histories of
     Louis XI and Charles VIII, King of France and of Charles the Bold, Duke of Burgundy;
     to which is added, The scandalous chronicle of the secret history of Louis XI*, trans.
     Andrew R. Scoble (London: George Bell, 1896–1900), vol. I, p. 265.

44   *CC*, p. 161.

45   *The memoirs of Philip de Commines*, II, p. 64.

46   R. H. Helmholz, 'The sons of Edward IV: A canonical assessment of the claim that
     they were illegitimate', in P. W. Hammond, ed., *Richard III: Loyalty, Lordship and Law*
     (York: Richard III Society and Yorkist History Trust, 1986), pp. 91–103.

47   Harley MS 433 III, p. 29. The argument that the text of the petition was
     enclosed with the letter to Calais does not seem convincing, as the letter
     clearly states that the petition 'will be sent unto Calais, and ther to be redd
     & understanded, togeder with thise presentes', i.e. it is not an enclosure,
     but will come on later. For arguments on both sides, see Anne Sutton,
     'Richard III's "tytylle & right": A new discovery', *The Ricardian* 4, no. 57
     (1977), pp. 2–8, and Charles T. Wood, 'The deposition of Edward V', *Traditio* 31
     (1975), pp. 247–85.

48 John Rous, *Historia Regum Angliae*, pp. 213–14 (noted in Sutton and Hammond, eds, *Coronation*, p. 24).

49 *CC*, p. 161; Armstrong, ed., *Dominicus Mancinus*, p. 113.

50 Armstrong, ed., *Dominicus Mancinus*, p. 109.

51 *CC*, p. 161.

52 Sutton and Hammond, eds, *Coronation*, p. 25.

53 See Jonathan Hughes, *Arthurian Myths and Alchemy: The Kingship of Edward IV* (Stroud: Sutton Publishing, 2002).

54 Hammond and Sutton, *Richard III*, p. 103.

55 See John Leland, 'Witchcraft and the Woodvilles: A standard medieval smear?', in Douglas L. Biggs, Sharon D. Michalove and A. Compton Reeves, eds, *Reputation and Representation in Fifteenth-Century Europe* (Leiden: Brill, 2004), pp. 267–88.

56 *PROME* Richard III January 1484, 1.

57 'Tabula eclipsis lunaris . . .' Royal MS 12 G I, ff.1–2r, quoted in Pearl Kibre, 'Lewis of Caerleon, doctor of medicine, astronomer, and mathematician', *Isis* 43 (1952), pp. 100–8.

58 Sylvester, ed., *St Thomas* More, p. 48.

59 Armstrong, ed., *Dominicus Mancinus*, p. 95.

60 Jo Appleby et al., 'The scoliosis of Richard III, last Plantagenet King of England: Diagnosis and clinical significance', *The Lancet* 383, no. 9932 (31 May 2014), p. 1,944.

61 Amy Licence, 'Was the downfall of Richard III caused by a strawberry?', *New Statesman* (31 August 2013).

62 Shore later married Richard's solicitor Thomas Lynom, to the king's astonishment (Harley MS 433 III, p. 259): see also Anne F. Sutton et al., 'The children in Richard III's care', *The Ricardian* 24 (2014).

63 'In the yeare of our lorde', in Lansdowne MS 762 63v–65v, discussed along with the other prophecies in Lesley Coote and Tim Thornton, 'Richard, son of Richard: Richard III and political prophecy', *Historical Research* 73, no. 182 (October 2000).

64 Alison Hanham, ed., *The Cely Letters 1472–1488* (Oxford: Oxford University Press, 1975), pp. 184–5 and note, pp. 285–6.

65 Charles Ross, *Richard III* (London: Yale University Press, 1981), p. 94.

66 Philip Schwyzer, *Shakespeare and the Remains of Richard III* (Oxford: Oxford University Press, 2013), p. 196.

Chapter 5

1   Mark Collins, Phillip Emery, Christopher Phillpotts, Mark Samuel and Christopher Thomas, 'The king's high table at the Palace of Westminster', *The Antiquaries Journal* 92 (2012), pp. 197–243.

2   *Grafton's Chronicle, Or History of England: To which is Added His Table of the Bailiffs, Sheriffs and Mayors of the City of London from the Year 1189, to 1558, Inclusive: in Two Volumes* (London: J. Johnson et al., 1809), vol. 2, p. 113.

3   Richard S. Sylvester, ed., *The Complete Works of St Thomas More.* Volume II, *The History of King Richard III* (London: Yale University Press, 1961), pp. 81–2.

4   *Great Chronicle*, p. 234, in P. W. Hammond and Anne F. Sutton, *Richard III: The Road to Bosworth Field* (London: Constable, 1985), p. 144.

5   Dominicus Mancinus [Dominic Mancini], C. A. J. Armstrong ed., *The Usurpation of Richard the Third: Dominicus Mancinus ad Angelum Catonem De Occupatione regni Anglie per Ricardum Tercium libellus* (Oxford: Oxford University Press, 1936), p. 113.

6   Harley MS 433 II, p. 2.

7   Psalm 102:3.

8   Armstrong, ed., *Dominicus Mancinus*, p. 123; more than 450 years later, a new king not wearing headgear was, apparently, still remarkable; '. . . the new suburb stretched beyond the run-way/Where a young man lands hatless from the air'.

9   Anne F. Sutton and P. W. Hammond, eds, *The Coronation of Richard III: The Extant Documents* (Gloucester: Alan Sutton, 1983), p. 43.

10   Armstrong, ed., *Dominicus Mancinus*, p. 123.

11   'The little device', in Sutton and Hammond, eds, *Coronation*, pp. 218–19.

12   According to the records of York, which mentions pageants at other towns (York Records, I, pp. 78–9).

13   Magdalen College Register, 11–12; see H. A. Wilson, *Magdalen College* (London: F. E. Robinson, 1899), pp. 46–7.

14   Harley MS 433 II, p. 6.

15   *PROME* Richard III: January 1484, item 18.

16   Harley MS 433 II, p. 7.

17   J. B. Sheppard, ed., *Christ Church Letters: A Volume of Mediæval Letters Relating to the Affairs of the Priory of Christ Church, Canterbury* (London: Camden Society, 1877), p. 46.

18   On Langton, see R. A. Griffiths, 'Richard III: King or anti-king?', in N. M. Herbert et al., *The 1483 Gloucester Charter in History* (Stroud: Sutton Publishing, 1983), pp. 33–4.

19 MS CCA-DCc-ChChLet/I/88 in Canterbury Archives.

20 Alison Hanham, *Richard III and His Early Historians 1483–1535* (Oxford: Clarendon Press, 1975), p. 50.

21 Hammond and Sutton, *Richard III*, p. 125.

22 See Pamela Tudor-Craig, ed., *Richard III*, catalogue to the National Portrait Gallery exhibition (London: National Portrait Gallery, 1973), for a link to the death of the princes.

23 'If I were to suggest that between the Earth and Mars there is a china teapot revolving about the sun in an elliptical orbit, nobody would be able to disprove my assertion provided I were careful to add that the teapot is too small to be revealed even by our most powerful telescopes. But if I were to go on to say that, since my assertion cannot be disproved, it is intolerable presumption on the part of human reason to doubt it, I should rightly be thought to be talking nonsense.' Bertrand Russell, 'Is there a God?' [1952], *The Collected Papers of Bertrand Russell*. Volume 11, *Last Philosophical Testament (1943–68)* (London: G. Allen and Unwin, 1983), pp. 547–8.

24 John Stow, *The annales of England* (London: R. Newbery, 1592), p. 762.

25 See L. Visser-Fuchs, 'He hardly touched his food: What Niclas Von Popplau really wrote about Richard III', *The Ricardian* 11, no. 145 (1999), p. 529.

26 The genealogy, in which Henry VII is still referred to as the Earl of Richmond, is Ashmole 1448 in W. H. Black, ed., *Catalogue of the Manuscripts of Elias Ashmole* (1845), p. 1,231 (my translation from the Latin); for the Colchester Oath book see John Ashdown-Hill, 'The death of Edward V: New evidence from Colchester', *Essex Archaeology and History* 3rd series, no. 35 (2004), pp. 226–30.

27 Original Latin quoted in Desmond Seward, *Richard III: England's Black Legend* (London: Folio Society, 2014), p. 253 n. 11.

28 For Edward II, see e.g. Ian Mortimer, 'The death of Edward II in Berkeley Castle', *English Historical Review* 120, no. 489 (2005), pp. 1,175–1,214, or Kathryn Warner, *Edward II: The Unconventional King* (Stroud: Amberley, 2014).

29 Henry VII's subsequent motives for executing the Earl of Warwick bear the point out, coming only after conspiracies that implicated the earl as a possible alternative to Henry. Warwick was a strong enough threat that his removal seems to have been a condition upon which Katherine of Aragon's parents Ferdinand and Isabella insisted before agreeing to their daughter's betrothal to Henry's eldest son, Arthur.

30 George Buck, *The History of King Richard III*, ed. A. N. Kincaid (Gloucester: Alan Sutton, 1982), p. 140.

31 Sylvester, ed., *The Complete Works of St Thomas More*, II, pp. 85–6.

32 Lawrence E. Tanner and William Wright, 'Recent investigations concerning the fate of the princes in the tower', *Archaeologia* 84 (1935), p. 18.

33   P. W. Hammond and W. J. White, 'The sons of Edward IV', in Hammond, ed., *Richard III: Loyalty, Lordship and Law* (York: Richard III Society and Yorkist History Trust), p. 128.

34   Alan Travis, 'Why the princes in the tower are staying six feet under', *The Guardian*, 5 February 2013.

35   Colin Richmond, '1483: The year of decision', in Gillingham, ed., *Richard III: A Medieval Kingship* (London: Collins and Brown, 1993), p. 53.

36   Welles's mother was Margaret Beauchamp, which made him Margaret Beaufort's half-brother. Later, he would be recognized as Henry VII's uncle, but there is no indication that he was part of a 'Tudor plot' this early. Harley MS 433 II, p. 7.

37   Harley MS 433 III, p. 33.

38   Harley MS 433 III, pp. 34–5.

39   Harley MS 433 III, pp. 49–50.

40   P. M. Kendall, *Richard III* (London: Allen and Unwin, 1955), p. 307.

41   Told in one of William Caxton's publications, the *Brut* chronicle, printed as the *Chronicles of England* in 1480.

42   Harley MS 433 II, pp. 14–15.

43   Harley MS 433 II, pp. 26–8. On the wine, Thomas Langton had hoped that he would do the same for the prior of Christchurch, though Richard and Anne preferred Burgundy to the prior's Bordeaux.

44   Caxton dedicated his first printing of the latter, in 1474, to Clarence. Although Caxton did reprint it in 1483, he did not make a personal re-dedication, recommending it instead to 'every astate and degree'. The book itself was as much about politics as it was about the game.

45   Harley MS 433 II, pp. 23–4.

46   Harley MS 433 II, pp. 47–8.

47   Harley MS 433 II, p. 25.

48   Harley MS 433 II, p. 42.

49   Sutton and Hammond, eds, *Coronation*, pp. 81–2 and 172–6; for a positive statement of the case that Tyrell did use this opportunity to kill the princes, see Alison Weir, *The Princes in the Tower*, p. 156, which does not, however, mention the Wardrobe editors' description of the mission as 'inconceivable'.

50   Hammond and Sutton, *Richard III*, pp. 140–1, from York Minster Library Bedern College Statute Book.

51   *CC*, p. 161.

52 Letter (in Latin) to the archbishops on the occasion of the investiture of the Prince of Wales, original and translation in Harley MS 433 I, pp. 82–3.

53 *CPR 1476–85*, pp. 465–6, and see Rosemary Horrox, *Richard III: A Study of Service* (Cambridge: Cambridge University Press, 1989), p. 151 n. 50, for a reference to uncalendared text for this entry.

54 *CC*, p. 163.

55 *CC*, p. 163.

56 Hammond and Sutton, *Richard III*, p. 145.

57 C. L. Kingsford, ed., *The Stonor Letters and Papers, 1290–1483* (London: Royal Historical Society, 1919), vol. II, pp. 41–2, 162–3.

58 See Horrox, *Richard III*, p. 143.

59 Thomas Stapleton, ed., *Plumpton Correspondence: A series of letters, chiefly domestick, written in the reigns of Edward IV, Richard III, Henry VII, and Henry VIII* (London: Camden Society, 1839), pp. 44–5.

60 Norman Davis, ed., *Paston Letters and Papers of the Fifteenth Century* (Oxford: Clarendon Press, 1971–6), vol. II, p. 443.

61 Hammond and Sutton, *Richard III*, pp, 146–7.

62 *CC*, p. 165.

63 See Chris Skidmore, *Bosworth: The Birth of the Tudors* (London: Weidenfeld and Nicolson, 2014), p. 54, and Glenn Foard and Anne Curry, *Bosworth 1485: A Battlefield Rediscovered* (Oxford: Oxbow, 2013), p. 33, for discussions, though it should be noted that John Cheyne, contrary to what the latter write, did not go with Henry in 1471, but only after Buckingham's rebellion in 1483.

64 Lewkenore's pardon, TNA C81/1531/48, transcribed in Colin Richmond, '1485 and all that', in Hammond, ed., *Richard III: Loyalty, Lordship and Law*, p. 198 n. 60.

65 See e.g. Charles Ross, *Richard III* (London: Yale University Press, 1981), p. 119.

66 Horrox, *Richard III*, p. 186.

67 *CPR 1476–85*, p. 371.

68 See Anne F. Sutton, Livia Visser-Fuchs and Hannes Kleineke, 'The children in the care of Richard III: New references. A lawsuit between Peter Courteys, keeper of Richard III's Great Wardrobe, and Thomas Lynom, solicitor of Richard III 1495–1501', *The Ricardian* 24 (2014), p. 53 (where the reference to 12 March 1483 should be 12 March 1484).

69 *CC*, p. 171.

70 A. J. Pollard, 'The tyranny of Richard III', *Journal of Medieval History* 3, no. 2 (1977), pp. 147–65.

71 See Horrox, *Richard III*, pp. 275–94.

Chapter 6

1   William Caxton, *The Game and Playe of the Chesse*, ed. Jenny Adams (Kalamazoo, MI: Medieval Institute Publications, 2009), vol. 4, ch. 2.

2   For Caxton's pardon, see Louise Gill, 'William Caxton and the rebellion of 1483', *English Historical Review* 112, no. 445 (1997), pp. 105–18.

3   *CC*, p. 169.

4   Journal 9 (London Metropolitan Archives COL/CC/01/01/009 f.39, f.84); and see Rosemary Horrox, 'Richard III and London', *The Ricardian* 6, no. 85 (1984), pp. 322–9, and R. Sharpe, *London and the Kingdom: A History* (London: Longmans, 1894), vol. I, pp. 324–6.

5   Exchequer Warrants for Issue E404/78/2/28 and 33 quoted in P. W. Hammond and Anne F. Sutton, *Richard III: The Road to Bosworth Field* (London: Constable, 1985), pp. 166–7.

6   Amy Licence, 'New evidence: Was Richard III guilty of murdering the princes in the Tower?', *New Statesman*, 5 March 2013, with a more cautious expansion at the author's blog, http://authorherstorianparent.blogspot.co.uk/2013/03/roads-hospitals-and-shrines-richard-iii.html. For records of Edward IV's and Richard III's Canterbury visits, Edward Hasted, *The History and Topographical Survey of the County of Kent,* Volume 12 (1801), 'Addenda to volume 12: Minutes of the records and accounts of the chamber', pp. 612–62 (entry under 1461 following).

7   *PROME* Richard III January 1484; for Russell's draft sermons for the cancelled Edward V parliaments and for Richard III's, see J. G. Nichols ed., *Grants etc from the Crown during the Reign of Edward the Fifth* (1854), pp. xxxix–lxiii.

8   Anne F. Sutton, 'Richard III's "tytylle & right": A new discovery', *The Ricardian* 4, no. 57 (1977), pp. 2–8.

9   Charter of Richard III to Gloucester, granted by letters patent 2 September 1483, in N. M. Herbert et al., *The Gloucester Charter in History* (Gloucester: Alan Sutton, 1983), p. 9.

10   *PROME* Richard III 1484, 1.

11   Michael Hicks, *Richard III* (Stroud: History Press, 2001).

12   *PROME* Edward IV November 1461.

13   *PROME* Richard III 1484.

14   John Paston to Sir John Paston, 26 March 1473, in Norman Davis, ed., *Paston Letters and Papers of the Fifteenth Century* (Oxford: Clarendon Press, 1971–6), vol. I, p. 589.

15   M. H. Keen, *England in the Later Middle Ages* (London: Methuen, 1973), pp. 392–3.

16 A. H. Thomas and I. D. Thornley, eds, *The Great Chronicle of London* (London: George Jones, 1928), p. 223.

17 *CC*, p. 173.

18 See Hammond and Sutton, *Richard III*, p. 202, for an example.

19 *PROME* Richard III January 1484.

20 Taylor Littleton and Robert R. Rea, eds, *To Prove a Villain: The Case of Richard III* (New York: Macmillan, 1964), p. 104.

21 *CPR* 1476–1485, p. 413.

22 As, surprisingly, Charles Ross does, in *Richard III* (London: Yale University Press, 1981), p. 174.

23 P. Schwyzer, *Shakespeare and the Remains of Richard III* (Oxford: Oxford University Press, 2013), p. 139.

24 Harley MS 433 III, p. 139.

25 Hammond and Sutton, *Richard III*, pp. 165–6.

26 Hammond and Sutton, *Richard III*, p. 165, for Richard's oath.

27 *CC*, p. 171.

28 See Pamela Tudor-Craig, ed., *Richard III*, catalogue to the National Portrait Gallery exhibition (London: National Portrait Gallery, 1973), which seems to be making that argument in connection with accusations referred to by Richard in a public proclamation ('Either he was a very advanced schizophrenic, or he had reason to believe himself innocent of the crimes to which he referred in his letter to Southampton').

29 Hammond and Sutton, *Richard III*, p. 191; for a discussion of the prayer and its context, see Anne F. Sutton and Livia Visser-Fuchs, *Richard III's Books: Ideals and Reality in the Life and Library of a Medieval Prince* (Stroud: Sutton Publishing, 1997), p. 56.

30 Ross, *Richard III*, p. 183.

31 See *CC*, p. 181.

32 *CC*, p. 173.

33 Von Popplau in German in *Darstellung der inneren Verhältnisse der Stadt Breslau vom Jahre 1458 bis zum Jahre 1526*, pp. 363–6 (available online); English translation by Livia Visser-Fuchs, 'He hardly touched his food: What Niclas Von Popplau really wrote about Richard III', *The Ricardian* 145, no. 11 (June 1999), pp. 525–30.

34 *CPR*, p. 493.

35 Hammond and Sutton, *Richard III*, pp. 191–3.

36 *Great Chronicle*, in Hammond and Sutton, *Richard III*, p. 196.

37 An exception is the Tudor historian Edward Hall, whom Charles Ross accuses of suppressing Collingbourne's treasonous activities to make his offence seem more trivial, and Richard's reaction all the harsher (Ross, *Richard III*, p. xxxiii).

38 Raphael Holinshed, *Chronicles of England, Scotland and Ireland* (1808), vol. III, p. 422.

39 Harley MS 433 III, p. 124.

40 Letter in Harley MS 787 f.2v, quoted e.g. in S. B. Chrimes, *Henry VII* (London: Yale University Press, 1972, rev. 1999), p. 39.

41 Letter of Charles VIII to Toulon, 3 November 1484, quoted by Michael K. Jones, 'The myth of 1485: Did France really put Henry Tudor on the throne?', in D. Grummitt, ed., *The English Experience in France c. 1450–1558: War, Diplomacy and Cultural Exchange* (Aldershot: Ashgate, 2002), p. 92.

42 Harley MS 433 I, pp. 201, 221, 247.

43 *CC*, p. 175.

44 Hammond and Sutton, *Richard III*, p. 199.

45 George Buck, *The History of King Richard III*, ed. A. N. Kincaid (Gloucester: Alan Sutton, 1982), p. 191.

46 A. N. Kincaid, 'George Buck senior and George Buck junior: A literary and historical mystery', in J. Petre, ed., *Richard III: Crown and People* (Langley: Richard III Society, 1985), pp. 245–51.

47 See J. Ashdown-Hill, *The Last Days of Richard III* (Stroud: History Press, 2010), pp. 27–33, for a discussion of the potential double marriage for Richard and Elizabeth of York into the Portuguese royal house.

48 Hammond and Sutton, *Richard III*, pp. 205–6.

49 *CC*, p. 173.

50 Harley MS 433 II, pp. 228–30.

51 Lesley Boatwright, 'Buckinghamshire six', *The Ricardian* 13 (2003), p. 65.

52 Glenn Foard and Anne Curry, *Bosworth 1485: A Battlefield Rediscovered* (Oxford: Oxbow, 2013), pp. 26–7.

53 *CC*, p. 173.

54 *CPR* 1476–85, p. 545.

55 Davis, ed., *Paston Letters*, II, pp. 443–4.

56 Foard and Curry, *Bosworth 1485*, p. 27.

57 C. Richmond, 'The nobility and the coronation of Richard III', *The Ricardian* 12, no. 148 (2000), p. 659.

Chapter 7

1 Glenn Foard and Anne Curry, *Bosworth 1485: A Battlefield Rediscovered* (Oxford: Oxbow, 2013), p. xix.

2 *Vita Henrici Septimi* in M. Bennett, *The Battle of Bosworth* (Stroud: Sutton Publishing, 1985), p. 163.

3 See Michael K. Jones, 'The myth of 1485: Did France really put Henry Tudor on the English throne?', in David Grummitt, ed., *The English Experience in France, c. 1450–1558: War, Diplomacy and Cultural Exchange* (Aldershot: Ashgate, 2002), pp. 85–105; and L. Visser-Fuchs, 'Phantom bastardy and ghostly pikemen', *The Ricardian* 14 (2004), pp. 116–22.

4 *CC*, p. 179.

5 Harley MS 433 I, p. 112.

6 Foard and Curry, p. 37.

7 *CC*, p. 179.

8 J. Ashdown-Hill, 'The Bosworth crucifix', *Transactions of the Leicestershire Architectural and Archaeological Society* 78 (2004), pp. 83–96.

9 *CC*, p. 181.

10 For the argument that Richard wore his crown, etc., see Michael K. Jones, *Bosworth 1485: Psychology of a Battle* (Stroud: Tempus, 2002), p. 22.

11 *Great Chronicle*, quoted by Colin Richmond, '1485 and all that', in P. W. Hammond, ed., *Richard III: Loyalty, Lordship and Law* (York: Richard III Society and Yorkist History Trust, 1986), p. 178.

12 Foard and Curry, p. 55.

13 Richmond, '1485 and all that', p. 173.

14 Harley MS 433 II, p. 112.

15 See Foard and Curry, esp. pp. 186–90, for the details of this suggestion.

16 Polydore Vergil in Bennett, *Battle of Bosworth*, pp. 165–6.

17 *CC*, p. 181.

18 Salazar in Juan de Valera, 'A Castilian report', in Bennett, *Battle of Bosworth*, p. 160.

19 Jo Appleby et al., 'Perimortem trauma in King Richard III: A skeletal analysis', *The Lancet* 385 (2015), pp. 235–9.

20 *CC*, p. 183.

21 Diego de Valera, in Bennett, *Battle of Bosworth*, pp. 159–60.

22 See Andrew Breeze, "A Welsh poem of 1485 on Richard III", *The Ricardian* 18 (2008), pp. 46–53.

23 R. Buckley et al., 'The king in the car park: New light on the death and burial of Richard III in the Grey Friars church, Leicester, in 1485", *Antiquity* 87, no. 336 (2013), pp. 531–5.

Chapter 8

1   Simon Farnaby, 'The King in the car park', Channel 4, 4 February 2013.

2   *PROME* Henry VII November 1485, part 1, item 18.

3   Proclamation of Henry Tudor, 22–23 August 1485, in Michael Bennett, *The Battle of Bosworth* (Gloucester: Alan Sutton, 1985), p. 155.

4   *PROME* Richard III January 1484, item 1.

5   Pamela Tudor-Craig, ed., *Richard III* (London: National Portrait Gallery, 1973), p. 41.

6   John Ashdown-Hill, 'The epitaph of King Richard III', *The Ricardian* 18 (2008), pp. 31–45.

7   Robert Davies, *Extracts from the Municipal Records of the City of York in the Reigns of Edward IV, Edward V and Richard III* (London: J. B. Nichols and Son, 1843), p. 221.

8   Josephine Wilkinson, *Richard: The Young King to Be* (Stroud: Amberley, 2009), p. 286.

9   Richard S. Sylvester, ed., *The Complete Works of St Thomas More*. Volume II, *The History of King Richard III* (London: Yale University Press 1961), p. 7.

10 William Shakespeare, *Richard III*, Act I, scene i; Act V, scene v.

11 The praise of King Richard III', in Taylor Littleton and Robert R. Rea, eds, *To Prove A Villain: The Case of Richard III* (New York: Macmillan 1964), p. 80.

12 Shakespeare, *Richard III*, Act I, scene i.

13 Tudor-Craig, *Richard III*, pp. 5–6.

14 George Awdry, *The Richard III Society, the First Fifty Years: A Personal Account* (Upminster: The Society, 1977).

15 https://www.le.ac.uk/richardiii/history/whowasrichard.html.

16 Letter to the *Ricardian Bulletin*, September 2014, p. 9.

17 See, for example, http://fuckyeahrichardiii.tumblr.com.

18 *Daily Mail*, 24 March 2015.

19 Edward Hall, *Henry VIII*, quoted in Philip Schwyzer, *Shakespeare and the Remains of Richard III* (Oxford: Oxford University Press, 2013), p. 127.

20 '"Entumbid Right Princely": The re-interment of Richard Beauchamp, earl of Warwick, and a lost rite', in *The Yorkist Age: Proceedings of the 2011 Harlaxton Symposium*, ed. Hannes Kleineke and Christian Steer (Donington: Shaun Tyas, 2013).

21 Fenwick in Market Street.

22 Mr Ibsen's mother, Joy Ibsen, had been identified by John Ashdown-Hill as directly descended from Richard's sister Anne (and therefore from their mother Cecily Neville) for an earlier project. Strictly speaking, of course, Richard III had no direct descendants, as his only legitimate child predeceased him without issue.

23 Francis Sandford, *A Genealogical History of the Kings of England* (London, 1677), p. 402, quoted in Lawrence E. Tanner and William Wright, 'Recent investigations regarding the fate of the princes in the Tower', *Archaeologia* 84 (1935), p. 8.

Bibliography

Adair, John. 'A Hanseatic merchant's account of Edward's campaign to regain the crown, up to the battle of Barnet', from 'The Newsletter of Gerhard von Wessel, 17 April 1471', *Journal of the Society for Army Historical Research* (1968).

Adams, Jenny, ed. *The Game and Playe of the Chesse by William Caxton* (Kalamazoo, MI: Medieval Institute Publications, 2009).

Appleby, Jo et al. 'The scoliosis of Richard III, last Plantagenet King of England: Diagnosis and clinical significance', *The Lancet* 383, no. 9,932 (2014), p1. 944.

Appleby, Jo et al. 'Perimortem trauma in King Richard III: A skeletal analysis', *The Lancet* 385, no. 9,964 (2015), pp. 253–9.

Armstrong, C. A. J. 'Inauguration ceremonies of the Yorkist kings', *Transactions of the Royal Historical Society* 4, no. 30 (1948), p. 53.

Ashdown-Hill, John. *The Last Days of Richard III* (Stroud: History Press, 2010).

Ashdown-Hill, John. *The Third Plantagenet: George, Duke of Clarence, Richard III's Brother* (Stroud: History Press, 2014).

Ashdown-Hill, John. 'The Bosworth crucifix', *Transactions of the Leicestershire Architectural and Archaeological Society* 78 (2004), pp. 83–96.

Ashdown-Hill, John. 'The death of Edward V: New evidence from Colchester', *Essex Archaeology and History* 35 (2004), pp. 226–30.

Ashdown-Hill, John. 'The epitaph of King Richard III', *The Ricardian* 18 (2008), pp. 31–45.

Attreed, Lorraine. 'Hanham redivivus: A salvage operation', *The Ricardian* 5, no. 65 (1979), pp. 41–50.

Attreed, Lorraine, ed. *The York House Books, 1461–1490*, 2 vols (Stroud: Sutton Publishing, 1991).

Awdry, George. *The Richard III Society, the First Fifty Years: A Personal Account* (Upminster: The Society, 1977).

Bahn, Paul, ed. *Written in Bones: How Human Remains Unlock the Secrets of the Dead* (Newton Abbot: David & Charles, 2003).

Baldwin, David. *Richard III* (Stroud: Amberley, 2013).

Baldwin, David. 'King Richard's grave in Leicester', *Transactions of the Leicestershire Archaeological and Historical Society* 60 (1986), pp. 21–2.

Barnardiston, K. W. *Clare Priory: Seven Centuries of a Suffolk House* (Cambridge: W. Heffer, 1962).

Barnfield, Marie. 'Diriment impediments, dispensations and divorce: Richard III and matrimony', *The Ricardian* 17 (2007), pp. 84–98.

Bayley, John, ed. *Calendars of the Proceedings in Chancery, in the Reign of Queen Elizabeth*, vol. 1 (London: Eyre and Strahan, 1827).

Beal, John P., James A. Coriden and Thomas J. Green, eds, *New Commentary on the Code of Canon Law* (New York: Paulist Press, 1999).

Bede, *History of the English Church and People*, trans. L. Shirley-Price, rev. R. E. Latham (Harmondsworth: Penguin, 1968).

Bennett, Michael, *The Battle of Bosworth* (Stroud: Sutton Publishing, 1985).

Bentley, Samuel, ed. *Excerpta historica or, Illustrations of English History* (London: privately printed, 1831).

Biggs, Douglas L., Sharon D. Michalove and A. Compton Reeves, eds, *Reputation and Representation in Fifteenth-Century Europe* (Leiden: Brill, 2004).

Black, W. H., ed. *A Descriptive, Analytical and Critical Catalogue of the Manuscripts of Elias Ashmole* (Oxford: Oxford University Press, 1845).

Boatwright, Lesley. 'The Buckinghamshire six at Bosworth', *The Ricardian* 13 (2003), pp. 54–66.

Botfield, Beriah. *Manners and Household Expenses of England in the Thirteenth and Fifteenth Centuries Illustrated by Original Records* (London: W. Nicol, 1841).

Breeze, Andrew A. 'A Welsh poem of 1485 on Richard III', *The Ricardian* 18 (2008), pp. 46–53.

Brown, Lucy. 'Continuity and change in the parliamentary justifications of the fifteenth-century usurpations', in *The Fifteenth Century VII: Conflicts, Consequences and the Crown in the Late Middle Ages*, ed. Linda Clark (Woodbridge: Boydell and Brewer, 2007), pp. 157–74.

Bruce, John, ed. *Historie of the arrivall of Edward IV in England and the finall recouerye of his kingdomes from Henry VI* (London: Camden Society, 1838).

Buck, George. *The History of King Richard the Third* (1619), ed. A. N. Kincaid (Gloucester: Alan Sutton, 1982).

Buckle, Alexandra. '"Entumbid Right Princely": The re-interment of Richard Beauchamp, earl of Warwick, and a lost rite', in *The Yorkist Age: Proceedings of the 2011 Harlaxton Symposium*, ed. Hannes Kleineke and Christian Steer (Donington: Shaun Tyas, 2013).

Buckley, Richard et al. 'The king in the car park: New light on the death and burial of Richard III in the Grey Friars church, Leicester, in 1485', *Antiquity* 87, no. 336 (2013), pp. 519–38.

Calendar of the Close Rolls Preserved in the Public Record Office: Edward IV, vol. II, *1468–1476* (London: HMSO, 1953).

Calendar of the Close Rolls Preserved in the Public Record Office: Edward IV, Edward V, Richard III, 1476–1485 (London: HMSO, 1954).

Calendar of the Patent Rolls Preserved in the Public Record Office: Edward IV, 1461–1467 (London: HMSO, 1897).

Calendar of the Patent Rolls Preserved in the Public Record Office: Edward IV, Henry VI, 1467–1477 (London: HMSO, 1900).

Calendar of the Patent Rolls Preserved in the Public Record Office: Edward IV, Edward V, Richard III, 1476–1485 (London: HMSO, 1901).

Calendar of the Patent Rolls Preserved in the Public Record Office: Henry VI, vol. VI, *1452–1461* (London: HMSO, 1910).

Carlin, Martha. 'Sir John Fastolf's place, Southwark: The home of the Duke of York's family, 1460', *The Ricardian* 5, no. 72 (1981), pp. 311–14.

Chrimes, S. B. *Henry VII* (London: Yale University Press, 1972; rev. ed. 1999).

Clarke, P. D. 'English royal marriages and the papal penitentiary in the fifteenth century', *English Historical Review* 120, no. 488 (2005), pp. 1,014–29.

A Collection of ordinances and regulations for the government of the royal household, made in divers reigns from King Edward III to King William and Queen Mary (London: Society of Antiquaries, 1790).

Collins, Mark, Phillip Emery, Christopher Phillpotts, Mark Samuel and Christopher Thomas. 'The king's high table at the Palace of Westminster', *The Antiquaries Journal* 92 (2012), pp 197–243.

Commynes, Philippe de. *Memoirs: The Reign of Louis XI, 1461–83*, trans. with an introduction by Michael Jones (Harmondsworth: Penguin, 1972).

Coote, L. and T. Thornton. 'Richard, son of Richard: Richard III and political prophecy', *Historical Research* 73, no. 182 (2000).

Cothi, Gwaith Lewis Glyn, Walter Davies and John Jones, eds. *The Poetical works of Lewis Glyn Cothi, a celebrated bard who flourished in the reigns of Henry VI, Edward IV, Richard III and Henry VII* (Oxford: The Cymmrodorion or Royal Cambrian Institution, 1837).

Davies, John Silvester, ed. *An English chronicle of the reigns of Richard II, Henry IV, Henry V, and Henry VI written before the year 1471* (London: Camden Society, 1856).

Davies, Robert. *Extracts from the Municipal Records of the City of York in the Reigns of Edward IV, Edward V and Richard III* (London: J. B. Nichols and son, 1843).

Davis, Norman, ed. *Paston Letters and Papers of the Fifteenth Century* (vols I and II: Davis, ed.; vol. III: Richard Beadle and Colin Richmond, eds) (Oxford: Clarendon Press; I and II, 1971–6; III, 2004).

Dockray, Keith. *Richard III: A Sourcebook* (Stroud: Sutton Publishing, 1997).

Du Boulay, F. R. H., ed. *Registrum Thome Bourgchier Cantuariensis archiepiscopi, A.D. 1454–1486* (Oxford: Oxford University Press, 1957).

Dupont, L. M. E., ed. *Anchiennes Croniques d'Engleterre par Jehan de Wavrin* (Paris: Renouard, 1858–63).

Edwards, Rhoda. *The Itinerary of King Richard III, 1483–1485* (London: Richard III Society, 1983).

Ellis, Henry, ed. *The New chronicles of England and France, in two parts by Robert Fabyan* (London: Rivington, 1811).

Ellis, Henry, ed. *Original Letters Illustrative of English History, Including Numerous Royal Letters from Autographs in the British Museum, the State Paper Office, and One or Two Other Collections* (1824) (London: Dawsons, 1969).

Evans, Howell T. *Wales and the Wars of the Roses* (Cambridge: Cambridge University Press, 1915).

Fiorato, Veronica, Anthea Boylston and Christopher Knusel, eds. *Blood Red Roses: The Archaeology of a Mass Grave from the Battle of Towton AD 1461* (Oxford: Oxbow, 2001).

Firth Green, Richard. 'Historical notes of a London citizen, 1483–1488', *English Historical Review* 96, no. 380 (1981), p. 588.

Firth Green, Richard. 'An epitaph for Richard, Duke of York', *Studies in Bibliography* 41 (1988), pp. 218–24.

Flenley, Ralph, ed. *Six Town Chronicles of England* (Oxford: Oxford University Press, 1911).

Foard, Glenn, and Anne Curry. *Bosworth 1485: A Battlefield Rediscovered* (Oxford: Oxbow, 2013).

Gaimster, David, Sarah McCarthy and Bernard Nurse, eds. *Making History: Antiquaries in Britain 1707–2007* (London: Royal Academy of Arts, 2007).

Gairdner, James. *History of the Life and Reign of Richard III, to which is added the story of Perkin Warbeck* (Cambridge: Cambridge University Press, 1898 revised edn).

Gairdner, James, ed. *Letters and Papers Illustrative of the Reigns of Richard III and Henry VII*, 2 vols (London: Longman, 1861–3).

Gairdner, James, ed. *Historical Collections of a Citizen of London in the Fifteenth Century* (London: Camden Society, 1876).

Gairdner, James, ed. *Three Fifteenth-Century Chronicles with Historical Memoranda by John Stowe* (London: Camden Society, and British History Online, 1880).

Gairdner, James, ed. *The Paston Letters* (London: Constable, 1896).

Gascoigne, Thomas. *Loci e Libro Veritatum*, ed. J. E. T. Rodgers (Oxford: Clarendon Press, 1881).

Giles, J. A. *Incerti Scriptoris Chronicon Angliae* (London: D. Nutt, 1848).

Giles, J. A., ed. *The chronicles of the White Rose of York: A series of historical fragments, proclamations, letters, and other contemporary documents relating to the reign of King Edward the Fourth* (London: James Bohn, 1845).

Gill, Louise. 'William Caxton and the rebellion of 1483', *English Historical Review* 112, no. 445 (1997), pp. 105–18.

Gillingham, John, ed. *Richard III: A Medieval Kingship* (London: Collins and Brown, 1993).

Gilson, J. P. 'A defence of the proscription of the Yorkists in 1459', *English Historical Review* 26 (1911), pp. 512–25.

Given-Wilson, Chris et al., eds. *Parliament Rolls of Medieval England* (Woodbridge: Boydell and Brewer, and British History Online, 2005).

Goodman, Anthony. *The Wars of the Roses: The Soldiers' Experience* (Stroud: Tempus, 2005).

Grafton, Richard. *Grafton's Chronicle, Or History of England: To which is Added His Table of the Bailiffs, Sheriffs and Mayors of the City of London from the Year 1189, to 1558, Inclusive*, 2 vols (London: J. Johnson et al., 1809).

Green, J. Alec J. 'Fotheringhay castle', *The Ricardian* 3, no. 45 (June 1974).

Griffiths, R. 'Richard, Duke of York and the crisis of Henry VI's household in 1450–51', *Journal of Medieval History* 38 (2012).

Griffiths, R. A. *The Reign of King Henry VI: The Exercise of Royal Authority, 1422–1461* (London: Benn, 1981).

Griffiths, R. A. 'Duke Richard of York's intentions in 1450 and the origins of the Wars of the Roses', *Journal of Medieval History* 1 (1975), pp. 203–5.

Griffiths, Ralph A., and James Sherborne, eds. *Kings and Nobles in the Later Middle Ages* (Stroud: Sutton Publishing/St Martin's Press, 1986).

Grummitt, David. *A Short History of the Wars of the Roses* (London: I. B. Tauris, 2013).

Grummitt, D., ed. *The English Experience in France, c. 1450–1558: War, Diplomacy and Cultural Exchange* (Aldershot: Ashgate, 2002).

Gunn, S. J. 'Early Tudor dates for the death of Edward V', *Northern History* 28 (1992), pp. 213–16.

Halliwell, J. O., ed. *Palatine Anthology: A collection of ancient poems and ballads relating to Lancashire and Cheshire* (London: privately printed, 1850).

Hammond, P. W. 'The bones of the "Princes" in Westminster Abbey', *The Ricardian* 4, no. 52 (1976), pp. 22–5.

Hammond, P. W., ed. *Richard III: Loyalty, Lordship and Law* (London: Richard III Society and Yorkist History Trust, 1986).

Hammond, P. W., and Anne F. Sutton. *Richard III: The Road to Bosworth Field* (London: Constable, 1985).

Hammond, P. W., Anne F. Sutton and Livia Visser-Fuchs. 'The reburial of Richard, Duke of York, 21–30 July 1476', *The Ricardian* 10, no. 127 (1994), pp. 122–65.

Hanbury, Harold Greville. 'The legislation of Richard III', *American Journal of Legal History* 6 (1962), pp. 95–113.

Hanham, Alison. *Richard III and His Early Historians, 1483–1535* (Oxford: Clarendon Press, 1975).

Hanham, Alison. 'Richard III, Lord Hastings and the historians', *English Historical Review* 87 (1972), pp. 235–48.

Harriss, Gerald. *Shaping the Nation: England 1360–1461* (Oxford: Oxford University Press, 2005).

Harvey, I. M. W. *Jack Cade's Rebellion of 1450* (Oxford: Oxford University Press, 1991).

Hasted, Edward. *The History and Topographical Survey of the County of Kent*, vol. 12 (Canterbury: privately printed, and British History Online, 1801).

Haward, W. I. 'Economic aspects of the Wars of the Roses in East Anglia', *English Historical Review* 41, no. 162 (1926).

Hays, Denys, ed. and trans. *The Anglica Historia of Polydore Vergil, A.D. 1485–1537* (London: The Royal Historical Society, 1950).

Heralds' commemorative exhibition, 1484–1934, held at the College of Arms: enlarged and illustrated catalogue (London: Printed for the Kings, Heralds & Pursuivants of Arms of England, 1936).

Herbert, N. M. et al. *The 1483 Gloucester Charter in History* (Stroud: Sutton Publishing, 1983).

Hicks, M. A. *False Fleeting Perjur'd Clarence: George, Duke of Clarence, 1449–78* (Gloucester: Alan Sutton, 1980).

Hicks, M. A. *Richard III and His Rivals: Magnates and their Motives in the Wars of the Roses* (London: Hambledon, 1991).

Hicks, M. A. *Richard III* (Stroud: History Press, 2000).

Hicks, M. A. *Anne Neville: Queen to Richard III* (Stroud: History Press, 2006).

Hicks, M. A. 'From megaphone to microscope: The correspondence of Richard, Duke of York, with Henry VI in 1450 revisited', *Journal of Medieval History* 25 (1999), pp. 251–2.

Hinds, Allen B., ed. *Calendar of State Papers and Manuscripts in the Archives and Collections of Milan: 1385–1618*. Online at www.british-history.ac.uk.

Hipshon, David. *Richard III* (London: Routledge, 2011).

Hoccleve, Thomas. *The Regiment of Princes*, ed. Charles R. Blyth (Kalamazoo, MI: Medieval Institute Publications, 1999).

Holinshed, Raphael. *Chronicles of England, Scotland and Ireland*, vol. III (London: J. Johnson et al., 1808).

Horrox, Rosemary. *Richard III: A Study of Service* (Cambridge: Cambridge University Press, 1989).

Horrox, Rosemary. 'Preparations for Edward IV's return from exile', *The Ricardian* 6, no. 79 (1982), pp. 124–7.

Horrox, Rosemary. 'Richard III and London', *The Ricardian* 6, no. 85 (1984), pp. 322–9.

Horrox, Rosemary, ed. *Richard III and the North*. (Centre for Regional and Local History, Department of Adult and Continuing Education, University of Hull, 1986).

Horrox, Rosemary, and P. W. Hammond, eds, *British Library Manuscript Harleian 433*, 4 vols (London: Richard III Society, 1979–83).

Hughes, Jonathan. *Arthurian Myths and Alchemy: The Kingship of Edward IV* (Stroud: Sutton Publishing, 2002).

Hughes, Jonathan. *The Religious Life of Richard III* (Stroud: Sutton Publishing, 1997).

Huizinga, J. *The Waning of the Middle Ages*, trans. F. Hopman (Harmondsworth: Penguin, 1955).

Jacob, E. F. *The Fifteenth Century, 1399–1485* (Oxford: Oxford University Press, 1961).

Jones, Michael K. 'Edward IV, the earl of Warwick and the Yorkist claim to the throne', *Historical Research* 70, no. 173 (1997), pp. 342–52.

Jones, Michael K. *Bosworth 1485: Psychology of a Battle* (Stroud: Tempus, 2002).

Jones, Michael K. 'Somerset, York and the Wars of the Roses', *English Historical Review* 104, no. 411 (1989), pp. 285–307.

Keen, M. H. *England in the Later Middle Ages* (London: Methuen, 1973).

Kekewich, M. 'The attainder of the Yorkists in 1459: Two contemporary accounts', *Historical Research* 55 (1982), pp. 25–34.

Kekewich, M. 'Edward IV, William Caxton, and literary patronage in Yorkist England', *Modern Language Review* 66, no. 3 (1971), pp. 481–7.

Kendall, P. M. *Richard III* (London: Allen and Unwin, 1955).

Kendall, P. M., ed. *Richard III: The Great Debate. Sir Thomas More's History of King Richard III and Horace Walpole's Historic Doubts on the Life and Reign of King Richard III* (New York: Norton, 1965).

Kibre, Pearl. 'Lewis of Caerleon, doctor of medicine, astronomer, and mathematician', *Isis* 43, no. 2 (1952), pp. 100–8.

Kingsford, C. L. *English Historical Literature in the Fifteenth Century* (Oxford: Clarendon Press, 1913).

Kingsford, C. L, ed. *The Stonor Letters and Papers, 1290–1483*, 2 vols (London: The Royal Historical Society, 1919).

Kleineke, Hannes. 'Alice Martyn, widow of London: An episode from Richard's youth', *The Ricardian* 14 (2004), pp. 32–6.

Lamb, Angela L., Jane E. Evans, Richard Buckley and Jo Appleby. 'Multi-isotope analysis demonstrates significant lifestyle changes in King Richard III', *Elsevier Journal of Archaeological Science* 30 (2014), pp. 1–7.

Lander, J. R. *The Wars of the Roses* (London: Secker and Warburg, 1965).

Langley, Philippa, and Michael Jones. *The King's Grave: The Search for Richard III* (London: John Murray, 2013).

Leland, John. *Joannis Lelandi antiquarii De rebus Britannicis collectanea. Cum Thomæ Hearnii præfatione notis et indice ad editionem primam, etc.* (Farnborough: Gregg International, 1774; facsimile 1970).

Licence, Amy. *Anne Neville: Richard III's Tragic Queen* (Stroud: Amberley, 2013).

Licence, Amy. 'New evidence: Was Richard III guilty of murdering the Princes in the Tower?', *New Statesman* (3 May 2013).

Littleton, Taylor, and Robert R. Rea, eds. *To Prove a Villain: The Case of Richard III* (New York: Macmillan, 1964).

MacGibbon, David. *Elizabeth Woodville: A Life* (Stroud: Amberley, 2013).

Mancinus, Dominicus, *The Usurpation of Richard the Third*, ed. and trans. C. A. J. Armstrong (Oxford: Oxford University Press, 1936).

Markham, Clements E. *Richard III: His Life and Character Reviewed in the Light of Recent Research* (London: Smith, Elder and Co., 1906).

Martí, Jordi Sánchez. 'Longleat House MS 257 – a description', *Atlantis* 27, no. 1 (2005), pp. 78–89.

Matheson, Lister M., ed. *Death and Dissent: Two Fifteenth-Century Chronicles* (Woodbridge: Boydell and Brewer, 1999).

Maurer, Helen. *Margaret of Anjou: Queenship and Power in Late Medieval England* (Woodbridge: Boydell and Brewer, 2003).

McFarlane, K. B. *England in the Fifteenth Century*, ed. G. L. Harriss (London: Hambledon, 1981).

McFarlane, K. B. 'The Wars of the Roses', *Proceedings of the British Academy* 1 (1964).

Molleson, Theya. 'Anne Mowbray and the Princes in the Tower: A study', *London Archaeologist* 5 (1987), pp. 258–62.

Morgan, D. A. L. 'Hearne's "Fragment" and the long prehistory of English memoirs', *English Historical Review* 124 (2009), pp. 811–32.

Morgan, Philip. 'The death of Edward V and the rebellion of 1483', *Historical Research* 68, no. 166 (1995), pp. 229–32.

Morris, Matthew, and Richard Buckley. *Richard III: The King under the Car Park* (Leicester: University of Leicester Archaeological Services, 2014).

Myers, A. R. 'Richard III and the historical tradition', *History* 53 (1968), pp. 181–202.

Myers, A. R., ed. *The Household of Edward IV: The Black Book and the Ordinance of 1478* (Manchester: Manchester University Press, 1959).

Nichols, J. G. *Grants, etc. From the Crown during the Reign of Edward V* (London: Camden Society, 1854).

Nicholson, R. G. *Scotland: The Later Middle Ages* (Edinburgh: Oliver and Boyd, 1974).

Orme, Nicholas. *From Childhood to Chivalry: The Education of English Kings and Aristocracy 1066–1530* (London: Methuen, 1984).

Palliser, D. M. *Medieval York: 600–1540* (Oxford: Oxford University Press, 2014).

Penman, Sharon. *The Sunne in Splendour* (London: Macmillan, 1982).

Penn, Thomas. *Winter King: The Dawn of Tudor England* (Harmondsworth: Penguin, 2011).

Petre, J., ed. *Richard III: Crown and People* (London: Richard III Society, 1985).

Pitts, Mike. *Digging for Richard: How Archaeology Found the King* (London: Thames and Hudson, 2014).

Pollard, A. J. *Richard III and the Princes in the Tower* (Stroud: Sutton Publishing, 1991).

Pollard, A. J. 'The tyranny of Richard III', *Journal of Medieval History* 3, no. 2 (1977), pp. 147–65.

Pollard, A. J. 'Richard Clervaux of Croft', *Yorkshire Archaeological Journal* 50, no. 9 (1978), pp. 151–69.

Potter, Jeremy. *Good King Richard?: An Account of Richard III and His Reputation, 1483–1983* (London: Constable, 1983).

Pronay, Nicholas, and John Cox, ed. *The Crowland Chronicle Continuations: 1459–1486* (London: Richard III Society and Yorkist History Trust, 1986).

Reid, R. R. 'The office of Warden of the Marches: Its origin and early history', *English Historical Review* 32, no. 128 (1917), pp. 479–96.

Richmond, C. F. 'The death of Edward V', *Northern History*, 25 (1989), pp. 278–80.

Richmond, Colin. 'Fauconberg's Kentish rising of May 1471', *English Historical Review* 85, no. 337 (1970), pp. 673–92.

Richmond, Colin. 'The nobility and the coronation of Richard III', *The Ricardian* 12, no. 148 (2000), pp. 653–9.

Riley, H. T., ed. *Registrum Abbatiae Johannis Whethamstede* (London: Longman, 1872–3).

Ross, Charles. *Richard III* (London: Yale University Press, 1981).

Ross, Charles. *Edward IV* (London: Yale University Press, 1983).

Ross, Charles. 'Some servants and lovers of Richard in his youth', *The Ricardian* 4, no. 55 (1976), pp. 2–4.

Rymer, Thomas. *Foedera*, vol. XII (The Hague: J. Neulme, and British History Online, 1739–45).

Schwyzer, Philip. *Shakespeare and the Remains of Richard III* (Oxford: Oxford University Press, 2013).

Seward, Desmond. *Richard III: England's Black Legend* (London: Folio Society, 2014).

Shakespeare, William. *Richard III*: ed. E. A. J. Honigmann (Harmondsworth: Penguin 2005).

Shakespeare, William. *Henry VI Part One*, ed. Norman Sanders (Harmondsworth: Penguin, 2005).

Shakespeare, William. *Henry VI Part Two*, ed. Stanley Wells (Harmondsworth: Penguin, 2005).

Shakespeare, William. *Henry VI Part Three*, ed. Norman Sanders (Harmondsworth: Penguin, 2007).

Sharpe, R. *London and the Kingdom: A History Derived Mainly from the Archives at Guildhall in the Custody of the Corporation* (London: Longman, 1894).

Sheppard, J. B. *Christ Church Letters: A volume of mediaeval letters relating to the affairs of the Priory of Christ Church, Canterbury* (London: Camden Society, 1877).

Skidmore, Chris. *Bosworth: The Birth of the Tudors* (London: Weidenfeld and Nicolson, 2013).

Spedding, Alison J. '"At the King's Pleasure": The testament of Cecily Neville', *Midland History* 35, no. 2 (2010), pp. 256–72.

Spencer, Mark. *Thomas Basin, 1412–1490* (Nieuwkoop: De Graaf, 1997).

Stapleton, Thomas, ed. *Plumpton Correspondence: A series of letters, chiefly domestick, written in the reigns of Edward IV, Richard III, Henry VII and Henry VIII* (London: Camden Society, 1839).

Stevenson, J., ed. *Letters and Papers Illustrative of the Wars of the English in France During the Reign of Henry the Sixth, King of England* (London: Longman, 1861–4), vol. 2, part 2.

Storey, R. L. 'The wardens of the Marches of England towards Scotland, 1377–1489', *English Historical Review* 72, no. 285 (1957), pp. 593–615.

Stow, John. *The Annales of England* (London: R. Newbery, 1592).

Sutton, Anne F. 'The return to England of Richard of Gloucester after his first exile', *The Ricardian* 3, no. 50 (1975), pp. 21–2.

Sutton, Anne F. 'Richard III's "Tytylle & Right": A new discovery', *The Ricardian* 4, no. 57 (1977), pp. 2–8.

Sutton, Anne F. 'And to be delivered to the Lord Richard Duke of Gloucester, the other brother', *The Ricardian* 8, no. 100 (1988), pp. 20–5.

Sutton, Anne F. 'Richard III as a fop: A foolish myth', *The Ricardian* 18 (2008), pp. 58–65.

Sutton, Anne F., and Livia Visser-Fuchs. *Richard III's Books: Ideals and Reality in the Life and Library of a Medieval Prince* (Stroud: Sutton Publishing, 1997).

Sutton, Anne, and Livia Visser-Fuchs. 'Richard of Gloucester and La Grosse Bombarde', *The Ricardian* 10, no. 134 (1996), pp. 461–5.

Sutton, Anne, and P. W. Hammond, eds. *The Coronation of Richard III: The Extant Documents* (Gloucester: Alan Sutton, 1983).

Sutton, Anne, Livia Visser-Fuchs and Hannes Kleineke. 'The children in the care of Richard III: New references. A lawsuit between Peter Courteys, keeper of Richard III's Great Wardrobe, and Thomas Lynom, solicitor of Richard III, 1495–1501', *The Ricardian* 24 (2014), pp. 31–62.

Sylvester, Richard S., ed. *The Complete Works of St Thomas More*. Volume II, *The History of King Richard III* (London: Yale University Press, 1961).

Tanner, Lawrence E., and William Wright. 'Recent investigations regarding the fate of the Princes in the Tower', *Archaeologia* 84 (1935), pp. 1–26.

Tey, Josephine. *The Daughter of Time* (London: Peter Davies, 1951).

Thomas, A. H., and I. D. Thornley, eds. *The Great Chronicle of London* (London: George Jones, 1938).

Thomson, J. A. F. 'The death of Edward V: Dr Richmond's dating reconsidered', *Northern History* 26 (1990), pp. 207–11.

Thornley, I. D., ed. *England under the Yorkists, 1460–85* (London: Longman, 1920).

Tudor-Craig, Pamela, ed. *Richard III* (London: National Portrait Gallery, 1973).

Turner, Wendy. *Madness in Medieval Law and Custom* (Leiden: Brill, 2010).

Vissa-Fuchs, Livia. 'Richard in Holland, 1461', *The Ricardian* 6, no. 81 (1983), pp. 182–9.

Visser-Fuchs, Livia. 'Richard in Holland, 1471–2', *The Ricardian* 6, no. 82 (1983), pp. 220–8.

Visser-Fuchs, Livia. 'He hardly touched his food: What Niclas Von Popplau really wrote about Richard III', *The Ricardian* 145 (1999), pp. 525–30.

Visser-Fuchs, Livia. 'Richard was late', *The Ricardian* 11, no. 147 (1999), pp. 616–19.

Warkworth, John. *A Chronicle of the First Thirteen Years of the Reign of King Edward the Fourth*, ed. J. O. Halliwell-Phillipps (London: Camden Society, 1839).

Warnicke, Retha M. 'Sir Ralph Bigod: A loyal servant to Richard III', *The Ricardian* 6, no. 84 (1984), pp. 299–303.

Warwick, Roger. 'Anne Mowbray: skeletal remains of a medieval child', *Archaeologist* 5 (1986), pp. 176–9.

Wavrin, Jehan de. *Recueil des croniques et anchiennes istories de la Grant Bretaigne: a present nomme Engleterre par Jehan de Waurin, seigneur du Forestel*, ed. William Hardy (London: Longman, 1864–91).

Weir, Alison. *The Princes in the Tower* (London: Bodley Head, 1992).

Wilkins, Christopher. *The Last Knight Errant: Sir Edward Woodville and the Age of Chivalry* (London: I. B. Tauris, 2010).

Wilkinson, Josephine. *Richard: The Young King to Be* (Stroud: Amberley, 2009).

Williams, Daniel. 'From Towton to Bosworth: The Leicestershire community and the Wars of the Roses, 1461–1485', *Transactions of the Leicestershire Archaeological and Historical Society* 59 (1984), pp. 27–43.

Wilson, H. A. *Magdalen College* (London: F. E. Robinson, 1899).

Wolffe, B. P. 'When and why did Hastings lose his head', *English Historical Review* 89 (1974), pp. 835–44.

Wood, Charles T. 'The deposition of Edward V', *Traditio* 31 (1975), pp. 247–86.

Wroe, Ann. *Perkin: A Story of Deception* (London: Jonathan Cape, 2003).

Wynne, W. E. W. 'Grant from Richard, Duke of Gloucester, to Reginald Vaghan 10 Edw. IV', *Archaeologia Cambrensis* 9 (1863).

Index